SYNCRETISM IN RELIGION

Critical Categories in the Study of Religion

Series Editor: Russell T. McCutcheon, Associate Professor, Department of Religious Studies, University of Alabama

Critical Categories in the Study of Religion aims to present the pivotal articles that best represent the most important trends in how scholars have gone about the task of describing, interpreting, and explaining the position of religion in human life. The series focuses on the development of categories and the terminology of scholarship that make possible knowledge about human beliefs, behaviours, and institutions. Each volume in the series is intended as both an introductory survey of the issues that surround the use of various key terms as well as an opportunity for a thorough retooling of the concept under study, making clear to readers that the cognitive categories of scholarship are themselves historical artefacts that change over time.

Forthcoming books in the series:

Ritual and Religious Belief
A Reader
Edited by Graham Harvey

Myths and Mythologies
A Reader
Edited by Jeppe Sinding Jensen

Syncretism in Religion

A Reader

Edited by

Anita M. Leopold

and

Jeppe S. Jensen

ROUTLEDGE
NEW YORK

First Published 2004
by Equinox Publishing Ltd.
Unit 6, The Village, 101 Amies St., London, SW11 2JW

www.equinoxpub.com

Published in 2005 in the USA and Canada
by Routledge
270 Madison Avenue, New York, NY 10016
Routledge is an imprint of the Taylor & Francis Group

This selection and introductory material
© Anita M. Leopold and Jeppe S. Jensen 2004.

Typeset by ISB Typesetting, Sheffield
Printed and bound in Great Britain by Antony Rowe Ltd, Chippenham,
Wiltshire

British Library Cataloguing in Publication Data
A catalogue record for this book is available from the British Library

Library of Congress Cataloging in Publication Data
A catalogue record for this book is available on request from the Library of
Congress

#58675333

ISBN   0 415 97361 9   (paperback)

CONTENTS

Contents

PREFACE

I was an undergraduate student in the History of Religions when I first became acquainted with the subject of syncretism. It was the study of Gnosticism, a Hellenistic religious movement, characterized as syncretistic, which directed me to the subject. Right from the beginning, I was intrigued by the complexity of the phenomenon, and how it simultaneously expressed the sense of multi-vocality, of alienation, and of rebellious creativity, much of which I felt myself as a child when I grew up in Denmark, which was a foreign country to both of my parents. Being of a mixed cultural background—the child of a German–Jewish father and a Swedish–Protestant mother—I never felt that I belonged to the place where I was born, although my friends always insisted that I was just like them—a Dane. However, the right to be different, to take in the qualities of my parents' origins and histories to form my own life, has at all times been valuable to me. Not just so that you can stand out in the crowd, or uphold particular political or ethnical rights, but also because it gives you an outlook on alternative positions in life. Probably, this personal stance has inspired me to examine the subject of syncretism from the angle of transformative and innovative dynamics in culture and in religion. My own view from a mixed cultural position (Creole—you might say) has made me realize how much we invent our religious, our cultural, and even our personal identities. I grew up with my father's tragic story of the Holocaust and my mother's romantic vision of Swedish rural idyll and both formed the basic background of my idiosyncratic invention of who I was and how I looked at the world that I lived in. I realized, though, that the parents' history easily becomes the children's mythology when we use it as legitimating for national, ethnic and political favouritism. This has become a particularly apparent problem in multi-cultural societies, or where the political power is in the hands of one particular religious or ethnic group of people, fighting against another group of people, a way of life or a religion. In short, we construct meaningful borders such as those of religious or national traditions around others and ourselves by way of the myth of belonging to a particular history. Syncretism confronts our certainty of belonging. This makes it such a controversial category to deal with socially as well as psychologically, but on the other hand, it also makes it so attractive to study because of its creative and transformative potentiality that may redirect and reformulate any cultural, religious and individual mode of belonging.

This is essentially what human history is about. That is why it is important to preserve the category of syncretism: to continue the discussion on the many relevant issues concerning the human invention and re-invention of religion, culture and identity. Therefore, any student of religion and of the humanities in general will benefit from confronting the issues discussed in this collection, even though the category has been considered one of the controversies in the study of religion, one that many scholars of religion would like to abolish. I have attempted to give a thorough introduction to the problematic history of the term syncretism with particular attention to the wide range of theoretical questions with which we have to deal in our efforts to isolate the crucial issues concerning the category. Despite my own theoretical interest in syncretism, I hope, by way of my selection of essays, to give students and scholars a fair impression of the many phenomena that come under the heading of "syncretism." In the introductions I have attempted to separate the different issues of syncretism, as presented in the essays, into different levels of analysis. This should give the reader a more lucid outline of the complex problems of the subject, and to give a key by which to examine each level of the subject without a mix-up of divergent empirical or theoretical matters of discussion. This form of analysis is also meant to help raise issues and questions about theory and method in the classroom. In my conclusion, I have taken the liberty to suggest an analytical model that advances my own theory of syncretism. Overall, the general introduction and the conclusion together with my introductions to each part form "a book in the book"; therefore, I recommend that the reader takes time to discuss my introductions and conclusion as if each was a reading in itself. Because of my personal commitment to solving the problems of syncretism instead of abolishing the category, I have chosen to contribute to the discussion with a theoretical model, which of course is open to debate.

I have made an effort to combine a selection of essays that represents the classical contributions and issues as well as some that are possibly not so well known to most in the field. Finally, there are some new essays published for the first time in this book. My selection is mainly theoretically oriented; therefore, it does not exhaust the range of sources that may be consulted on the topic of syncretism. For that reason, I have included a list of references for further reading in addition to the references that accompany each essay.

Finally, although instructors will no doubt use the anthology in various ways, I would recommend that the collection would be the most constructive if the essays are read in the existing order, because the problem of syncretism increases as the anthology progresses.

For the major assistance in the technical work of reading and revising the mass of work on this volume, and for all the clever advice he has given me through my years of studying syncretism, I must thank Jeppe Sinding Jensen, my husband and colleague at the University of Aarhus. He deserves my heartfelt thanks because he accepted, on very short notice, to become my co-editor when I needed help most urgently. I could not have done without his patience and expertise in the editorial work. I must also thank David Warburton, also my colleague at the University of Aarhus, for his translations of German texts into English and for discussing the subject with me, and our graduate student Christian Koch Ramsing for scanning the texts in print and kind assistance when needed. Furthermore, Russell McCutcheon, editor of the series "Critical Categories in the Study of Religion," and Janet Joyce, publisher at Equinox, deserve my sincere thanks for entrusting me with this work and for being so patient with me when behind schedule. Special thanks go to Russell for his friendly advice on the editorial work. I enjoyed our little talks about everything from family to the weather forecast; there has been quite a traffic of e-mail between us—from Alabama to Aarhus—that I have enjoyed immensely. I also thank Valerie Hall from Equinox for being such a competent, helpful and friendly adviser on editorial issues.

Finally, Luther H. Martin deserves my heartfelt thanks for being my major support and mentor. He has been there to back me up right from the beginning when not many believed that syncretism was a subject worth studying any more. I must also thank him for suggesting me to Russell McCutcheon and Janet Joyce as the editor of this volume. Thanks also to Armin W. Geertz, friend, colleague, and PhD supervisor, for much interest and support along the way. I wish also to express my gratitude to Hans G. Kippenberg, Michael Pye, Panayotis Pachis, Ulrich Berner, Gustavo Benavides, Kirstine Munk, and William Cassidy for discussing various issues and contributing to this project—and to the participants in the workshops in the 2000 Durban IAHR (International Association for the History of Religions) congress where many of the problems and issues were debated in a spirit of true scholarship. Finally, I wish to thank Professor Per Bilde, the head of the PhD School of Religion, Identity and Culture at the Faculty of Theology, University of Aarhus, for taking much interest in the subject of syncretism, and my friends and colleagues in KRAKA, a research network of women scholars which has generated great support and discussions.

Anita Maria Leopold
Aarhus, Denmark

SOURCES

PART II

Hans G. Kippenberg, "In Praise of *Syncretism*: The Beginnings of Christianity Conceived in the Light of a Diagnosis of Modern Culture." Published in this volume.

Hendrik Kraemer, "Syncretism." In *idem*, ed., *The Christian Message in a Non-Christian World*, 200–211. New York: Harper & Brothers, 1938. Reprinted with the permission of the World Council of Churches.

Robert Baird, "Syncretism and the History of Religions." In *Essays in the History of Religions*, 59–71. New York: Peter Lang Publishing Inc., 1991. Reprinted with permission of Peter Lang Publishing Inc.

Michael Pye, "Syncretism and Ambiguity." *NUMEN* 18 (1971): 83–93. Reprinted with permission from Brill and the author.

Kurt Rudolph, "Syncretism—From Theological Invective to a Concept in the Study of Religion." Translated by David Warburton from "Synkretismus-vom Theologischen Scheltwort zum Religionswissenshaftlichen Begriff." In *Geschichte und Probleme der Religionswissenschaft*, 193–213. Leiden: Brill, 1992. Reprinted with permission of Brill and the author.

PART III

Gerardus van der Leeuw, "The Dynamic of Religions. Syncretism. Mission." In *Religion in Essence and Manifestation: A Study in Phenomenology*, translated by J. E. Turner, 609–612. Princeton: Princeton University Press, 1933, 1938. Copyright © 1986 by Princeton University Press. Reprinted with the permission of Princeton University Press.

Hendrik M. Vroom, "Syncretism and Dialogue: A Philosophical Analysis." In *Dialogue and Syncretism: An Interdisciplinary Approach*, ed. J. D. Gort, H. M. Vroom, R. Fernhout, and A. Wessels, 26–35. Grand Rapids, MI: Eerdmans, 1989. Copyright © by William B. Eerdmans. Used with permission; all rights reserved.

Roger Bastide, "Problems of Religious Syncretism." In *The African Religions of Brazil: Toward a Sociology of the Interpenetration of Civilizations*, translated by Helen Sebba, 260–84. London: The Johns Hopkins University Press, 1960, 1978. © 1978 Reprinted with the permission of The Johns Hopkins University Press.

Sources

PART IV

Andrew Apter, "Herskovits's Heritage: Rethinking Syncretism in the African Diaspora." *Diaspora: A Journal of Transnational Studies* 1(3) (1991): 235–60. © Reprinted with the permission of University of Toronto Press Inc.

Carlos Guillermo Wilson, "The Caribbean: Marvelous Cradle-Hammock and Painful Cornucopia." In *Caribbean Creolization: Reflections on the Cultural Dynamics of Language, Literature, and Identity*, translated by E. D. Birmingham and L. A. Jiménez, ed. K. M. Balutansky and M. A. Sourieau, 36–43. Gainesville: University Press of Florida, 1998. Reprinted with the permission of University Press of Florida.

Gustavo Benavides, "Syncretism and Legitimacy in Latin American Religion." In *Enigmatic Powers: Syncretism with African and Indigenous Peoples' Religions among Latinos*, ed. A. M. Stevens-Arroyo and A. I. Pérez y Mena, 19–46. Program for the Analysis of Religion among Latinos, 3. New York: Bildner Center for Western Hemisphere Studies, 1995. Reprinted with the permission of PARAL, the Program for the Analysis of Religion Among Latinos/as, Anthony M. Stevens-Arroyo, Andres I. Pérez y Mena and the author.

André Droogers, "Syncretism, Power, Play." In *Syncretism and the Commerce of Symbols*, ed. Göran Aijmer, 38–59. Göteborg: The Institute for Advanced Studies in Social Anthropology (IASSA), 1995. Reprinted with the permission of Göran Aijmer and the author.

Armin W. Geertz, "Worlds in Collusion: On Social Strategies and Misrepresentations as Forces of Syncretism in Euro-American and Native American Affairs." In *Syncretism and the Commerce of Symbols*, ed. Göran Aijmer, 38–59. Göteborg: The Institute for Advanced Studies in Social Anthropology (IASSA), 1995. Reprinted with the permission of Göran Aijmer and the author.

PART V

Charles Stewart, "Relocating Syncretism in Social Science Discourse." In *Syncretism and the Commerce of Symbols*, ed. Göran Aijmer, 13–37. Göteborg: The Institute for Advanced Studies in Social Anthropology (IASSA), 1995. Reprinted with the permission of Göran Aijmer and the author.

Luther H. Martin, "Syncretism, Historicism, and Cognition: A Response to Michael Pye." *Method & Theory in the Study of Religion* 8(2) (1996): 215–24. Reprinted with the permission of Brill and the author.

Ulrich Berner, "The Concept of 'Syncretism': An Instrument of Historical Insight/Discovery?" Translated by David Warburton from "Der Begriff 'Synkretismus'—ein Instrument historischer Erkenntnis?" *Saeculum* 30 (1979): 68–85. Reprinted with the permission of Verlag Karl Alber and the author.

PART VI

Timothy Light, "Orthosyncretism: An Account of Melding in Religion." In *Perspectives in Method and Theory in the Study of Religion*, ed. A. W. Geertz and R. T. McCutcheon, 162–86. Leiden: Brill, 2000. Reprinted with the permission of Brill.

Panayotis Pachis, "Religious Tendencies in Greece at the Dawn of the 21st Century—An Approach to Contemporary Greek Reality." Published in this volume.

Kirstine Munk, "Medicine-Men, Modernity and Magic: Syncretism as an Explanatory Category to Recent Religious Responses and Magical Practices among Urban Blacks in Contemporary South Africa." Published in this volume.

In memory of my mother and father,
Greta Maria Skålberg and Alfred Leopold

Part I

General Introduction

GENERAL INTRODUCTION

The idea that religion, culture and ethnicity are pure entities, which may become mixed when in encounter, just as when biological organisms cross-breed, is an idea that relates to the traditional definition of syncretism. According to this view, the mixture of different religious origins may again lead to the parentage of new, but impure, hybrid forms, instead of the stable reproduction of pure religious or cultural traditions. This description echoes a more or less folk-scientific understanding of the propagations of religion and culture as similar to that of biological organisms. Similar to the pro-creation of biological organisms there are two ways of propagating religion and culture: you can breed either by reproduction/cloning or by genetic mixing/sexual breeding. The first form illustrates how people imagine tradi-tions reproduce by unchanged "cloning" through history, whereas the latter form suggests the illegitimate or impure cross-breeding between traditions.

Permit me to introduce my interest in the "problem of syncretism" by way of a bit of autobiography. I remember my childhood dog, "Bamse," who was a mongrel of a Danish farm dog and who knows what else. She was the only survivor out of a litter that otherwise suffered death by drowning, because few people want mongrel dogs. But Bamse was saved because she was meant for the job as watchdog on the neighbouring farm. However, this small, black and yellow, and terribly plump-looking dog with a temper like a German shepherd really had caught my heart. Incidentally, the name I gave her trans-lates into "Teddy" in English, thus the name itself introduced some measure of a blending of categories. So to save her from a sad life as a watchdog on a farm, I dared to ask my father permission to keep this dog, although I knew he was against having pets. Regrettably, Bamse did not have anything to offer with regards to looks or pedigree. But my father surprised me by allowing me this dog, without further ado, because, as he explained, he, who was a German Jew, could prove a pure genealogy all the way back to the time of Jesus Christ. "So what harm is there," he said, "in importing a little drop of mongrel blood into my family!"

I was, of course, thrilled by the fact that I had got myself a dog, but I was also intrigued by my father's answer, because I knew that my mother was not of the same descent as he. Being a Swede of the Protestant church, she was neither Jewish nor German. Consequently, did the fact that my parents were of different descent make me a "mongrel" too? This example from my childhood illustrates how we humans tend to think in kinship terms. Cate-gories such as blood relations and family extraction play an enormous role in social interaction, as well as in the interaction between religions and cul-tures. In this framework, mixed origins present a challenge to the human mind. To pose questions about why this is so is also the challenge of posing questions about the very category of *syncretism*.

The Essence of Mixing

The anthropologist Pascal Boyer, who is particularly attentive to evolutionary psychology, observes how children believe that kinship refers to a special kind of "essence" shared by people with a common genealogy. He refers to anthropologist Larry Hirschfeld's term "naive sociology" in order to explain why children, as well as adults, tend to be open to particular ideologies that understand groups of people as naturally different from others, which may, in further consequence, lead to the formation of racial or racist ideas:

> ... we all – seem prepared to think of social groups in terms of natural difference ... Our "naive sociology," then, is an attempt to make sense of our own intuitions about the social world around us ... If your village has always fought (note the anthropomorphic term) against the next village, then in a sense the interaction transcends the existence of its participants. So it makes perfect sense to think of villages and other such units as abstract persons or living organisms, because that helps explain stable interaction. People often say that all members of a village or a clan have the "same bones," that they share some essence that is the eternal life of a social group. (Boyer 2001, 252–53)

As a result, we may understand, in terms of evolutionary psychology, why syncretism has become such a debated and controversial category in the study of religion, and that is because it has as a prerequisite the idea of natural difference. It is related to issues about the nature of the social world of humans, and how groups of people are inclined to think about cultural and religious mixing in terms of kinship codes. It is a case of naïve sociology, or even naïve biology, when humans view their belonging to a group with reference to the idea of blood relation that "the essence of the clan is inside us." Boyer remarks that this expresses the intuitions that groups have of the otherwise complex aspects of social interaction (253).

That a notion such as syncretism gives the impression of impurity is because we have such a propensity for essentializing our belonging to a set of ideas, just as we do according to our belonging to a particular group. To be a Dane is essentially different from being an American, and to be a Lutheran Christian is essentially different from being a Jew—that goes without explanation for most people. But to be an American Dane, or to be a Jewish Lutheran is a mixing up of domains that will require some additional explanation and perhaps even a legitimation of some kind. Syncretism, subsequently, is about the negotiation and interaction of new elements into a particular group or domain that stem from "essentially" different groups or domains. This adaptation or mixing of alien elements into a particular group, category or domain may sometimes evoke fear of "contamination" or "interpenetration" of the essence of a known life form. It goes without saying then that the category syncretism represents elements of struggle in the transmission of religion. The phenomenon may be compared with the "trial and error" processes of social life, wherein the interaction of religious and cultural products is an ongoing process resulting in changes and innovations. Mostly, those changes or innovations go unnoticed, but at other times they evolve from more violent clashes between religions, discourses or groups of people.

Syncretism as Taxonomy

The notion of syncretism is connected to the transmission of religion in general. Students of religion usually describe the category as "a generalization about diverse elements incorporated into some target religion from external religious or secular source or sources" (Martin and Leopold, in press). The causes, as well as the effects, of historical processes that lead to syncretistic formations vary a great deal depending on the historical, cultural, political and social climates.

Most syncretistic formations go unnoticed as they appear as the natural results of interaction. Some scholars call this an "unconscious" mode of syncretism (see André Droogers and Kurt Rudolph, in this volume). This is most salient between similar, but sometimes competing, religious types or elements, and is also referred to as "the finding of one's own in the other" (Schenk 1989, 100), and this would rarely be registered as an innovation but rather be considered an adaptation, amalgamation or assimilation. An example of this is the comparison or parallelization of Isis and Demeter in the Hellenistic age that finally resulted in an identification of the two goddesses (Pakkanen 1996, 94–100).

Other syncretistic formations have emerged as the consequence of a dominant culture forcing on or "interpenetrating" (see Roger Bastide, in this volume) a culture of minority its own religion such as to make it the official religion. In those cases, syncretism may be seen as a result of a resistance to power and a means to preserve indigenous gods in the clothing of the gods of the dominant culture. In certain cases, this form has been called "creolization" with reference to the dominance of the Christian culture upon Afro-Caribbean or Afro-American cultures (see Part IV, in this volume). However, innovations are not necessarily the result of inter-cultural contact, but they may arise independently as part of discursive differences in competing factions of shared religious and cultural backgrounds. New religious movements or new myth-making often incorporate "borrowed" elements from other religious (or secular) sources as a way of legitimating new contemporary values, often disguised as old religious teachings as a means to contest orthodox values (see Panayotis Pachis, this volume). The break between early Christianity and Judaism produced new myth-making, together with the many factions of Christian movements such as the Gnostic movements which gave rise to a rich and innovative mythology disguised as revelations of earlier teachings. Universalists, such as the nineteenth-century Deists as well as certain groups inside the New Age movement, can be compared to this type of innovative mythology because they aim to explain all religions as being the same and encompassed in a unifying religious paradigm. There are, of course, many more "syncretisms" than mentioned here (see Ulrich Berner, in this volume).

Using syncretism taxonomically, as I have just demonstrated here, seems relatively unproblematic. However, many students of religion have rightly accused the category as too vague and indefinite to be of use in classifying its object. If we are trying to isolate it as an historical phenomenon, how do we differentiate among random historical processes in order to pinpoint which one is syncretistic and which one is not? The history of religion confirms that every religion is in "essence" syncretistic—there are no pristine origins or essences. Nevertheless, historical-genetic descriptions may only lead us to depict particular fusions of religion and typologies of fusions. The criticism of the category has drawn attention to the lack of precision of the fundamental levels of explanation.

A Theoretical Invention

Discussions related to the category of syncretism include many focal theoretical issues in the study of religion in general. In particular, this concerns methodology, and how to use the historical-genetic approach to explain diffusion and fusion of religion. There is also the socio-political view of the power-related consequences of religions in contact, the phenomenological entry to syncretism as a dynamics of religion, and finally, the attempt to use cognitive or evolutionary theories to explain religious transmission and innovation in the light of the architecture of the human mind. These methodological and theoretical questions, among others, relate to the problem of defining the notion of syncretism. In order to attain some degree of clarification one may set out by asking whether the syncretic formations take place at the individual psychological or cognitive levels, at the linguistic levels of discourse or symbolism, or at the social and political levels of power and control in interaction. That is: do we locate syncretism in mind, in culture or in politics? It is our choice; we invent the levels that are methodologically relevant.

The historian Petra Pakkanen has termed syncretism a "theoretical invention" that has no correspondence in contextual reality (Pakkanen 1996, 86). She, among other scholars, has raised the question of the usefulness of the category in as much as it gives the idea of "explaining the phenomenon of syncretism with syncretism," one that explains nothing at all, as she claims (87). Pakkanen suggests, instead, that the category syncretism is applicable as a heuristic tool for discovering otherwise "hidden antecedents of historical facts and to interpret them." She aims to relate the category directly to the object of study on a descriptive level, so that it may help illuminate the religious processes of the past (86). In her case, it is used as an archaeological category to help dig up the traces of particular historical developments, which can be useful to historians and archaeologists who are forced to deduce the "leftovers" of history, and come up with whole pictures of the past. However, a narrow connection between category and object makes for narrow explanations; in other words, a category only proves useful if it can say something new about the object in question. Therefore, I would suggest that there is not much interest in retaining the category of syncretism if its only application is to describe historical processes that are already evident in the historical data. The benefit of the category should lie, first, in its ability to function as a heuristic tool, to aid us in pointing out a phenomenon and telling us *what* it is, and second, as an aid in explaining, that is, to tell us *why* and *how* it is the way that it is.

Descriptions versus Explanations

In an extension of Pakkanen's criticism of the category syncretism as a theoretical invention we may consider what kind of inference a scientific category must contain to best be able to say something new about a certain object. A scientific category must say more than what is commonsensical and what can be stated in everyday language. A scientific category must relate to a theoretical framework and to methodological reflections on how to proceed. However, there is not always agreement about theory, nor on methodology. This issue concerns the discussion going on in the study of religion as to whether our scientific categories should be explanatory or descriptive. Certainly, it seems that they could be both, according to the theoretical object and purpose of the relevant analysis. Moreover, no matter whether one favours explanatory or descriptive categories, all categories we employ are always interpretive and they are always related to models—and not just to any fact "in themselves." A simple and telling example of this is van Gennep's tripartite structural model of "rite de passage" as the categories associated with it are part of the model—not of the rituals.

Given the enormous amount of historical data that can be classified as syncretistic, the many subjects in various religious traditions are so multifaceted and complex that bewildered scholars tend to redefine the category each time there is a new subject under study. The variety of approaches in the essays presented in this book will prove that a fact. One reason for the inconsistency in definition is that students of religion mostly indulge in describing what seems to be a general phenomenon from the study of single traditions and often on rather detailed items. The challenge of description is to find a common denominator. The challenge, as far as the category of syncretism goes, is that there appears to be no common denominator on which scholars can agree. Rather, the fields of study seem to denote a variety of phenomena that are all listed under the heading of syncretism without any obvious link of explanation or theoretical justification.

As the category of syncretism is a theoretical invention, then scholars must decide the theory or theories to which the concept of syncretism applies. The challenge of the explanatory approach is that we risk finding evidence that goes in another direction, or even runs counter to, the assumptions we started out with, so that we need to redirect the definition of the category altogether. Explanatory approaches of interest to the question of syncretism may be divided into two quite different kinds. One is the mode of structural or analytic explanation and the other is the causal mode of explanation. A structural, or formal analytic, explanation explains why the object is what it is in terms of the rules and conditions that may account for it, such as the rules of syntax and grammar. A causal explanation explains what causes a phenomenon to be the way it is. Some causal explanations, i.e. those termed "nomothetic," are linked to theories, or hypotheses, in such a way that they may predict the outcome, or the effects, of certain causes in a law-like manner. Such explanations are common in, say, chemistry.

A theory does not always have to correspond solely to its immediate contextual reality; in fact, the best theories employing causal explanations are able to make predictions about another level of reality not directly observable in the context, for instance if it can be shown that sociological causes have psychological effects or vice versa. The anthropologist Harvey Whitehouse has stated that: "What matters is that the variables with which the theory is concerned conform to patterns of relationships that the theory predicts, and that all this is formulated in such a way that we could agree on what would constitute counter-evidence with regards to the theory's predictions" (conference report 2002). A quest for a full-blown nomothetic, causal explanation of syncretism seems unlikely to succeed, but even when restricted to more modest analysis of the conditions under which certain patterns emerge and make sense at various levels, will an explanatory approach be an advance on the present situation. The focal point in unfolding what syncretism is lies between the descriptive and the explanatory outlines, which do not always conform. However, they are the framework for the critical agenda of defining the category.

A Pejorative Criticism

The main criticism against the category syncretism has been that it carries pejorative connotations that are historically linked to theological disputes in Christianity. Students of religion have criticized the category for having absorbed the negative theological assumptions about religions of mixed origins. Therefore, there is an ongoing debate about the political consequences, in both the history of religion and in anthropology, of the use of the notion, which cannot be ignored. Several attempts have been made to redefine syncretism into a scientifically-sound category freed from its theological bias. Nonetheless, even though most scholars can agree on the disposal of its pejorative past, the consequences of the concept's history linger in the consciousness of believers of various traditions that are part of or in contact with the Christian world. To reach an agreement on the topic of syncretism demands a thorough study of all the aspects connected to the category, whether we are talking about syncretism as a descriptive, a taxonomic, a discursive, a political or an explanatory term.

Would it not be better, then, to dispose of the category syncretism altogether? This has been the suggestion of several scholars. Judging from the vast production of books and essays about the subject there is a lot to say about it. Borrowing, blending and influencing are both inevitable and universal, and represent the history of human negotiation. However, inter-religious disputes about well-protected revelations, and questions about the essence of religion are provoked by the term. The use of syncretism in the more theological (mostly Christian) sense has often been used to appoint and control what has been thought of as illegitimate correlations between competing religious movements, traditions or discourses. The heritage from the theological use of syncretism represents a problem in definition for the study of religion. Nevertheless, we need a concept to describe what happens when religions travel to help us obtain an image of how changing contexts influence religious meaning in the minds of people.

When Religion Travels

On the concept of syncretism, Pascal Boyer observes, with reference to the Javanese ritual "slametan," that it refers to "a situation where there is a mixture of heterogeneous elements" (Boyer 2001, 268). However, he continues to note that, "the term *syncretism* is misleading if it suggests that people are confused." On the contrary, it seems to imply that the activity of fusing, "mixing" or "blending" different domains does not present a problem to the human mind. Although the way we think appears to be domain-specific, in accordance with the mode that thought is expressed in language, syntax and concepts, it seems as if the meaning itself evolves *ad hoc* from the blending of different domains. We may compare this with the travel of religion. A Christian saint changes domicile to the African company of "Orixas" (in reference to the Shango cult and the Brazilian syncretistic forms of Afro-Christian cults; see Roger Bastide in this volume, Part III) but that does not mean that the two religious systems are "confused" or simply "fused" in the minds of people.

Studies in the cognitive sciences suggest that the human mind is so composed that it makes particular selections out of the various impressions it is given, rather than having a whole system of thought, such as a religious system, implanted into it. Instead it is suggested that the mind "comprises lots of specialized explanatory devices, more properly called *inference systems*, each of which is adapted to particular kinds of events and automatically suggests explanations for these events" (Boyer 2001, 17). It makes sense, then, to consider the mixing of religious elements in the light of how they form inferences to particular religious categories amongst groups of people. Therefore, when a Christian saint is selected in a new religious or cultural domain it is because of the particular quality of the saint as participating in a certain religious category. On the other hand, Christian saints do not carry with them the whole package of Christian theology to implant in the minds of their new adherents. The saint adds to that certain category some new quality from the original domain that may not have been there before, one which may eventually transform elements of meaning as well as structure.

Is "Blending" the Way We Think?

The pattern for a syncretistic formation is similar to how we think in general—at least if we trust scholars in cognitive science, Mark Turner and Gilles Fauconnier, who are spokesmen for a theory that proposes that our way of thinking is based on the blending of different mental spaces. "Blending" refers to a general cognitive operation of conceptual integration—a mental capacity, which is unconscious to the mind (Fauconnier and Turner 2002, 18). They describe this operation as follows:

> In blending, structure from input mental spaces is projected to a separate "blended" mental space. The projection is selective. Through completion and elaboration, the blend develops structure not provided by the inputs. Inferences, arguments, and ideas developed in the blend can have

effect in cognition, leading us to modify the initial inputs and to change our view of the corresponding situations. (Fauconnier and Turner 1998, 1)

This theory presents a challenging proposition concerning the pattern of syncretistic formations, one that may say something about the fundamental structure of the phenomenon that goes beyond the historical descriptive opaqueness, and the theological negative connotations of "impurity." However, if we explain syncretism as just an extension of our thinking, do we not then drown the whole idea of the concept, as happened to the siblings of my childhood dog, Bamse? When scholars find more fundamental laws or rules of syncretistic formations, does that mean that there will then be a place for a mongrel dog in the litter of pedigrees? Most likely not, considering the way humans think. The issues of syncretism presented in this volume prove, otherwise, that the social mode of groups of humans is determinative on the acceptance of heterogeneous groups or beliefs. However, the many dissimilar aspects of the essays unveil the very complexity of the category that calls for a study on different levels. How do we solve the fundamental questions about how humans think about the "other," the odd and the deviant, which is obviously linked to the natural human affairs of mixing everything from blood to concepts? We have already touched upon the discrepancy between the common fact of mixing and the discrimination against it. How do we deal, on the one hand, with the discourses of the concept referring to the consequences of its tangled history; and, on the other hand, with the phenomenon of mixing itself? It is the intention of this volume to take a closer look at the many levels of the study of syncretism and to suggest a way of solving the seeming incompatibilities of the study.

The Plan of the Book

This volume provides an insight into the scholarly discourse about the category syncretism. However, predisposed by its past use in theology as a pejorative term it has entered the study of religion, including anthropology, for the purpose of describing processes in religion of integration, acculturation, transformation and innovation in various fields of study. Each part of the volume contains an introduction to the particular topic as well as to each essay, which will give the reader a better understanding of the discussions contained therein. The intention is to give a deeper insight, while also clarifying the problem of the category. There is a guiding line throughout the volume that highlights the main issues and, at the same time, directs the reader to focus on different ways of addressing the problem of syncretism. In addition, the reader can follow the pursuing argument in order to suggest a solution to the problem.

Part II defines the problem of the category syncretism in the study of religion including extracts of or references to source material that refer to the term's historical and etymological background. It offers a selection of classical readings from the field of study of religion and theology that are pivotal to understanding the discussions of the problem of definition up to the present day; this will be apparent throughout the volume. In particular, we will engage in discussion of the term's problematic past and negative use in theology; and as a consequence, the disagreement over an adequate definition of it in the study of religion.

Part III concerns the definition of syncretism as historical processes of encounter and assimilation of religion. In this part, I will present a wide range of classical readings from the field of the history of religion, the philosophy of religion and anthropology. The essays represent different starting points as to methodology and empirical data, ranging from early Christianity to Afro-Brazilian cults, but they all refer to syncretism as a common inner dynamic of historical processes.

Part IV defines syncretism in relation to theories of power, which include the contradicting outlook of anti-syncretism. This further relates to issues about the problem of the "insider" and "outsider" view in reference to the diffusion of the scholarly and theologian discourses to the different religious communities, which are defined as syncretistic as a consequence of a power-related influence of another religion. The topic of "creolization" is also discussed in connection with questions about the acquisition of religion. The readings represent studies from the field of religion, anthropology, linguistics and literature.

Part V relates to the ongoing and unsettled discussion on "Whether to use or not to use syncretism"[1] or on how to use syncretism. This is also a question about whether syncretism should be a descriptive or an explanatory term, which refers, yet again, to the problem of redefining syncretism in relation to a theory or theories that may grant the category some explanatory value.

Part VI is a collection of recent studies of syncretism that will give the reader an impression of the direction in which the study is heading. There is less reservation against using the term in the three contributions from the study of religion than there was in the earlier studies. We notice that the study of syncretism is now moving from the problem of defining the category of syncretism towards finding new aspects of syncretism and explaining them in different ways.

Part VII is the conclusion where we will offer to set out some of the questions on method and theory presented in the readings. Together with points of debate about syncretism as introduced in the General Introduction we shall sum up those positions, presented in the essays, which we consider relevant for making the subject more transparent to the reader. As such, it is our intention to come up with a suggestion of how we may retain the term syncretism as a descriptive category in the study of religion and simultaneously provide it with an amount of explanatory value.

This volume is designed so that it allows instructors and students to trace several coherent, competing approaches to one uniform problem in the study of religion. Furthermore, the reader will become familiar with a number of related issues in the field as well as a number of authors, past and present, who have made significant contributions. By its very nature, this problem is equally applicable to many other sciences of the human condition, and so, despite the high degree of specificity of the readings, the collection should certainly also be of relevance to students outside the study of religion.

There is no single prescribed way of using this collection of readings. However, their order and presentation suggest a format in which each reading or position as a whole is explored descriptively and then investigated in class debates or seminars where students are encouraged either to develop, and apply in greater detail, the position in question, or to delineate a line of reasoning capable of criticizing its assumptions and findings.

Note

1. This is the title of Luther Martin's article in *Historical Reflection/Refléxions Historiques* 27(3) (2001): 389–400.

References

Boyer, Pascal. 2001. *Religion Explained: The Evolutionary Origins of Religious Thought*. New York: Basic Books.

Fauconnier, Gilles, and Mark Turner. 1998. "Conceptual Integration Networks." *Cognitive Science* 22(2): 133–87.

—2002. *The Way We Think: Conceptual Blending and the Mind's Hidden Complexities*. New York: Basic Books.

Martin, Luther H., and Anita M. Leopold. (In press.) "New Approaches to the Study of Religion." In *New Approaches to the Study of Religion: Comparative Approaches*, ed. Peter Antes and Armin W. Geertz.

Pakkanen, Petra. 1996. "Definitions: Re-evaluation of Concepts. 1. Syncretism." In *idem, Interpreting Early Hellenistic Religion: A Study Based on the Mystery Cult of Demeter and the Cult of Isis*, 85–100. Papers and Monographs of the Finnish Institute at Athens, 3. Athens: D. Layias and E. Souvatzidakis.

Schenk, Wolfgang. 1989. "Interpretatio Graeca—Interpretatio Romana. Der hellenistische Synkretismus als semiotisches Problem." In *Innovationen in Zeichentheorien: Kultur- und wissenschaftsgeschictliche Studien zur Kreativität*, ed. P. Schmitter and H. W. Schmitz. Münster: Nodus Publikationen.

Part II

THE HISTORICAL BACKGROUND OF THE TERM
SYNCRETISM: THE PROBLEM OF DEFINITION

INTRODUCTION TO PART II

The problem of defining syncretism is related to its complex history and conflicting etymology. Syncretism first occurred in the treatise of the Greek historian Plutarch (ca. 50 AD–120 AD). In the chapter "On Brotherly Love" in his *Moralia*, Plutarch uses the term to illustrate "how the Cretans did" when they suspended their mutual disagreements and united to face a common enemy:

> Then this further must be born in mind and guarded against when differences arise among brothers: we must be careful especially at such time to associate familiarly with our brothers' friends, but avoid and shun all intimacy with their enemies, imitating in this point, at least, the practice of Cretans, who, though they often quarrelled with and warred against each other, made up their differences and united when outside enemies attacked; and this it was which they called "syncretism." (Plutarch, 313)

Etymologically the Greek term *syncretismos* stems from a combination of the Greek prefix *syn* with *kretoi*, the word for Cretans, or *kretismos*, "the Cretan behaviour" (Pakkanen 1996, 86 n. 10). The notion of syncretism is used proverbially, in the best style of the Hellenistic writer, to warn close friends or kindred not to stay divided unless they want to get slain by intruders. It essentializes the sense of belonging to a particular group of people, and emphasizes the political meaning of "self-defence" (Moffatt 1922) in the attempt to preserve a community in a perilous situation. But similar proverbs (without the notion of syncretism) are known from the Christian literature to warn against people that are divided in faith (e.g. *Gospel of Thomas*, saying 47; see Koester 1990, 131).

The Syncretistic Strife

Plutarch's irenic version of syncretism has been criticized for having nothing to do with the modern reference to religious syncretism. Rather, the modern version of syncretism stems from a neo-etymologism deriving from *synkerannumi* which means to "mix" things that are incompatible (Usener 1896, 337–40). This form was used in a polemical sense to denote ecumenical betrayals against the Reformed orthodoxy by Protestant theologians of the sixteenth and seventeenth centuries. The syncretistic strife of Protestant theologians was a secondary reaction to cancel out the term *synkretizein* that, in a similar sense to Plutarch, meant to combine, or to reconcile the confessional differences of the competing Reformed sects. The humanistic theologians Erasmus of Rotterdam (1469–1536) and Georg Calixt (1586–1656) tried, in the sense of *synkretizein*, to reconcile the competing Christian parties. Erasmus propagated what he called the *bonae litterae*, i.e. the "good science," which was a combination of Greek philosophy and the *philosophia Christi* which formed what he thought was a humanistic Christianity. It was in the defence of good science that he proposed the reconciliation (*synkretizein*) of scholars of all parties against the barbarians (Moffatt 1922, 155). In the vein of Erasmus, Calixt, a Danish theologian and prominent scholar at Helmstedt (in Germany), saw in the pagan literature, especially in Aristotelian philosophy, the rational proof of the truth in Christianity (Engel 1976, 19–21). Calixt called it "the theological evidence," the revelation of a universal truth that he hoped would unify all Christians despite their confessional differences (150). His ecumenical efforts was meant to be the continuation of the Reformation as the restoration of the universal truth that was once present in the old Church, *antiquitas ecclesiastica*, which, in Calixt's view, had been corrupted through history by erroneous human interpretations and the "tyranny of the papacy" (123).

The theologian Peter Engel, referring to the study by the theologian Arnold Schleiff, defends Calixt's striving towards unification against the accusations of syncretism:

> Schleiff pointed out that it is not accurate to speak of "syncretism" in Calixt, as Calov and Calixt's other opponents did. "For him it was not a matter of making an emergency alliance against the common foe— the Roman Antichrist—but rather a union, a union even with the Catholics." The reproach of syncretism includes the implicit accusation that Calixt's betrayal of the teaching and the faith was committed for opportunistic reasons, in the interest of a superficial unity of the church. This cannot be correct because his efforts at reconciliation were aimed solely at establishing the general and obligatory recognition of the one true and divine teaching. (Engel, 1976, 127, transl. D. Warburton)

Notice that Engel defines syncretism as "opportunistic" in reference to its political sense of human affairs, in contrast to Calixt's inspiration of faith. This noticeably outlines the negative sense of the notion in theology: that syncretism is secular in essence, contrary to true religion that is divine revelation. The accusations of syncretism against Calixt were bound up with the aftermath of the Reformation that propagated sectarian individuality. The reaction against a possible union of the Lutheran Church with the many Reformed Churches was as old as the Lutheran Church itself (Schmid 1846, 309–311), and that was a resistance against a union of confessions.

The allegation against Calixt was as much one against an apostatized Lutheran (Schmid 1846, 337). His theology was regarded as dangerous and pro-Catholic, and "seemed to repudiate not only medievalism, but the Reformation itself" (McNeill 1964, 272). His ecumenical attempt failed to have any effect even though it had many followers both in the Reformed Churches and the Roman Church. The historian J. Moffatt concludes that in view of the Roman Peril, Reformed churches were warned against syncretism:

> ... a betrayal of principles or as an attempt to secure unity at the expense of truth. The "syncretistic controversy" was a quarrel over peace, and such quarrels are not the least bitter upon earth. What the "syncretists" in Plutarch's sense of the term called a harmony, their opponents called a "hybrid." (1922, 155)

The changing interpretations of syncretism were dependent upon the changing historical contexts and additional political agendas. In this line of inquiry, the negative use of syncretism by the theologians of the sixteenth and seventeenth centuries can be seen as an inversion of the irenic definition of Plutarch, Erasmus and Calixt. As such, none of them can be used to define syncretism in terms of a category for the study of religion. But as objects of study, the changing etymologies are a theme related to the category when definitions are viewed in the light of the polemics and politics of negotiating religious divergence. On this level of inquiry syncretism refers to issues about power in relation to the encounter of religion in the historical as well as social strata.

Syncretism and Christian Mission

Even now syncretism provokes anti-syncretism as it did in the days of Erasmus and Calixt. This is mainly caused by the Christian propaganda against it. It has been argued, accordingly, that in modern times syncretism has mainly been a Christian missionary problem.

The expansion of Christianity in the sixteenth century was the basis on which the notion became part of the mission policy. It was in the irenic sense of the term that the Franciscans and Dominicans in Mexico planned in 1524 and in the tradition of Erasmus, "to settle the Indians around churches...and convert them by colourful ceremonies" (McManners 1992, 305–308). In the east, Jesuits regarded syncretism as a means to expand their mission, in a similar way to the Jesuit Francis Xavier (1542), who worked out a scheme to convert Japanese lords to Christianity by adapting Christianity to Japanese culture. As a consequence, local customs not directly in contradiction to Christianity were to be accepted (McManners 1992, 315). In China, another Jesuit, Matteo Ricci (ca. 1600), accepted Confucian rites and ancestor worship as a way of serving missionary purposes. He even wore the robes of a Confucian scholar. In 1622 Rome set up the congregation for the propagation of the faith as a direction for missionary work that specified that indigenous clergy was to be accepted along with customs of the various peoples. But, in the beginning of the eighteenth century, forces against the Jesuits turned the tables and resulted in Rome abandoning the irenic policy of syncretism such as dressing Christianity in foreign customs.

In North America, especially in the United States, the demand for oneness led to a kind of "civic faith" that became the umbrella of a pluralism of many faiths, because of the many persecuted European religious minorities that had abandoned the Old World (Marty 1992, 385–88). The Christian mission, Protestant as well as Catholic, added to that pluralism in its efforts to convert Native Americans and black slaves. The relatively few conversions of Indians resulted in forms of syncretism where Christian beliefs were mixed with Native American beliefs about spirits, nature, and tribe; forms that were dismissed by the missionaries as paganism (401). When the slave-masters eventually began to care about the souls of their slaves, they encouraged the organization of Methodist and Baptist congregations among them. This resulted in a new ethnic formation of black Methodist and Baptist churches that, even though they were supervised by whites to prevent the rise of literacy among slaves, "helped create the very 'manyness' they professed to want to discourage" (402). Supported by the nineteenth-century racist theories, the division of "black" and "white" churches was legitimated and established the inferiority of the Afro-American population.

The idea of the American "oneness" is compounded of both an irenic and an antipathetic currency of syncretism that has depended on the shifting politics of racial tolerance in the different historical contexts. Due to the violent history of the encounter with the "Indians," Native Americans were not integrated into white America, but isolated on reservations. Therefore, syncretism as a way of integration between Christianity and Native religion could not be tolerated, because it did not guarantee a safe integration of Native America (Marty 1992, 401). The situation for the black Americans, although they were distinguished as an inferior race, was different because they had already been integrated into the white families as slaves. This allowed Afro-Christian syncretism to move a further step towards integration into the white society. The concept of "black theology," shaped by Christian Afro-Americans, is a theological reflection on how the black struggle for justice and liberation is part of the Christian message, which was also a major element of the programmes of Martin Luther King, Joseph Washington as well as Malcolm X (Marty 1992, 417; Cone 1985, 94). It was Washington who combated the discriminatory idea of the whites that "black" churches were less genuine than "white" churches. In the eyes of the whites, he concluded, blacks have only "folk religion," and as such "Negro congregations are not churches but religious societies—religion can choose to worship whatever gods are pleasing" (Cone 1985, 95).

Modern Ecumenical Attempts

Syncretism has once more become an issue of ecumenical thinking in the post-colonial era as a result of the various Christian communities' demand for a new theology that emerged from the encounter with the Christian mission. In the words of James H. Cone, a member of the Ecumenical Association of Third World Theologians (EATWOT), Third World theologians have been attempting to develop a new way of doing theology: "The liberating character of their spirituality can be seen in the way their faith in God evolves out of their cultural and political aspirations" (Cone 1985, 101).

Cone's words reflect a modern ecumenism, which does not aspire to a unity of Christianity in the sense of Calixt, but rather encourages the acceptance of "Christianities" in the plural. The task of EATWOT is to reformulate Christian theology to be "the spirituality of justice and liberation" of the oppressed peoples seeking equality in theology (Torres 1985, xviii–xix). The agenda for a new "liberation theology" is to fight the cultural imperialism of First World theologians, and to recover indigenous cultures and values in their traditional religions and cultures denigrated by christianization and westernization:

> Ultimately the cultural aspect of liberation theology is a struggle for values that enhance rather than truncate human life. Christianity itself is renewed in the process, as it is rescued from its imprisonment in death-producing forms of domination and restored as a message of liberation. (Fabella and Torres 1985, 185–86)

The Second Vatican Council

Ever since the syncretistic strife that was the outcome of the Reformation, the Protestant Church has been more anti-syncretistic than the Roman Catholic Church. However, the Roman Catholic Church has, as result of a longer tradition of mission, developed a wider frame for adapting new or foreign elements within the frame of Church theology and policy. In the 1960s, a new turn in Church policy promised a more irenic attitude toward syncretism following the more severe accusations against it in the eighteenth century. The effects of the Christian mission not merely left traces of more or less accidental blends between, for example, Catholic saints and indigenous gods, but it also provoked Christian clergy from different ethnic origins to interpret Christianity differently from the orthodoxy of the Church in their efforts to make the Christian faith meaningful to peoples with very different backgrounds. It is not surprising that the unionism expressed by

EATWOT favours syncretism as a way of surviving in a divided world (Fabella and Torres 1985, 191).

It happened to be in the wake of post-colonialism that an opening for a more tolerant policy, towards variations of faith by the members of the Catholic Church all over the world, was voiced in the decree of the Second Vatican Council in 1965. This Council gave stimulus to both unity of Christians (Marty 1992, 417) and the redrawing of the boundaries around syncretism by accepting some degree of cultural adaptation (Stewart, this volume, Part V). Nonetheless, there was still reluctance towards syncretism in the following words of Pope Paul VI, which reveal that the prejudice against the notion itself has not changed:

> The young churches ... borrow from the customs and traditions of their people, from their wisdom and their learning, from their arts and disciplines, all those things which can contribute to the glory of their Creator, or enhance the grace of their Saviour, or dispose Christian life the way it should be. To achieve this goal, it is necessary that in each major socio-cultural area, such theological speculation should be encouraged ... Thus it will be more clearly seen in what ways faith may seek for understanding, with due regard for the philosophy and wisdom of these peoples; it will be seen in what ways their customs, views on life, and social order, can be reconciled with the manner of living taught by divine revelation. From here the way will be opened to a more profound adaptation in the whole area of Christian life. By this manner of acting, every appearance of syncretism and of false particularism will be excluded, and Christian life will be accommodated to the genius and dispositions of each culture. (Pope Paul VI 1965; also ref. to Abbott 1966 in Stewart, this volume, Part V)

In the narrow sense of Christian theology, it is clear why the notion of syncretism represents a dilemma, that is: on one hand its intention of being a universal religion is set out to encompass all peoples of the world, but on the other hand its further existence as a dogmatic religion by the book demands total loyalty from its members of congregations to remain faithful to the canon of the Bible. From the logic of the system of Christianity and its history of doctrinal differences, the plurality of cultural and religious inputs may become fatal, but so too would an over-anxious control against syncretism; the Roman Catholic church became conscious about this in the 1960s.

If we are to conclude a meaning of syncretism from the history of Christian mission, then it is very much in the Plutarchian sense of a politicized term subject to the aspects of amities as well as enmities. In a broader sense, if the concept should prove useful as a scientific and generalizing category it cannot be isolated to a particular religion or phenomenon. Therefore, it must be put to the test with other types of empirical data that may reflect differently the transforming and the making of religions. However, the inquiry on syncretism in mission history represents important data for understanding religion as social and political fact, in as much as the theological use of the term mirrors the politics of religious difference in the history of religions in encounter with Christianity.

Syncretism in the Study of Religion

The notion of syncretism became an issue in the study of religion in the late nineteenth century and the beginning of the twentieth century owing to some major influences from the German philosopher Georg Wilhelm Friedrich Hegel (1770–1831) upon the German school of History of Religion and in particular through the inspiration from historian Johann Gustav Droysen (1808–1884), the architect behind the notion of Hellenism (as roughly referring to a period of time from 300 BC to 300 AD).

Droysen introduced the notion of Hellenism to classify a period of fusion of the occident with the orient that he saw as a result of the conquests of Alexander the Great (356–323 BC). His reading of the Hellenistic period was much coloured by the "Great man view of history" (Martin 1983, 132) that emphasized Alexander's influence on the cause of history. It was the inspiration from Hegel's philosophical view of history (whom Droysen's own father had been a student of), which gave meaning to the notion of Hellenism. Hegel's view of history refers in short to a development of consciousness that is in its entirety an idealization of history. To him, Jesus of Nazareth represented a turning point in the history of the world's consciousness that was prepared through the reconciliation of the occident with the orient, in particular the settlement of the Greek philosophical enlightment and the belief in the one god by the people of Israel (Bichler 1983, 70–71). Because of the inspiration from Hegel, Droysen pictured the fusion of the East and the West to be the aftermath of Alexander's efforts to form a "cosmopolitan" state through the diffusion of the Greek language and culture to the non-Greek areas of his conquests (Droysen 1952–53, bd. 3, 11, 14, 21). Later in his study, Droysen altered his Hegelian outlook to see the Hellenistic culture more as a "mixed product" of influences flowing from both the occident as well as from the orient (Bichler 1983, 59). This view motivated other scholars to use the notion of syncretism about this particular era in history. Although most of his contemporaries saw this as a sign of a degeneration of Greek culture he chose to interpret this "corruption" in the light of the new potentials that the Hellenistic period fostered.

In this line of understanding, Droysen defined Hellenism as the modern era of antiquity. The term came to signify in a twofold sense the religious "mixture" (*Verschmelzung*) of the east–west encounter by referring, partly, to the *interpretatio Graeca* corresponding to the identification of foreign gods by Greek equivalents (Martin 1983, 134, and Droysen 1952–53, 18), and partly to the new religious forms he saw emerging as a result of the fusion of eastern and western cultures. The term Hellenism qualified for both a Hegelian idealistic view of history leading to the making of Christianity as well as its inclusive explanation of how the new religions of that period emerged from syncretism (Jonas 1958, 12). In Droysen's characterization, religious "mixture" (*Verschmelzung*) was caused by the cosmopolitical universalism of Alexander. Later in the study of Hellenism, and owing to Droysen's definition of the term *Verschmelzung*, syncretism became a "politico-historical" term that was employed to explain the religious reactions following Alexander's conquests (Martin 1983, 137).

The universal trend that Droysen read into Alexander the Great and the Greek–Roman history was much influenced by the national-political views of his time that favoured nationalistic currents and the idealization of Christian universalism. From that point of view the Hellenistic period marked an end to paganism and the passage to the victorious Christianity (Droysen 1952–53, 462). Thus, the term "Hellenistic" became a concept to denote a time of transformation caused by the political re-adjustment after Alexander the Great (Moffatt 1922, 156). According to this view, Hellenism became synonymous with syncretism (as in Droysen's *Verschmelzung*), a "transitional" concept in a "transitional" period in history. Consequently, the notion of syncretism was explained later in the study of religion through an idealized conception of human history—that the unsteadiness of its nature is but a stepping-stone to more complete stages in the histories of religions.

The "History of Religion School"

The use of the term syncretism in historical studies carried an ambiguity much like it did in theology. It signified the heterogeneity of historical processes as opposed to the idealized homogeneity that the Hegelian philosophy of history proposed. The tendency, in the nineteenth and twentieth centuries, to prefer monolithic/uniform cultures over heterogenous cultures has influenced the historico-descriptive use of syncretism in that it was mainly used in a search for "survivals" of older traditions in the confused compositeness of syncretistic traditions.

In the beginning of the twentieth century, the German "History of Religion School" ("Die Religionsgeschichtliche Schule") marked a shift from the earlier negative use of the notion in theology as illegitimate mixing towards a more positive application of the notion onto the school's own understanding of "religiosity" as reflecting the subjective creativity of religion. In his introduction to the school, represented below, the historian of religions Hans

Kippenberg stresses that the notion of syncretism re-emerged in Wilhelm Bousset's writings, as well as in the work by other members of the school, as a positive term connected with a clash of paradigms against the previous views of early Christianity as having originated directly from Judaism. Thus, ironically, the notion of syncretism became reformulated as a positive term in support of the idea of the uniqueness of Christianity by its reference to it as a new formation resulting from the syncretistic milieu of Hellenistic–Jewish tendencies. In this way Bousset and other members of the "History of Religion School" saw Christianity freed from the legalist forms of Judaism. Kippenberg observes that this revised view of Christianity, together with the reformulated concept of syncretism, answered to the anti-Semitic paradigm of the time. This was, furthermore, occasioned through a reinterpretation of Hegel's philosophy of history (Bichler 1983, 162).

Besides this utmost problematic purpose for the use of the term, it was applied in order to distinguish between "religion" and "religiosity," or between objective and subjective religiosity. This differentiation indicates two very different modes of religiosity: (a) the clerical or canonical forms of religiosity versus (b) the popular forms of religiosity. The notion of syncretism typically operates at the level of popular and individual religiosity to explain how mutual influences get "subjectivized" historically in the making of new religious forms. Kippenberg points both to Hegel and to the German–American ethnographer Franz Boas and their influence on the changing notion of syncretism by introducing a shift from the ideas of unilinear evolution in religious change to that of mutual influences and diffusion. As such, he observes how the notion became the "cultural matrix" of historical description of the Roman Empire as well as in modern multi-culturalism, whilst the notion has changed definition according to the different roles it has played in the scholarly culture-critical discourse of the modern age.

The Problem of Definition

The persistent discussion on syncretism in the study of religion cannot resist the effects of the history of the term, a history that makes it quite an ambiguous affair to define the category of syncretism without falling back to its past definitions in theology. The five contributions in this part of the volume represent the work of Hans Kippenberg, a historian of religions; Hendrik Kraemer, a theologian; Robert Baird, a historian of religions; Michael Pye, a historian of religions; and Kurt Rudolph, also a historian of religions. Apart from Kippenberg's introduction to the German school of history of religion (see above), Baird, Pye and Rudolph all represent critical voices towards Kraemer's definition of syncretism. Baird is particularly unfavourable to the category of syncretism, whereas the other two, Pye and Rudolph, suggest a redefinition of the category.

Baird's criticism is particularly aimed at Kraemer's theological use of the term. Kraemer, who was professor of the History of Religions in Leiden, was engaged in the International Missionary Council, which asked him to write the book *The Christian Message in a Non-Christian World* (1938). In the preface of the book Kraemer wrote:

> The Christian Church and the missionary enterprise to-day stand in dire need of coming back to this which is, as it were, the heart from which the life-blood gushes forth through all the parts of the body. All the ways in which the Church expresses and manifests itself in the non-Christian world, either in word or in deed, have to be impelled and inspired by its prime apostolic obligation of witness bearing to the world. (Kraemer 1938, vii)

These words bore witness to Kraemer's deeply felt engagement in the Christian mission. And his twofold engagement in the opposing fields of Christian mission and the history of religions has influenced his approach to syncretism. To Kraemer, syncretism is first of all a non-Christian phenomenon although he admits that syncretism is inevitable and part of even anti-syncretistic religions such as Christianity and Islam (Kraemer 1962, 567). However, contrary to Christianity, he claims that the non-Christian religions have an *innate syncretistic apprehension*, which, in comparison with Christianity, displays the connotations of illegitimate mingling of religions.

Although he rightly points out that there are different attitudes towards syncretism in the oriental religions and Christianity, Kraemer uses the term to denote fundamental differences between other religions and Christianity that suggest that syncretism represents a rupture from authentic religious truth. This is the reason why Robert Baird and others have criticized Kraemer for using the term as a pejorative and value-laden description of non-Christian religions.

"Insider/Outsider"—A Question of Taxonomy

Baird warns against using the notion of syncretism in the normative sense, because it tends to hold the "outsider's" view instead of the "insider's." He remarks that the "outsider" fails to recognize the significance of the more "pragmatic," non-conflicting attitude towards syncretism, and that that makes syncretism quite irrelevant for the "insider." Therefore, he concludes, if the notion inclusively represents an anti-syncretistic stand then we have no use for the term except to describe it as a specific Christian phenomenon. This leads us to the question about taxonomy. Is it, as Baird suggests, among the definitional criteria for an academic taxonomy that it must correspond to the believer's taxonomy? Or, may it be that an academic category cannot be other than a "construction of a constructions" (Jensen 1996, 27)? We must be aware of not to "ontologize" our categories, but rather use them as "theoretical point of departure" (27) for analysing a specific phenomenon. Jensen suggests that instead of disputing about specific definitions as if they had a direct correspondence with their referents, we should agree to use a *generalized interpretation* about a subject (Jensen 1996, 29).

Baird's criticism of syncretism can be summed up as a critique of its many inadequate uses, whether it refers to the ambiguous theological tone, or it merely refers to "a dictum of historical knowledge," i.e. pointing to a self-evident and universal phenomenon without much descriptive value. His critique is essential to the discussion on syncretism in the following readings, which do not just discuss *whether-or-not-to-use* syncretism, but also *how-to-use* syncretism. For an understanding of the discussion it is absolutely indispensable to review the variety of ways in which the concept of syncretism is defined, so that it may serve as a platform of information for the creation of a more viable generalized interpretation of the category. It will never simply be a "one-to-one" relation between the *concept* and the *phenomenon* of syncretism that makes the category a good taxon. The idea that it should be so produces a confusion of unclear statements instead of intelligibility.

The Ambiguity of Syncretism

Can any category be free of ambiguity? This is the keyword to Michael Pye's discussion on syncretism. At the outset of the discussion, he considers J. H. Kamstra's view of syncretism. Kamstra is another Dutchman, who, contrary to Kraemer, took a phenomenological approach to the notion. He stressed, as did van der Leeuw (below, Part III) that we must look for the *dynamics* of syncretism in order to explain the phenomenon. This phenomenological understanding of syncretism, says Pye, meets the frontier between phenomenology and theology. Therefore, he challenges Kamstra's idea of "alienation" from within a religion to be too narrow a criterion for syncretism, because it refers to a theological standpoint. On the other hand, he accepts Kamstra's phenomenological approach as a method for comparing different ongoing hermeneutical activities in theology, as well as in other equivalents, that may help uncover the nature of the phenomenon.

In contrast to Kamstra's emphasis on "alienation," Pye perceives the nature of syncretism as "ambiguity," because various meanings of syncretism are presupposed in the different religious traditions that also give the notion its many phenomenological descriptions. Therefore, he stresses, specific meanings of syncretism must refer back to a general meaning of syncretism, that is, a general theory about the category. With reference to the notion of "transpositions" as found in the work of both van der Leeuw and Kamstra, the nature of syncretism displays, according to Pye, an aspect of ambiguity that is found in the very nature of religion as well as in the nature of man. Pye's observation on ambiguity in the nature of man locates his theory of syncretism at the level of culture as well as in psychology. According to scholars in the field of cognitive studies, individuals do not think in complete coherent systems of knowledge. Rather, humans select knowledge in smaller units of "mental spaces" that can be combined in various ways, all depending on our situation in social, religious and cultural contexts. This may in fact have an effect on how individuals organize their different inputs of beliefs according to the religious systems with which they come into contact. While the sense of ambiguity may seem particularly active in religion, it may very well be the manifestation of the difference between how individuals think and act, and how systems agree on how individuals think and act. Although Pye's statement with regard to religion in general is important, he relies particularly on his empirical data from Japanese religion when generalizing about syncretism exactly in the same manner as Kamstra relied on his characterization based on prophetic religion. However, in his refutation of Rudolph's critique of him, Pye's suggestion of a generalization is not meant as an attempt to essentialize syncretism or *ambiguity* for that sake, as he has emphasized in later works (Pye 1994)—even though, as I see it, the issue of ambiguity is more frequently present in the discourse about syncretism than it is in the phenomenon itself. Moreover, we must be aware not to accumulate definitions about syncretism that are mistaken for a particular *nature* or *essence* in the general discussion. This accumulation of definitions has tended to add to the problem of definition because of the inclination to fabricate *a* final definition both in the study of religion and anthropology. Instead, we should consider each definition as one more piece in the full puzzle of the syncretism phenomenon.

Turning now to Pye's conclusion, he restricts the use of syncretism to refer to a temporary process that, because of the ambiguous clash of meanings, leads to one of three solutions: (1) *assimilation*, (2) *a new religion*, and (3) *dissolution*. Although it makes good sense to limit syncretism to a process towards a more definite structure, it can be problematic to divide between process and result because it is not always possible to establish the historical antecedents of syncretistic formations. However, Pye's descriptive use of the term has the great advantage of defining syncretism as a mode of production of religion rather than a deviation from it. As such, he emphasizes the dynamic processes between religious systems, regarding them as fluid, negotiable traditions rather than fixed entities. Finally, his suggestion concerning the ambiguity of the category gives a good indication to the problem of definition.

The Interlock of Contact

The problems of definition tend to build up in the discourses on defining the problem. This is the main point in Kurt Rudolph's very extensive and thorough evaluation of the field of study of syncretism. Thereby he maintains that terminological awareness is essential for constructing one's own methodology according to the subject, which he mainly identifies as a category of philological-historical scholarship.

After a careful and critical review of various definitions stemming from the results of two symposia on syncretism, in Turku in 1966 and in Reinhausen in 1971, Rudolph presents his own definition of syncretism emphasizing the universal and value-free use of the concept to indicate types of cultural and religious encounters that may be described as "blendings." He restricts the definition of the phenomenon to the open form of the dynamics of religion from which he sees the three universal conditions for syncretism, *the encounter, the contact,* and *the confrontation,* because, he concludes, no terminology or typology has so far resulted in a unified definition of the nature of syncretism. Thus, Rudolph is in agreement with G. van der Leeuw (below, Part III) and others who understand syncretism as a historical fact of every religion. From this point of view, syncretism is embedded in the historical processes by the motivation of the three universal conditions mentioned above. However, Rudolph realizes the difficulty in generalizing about these three conditions without considering the many variations of encounter that result in different syncretistic forms. He suggests, therefore, that we may have to look for internal structures, social as well as psychological, that play a part in the differentiation of formations of syncretism, and which finally may constitute a typology of syncretism.

"Conscious" or "Unconscious"—Modes of Syncretism?

First of all, Rudolph differentiates between "conscious" and "unconscious" syncretism. Unconscious syncretism is defined as "naïve," "spontaneous" and "vegetating," but it refers mainly to the basis of religious/cultural development. Typical of unconscious syncretism is, according to Rudolph, a tendency towards identity-preservation in spite of changes. On the other hand, the conscience syncretism, he states, is the reflected religiosity of the founder of a religion that may lead to new religious formations.

The differentiation between conscious and unconscious syncretism is not without problems if it is carried out without absolute theoretical clarity as to what is meant by these concepts. In that respect, it could be seen as problematic that Rudolph associates the "conscious" part with the founders of religion, and the "unconscious" with the followers or users of religion, because his model for distinguishing syncretistic modes comes close to a classical Judeo-Christian distinction between founders of religion and lay-people. In this aspect, his view is similar to that of Kamstra and Colpe, whom he criticizes because they create the modes of syncretism based on a Christian distinction of religion or religiosity. It also serves to assert that only founders of religions are consciously motivated towards the innovative, and to maintain that lay-people have no conscious influence on religion—for they do so at least when it comes to confirming or invalidating the innovations of the founders.

According to the overall picture of the dynamics of syncretism that Rudolph presents, it is, in short, the interlock of contact of difference that prevails during the historical processes of every religion. And he is right to accentuate the reciprocity of historical processes and social and psychological mechanisms to determine syncretistic change in religion, and to take into consideration the complex interlocked processes going on at different levels, instead of simply describing syncretism as a *one-essence-phenomenon*.

The Historical-Descriptive Level of Explanation

The readings discussed in this chapter have predominantly defined syncretism on the historical-descriptive level of explanation. However, even the historical definition of syncretism raises questions that are in need of clarification. It should be obvious now, from the readings in this part, that the mere statement that the dynamics of syncretism are historical processes will not do alone without empirical data to back it up and theories to substantiate it. We need, therefore, to distinguish between other levels of explanation than the historical-descriptive to form an idea of the complexity of the nature of syncretism. The readings in the next part will suggest different approaches to clarify the dynamics of syncretism.

References

Abbott, W., ed. 1966. *The Documents of Vatican II*. London: Geoffrey Chapman.

Bichler, Reinhold. 1983. *'Hellenismus'. Geschicte und Problematik eines Epochenbegriffs*. Darmstadt: Wissenschaftliche Buchgesellschaft.

Cone, James H. 1985. "Black Theology: Its Origin, Methodology, and Relationship to Third World Theologies." In *Doing Theology in a Divided World*. Papers from the Sixth International Conference of the Ecumenical Association of Third World Theologians, ed. V. Fabella and S. Torres, 93–105. Maryknoll: Orbis Books.

Droysen J. G. 1952–53 [1836–78]. *Geschichte des Hellenismus*, bd. 1, 2, 3, ed. E. Bayer. München: Deutscher Tashenbuch.

Engel, Peter. 1976. *Die eine Warhrheit in der gespaltenen Christenheit. Untersuchungen zur Theologie Georg Calixts.* Göttingen: Vandenhoeck & Ruprecht.

Fabella, V., and S. Torres, eds. 1985. *Doing Theology in a Divided World.* Papers from the Sixth International Conference of the Ecumenical Association of Third World Theologians. Maryknoll: Orbis Books.

Jensen, Jeppe Sinding. 1996. "On Intentionally Putting Religions in Contact." In *Religions in Contact,* ed. I. Dolezavola *et al.,* 19–30. Brno: Czech Society for the Study of Religion.

Jonas, Hans. 1963 [1958]. *The Gnostic Religion: The Message of the Alien God and the Beginnings of Christianity.* Boston: Beacon Press.

Koester, Helmut. 1990. *The Nag Hammadi Library,* ed. James M. Robinson, 124–38. New York: HarperSanFrancisco.

Kraemer, Hendrik. 1938. *The Christian Message in a Non-Christian World.* New York: Harper & Brothers; London: Edinburgh House Press.

—1962. "Synkretismus." In *Die Religion in Geschichte und Gegenwart. Handwörterbuch für Theologie und Religionswissenschaft.* Dritte Auflage, Band 6, 563–68. Tübingen.

Martin, Luther, H. 1983. "Why Cecropian Minerva? Hellenistic Religious Syncretism as a System." *NUMEN* 30: 134–37.

Marty, Martin. 1992. "North America." In *The Oxford Illustrated History of Christianity,* ed. John McManners, 384–419. Oxford: Oxford University Press.

McManners, John. 1992. "Enlightenment: Secular and Christian (1600–1800)." In *The Oxford Illustrated History of Christianity,* ed. John McManners, 267–300. Oxford: Oxford University Press.

McNeill, John Thomas. 1964. *Unitive Protestantism.* New York: Abingdon Press.

Moffatt, J. 1922. "Syncretism." In *Encyclopaedia of Religion and Ethics,* ed. J. Hastings, vol. 12, 155–57. New York: Charles Scribner's Sons.

Pakkanen, Petra. 1996. *Interpreting Early Hellenistic Religion: A Study Based on the Mystery Cult of Demeter and the Cult of Isis.* Papers and Monographs of the Finnish Institute at Athens 3. Athens: D. Layias and E. Souvatzidakis.

Paul VI. 1965. *Decree on the Mission Activity of the Church.* http://www.ccel.org/contrib/catholic/church/vaticann/v2miss.txt

Plutarch. *Moralia,* vol. 6, Loeb edition. Cambridge: Harvard University Press.

Pye, Michael. 1994. "Syncretism versus Synthesis." *Method & Theory in the Study of Religion* 6: 217–29.

Schmid, Heinrich F. F. 1846. *Geschichte der syncretischen Streitigkeiten in der Zeit des Georg Calixt.* Erlangen: Carl Heyder.

Torres, Sergio, ed. 1985. "Preface." In *Doing Theology in a Divided World.* Papers from the Sixth International Conference of the Ecumenical Association of Third World Theologians, ed. V. Fabella and S. Torres, ix–xix. Maryknoll: Orbis Books.

Usener, H. 1896. *Götternamen. Versuch einer Lehre von der Religiösen Begriffsbildung.* Bonn: F. Cohen.

IN PRAISE OF *SYNCRETISM*:
THE BEGINNINGS OF CHRISTIANITY CONCEIVED IN THE LIGHT OF A DIAGNOSIS OF MODERN CULTURE[*]

Hans G. Kippenberg

Early Christianity was a syncretistic religion. This thesis, defended by Hermann Gunkel (1903, 88), summarizes a new revolutionary approach to the beginnings of Christianity. The Greek word 'syncretism,' originally indicating the practice of the people of Crete, who in times of external threat neglected their internal conflicts, became a boo-word in the theological debates after the Reformation. Surprisingly, with the *Religionsgeschichtliche Schule* the notion was evaluated positively (Rudolph 1992, 193–96). The new assessment was part of a new paradigm that Wilhelm Bousset, scholar of New Testament studies, explained in 1904 in three basic articles. Not long before then, the students had been taught, in particular by Albrecht Ritschl, that the writings of the New Testament stood in close connection to the Old Testament. Only through a consideration of this context could they be understood. Only few years later, the situation had changed completely. As Bousset observed:

> Gradually we then learned to recognize that there was not empty space between the time and literature of the Old Testament and of the New Testament that could simply be omitted, but rather a momentous development of religions had taken place, and without knowing and understanding it, the literature of the New Testament could not be understood. In an indefatigable work, the material was compiled, sifted, processed, and many new things were added to what was already known... Today, the material of the later Jewish literature has been so comfortably

processed and almost completely presented by Kautzsch in the two volumes of the *Apocrypha* and the *Pseudepigrapha*, so that the time has now come when even those who study theology may no longer ignore these things. But what became most important is that this literature is now really grasped and understood in its historical context. And the historical significance of what previously looked like a collection of curiosities … is now appreciated and understood. Gradually the lines are extended and we now recognize the significance of the knowledge of the later literature of Judaism for the understanding of the New Testament, that it presents their contemporary milieu, from which the New Testament, especially the Gospels, arose, and with which they are bound by endless fine and coarse threads. The sensation excited by all works that advanced vigorously in this direction showed that a virgin forest was being cleared here and a decisive advance achieved in theological work. (Bousset 1904, 267–68)

Sources Severing Christianity from Judaism

The new approach replaced the Old Testament by the *Religionsgeschichte* (simultaneously a historical theory of religions and a designation of a school of scholars) as the main frame of reference. A new generation of scholars was realizing that there was indeed "not empty space" between the Old and the New Testaments and gradually filled it by hitherto unknown sources and a new method of interpreting them. A host of scholars of various disciplines started tracing, editing, translating and analyzing writings that have been excluded from the Hebrew and the Greek Bible. These writings, the *Apocrypha* and *Pseudepigrapha*, they declared to be the "main bridge between the Old and the New Testament" (Gressmann 1914, 37–38). They belong to a "syncretistic new formation," that brought together Jewish and Hellenistic ideas and practices and became crucial in the rise of early Christianity (Bousset 1904, 273).

Bousset demonstrated the superiority of the new approach in three fields. The specific kind of Judaism between the Old and the New Testament (*Spätjudentum*) could no longer be explained as a logical unfolding of the biblical religion. It represented a soil of its own, to which other religions have contributed, in particular Iranian, Babylonian, Syrian and Hellenic ones. The same holds true for the gospels and the apostle Paul, who likewise operated in a religious context broader than the Old Testament. Scholars dedicated to that program developed the notions of eschatology, apocalypticism, gnosticism and mystery religions in order to determine the types of religiosity generated by that fertile matrix. In 1919, looking back at this new approach,

Bousset describes how this approach has contributed to a revised view of early Christianity:

> It was clear to us that Ritschl's statement was wrong since there is still a large, unresearched land between the Old and the New Testaments, late Judaism. And as we set about this research, it became clear to us that the most important basic notions of Jesus' preaching, the Son of Man and the Kingdom of God, first came to light in this later time and its literature, that the growth of early Christianity in the world cannot be understood without a knowledge of Diaspora Judaism, its religious worship and its liturgy. And as soon as our eyes grew accustomed to the new discoveries that arose here, our scholarship needed to take a second big step. We discovered that we could not understand Paul and John in many essentials without precise knowledge of the world of Hellenistic religion, the world in which Christianity conquered its new homeland, especially by Paul. (Bousset 1919, 41)

It was not by chance that a Jewish scholar objected to this approach and exposed its weakness by means of a compelling analogy. Reviewing W. Bousset's book *Die Religion des Judentums*, George Foot Moore wrote:

> The author uses as his primary sources almost exclusively the writings commonly called Apocrypha and Pseudepigrapha, with an especial penchant for the apocalypses; and only secondarily, and almost casually, the writings which represent the acknowledged and authoritative teachings of the school and the more popular instruction of the synagogue. This is much as if one should describe early Christianity using indiscriminately for his principal sources the Apocryphal Gospels and Acts, the Apocalypses of John and Peter, and the Clementine literature. (Moore 1920–21, 243)

Bousset evaluated these Jewish writings so differently from Moore because he suspected them to be witnesses of popular beliefs, uncontrolled by Jewish authorities. Religions, practiced by ordinary people, are not derived from authoritative teachings, he assumed. The *Apocrypha* and *Pseudepigrapha* are valuable sources of that popular current. In order to analyze them according to their scholarly point of view, scholars introduced the notion *syncretism*. It served as a category of describing and explaining processes of generating new forms of religiosity.

A Method Privileging Unwritten Practice in Favor of Written Representation

Part of the new approach was a marked methodological twist, one that distinguished Bousset and his fellows from previous scholarship. In contrast to the preceding but still living generation of scholars (e.g. Julius Wellhausen or Adolf Harnack) that had focused on the history of the sources and literary forms of the Bible, they searched for unwritten beliefs and practices, since these may reflect subjective religiosity much closer than written texts. 'Religiosity' was a crucial notion at that time (Krech 2001, 51–75). The methodological point of view was elaborated convincingly by Hugo Gressmann. What is vital and historically effective never has its ultimate basis in books, but rather in persons, their experiences and in the history they are rooted in. "How often is the unwritten more important than the written"! (Gressmann 1914, 30). One has to go beyond the literary text in order to grasp the "real," "living" religion. It is religiosity that counts, not the literary representation. Nevertheless, literary representations remain unavoidable for the scholar looking for such religiosity. Since any author of a text has to take into account the expectations and experiences of distant readers, he has to draw from that common unwritten stratum; otherwise there would be no communication between both parties. So also, a historian of religions, studying texts, is able to recover "popular" religion from these writings. By collecting reliable information about popular beliefs from other sources, comparing it with the content of the literary works and by isolating oral traditions in literary work, the scholar is able to disclose religiosity.

Implicit in this approach is the assumption that genuine religion ultimately evaded any rational fixation. It is directly and clearly declared by Heinrich Hackmann, a less prominent member of the *Religionsgeschichtliche Schule* (Rollmann 1982, 276–79). W. Bousset agreed with that view, but resisted the wholesale reduction of religion to an irrational force, a position argued by Rudolf Otto in his best-selling book *The Idea of the Holy: An Inquiry into the Non-Rational Factor in the Idea of the Divine and its Relation to the Rational*, published in 1917. Bousset objected:

> Religion is not purely and simply irrational power... All religions contain a twofold aspect: the divine, the deity confronts man as the stranger, the almost uncanny power that is purely and simply superior to him, before which his soul quakes in fear and awe, and yet on the other hand, as the blessing power, to which he secretly feels drawn powerfully in the depths of his being. If religion were only that irrational aspect, it would be something purely and simply uncanny, destructive, fatal. (Bousset 1919, 36)

Though the popular experience of religion appeared to W. Bousset to be more genuine than its literary representation, this experience is not immediate, but shaped by ideas and concepts. Rational reflection remains fundamental to any discourse on religion. That enables the scholar to identify the forms of practiced religion. Gnosticism, eschatology, dualism, apocalyticism are the outcome of such inquiry.

Along with other scholars of the *Religionsgeschichtliche Schule*, Bousset reconstructed the rise of early Christianity as part of that syncretistic religious milieu. In contrast to William Robertson Smith and Julius Wellhausen who had conceived of the history of Israel in analogy with the later development of Arab tribes, Bousset assumed substantial influences and borrowings from adjacent Near Eastern and Hellenistic cultures. This coincided with a simultaneous shift in social anthropology. Since the 1890s the theory of an universal unilinear evolution of all human societies, independent of each other, gradually lost its plausibility as an all-explaining law. Anthropologists doubted the underlying assumption that the rise of similar beliefs and institutions in human history was always due to similar causes. Was it not evident that similarities between cultures were increasing and decreasing according to geographical parameters? There were good arguments for replacing the paradigm of unilinear evolution with that of mutual influences and diffusion. German-American scholar Franz Boas nicely presented the arguments: as one of the leading anthropologists he pleaded for diffusion in place of evolution as an explanation for similarities between cultures (Boas 1896).

Syncretism: Shifting the Focus from Product to Producer

German Protestant scholars at that time conceived of post-exilic Judaism as primarily a religion of law obedience. When employing the category *syncretism*, they constructed the idea of a prolific cultural milieu, one that severed Christianity from a legal type of Judaism. A vivid religiosity had poured into Judaism and enabled Jews to overcome a tradition-bound ethics. The entire construction was part and parcel of a Protestant anti-Semitism of those days. "We Christians have absolutely no reason for the assumption that everything good and valuable in religion could come only from Israel; such Jewish chauvinism would sound very curious in our mouth"—Hermann Gunkel once stated.[1] That scholarly operation deeply affected the understanding of early Christianity. While the former liberal theologians understood Jesus' 'Kingdom of God' as a kind of moral authority, similar to Kant's categorical imperative, the new generation of scholars realized that Jesus' ethics were conditional upon his apocalyptic expectations. His demands did not come from an ideal of human community and had nothing to do with generally valid moral norms. They came from the dreadful seriousness of the present view of the end of days. "The greatest crisis of world history is at the gates. The most blessed salvation and the most awful doom lie hidden in the dark of the nearest future. Once more, at the eleventh hour, is the decision about his own fate given to everyone. The time is short" (Weiss [1892] 1964, 138). There is only one salvation: everyone had to repent and atone if he/she did not want to perish in the messianic judgment (Luke 13:3, 5). Weiss's discovery offered a new choice for the study of the life of Jesus. As Albert Schweitzer put it: to understand Jesus either eschatologically or not at all ([1913] 1951, 232). These scholars did not conceive of religion as establishing a harmony between man and world, but as a power of world rejection (Kippenberg 2002, 113–24).

That point of view ultimately derived from Georg Wilhelm Friedrich Hegel, who had argued, against Friedrich Schleiermacher, that religion does not create a harmony between the human mind and the natural world, between subject and object. In contrast to that romantic view, religion is a major power in establishing a split between them. In his comparison of Indian and Christian religions, Hegel distinguished different strategies of establishing the relation between both realms. In India, the individual believer could overcome it by contemplating the divine essence, while in Christianity the believer had to endure that tension by practicing world rejection. Hegel was the first to distinguish two different, even opposite, modes of world rejection: contemplation/mysticism on the one hand, asceticism on the other. While Hegel frankly confessed his sympathy with the Christian type of world rejection, Arthur Schopenhauer favored the Indian one. In this context, Schopenhauer contemplated the possibility that in the beginning, Christianity had been a religion of the Indian type. World-rejection and contemplation were the hallmarks of genuine Christianity (1969, vol. II, ch. 48). Schopenhauer's view was later adopted by members of the *Religionsgeschichtliche Schule*. It answered exactly to their interests to view religion as a subjective principle behind the written texts. The notion of *syncretism* held a firm place in that shift of interest from objective literary texts to the level of subjective religiosity. I have addressed here a process in which established religions were reshaped as subjective worldviews and ethics.

Syncretism and Multiculturalism

Syncretism required the existence of a cultural matrix, which could contain the diverse elements deriving from different sources: from Jewish and from Greek religions. For Wilhelm Bousset, Jewish and Greek religions had different linguistic genealogies and accordingly they were of different stock: one was Indo-European, the other Semitic (Bousset 1906, 181). As did many other scholars of his time, Bousset embraced the conception of Friedrich

Max Müller, revised by Cornelis Petrus Tiele, that Indo-European religions conceived of the Gods as revealing themselves in the veil of nature, while Semitic religions conceived of gods as revealing themselves in prophets and the course of history. Whether the differences can be described along these lines or not, there is no doubt that the ancient city fostered pluralism.

In Hellenistic and Roman Empires, traditional religions were officially recognized (Kippenberg 1991). Although the cities were gradually losing political independence, emperors guaranteed the autonomy of local religions until the age of Constantine. Citizens were expected to run their communities according to their "ancestral laws," which were tied to local religions and cults. This recognition applied not only to pagan cults; the Seleucid Emperor Antiochos III also granted the privilege of governing their community in accordance with their "ancestral laws" to the Jews of Jerusalem. Roman Emperors, who extended the privilege to Jews in the Diaspora, later followed his example. In cities of Asia Minor, Syria and Egypt (Alexandria) Jews were allowed to form separate political communities, called *politeuma*. Jews and pagans shared citizenship in these cities, though they belonged to different, even opposed, religious communities. Since Jews rejected the pagan cults as idolatry, common citizenship and religious conflicts went hand in hand. I suspect that as a matrix, this system fostered not only conflicts, but also exchange and interactions between different religious traditions. In his study on African religions in Brazil, Roger Bastide has demonstrated that diverse religions can operate in a common social matrix without merging (Bastide 1971; Reuter 2000, 210–96). In this regard, the ancient processes of *syncretism* were similar. Comparable also is modern Western *multiculturalism*, which functions similarly by merit of a political recognition of religious diversity (Taylor 1994). Peter van der Veer has made the pertinent remark that the notion of *multiculturalism* appears to have replaced the notion of *syncretism* (1994, 209).

This brings me to my final point. The use of *syncretism* in the *Religionsgeschichtliche Schule* echoes the debates about the fate of religion in the modern scientific and industrialized world. It is not by chance, that at the very same time, when historians of religions hailed ancient *syncretism* as a matrix for creating new worldviews and ethics, contemporary intellectuals embraced non-Christian religions as a means of opposing a culture, which they accused of disenchanting nature, man and history. They held the Jewish–Christian notion of *creatio ex nihilo*, to be guilty of producing the view of a world ruled by mechanical laws. In their understanding, that worldview and its associated ethics spoiled the spontaneity of life. The German publisher Eugen Diederichs answered the needs of these intellectuals through his publication activities (Hübinger 1996). His publishing house clearly had a mission: It should help creating a "living religion"—part of a genuine German culture, as Diederichs understood it (Graf 1996). Esotericism, mysticism and theosophy were expected to be able to preserve the human person from perishing in a mechanistic world more efficiently than official Christianity was able to. "Today it would not be necessary to speak about religion at all, has [*sic*] not the overestimation of intellectual knowledge and the one-sided preference of economic activities silenced the voice of the inner demon," Diederichs pointed out in a leaflet. Only through an infusion of religions that re-enchant nature, man and history could the individual be cured from the disease of modern civilization. Diederichs published a series called *The Religious Voices of the Nations (Die religiösen Stimmen der Völker)*, in order to serve that task. In his conception, these books presented "the religious documents of all positive religions—to begin with the primitive people, Confucius, Buddhism, Parsism, Greek religion to Islam and Talmud—in handy volumes explained by outstanding experts" (Diederichs 1967, 35). He hoped that Henri Bergson would be able to supply the speculative foundation for his venture, since this kind of religion embraced the principle of genuine life. By means of contemplation and mysticism man could emancipate from "iron-cage" traditions and rescue his personal identity from modern rationality. Only religious experience can open the doors to a world remote from rationality, but close to the stream of genuine life.

Summary

When the notion 'syncretism' appeared in the German *Religionsgeschichtliche Schule* at the beginning of the twentieth century, it served two functions. First: as an historical notion it was introduced into the study of early Christianity in order to indicate a context that separated Christian beginnings from Jewish roots. Non-canonical texts became the key to an understanding of early Christian religion. Second: historians of religions introduced a dimension of cultural critique into their arguments. They saw ancient Judaism as a barren religion of law obedience that urgently deserved a healthy 'infusion' of Hellenistic religious spirituality. This perspective had its place in intellectual debates on modern rational culture that was regarded as an outcome of the Jewish-Christian tradition. The construction of the historical notion of syncretism was thus also dependent on a diagnosis of the modern world.

Notes

* The paper was presented on a panel of *Greco-Roman Religions Section* of the American Academy of Religion in San Francisco, 1997. In my revision I made grateful use of the corrections and ideas of Professor William Cassidy, who was in charge of that panel.
1. Hermann Gunkel 1903, 14—quoted by Martin Rade in his article "Religionsgeschichte und Religionsgeschichtliche Schule," RGG, 4, Tübingen 1913, p. 2187.

References

Bastide, Roger. 1971. *African Civilizations in the New World.* Trans. Peter Green. New York: Harper & Row.
Boas, Franz. 1949 [1896]. "The Limitations of the Comparative Method of Anthropology." In *idem, Race, Language and Culture,* 270–80. New York: Macmillan.
Bousset, Wilhelm. 1982. *Jesu Predigt in ihrem Gegensatz zum Judentum. Ein religions-geschichtlicher Vergleich.* Göttingen: Vandenhoeck & Ruprecht.
—1904. "Die Religionsgeschichte und das neue Testament." Parts I, II, III. *Theologische Rundschau* 7: 265–77; 311–18; 353–65.
—1906. *Das Wesen der Religion.* Halle: Gebauer.
—1919. "Religion und Theologie." In *idem, Religionsgeschichtliche Studien. Aufsätze zur Religionsgeschichte des Hellenistischen Zeitalters,* ed. A. F. Verheule, 29–43. Leiden: Brill.
—1924. *Die Religion des Judentums im späthellenistischen Zeitalter* (1st edn 1903; 2nd edn 1906). 3rd edn by Hans Gressmann. Tübingen: Mohr (Siebeck).
Diederichs, Eugen. 1967. *Selbstzeugnisse und Briefe von Zeitgenossen.* Düsseldorf/Köln: Diederichs.
Graf, Friedrich Wilhelm. 1989. "Rettung der Persönlichkeit. Protestantische Theologie als Kulturwissenschaft des Christentums." In *Kultur und Kulturwissenschaften um 1900. Krise der Moderne und Glaube an die Wissenschaft,* ed. Rüdiger vom Bruch, Friedrich Wilhem Graf and Gangolf Hübinger, 103–31. Wiesbaden: Steiner.
—1996. "Das Laboratorium der religiösen Moderne. Zur 'Verlagsreligion' des Eugen Diederichs Verlags." In *Versammlungsort moderner Geister. Der Eugen Diederichs Verlag—Aufbruch ins Jahrhundert der Extreme,* ed. Gangolf Hübinger, 243–98. München: Diederichs.
Gressmann, Hugo. 1914. *Albert Eichhorn und Die Religionsgeschichtliche Schule.* Göttingen: Vandenhoeck & Ruprecht.
Gunkel, Hermann. 1903. *Zum religionsgeschichtlichen Verständnis des Neuen Testaments.* Göttingen: Vandenhoeck & Ruprecht.
Hübinger, Gangolf, ed. 1996. *Versammlungsort moderner Geister. Der Eugen Diederichs Verlag—Aufbruch ins Jahrhundert der Extreme.* München: Diederichs.
Kippenberg, Hans Gerhard. 1991. *Die vorderasiatischen Erlösungsreligionen in ihrem Zusammenhang mit der antiken Stadtherrschaft.* Heidelberger Max Weber-Vorlesungen 1988. Frankfurt: Suhrkamp.
—2002. *Discovering Religious History in the Modern Age.* Trans. Barbara Harshaw. Princeton: Princeton University Press.
Krech, Volkhard. 2001. "Religiosität." In *Max Webers Religionssystematik,* ed. Hans G. Kippenberg and M. Riesebrodt, 51–75. Tübingen: Mohr (Siebeck).
Lüdemann, Gerd. 1987. "Die Religionsgeschichtliche Schule." In *Theologie in Göttingen,* ed. Bernd Moeller, 325–61. Göttingen: Vandenhoeck & Ruprecht.

—1992. "Das Wissenschaftsverständnis der Religionsgeschichtlichen Schule im Rahmen des Kulturprotestantismus." In *Kulturprotestantismus. Beiträge zu einer Gestalt des modernen Christentums*, ed. Hans Martin Müller, 78–107. Gütersloh: Mohn.

Moore, George Foot. 1920–21. "Christian Writers on Judaism." *HThR* 14: 197–254.

Pfleiderer, Georg. 1992. *Theologie als Wirklichkeitswissenschaft. Studien zum Religionsbegriff bei Georg Wobbermin, Rudolf Otto, Heinrich Scholz und Max Scheler*. Tübingen: Mohr (Siebeck).

Reuter, Astrid. 2000. *Das wilde Heilige. Roger Bastide (1898–1974) und die Religionswissenschaft seiner Zeit*. Frankfurt: Campus.

Rollmann, Hans. 1982. "Duhm, Lagarde, Ritschl und der irrationale Religionsbegriff der Religionsgeschichtlichen Schule. Die Vita hospitis Heinrich Hackmanns als geistes- und theologiegeschichtliches Dokument." *Zeitschrift für Religions- und Geistesgeschichte* 34: 276–79.

Rudolph, Kurt. 1992. "Synkretismus—vom theologischen Scheltwort zum religionswissenschaftlichen Begriff." In *idem, Geschichte und Probleme der Religionswissenschaft*, 193–213. Leiden: Brill.

Schopenhauer, Arthur. 1969. *The World as Will and Representation*. Trans. E. F. J. Payne, 2 vols. New York: Dover.

Schweitzer, Albert. 1951. *Geschichte der Leben-Jesu-Forschung* (2nd edn 1913). Tübingen: Mohr (Siebeck).

Taylor, Charles. 1994. *Multiculturalism: Examining the Politics of Recognition*. Princeton: Princeton University Press.

van der Veer, Peter. 1994. "Syncretism, Multiculturalism and the Discourse of Tolerance." In *Syncretism/Anti-Syncretism: The Politics of Religious Synthesis*, ed. Charles Stewart and Rosalind Shaw, 196–211. London: Routledge.

Weiss, Johannes. 1964. *Die Predigt Jesu vom Reiche Gottes* (1892; 2nd edn, 1900) 3rd edn edited by Ferdinand Hahn. Göttingen: Vandenhoeck & Ruprecht.

SYNCRETISM

Hendrik Kraemer

In conversing on religious subjects with people in Java, one almost inevitably has some such experience as the following. In more than ninety out of a hundred cases, one hears the stereotyped remark: "All religions are ultimately one." It comes from the lips of the intellectuals as well as from those of the illiterate villager. This saying expresses a worldwide opinion, worldwide in place and in time. All the religions of antiquity and all the naturalist non-Christian religions today are deeply imbued with this conviction. The religions of revelation are the sole exception to this rule.

Everywhere in the world, in the religious world of the Roman Empire as well as in all the great naturalist non-Christian religions, the practice of a bewilderingly indiscriminative (as we might say) assimilation was and is the order of the day. In Syria every village-saint is the object of inter-confessional worship, for behind this cult-object stands the primordial Semitic God of their ancestors, who personified universal life and is still persistent in the minds of the people. In Japan the pilgrims and tourists sacrifice their homage-coin (*saisen*) alike at Buddhist temples, Shinto shrines and Roman Catholic cathedrals. In India, Hindus and Muslims have been known to worship simultaneously at each other's shrines. It would be easy to multiply by the hundred instances of this truly universal phenomenon.

One of the best-known features of Chinese universism is that the three religions—Confucianism, Buddhism and Taoism—are virtually treated as one. The religious allegiance of the average man is not related to one of the three religions. He does not belong to a confession or creed. He participates, unconcerned as to any apparent lack of consistency, alternatively in Buddhist, Taoist or Confucian rites. He is by nature a religious pragmatist. Religiously speaking, we find him *prenant son bien où il le trouve* (taking his due where he can find it). It is very significant to note that Mohammedanism, which by its prophetic origin has a more rigid and clear conception of religious truth, has never been allowed to enter the Chinese League of Religions, although there is no objection whatever to it from the standpoint of the three great religions—Islam has been established for many centuries in China.

A really gigantic and systematic attempt towards religious syncretism is Ryobu-Shinto (bi-lateral Shinto). In it Buddhism and Shinto have thoroughly amalgamated on the basis of naturalistic kinship. The great leader in this enterprise of religious amalgamation has been Kobo Daishi, the founder of Shingon. The procedure was an extraordinarily easy one. Hotoke (Buddhas, Bodhisattvas and Arhats) were identified with the Shinto Kami. Vairocana and Amatera-su became interchangeable. Buddhist-Shinto temples were built as places of worship. Even now every Japanese, if he is not a pure Shintoist or Buddhist (as is the case of Shinto sects and the Puritan Shinshu of Buddhism), is registered as a member of a Buddhist sect and worships in a Buddhist *tera* (temple) as well as in a Shinto *miya* (shrine). He participates in Shinto *mat-suris*, but his funeral rites are performed by Buddhist monks. In his house he has a kami-altar (*kamidan*) and a Buddha-altar (*butsudan*) and he sacrifices and prays to both. In China one can meet many similar conditions. The pragmatist attitude in religion and the natural innate syncretistic apprehension dominate the religious scene in all naturalist religions, whether in the past or in the present. The religious philosophies of India, China and Japan find in the justification of these two dominant characteristics one of their two main themes, the other being the speculation about Absolute Pure Essence and Reality. Japan and China, however, force these characteristics upon the attention of the onlooker still more emphatically than India does, because the man- and clan-centred mind of the Chinese and the nation-centred mind of the Japanese bring it about that religion in its different forms is preponderantly conceived as a means to satisfy the welfare of the individual and of the community. India's attitude and apprehension are not less pragmatic and syncretistic. When compared with that of China and Japan, however, it might perhaps be said to be somewhat disguised, for two reasons. The numerous *dharmas* contained in the caste-system are all clear symbols of the pragmatist attitude, and in Indian religious philosophy they are explained and justified by the same relativism which animates all naturalist religions. In practice, however, each *dharma* gets an aspect of practical absoluteness by the rigid separation between the different castes. In the second place, India, through the peculiar nature of its religious history, instinctively emphasizes in the way it conceives religion the aspect of openness to a world of indestructible spiritual reality.

We are repeatedly told, especially of the Chinese and the Japanese (but one can safely extend it to all other peoples which adhere to one of the naturalist religions), that they have a deep-rooted indifference towards dogma and doctrinal differences. In the Roman Empire it was the same. Apuleius invokes in his well-known prayer in one breath Isis, Minerva, Venus, Diana, Proserpina, Juno and Kybele as one deity, calling them all *rerum naturæ parens* (parent of the nature of things) and *elementorum omnium domina* (mistress of all elements). Nock in his book on *Conversion* says: "It was commonly held that the gods of different nations were identifiable, that the Egyptians worshipped Athena and Zeus under other names." In a foreign country one paid homage to its gods as a matter of course. About the whole area of naturalist religions, including those of antiquity, the testimony is given again and again that they are exceedingly tolerant.

All these instances demonstrate in an impressive way the underlying inherent unity of all these religions. The reason for this inherent unity is the fact of their being products of the primitive apprehension of existence and their naturalistic monistic framework.

We are accustomed to call the phenomenon illustrated by the preceding instances by the name of syncretism. From all that has been said in this chapter it will be clear as daylight that syncretism and religious pragmatism are necessary and normal traits in the religions that live on the primitive apprehension of existence. In view of the fundamental nature and structure of these religions it is nothing capricious or unprincipled; it is consistency itself. It would be abnormal if this were not so. One can safely speak about a fundamental syncretistic and pragmatist predisposition of those religions. It is rather interesting to note that the term syncretism is, properly speaking, inadequate if we judge this phenomenon from the standpoint of the fundamental nature and structure of the religions in which it occurs, which, scientifically considered, is the only legitimate method to be followed. The term syncretism has always more or less had the connotation of expressing the *illegitimate* mingling of different religious elements. This peculiar conception of syncretism could only grow in a Christian atmosphere—and has actually grown there, for the word and the concept are a result of theological controversies in seventeenth-century Protestant theology—where it is legitimate and obligatory to speak about illegitimate mingling, because an absolute standard of reference is implicitly assumed. From the standpoint of the naturalist religions, however, it is not correct to speak of syncretism as an illegitimate and unexpected proceeding, because it is just what one should expect to happen. A more adequate term, devoid of any value-judgment, would be amalgamation. Ryobu-Shinto is a special case in so far that it is a deliberate attempt at the amalgamation and harmonization of two religions, whereas in most cases syncretistic attitudes are practised without deliberate purpose, because it is as natural as breathing.

This amalgamation, the universal pragmatic attitude, the typical tolerance, the aversion to doctrinal borderlines, the relativist and, ultimately, very subjectivist (despite all seeming indications to the contrary) conception of religion, are all the natural products of the naturalistic monism in these religions.

Every form of religion, every system of religious tenets and practices, is to the mind that consciously or unconsciously lives on the naturalistic-monistic apprehension of existence one of the many possible and available ways and methods for the *realization* of a purpose or end that human beings have set themselves. That may be a base, a decent, or an exceedingly noble end, for example, one's wishes for a good life, consisting of riches, ease, and many children; for rebirth in better conditions of life; for the entrance into Amida's Paradise; for communion with God and experience of his exquisite love; for enlightenment and final deliverance. This is the reason why in this sphere of naturalist religions there are so many forms of religious life that are virtually huge hedonistic machineries, and others that are marvellous expressions of self-mastery and metaphysical serenity.

Religion, in its many positive forms, necessarily belongs in this sphere of naturalist religions to the domain of human *psychology*. It is sought primarily for its experience-value, not for its truth-value. It is exceedingly important to grasp the significance of this fact; it is another way of expressing the fundamental relativism of naturalist religions. On account of this fact, it becomes at once clear why the quality and nature of religious experience are always taken as the standard to measure the value of a religion. The pragmatist question: "What value does it have, what results does it yield?" is, as a matter of course, considered to be the decisive question, and not the question of truth and objective validity.[1] Why should one pose the question of truth? This whole world with all its forms of life belongs to the sphere of the relative, the unreal. Religion as manifest in different systems and ways, all belonging to the relative sphere of this phenomenal world, stands by the nature of the case outside the question of absolute truth. It is an endeavour of man to realize his ends, and as such altogether a social and psychological affair. A good illustration of this is that many *bhaktas*, although they are convinced and avow that real ultimate *moksha* is the supreme moment of *tat twam asi* (thou art that), openly proclaim that they "value" the "experience" of *bhakti* much more than ultimate *moksha*, which is the only *moksha* that wholly deserves the name. Psychological pragmatism here quietly takes precedence over truth and ultimate reality.

The latitude towards doctrine or creed does not mean indifference to doctrine in the sense of having a doctrine-less religion. The three great religious civilizations of India, China and Japan have been profusely creative in the field of doctrine and metaphysical speculation. But in accordance with their fundamental nature as naturalist religions they envisage doctrines as expressions of relative truth, which consequently can also only be relative. They are relative, intellectual realizations of man in the whole of his endeavour towards self-realization. Radhakrishnan in his *The Heart of Hindustan* praises Hinduism highly for this latitude towards doctrine and creed, which are all relative to the general character of the people who profess them. "That different people," says he, "should profess different faiths is not unnatural. It is all a question of taste and temperament." This doctrinal latitude and relativism could not be expressed more strongly. Gandhi, though he declares Truth to be God and though he is a man of deeply moral temperament, treats positive religion with the same easy-going relativism, as is demonstrated by his passionate *swadeshi*-ism in religion. And here we have the same remarkable phenomenon to state as in the pseudo-religious nationalisms of Europe. Gandhi stresses the relativist nature of all religions, for they are products of the country, and Truth Itself is unattainable. Yet, in practice, this fundamental relativism behaves, itself, as a militant absolutism.

This applies not only to the religious doctrine, but also to moral doctrine. In this whole naturalistic monistic world-conception with its cardinal division into the phenomenal relative world of unreality and the absolute world of reality, all moral systems—even morality as such, because it presupposes activity—belong to the relative sphere. They are means—in noble or dubious forms—to an end. God or the Divine in the fully valid sense of the word—not in any way qualified or accommodated—does exclusively belong to the absolute sphere. God is above all morality, for what has the Pure Essence to do with good and evil, with choice and responsibility, with activity and purpose? The deep-rooted universal conviction in the East, that the acceptance of the absolute antagonism of good and evil is a rather childish and narrow-minded idea and that the only conception which behoves him who really "knows" is the "*Jenseits von Gut und Böse*" (beyond good and evil), appears thus to be a quite natural and logical conviction.

For the same reason it is quite natural to the average Easterner, who has drunk deeply from the waters of naturalistic-monistic religion, to explain traits in his chief gods that are, according to common moral feeling, scandalous—for example, Krishna's well-known erotic adventures—as "divine condescensions." In this light, the well-known tolerance of those religions becomes clear, and also the amiable, suave quality it always shows, which so often evokes enthusiastic admiration. The enthusiasm and the admiration are in many cases understandable against the background of harsh and detestable intolerance with its bickering and petty controversies, which is the result of the distorted intellectualist conception of truth that corrupts so many human minds. But this admiration is no contribution whatever to the comprehension of the real character of this kind of tolerance. Tolerance, real tolerance, is equally rare everywhere in the world, and intolerance is equally common everywhere in the world, whether in the West or in the East. We are receiving today in both respects the most drastic and unforgettable lessons. The proverbially "tolerant" area, of the naturalist religions with its extreme "tolerant" temper in the realm of religious truth, is extraordinarily intolerant with respect to the social aspect of religion. The law that rules all corporate religious life in the religions that spring from the primitive apprehension of existence, the "tribal" religions as well as the cults and religions that belong to the three great religious civilizations of India, China and Japan, is the absolutely obligatory observance of, and conformity to, the traditional religious behaviour of the group. To break away from this conformity, however strong the call of conscience or truth may be, is unpardonable sin and *défaitism*. Rigorous intolerance is then considered the most natural thing in the world and is unhesitatingly applied. The caste system and its rules are a clear illustration of this intolerance in a land as "religiously" tolerant as India. Religious persecutions have been as common in Japan and China as anywhere else in the world, because everywhere in the world, East and West, North and South, man in different forms is the same self-assertive being and therefore prone to intolerance. The "religious" intolerance of these persecutions, however, had little to do with religious doctrine or truth (for there the usual doctrinal latitude obtained), but sprang from political or social motives.

The universality and intensity of intolerance in the realm of the naturalist religions suggest strongly that the no less marked phenomenon of tolerance needs some qualification. This tolerance in the realm of religious truth has to be interpreted in connection with that basic religious relativism, pragmatism and subjectivism which are a necessary consequence of the nature of the naturalist religions. It follows from the secret religious agnosticism that lies at the bottom of the naturalistic monistic life-apprehension. For the sake of clarity, it would be advisable not to speak of religious tolerance with regards to this phenomenon, but of truth-equalitarianism. In many cases, truth-indifferentism might even be more appropriate.

The amiable suavity, which often sweetens this pseudo-tolerance so agreeably, ought not to blind our eyes to the fact that it is dearly bought at the price of a radical relativism. In the same way the repellent impression that detestable intolerance makes must not make us forget that it at least, though in a very perverted way, evinces awareness of one of mankind's most precious gifts, the persistent demand for absolute truth as a matter of life or death, for *everyone* and not only for the elect. Where in the sphere of the naturalist religions in some form the problem of truth becomes paramount, the fierce struggle for it easily and deplorably takes on an aspect of intolerance, because the art of real tolerance belongs to the highest arts of life, in all climes and times rarely achieved. A very illuminating instance of this easy sliding off to intolerant bitterness is the way in which Ramanuja vehemently refutes in his *Shribhashya* Shankara's acosmist monism. Why was this noble seeker for the precious pearl of loving *bhakti* to the God of infinite mercy such a vigorous and mordant fighter in the field of religious dialectics? Because he had the sincere conviction that he had to defend religious values of supreme value, for himself and for others.

Real tolerance is an arduous lesson to be learnt. It presupposes the combination of unswerving obedience to, and vindication of, the authority of absolute and evident truth with acceptance of the liberty of others to reject it or to adhere to other convictions, even though they be considered erroneous. The breeder of all doctrinal intolerance is an intellectualist conception of truth. Real tolerance can only grow when it is fully recognized that truth can only be really obeyed in perfect spiritual freedom, because anything else or anything less is disobedience to and misunderstanding of the real character of truth. The possibility of achieving the most dynamic form of real tolerance is to be found in the purely apostolic attitude of being an obedient and joyful *witness* and not a *possessor* of the truth that God has mercifully revealed, and entreating humankind to join in accepting and obeying it.

The spirit of syncretism, relativism, pragmatism and subjectivism that runs through the veins of the naturalist religions has of course various and different incarnations. Primarily there are its practical forms in the life and practice of the millions. Secondly, however, there are various rationalized forms in the shape of the many religious philosophies, which all contain a justification of the many types of religious life and purpose. The philosophical or epistemological background of these rationalized forms is the juxtaposition of the illusory world of relative, empirical existence and the real world of pure, absolute Essence, to which we have alluded already. All religions and what they tell about God, man, the world, deliverance, and so on, belong, in these rationalized forms, to the sphere of illusory relative existence. Truth pertains exclusively to the sphere of absolute pure Essence. All religions therefore at their best can only be accommodated truths. All differences and contrasts have already a sameness, and therefore are at the bottom irrelevant. There is in this abstract ontological conception of Ultimate Reality or Truth no relation whatever between the Divine and empirical man, because man in his essence is one with relationless Essence. Its counterpart is the doctrine of the unreal character of the phenomenal world and of the positive forms of religion. Through this theory the syncretistic and relativistic attitude, which is implied in naturalistic-monistic apprehension, is rationalized. From the standpoint of Pure Essence all is sameness; from the standpoint of accommodated truth all is difference. Monism and pluralism, polytheism and monotheism can equally be true, while equally false, and they have therefore the right to co-exist.

In India this "tolerant" justification and sanctioning of the religious status quo—for that is what it comes to—uses still more persuasive arguments. In the sphere of relative empirical existence, all religions and confessions have their significance and value. For every individual the religion and confession in which he is born is, so to speak, the religious place assigned to him by *samsara* and *karma*. For the same reason *mukti*, or deliverance, is only possible for him in this religion and this confession, for the law of *karma*, which determined all the physical, social and other circumstances of his birth, is the supreme disposer. Although of relative value, to him this religion and this confession are his predestined stage of apprehension of religion and truth. As always, naturalistic monism or the ontological apprehension of existence appears here, notwithstanding the seeming capriciousness of its variegated forms, to be extremely logical. It does not even shrink in its ontological absolutism and its empirical relativism from declaring that the obtaining status quo of conditions and standpoints is the normal and inevitable state of things in every given period of history. It does not account for any real change, and thereby makes the world meaningless. In the last instance, this follows logically from the axis on which this monism turns. The Sole and Ultimate Reality is motionless, actionless Pure Essence. The ever-recurring cyclic process of nature, which is in non-speculative naïve naturalistic monism the world-process as it is enacted, becomes in its rationalized speculative form a mirage.

What has been said shows clearly how abysmal is the difference between the ontological apprehension of Ultimate Reality in the naturalist religions and the voluntarist apprehension in Biblical realism. In the first the Ultimate is relationless, actionless, blissful, Pure Essence; in the second it is the "God and Father of our Lord Jesus Christ," who yearns for the relation with his prodigal sons and who constantly acts and creates anew. In the first, the world is a gorgeous and yet nauseating pageant, an endless series of variegated and fascinating but at the same time disgusting processes of life, all ultimately unreal and meaningless; in the second the world is the creation of God, enigmatically perverted by sin, but yet God's working place, led by Him to its consummation, desperately real, and the place of responsible decisions between God and man.

It is not to be marvelled at that the prophetic religion of Biblical realism does not show this syncretistic, pragmatist, relativist and subjectivist trend of the naturalist religions. It contrasts entirely with the endless assimilative and adaptative elasticity of naturalistic monism. It is disturbing by its "exclusivist" attitude, that is not lessened in the least by the fact that the Bible radiates with the lustre of love and freedom of the Spirit, and with the personality of Christ who sovereignly breaks through all limitations and proclaims the truth that "sets free." This enigmatic "exclusivism" brought it about that amidst the tolerant and conforming mystery-cults Christianity stood alone "intolerant" and nonconformist. At present, the International Buddhist Society, founded in 1934 by Inoue Tetsujiro, has defined as one of its objects the absorption of Christianity. From the standpoint of Mahayanist Buddhism, whose monistic all-embracing tendency has been made clear in our discussion, this is a very reasonable object. Radhakrishnan in the book just quoted is of the opinion that there is not much serious difference between Hinduism and Christianity on the question and the nature and

46

means of salvation. This is certainly a mistaken opinion, for Christianity pro-claims salvation from sin by forgiveness of sins, which implies a religious world totally different from Hinduism, which preaches salvation from transiency and ignorance.

More significant for our present discussion are, however, the sequel of Tetsujiro's and Radhakrishnan's arguments. The Buddhist Society, while disclaiming any objection to the Christian message of salvation, emphatically rejects the Christian apprehension of God, the Creator and Judge of the world, and the Christian claim to proclaim the exclusive truth. Soteriological Mahayanism thus claims agreement with Christian soteriology, but not with its theocentric core. Radhakrishnan, although in his opinion the Cross is not an offence or a stumbling-block to the Hindu as showing how love is rooted in self-sacrifice, strongly rejects, however, atonement and reconciliation. Evidently he is not aware that, in the theocentric religion of Biblical realism, salvation has its real meaning in atonement and reconciliation because in it is expressed the fact that God solely and really creates a way where there is no way.

Note

1. The Greeks expressed the pragmatist conception of religion they had by the unequivocal words: Χρῆσθαι τοίς θεοίς. This is wholly appropriate to the religions we are discussing.

SYNCRETISM AND THE HISTORY OF RELIGIONS

Robert D. Baird

One of the purposes of the study of World Religions today is to enable us to understand the faiths of other people. It is with this purpose in view that Wilfred Cantwell Smith proposes that "it is the business of comparative religion to construct statements about religion that are intelligible within at least two traditions simultaneously" (1959, 53). This means that a description of Hinduism or Buddhism or Islam[1] that is to be considered valid must be both intelligible to outsiders and acceptable to that religion's believers. "Anything that I say about Islam as a living faith is valid only in so far as Muslims can say amen to it."[2] Our present concern is to inquire to what extent, if any, the concept of syncretism contributes to such understanding.

The concept of syncretism has been used frequently to describe certain manifestations in the history of religions. Although seldom defined, the term is usually assumed to be abundantly clear, even though examination of its usage reveals that it is used in various and conflicting ways. The term does not always communicate anything definite, and the meaning that is intended could often be more clearly expressed if another term were used.

Among those who have studied the history of religions few have used the term as frequently as Hendrik Kraemer. He has written on this theme at some length as both a theological problem and as a missionary problem.[3] Even in Kraemer's writings, however, the term is used with several meanings, and there are times when he employs the term in a manner which he has elsewhere stated is a confusing and misleading use of the word. There are, for example, those instances where he states explicitly that syncretism is inevitable, necessary, and universal:

> One could go on enumerating, but these examples may suffice to demonstrate the simple fact that syncretism, cultural and religious, is for many reasons a persistent and universal phenomenon in human history. It cannot but happen, unless peoples live in entire isolation. (1956, 389)

In this sense it would be possible, one would think, to agree with Radhakrishnan when he says that Christianity is a syncretistic faith, and with Hermann Gunkel whose history of religions approach to the Bible led to the same conclusion.

In another context, however, Kraemer denies that Christianity and Islam are syncretistic religions and that to so label them is misleading. It is, in his view, the Eastern religions which are by nature syncretistic, and that clearly includes Radhakrishnan himself (Kraemer 1956, 406). Kraemer would contend that while one can, in a certain sense, hold that the Christian Scriptures and also the Qur'an are syncretistic, this is not the best use of that term. Nevertheless, the confusion in usage remains when he also maintains that syncretism is inevitable and universal.

This much should be abundantly clear. Although the term has been used by not a few historians of religions, and although the term is assumed to communicate its own meaning, that meaning varies not only from one writer to another, but also within the writings of a single author. Some have apparently sensed this ambiguity when they distinguish between conscious and unconscious syncretism.

> In a certain sense every religion, "primitive" as well as religions related to a big cultural area or claiming to be world-religions, may be and often are called syncretistic to some degree as a result of their growth through history. In these cases, however, the word has various connotations. It then means that rites or conceptions of different origin, or of a different degree of affinity, have become incorporated in a given religion and have been adapted to its dominant spirit and concern in such a way that they have become a genuine and accepted part of this religion. This, however, has nothing to do with syncretism as a *conscious*, organizing religious principle, such as we have described in the form of genuine, full-fledged syncretism in the Roman Empire. (Kraemer 1956, 297)

This distinction is similar to the one that differentiates syncretism as naïve or indiscriminative and intentional or reflective (Kraemer 1963, 200; 1956, 401). Such distinctions do not solve the problem of varied usage, however, for in either case the meaning of syncretism is determined by what practices or ideas are synthesized and into what kind of apparent unity they are brought, rather than whether it was a conscious synthesis on the part of the participants.

It is my contention that the concept of syncretism has been used in both a historical and a theological sense. An analysis of these two general uses will show that in the former case the term serves no useful purpose at all. The only legitimate use of syncretism theologically is not applicable to the faith of those it is sometimes used to describe, but is in reality a barrier to understanding those faiths.

Syncretism as a Historical Phenomenon

Historical analysis limits itself to an explanation of events, persons, movements or ideas which is on the plane of history. While it may or may not be theologically true that the source of the Qur'an is Allah, it is not legitimate to make that judgment within the limits of historical knowledge. It has been this concern for historical explanation that has led to the historian's preoccupation with the "roots" of certain movements, or the "sources" of a person's thought. The historian is led to relate the contents of the Qur'an to its Arabian setting, and to attempt to show how the Meccan suras and the Medinan suras exemplify a different emphasis, no matter how theologically disconcerting it may be to some Muslims. Historicism goes so far as to imply that an entity cannot be understood unless its history has been traced, and that the significance of the twentieth-century approach to life is not that it is scientific, but that understanding itself has become historical. This type of approach goes some distance toward explaining the quest for origins whether it be a search for the Jesus of history, the authentic preaching of the early Christian church, or the authentic teaching of the Buddha.

But such a concern for origins runs counter to the very method that is employed. Within the historical method there is no real room for a beginning, a first cause. The historian must jump into the stream of history somewhere if he or she is to study anything. The study of Buddhism might possibly begin with Sakyamuni, but that is not to deny the historical legitimacy of another study showing the Brahmanical context that made Sakyamuni's position relevant, or still another study showing the features of the Vedic Age which preceded both. The only limitation placed on the historian's quest is in the limits of the information available as one moves into the remote past. However, this is not a logical limitation imposed by method but a limitation imposed by the availability of data. If and when more material becomes available, the historical method will push the historian back still further in a search for historical antecedents.

If the appeal is made to divine revelation such as in the Qur'an or the New Testament, the same search is relevant. Even if the Qur'an is professed to come from Allah, it was communicated by human beings and written in Arabic—an Arabic used and understood by the people of Muhammad's day.

It has been this search that has involved historians of religions when they apply their method to the study of the Bible. The result has been an insight into the historical relationship between the ideas and practices of the Old Testament and those of the ancient Near East, and the relationship between the New Testament and the Greco-Roman world. Such endeavors are legitimate historical quests even though they may not have the theological implications that have sometimes been attached to them.

One use of the term "syncretism" is to describe the interrelationship between ideas and movements historically. In this sense syncretism is universal and inevitable. Here it is merely a term which is used to describe a dictum of historical knowledge—any subject fitting for historical research has historical antecedents.

> Commercial intercourse, political events, the extension of power from a certain centre, often shows such spiritual, religious or cultural encounters and struggles as a mostly unintended consequence. We see, therefore, in the history of mankind many samples and varieties of syncretism. Everywhere, where genuine "culture-contact" take place, it appears as an inevitable effect. (Kraemer 1956, 389)

It is this method of history which led Hermann Gunkel to say that Christianity is a syncretistic religion. For Gunkel, extraneous elements did not wait until the fifth century to enter the church, but were detectable in the Apostolic Age itself. Following a historical method, he located elements in early Christianity that were found in other contexts in the Greco-Roman world and concluded that indeed Christianity is "a syncretistic religion." It is this same observation that lends some point to Radhakrishnan's judgment that "Christianity is a syncretistic faith, a blend of various earlier creeds ..." (Radhakrishnan 1933, 62).

Now, if it is true that such borrowing and blending and influencing on the plane of history is part of the whole historical process and is both inevitable and universal, then no real purpose is served by applying the term syncretism to such a phenomenon. Historically speaking, to say that "Christianity" or the "mystery religions" or "Hinduism" is syncretistic is not to say anything that distinguishes it from anything else and is merely equivalent to admitting that each has a history and can be studied historically. Although Kraemer himself calls this historical phenomenon syncretism, on other occasions he seems to sense that this usage is inadequate, as when he says:

> The smell of the earth, the brightness of the sky, the natural and spiritual atmosphere, which in the course of ages wrought the soul of a people, have to manifest themselves in the kind of Christianity that grows there. This is far from being syncretism in the technical sense in which it is

currently used, but it is a certain kind of coalescence, of symbiosis without losing identity. (1956, 390–91)

I propose, however, that the term syncretism be dropped as a designation of a historical phenomenon. Since in this sense it applies equally well to all expressions of religion, to use it to describe a particular expression tells us nothing specific.

Syncretism as a Theological Phenomenon

When we turn from the meaning of syncretism as a historical phenomenon to what syncretism might mean theologically, we find a certain confusion in the way the term is used. To distinguish between a syncretism that is reflective and conscious and one that is spontaneous may be interesting but it is not a significant distinction logically. Here we are interested in what takes place theologically when one uses the term syncretism, whether that which takes place does so consciously, unconsciously or both.

We shall begin by pointing out that merely to define syncretism as the uniting of religious elements of different origin, or merely as the "fusion of various beliefs and practices," is too general to avoid the application of the concept to any religious expression.[4] The origin of the elements to be united is not of prime import, and that various beliefs and practices are fused says nothing that would distinguish one movement from another.

Usually, when the concept of syncretism is applied, it connotes an element of conflict or inconsistency. Care must still be taken, however, lest the term be used in a manner which is meaningless. To say that syncretism is what takes place when one brings two conflicting ideas or practices and unites them into a harmonious whole is to say nothing coherent. If the two original ideas or practices are in conflict, then they cannot, without modification, produce a harmonious unity. If a harmony is produced, then it follows that either the two original elements were only apparently in conflict, or that changes have been effected so that it is not actually the two conflicting elements that produce the harmony but a modification of those elements that produces elements no longer in conflict. To say that two genuinely conflicting concepts were harmonized is a contradiction.

When elements which have come from differing sources are united into a harmonious unit then the term synthesis might be used to describe the phenomenon. This term indicates the unity achieved without implying the logically impossible statement that the harmony is produced by the union of two contradictory practices or ideas.

What, then, can be intended by the concept syncretism? This term should be reserved for cases where two conflicting ideas or practices are brought together and are retained without the benefit of consistency. Syncretism occurs only when the result is not a harmonious unity. Kraemer expresses this view in the following manner: "It is in these circles taken in the sense of a systematic attempt to combine, blend and reconcile inharmonious, even often conflicting, religious elements into a new, so called synthesis" (1956, 302). The same idea is found in Hocking when he mentions the view whereby one brings together elements from various sources into a whole "devoid of any principle of coherence" (Hocking 1956, 146). The same essential lack of unification in syncretism is implicit in H. R. Mackintosh's definition: "To be strict, syncretism is only present when elements derived from various religions are admitted on equal terms ..." (Mackintosh 1956, 185). Here various elements stand side by side without an attempt to reconcile or give priority to either one.

If, on the other hand, a unity is produced by modifying one's religious complex so that the previously extraneous element is comfortable in that context, then one is referring to what Hocking called "reconception":

> Either that good thing you have found belongs uniquely to the religious organism from which it came—in which case you must adopt *that* unity—or it belongs to *yours*—in which case you must *reconceive* the essence of your own faith, to include that new element. You cannot live religiously within a divided house, or a house whose roof covers only part of its floor area! (1956, 147; original italics)

From a theological point of view, reconceptionism may be as unhappy a situation as syncretism but the two are not the same. In reconceptionism, the result is a unity which has been effected through a modification of the very essence of a religion. This concept, of course, can only be used when one defines the essence of one's religion theologically. The attempt to arrive at the essence of a religion by examining its numerous historical manifestations has been unsuccessful. Syncretism, however, merely retains the conflicting elements without having successfully reconciled them.

I conclude, then, that this is the only meaningful use of the concept of syncretism, and that although the term has been used to designate other types of religious expressions as well, it is, in such contexts, misleading and confusing. The pejorative connotation attached to the term now becomes partially understandable. What could be objectionable in synthesizing religious elements which are not in conflict? It is the willingness to maintain contradictory elements side by side that has been objectionable.

Syncretism, a Barrier to Understanding

The term syncretism is usually not used by a believer to describe his or her own religion. One of the most common uses of the term in the history of religions is to describe certain Eastern religious expressions. Ryobu-Shinto is described as "syncretism" (Noss 1963, 436; Holtom 1938, 38), as is the Hindu philosophy of Shankara, or the Chinese attitude which enables one to be simultaneously a Buddhist, Confucianist, and Taoist.

> In the grand Mahayanist and Hindu philosophies of religion, for instance, elaborated in Japan in Ryobu-Shinto or in India by Shankara, every stage and expression of religion, from the "highest" to the "basest" gets, on this basis, full recognition and justification as to its necessary and relative value. On this syncretistic approach, the claim of absolute tolerance, the pride of all genuinely eastern spirituality, depends. Radhakrishnan is, as we have seen, a modernized but essentially unchanged defender of this syncretistic philosophy. (Kraemer 1956, 401)

It seems to be implied that in each case the Eastern religious expressions have brought elements together that are conflicting and illegitimate. This is never the religious attitude of those involved, however, who sense no such logical problem. The failure to find a recognition of inconsistency where it might be expected has been problematic for Western scholars.

In the thought of Shankara, for example, there are both levels of Being and stages of experience. What is true of one level is not necessarily true of another level. All distinctions, including logical ones, are part of the phenomenal world of appearance. The world of appearance, however, is *māyā*, that is, illusory from the vantage point of the indescribable and undifferentiated Nirguna Brahman. The phenomenal world is valid on its own level, but it can be transcended:

> So long as the right knowledge of the Brahman as the only reality does not dawn, the world appearance runs on in an orderly manner uncontradicted by the accumulated experience of all men, and as such it must be held to be true. It is only because there comes such a stage in which the world appearance ceases to manifest itself that we have to say that from the ultimate and absolute point of view the world appearance is false and unreal. (Das Gupta 1922, 446)

From the standpoint of Brahman, then, all distinctions of the phenomenal world are obliterated, including ideas and practices that are contradictory to the lower level of being. There is no uncomfortable sense of living with conflict in Shankara's total system. The conflict exists for those who reject the notion of levels of Being and who deny the ultimate reality of Nirguna Brahman.

> Another supposed illustration of syncretism is a Chinese expression. One of the best-known features of Chinese universalism is that the three religions—Confucianism, Buddhism and Taoism—are virtually treated as one. The religious allegiance of the average man is not related to one of the three religions. He does not belong to a confession or creed. He participates unconcerned as to any apparent lack of consistency, alternatively in Buddhist, Taoist or Confucian rites. He is, by nature, a religious pragmatist. (Kraemer 1956, 201)

The important point here is noticed by Kraemer himself. To the Chinese believer there was no inconsistency in such a religious practice for they were treated virtually as one. The reason for this is that there was a broader and over-arching religious attitude which made it possible to incorporate all such practices and beliefs as seemed useful. Kraemer says that the Chinese believer was in this case a pragmatist by nature. If that be true, then that was his/her religious attitude, and it was hardly inconsistent to act in the described manner. It is the outsider who does not share such an attitude, and fails to recognize its significance. It is also the outsider who uses the term to describe the phenomenon.

Ryobu-Shinto is often given as a good example of syncretism. Here the Shinto kami and the Buddhist bodhisattvas are identified and the two religious expressions are merged.

> A really gigantic and systematic attempt towards religious syncretism is Ryobu-Shinto (bi-lateral Shinto). In it, Buddhism and Shinto have thoroughly amalgamated on the basis of naturalistic kinship. The great leader in this enterprise of religious amalgamation has been Kobo Daishi, the founder of Shingon. (Kraemer 1956, 201)

Here again, however, Kraemer recognizes a basic kinship. The system of Ryobu-Shinto conceives of Ultimate Reality, or the unobservable source of all existent things, as the cosmic Buddha Maha-Vairochana or Dai Nichi. The universe is the body of Dai Nichi.

> In this manifestation of the Great Life of the Universe on the side of the observable events of experience, the *kami* of the Shinto pantheon appear as the avatars of the divine beings of Buddhism, and thus these two faiths are in essence one and the same. (Holtom 1938, 38)

In this system, every Shinto god or goddess becomes a manifestation of the special Buddhist divinity. Hence, Amaterasu-Omikami becomes a particular manifestation of Maha-Vairochana or Dai Nichi.

That some were opposed to Ryobu-Shinto and that others made attempts to eliminate those aspects which were foreign, is no refutation of the unity here expressed but merely underlines the well-known fact that the terms

"Hinduism," "Buddhism," "Christianity," or "Shinto" do not correspond to a clear and always consistent system of practices and ideas. "Every faith appears in a variety of forms" (Smith 1962, 2).

Buddhism had long shown the ability to adjust to Chinese religion. Shinto had a similar history of adjustment. As Anesaki puts it, "Now this Double Aspect Shinto was an expression of the compromising attitude so characteristic of the Japanese mind" (Anesaki 1930, 137). Of the utmost importance here is that those involved did not look on their amalgamation as involving opposing or conflicting positions. Rather it was a unification that appeared to those involved to be quite legitimate and natural.

Syncretism, then, is irrelevant to those who are inside the so-called syncretistic faiths. "For those naturalistic religions, which are by nature syncretistic, syncretism is no problem at all. They cannot see it" (Kraemer 1956, 402). If, then, one is attempting to understand such faiths or is attempting to communicate the meaning of such faiths, the term is misleading since it does not correspond to the believer's understanding of his/her faith.

Syncretism and the Encounter of Religions

Kraemer labels most Eastern religions as expressions of religious syncretism. Mahayana Buddhism, Advaita Vedanta, Chinese religions in general, Ryobu-Shinto, and the so-called primitive faith encountered in Java, are all syncretistic because they are basically naturalistic (naturalistic-cosmic or naturalistic-monistic) (Kraemer 1956, 403). It has already been observed that the insiders in the above cases sense no conflict in their approach. "In view of the fundamental nature and structure of these religions it is nothing capricious or unprincipled; it is consistency itself. It would be abnormal if this were not so" (Kraemer 1963, 203). The term serves no real purpose *within* the value system of these religions, but reflects instead the value system of the one who uses it. Such an observation is basic to understanding what is involved when the concept of syncretism is used.

We have argued that the only fruitful use of the term "syncretism" is to describe a situation in which conflicting ideas or practices are brought together into a new complex which is devoid of coherence. But the religious complexes represented by the above illustrations of syncretism are not devoid of coherence to the believers. The term syncretism most clearly denotes not only a lack of coherence in the new complex of ideas and practices, but also the distinction between the insider or person of faith and the outsider or observing scholar.

It is no secret that the term syncretism commonly carries a pejorative connotation:

> The scholars intended their statements to be taken objectively and scientifically, but they allowed subjective overtones to creep in. This is well seen in the concept of "syncretism" which has a deprecatory connotation. If a religion is said to be "syncretistic," it is held to be *ipso facto* inferior. (Watt 1963, 61)

This pejorative connotation is readily understandable when it is realized that the concept not only implies a contradiction, but that it is applied from outside the circle of a given faith. The concept of syncretism not only describes the encounter of religions, but is itself a part of that encounter. Syncretism is a concept applied to a religion by those who stand outside its circle of faith and hence fail to see or to experience its inner unity. Hence, Kraemer can say that Shankara's philosophy is syncretistic and Radhakrishnan can hurl the same label at Christianity.

Basically, syncretism is a concept that not merely points to the encounter of one religious complex with another but it is itself a part of that encounter. Hence, its use must be guarded. If one of the purposes of the history of religions is to come to an understanding of the faith of other people, then it is imperative that the term be avoided since it implies a conflict which is not experienced by the insider.

> It is rather interesting to note that the term syncretism is, properly speaking, inadequate if we judge this phenomenon from the stand point of the fundamental nature and structure of the religions in which it occurs, which scientifically considered, is the only legitimate method to be followed. (Kraemer 1963, 203)

If, however, one's purpose carries one to theological evaluation of other religious practices and ideas (and this is a legitimate purpose as well), then the word is legitimate but of limited service. To label a religious complex syncretistic is to say it is inconsistent—in which case more specific arguments are required.

Those works, of which the purpose is descriptive rather than normative, should avoid the label "syncretism" since, rather than assisting communication, the concept proves to be a barrier.

Notes

1. Since his article in the above volume, Smith has rejected these designations in favor of "the faith of Hindus" or "the faith of Buddhists," designations more in keeping with his personalist approach. Cf. *The Faith of Other Men* (1962) and *The Meaning and End of Religion* (1963).

2. Smith 1958, 43. We are not implying that there is no place for theological studies or critical evaluations which involve the truth question, but merely that understanding is a prior task for the history of religions.
3. Kraemer 1963, 200–211; 1956, 387–417. Asked to contribute an article to *The Theology of the Christian Mission*, Kraemer responded with a letter indicating that he could say little more on the subject than he had already said.
4. "Syncretism." In *The Oxford Dictionary of the Christian Church*, 1314. London: Oxford University Press, 1957.

References

Anesaki, M. 1930. *History of Japanese Religion*. London: Kegan Paul.

Das Gupta, S. 1922. *A History of Indian Philosophy*, vol. 1. Cambridge: Cambridge University Press.

Hocking, W. E. 1956. *The Coming World Civilization*. New York: Harper & Brothers.

Holtom, D. C. 1938. *The National Faith of Japan*. London: Kegan Paul.

Kraemer, H. 1956. *Religion and the Christian Faith*. Philadelphia: Westminster Press.

—1963 [1938]. *The Christian Message in a Non-Christian World*. Grand Rapids: Kregel Publications.

Mackintosh, H. R. 1956. *Types of Modern Theology*. London: Nisbet and Co.

Noss, J. B. 1963. *Man's Religions*. 3rd ed. New York: Macmillan.

Radhakrisnan, S. 1933. *East and West in Religion*. London: George Allen and Unwin.

Smith, Wilfred C. 1959. "Comparative Religion. Whither—and Why?" In *History of Religions: Essays in Methodology*, ed. M. Eliade and J. Kitagawa. Chicago: University of Chicago Press.

—1962. *The Faith of Other Men*. New York: New American Library.

—1963. *The Meaning and End of Religion*. New York: Macmillan.

Watt, W. M. 1963. *Truth in the Religions*. Edinburgh: Edinburgh University Press.

Syncretism and Ambiguity

Michael Pye

D r J. H. Kamstra has recently published a lecture about the significance of syncretism for the phenomenology of religion, and its connection with theology (1970).[1] His interest in this topic arose out of his experience of the mutual resistance set up between the syncretistic Japanese and Christianity, and out of his detailed study of the oldest case of syncretism in Japan, namely that brought about through the arrival of Buddhism in that country (Kamstra 1967). He complains that since the work of H. Kraemer (1937), little has been done in the analysis of syncretism, and that it has been neglected in the general study of religion. No reference to it is made at all, for example, in the 634 pages of Geo Widengren's recent *Religionsphänomenologie* (1969). Moreover, most practitioners of the study of religion are strongly influenced by Christianity and tend to see syncretism as an illicit contamination, as a threat or a danger, as taboo, or as a sign of religious decadence.

Kamstra notes that the word *synkretizein* was first used by Plutarch to mean "to come to concord, just as the Cretans do when threatened by a common enemy" and that Erasmus used it in the sense of reconciliation. Theologians in the seventeenth century began to also use it pejoratively. Kamstra himself proposes to use the word to mean: "the coexistence of elements foreign to each other within a specific religion, whether or not these elements originate in other religions or for example in social structures" (1970, 10). He elaborates the various ways in which these elements can be related, and then divides his attention between (1) "the theological approach to syncretism: the real roots of syncretism" and (2) "the phenomenological approach to syncretism: the dynamics of syncretism."

In the context of theological approaches to syncretism, Kamstra pays special attention to the analysis of Hendrik Kraemer. Kamstra considers it important to move away from analyses that are theologically loaded and to move instead to a phenomenological base. His criticism of Kraemer, with this in view, is particularly illuminating because, sensing that Kraemer's analysis was theologically conditioned, he turned his attention precisely to that religion which Kraemer had claimed was not in principle syncretistic, namely Kraemer's own religion, and found the roots of syncretism there. Or rather, as he further explains, the roots of syncretism lie neither in the "naturalism," whether primitive or monistic, of which Kraemer had spoken in distinction to the "prophetic" religions, but rather in the very structure of human existence. "To be human is to be a syncretist," he writes (Kamstra 1970, 23). And by this he means: "Even a prophet—however filled he may be with the divine—simply needs the speech and the situation of his audience in order to be comprehensible at all" (Kamstra 1970, 23–24).

In the text of his lecture, Kamstra appeals to the authority of Paul to illustrate this point, while in a note thereto he suggests that Buddhism can provide a helpful nuance in its distinction between *samvriti* and *paramārtha satya*, that is, between conventional and absolute truth. It seems that it would be possible to elaborate Kamstra's thesis at this point on a stronger comparative base. Perhaps this should strictly speaking be done, if what he says is to be allowed to stand as a generalization in the study of religion. On the other hand, there is little point in tediously going over what will almost certainly not be seriously challenged. However, I would emphasize briefly that there may be a slight problem here in that Kamstra's position could be taken as representing an alternative *theological* standpoint to that of Kraemer with regard to the interpretation of the nature of prophetic religion in general and the Christian religion in particular. After all, one remembers that the very title of Kamstra's fascinating book *Encounter or Syncretism* involved the use of a word fashionable in twentieth-century Christian theology, even though the book itself dealt with a completely different area of the history of religion. I do not myself consider that Kamstra's analysis of the roots of syncretism does suffer from this defect but it might have been better to free his analysis from the strains set up by the fact that it was conceived in reaction to Kraemer's theologically conditioned view.

In support of Kamstra at this point, one might add a complementary voice from a different quarter, namely that of Professor G. Maeda, who has argued that Christianity is a Mahayanistic (*daijoteki*) religion (Maeda 1962). By this he meant that it takes in elements foreign to itself and in this way extends its influence. That Maeda should make this point and should illustrate it also in the context of Israelite religion in Canaan (in spite of the prophetic reaction to which I referred above, which is really part of the total process), independently strengthens Kamstra's contention that syncretisms may be generally discerned also in those "prophetic" religions thought by Kraemer to be in principle not syncretistic.

Having freed himself from theology Kamstra goes on to approach the question of syncretism from a phenomenological point of view. As a matter of fact, by doing this he opens up a field for a better understanding of theology and eventually returns to it. While agreeing that this can be done, my own argument will find it necessary to return to theology *and its equivalents* rather sooner, and in this way, I believe, will reduce the no-man's-land which Kamstra has left between theology and phenomenology. As will be seen, the frontier between the two is perhaps as tight as anywhere when one is considering the nature of syncretism.

Kamstra finds, as I have found (Pye 1969, 234 ff.), that only one author, namely G. van der Leeuw (1938), has dealt to any extent with the question of what he calls the "dynamics" of religion.[2] He singles out especially van der Leeuw's conception of "transposition" (*Verschiebung*) as a clue on which to build further. This simply means that religions are changing all the time, and that therefore the meanings of different elements within different religions, many of which they borrow from each other, are also likely to change according to the context. Kamstra is particularly impressed by the fact that very frequently elements continue to exist within a religion even though they have really lost their original meanings, and intriguingly calls this "syncretism from within." This syncretism from within is a kind of alienation (*vervreemding*) within a religion with regard to items in its structure, which continue to exist there simply because of their familiarity. I believe Kamstra has touched here on a kind of religious or spiritual experience which many have known in modern times, especially in the West with regard to Christianity but perhaps also in the East with regard to various traditions, notably Buddhism in Japan. As Kamstra himself says (with an unfortunate unguarded theological allusion), "Examples of this syncretism from within are in our time legion" (1970, 7).

However, it seems to me that it is also at this point that there is a major error in Kamstra's argument. He writes, "After all that we have said, syncretism is therefore also the result of alienation in an existing religion. This alienation can arise as a result of all kinds of structural changes. The *criterion* for syncretism is therefore alienation: something which either comes in as alien from without or which is alienated from within—whichever it is" (1970, 27). I would challenge the view that alienation is "the criterion" for syncretism of all kinds. Kamstra found he needed to use the word "alienation" to characterize syncretism from within, but he has by no means shown that it is an appropriate word to characterize syncretism from without, which he has now simply slipped in along with the former. Indeed, fascinating though I find the idea of syncretism from within, it seems to distort our general vision of syncretism for two other reasons. Firstly, the word "alienation" is itself unsatisfactory because it is too reminiscent of prophetic religions. It tends to suggest that we are estranged from that to which we should turn, we have wandered from our true home, we are cast out from the Garden of Eden, and so on. Secondly, Kamstra is at this point too fascinated by the idea of "the within" of a religion, too introvert, feeling too much that religions are declining things being dissolved from within and attacked from without, no longer sensing the urge which many religions have to move out and to move on. Hence he sees syncretism "from without" as indeed a threat to an existing constellation. Why speak, one may ask, of syncretism "from without"? Why not "*towards* without"? If we speak of syncretism as something which can be "towards without" it cannot be said that alienation is the chief category for understanding it. It is perhaps not too much to say that Kamstra's analysis here, if not theologically conditioned as he had shown Kraemer's analysis to be, is at least spiritually conditioned, and that while this leads to some valuable insights, it also leads to a distortion of the true nature of syncretism.

Before attempting to grasp the nature of syncretism by another route, one of the by-products of Kamstra's approach is worth noting. This is, that as a result of his emphasis on syncretism "from within" he is able to recognize a parallel hermeneutical activity in quite diverse traditions. In any religion considered dynamically, syncretisms may be seen to be in the process of being unmasked and broken off while at the same time new ones are being built up again. Kamstra says that in this sense every theologian and every theological faculty moves in a frontier territory. More significant methodologically, however, is perhaps the frontier to which the comparative basis for these remarks leads, not the frontier of theology with the world, but the frontier between phenomenology and theology. It would seem that if theology, buddhology and other equivalents, considered as ongoing activities contributing to the dynamics of their respective religions, can in fact be studied in parallel or comparative terms, then this opens the way for a much more precise attempt to indicate the ways in which they operate. This in turn would lead to the possibility of experts acquiring a grasp of the principles and variables involved, so that theologians (and their equivalents) would no longer work on the basis of an intuitive sensitivity to the strains and stresses and possibilities of their own tradition, sometimes throwing up an effective new syncretism and more often not. Rather they would proceed on the basis of a scientific grasp of the nature of the dynamics of religion, so that while their activity would still be an imaginative one compared with some activities it could also be considered as a technological one. Building sacred bridges, or helping people to recognize them when they appear on the initiative of divinities (for in phenomenology we dare not beg the question about the divine initiative), would become analogous to building ordinary bridges (except with regard to leaving open the matter of divine initiatives). A comparative and phenomenological study of the dynamics of religion, with special reference to the hermeneutical activities of individuals acting with varying degrees of self-consciousness, would therefore become part of the fundamental equipment of any would-be theologian or buddhologian. Indeed, insofar as technological know-how indicates the viability of various options open to the engineer, the phenomenology of religion would begin to put pressure on its frontiers with theology, by no means necessarily with a deleterious effect. However, this is not the place to begin to develop such a comparative science of hermeneutics.[3] It is necessary for the time being to return to the specific problem of syncretism.

As I said above, it is necessary to return to theology and its equivalents rather sooner than Kamstra does, in order even to understand the nature of syncretism. Note however that we do not turn to theology in a concealed way. Nor should we be swayed by sensitivity to one religious situation. It is necessary to turn to theology *and its equivalents* comparatively and hence phenomenologically (since one cannot be a committed exponent of all the equivalents at once), in order to approach the *meanings* of syncretism. The meaning, if there is a meaning, can only be found through the meanings. Here therefore theology and its equivalents put pressure on phenomenology. Indeed if some of the equivalents are thought to be particularly helpful in elucidating the meaning of syncretism, the pressure of those equivalents will be particularly strong, and care should be taken to see that the presuppositions of no one religious tradition distorts our view even when it is not our own religious tradition. Although Kamstra is very interested in the meanings of syncretistic situations, his definition of syncretism quoted above contains no reference, direct or indirect, to meanings. This can be rectified, but it should be done in such a way that no one religion is called upon to supply the meaning. I hope to indicate that meanings can be referred to in an indirect and neutral way, such that the general theory of syncretism points back again for its specific meaning to specific cases.

A further curiosity of Kamstra's definition of syncretism is that it also contains no reference at all to one of his other main concerns. Again and again he emphasizes the importance of the dynamics of religion, but this does not appear to have influenced his formulation in any noticeable way. This is a second point to which attention will be paid below.

It is on the notion of the coexistence of elements foreign to each other that we must build. As a clear case of syncretism I should like to refer to the relations between Buddhism and Shinto, especially as developed under the influence of the theory of *honji-suijaku*. These relationships have been referred to in various publications and have been examined in detail recently by Alicia Matsunaga (1969). It is interesting that this writer traces the Buddhist ideas underlying this theory back to the Chinese Buddhist distinction between *pen* and *chi* and thence to the Indian Buddhist distinction between *samvriti* and *paramārtha satya*, referred to earlier. I think it would be generally agreed that the relations in question are a clear case of syncretism in that they obviously involve the coexistence of elements foreign to each other in a single religious context.

We must now approach the matter of the meanings. For the Buddhist, the meaning was that in the form of a local divinity (*kami*) there was latently present the being of a Bodhisattva or a Buddha. Thus the *kami* Ōmiya was considered to be a manifestation of Shakyamuni, the *kami* Hachiman was sometimes considered a manifestation of Amida, etc. In this way, existing focal points of religious devotion were drawn into a syncretistic field and interpreted in terms of Buddhist meaning. It appears from the Shinto side that the movement into syncretism may at first have been one of self-defence, in that the alternative to accommodation would have been the extinction of Shinto meanings altogether (Eliot 1959, 243). However that may be, there is no doubt that in this way Shinto meanings were able to persist, and in due course there came the Shinto reaction known as *han-honji-suijaku*, that is, *honji-suijaku* in reverse, in terms of which the Buddhist meanings were treated as but superficial manifestations of the more profound Shinto *kami*. The point about all this is that the elements under consideration became *ambiguous*. They were able to bear two distinct meanings depending on the different points of view of the people involved with them. These meanings were tussled over again and again, and it is a mark of the resilience of the Shinto religion that its *kami* were not after all completely assimilated. Syncretistic tension continued to be felt until there was a remarkable attempt at recoupment from the Shinto side. It is important not to allow either one of the two possible meanings of a symbol being used in *honji-suijaku* terms to overwhelm the phenomenological approach to syncretism. Of course it is the meanings which matter, but we can neutrally seize the importance of the various meanings here by recognizing the *ambiguity* of the situation.

It should not be thought that this type of relationship between Buddhism and Shinto can be observed only in cases where the theory of *honji-suijaku* can be applied. Consider, for example, the story of the visit of the monk Gedatsu to the Grand Shrine of Ise, as told in the *Taiheiki*:

> Once this holy man went to the Grand Shrine of Ise to worship at the Outer and Inner Shrines and speak secretly of the delights of complete response to the teachings of Buddhism. These shrines are not as other shrines, for their bargeboards are not curved, nor do their pointed boards bend backward. Wherefore it seemed to Gedatsu that they were as "the straight way that rejects what is roundabout." And beholding the ancient pines lowering their branches and the old trees spreading out their leaves, he likened them to bodhisattvas descending from heaven to save living things here below. Although the names of the Three Treasures of Buddhism may not be spoken here, he thought weeping, yet in this way too men may reach salvation. (McCullough 1959, 368)

Or consider the following spell used by *yamabushi* to exorcise the malevolent influence of the god Konjin over certain quarters of the compass.

> Because of ignorance the three worlds are a prison,
> Because of enlightemnent the ten directions are free.
> In truth there is neither East nor West,
> Where then are South and North? (Renondeau 1964, 140)

This spell clearly operates on two quite distinct levels or in two quite distinct spheres of meaning. Moreover the two spheres of meaning are mutually exclusive. If one really believes that the exorcism is desirable or necessary one clearly has not yet reached the point of insight into the nature of phenomena to which Buddhist philosophy tends. Yet the spell makes use of Buddhism to allay fear. Conversely if one takes the Buddhist analysis to heart, the spell becomes redundant. Yet the two are coexisting in a single religious pattern even while the ambiguity shows signs of being intolerable.

Nor is the relevance of this analysis restricted to the Buddhist-Shinto situation. The transpositions referred to by van der Leeuw and by Kamstra all display this character of ambiguity. They all refer to elements within a coherent religious pattern around which pivot two or more sets of meanings. Again, the notion of ambiguity does not restrict us either to what Kamstra would call "syncretism from without," which is what the cases we have examined are. It is equally crucial, and is equally neutral with regard to particular meanings (unlike the loaded word "alienation"), in the context of "syncretism from within," where the circles of meaning turning around particular elements in a tradition sometimes seem to move and slide like shifting sand, so that the specific elements themselves are ambiguous.

To take ambiguity as the main characteristic of syncretism is consistent also with Kamstra's view that it stems from humankind's very nature in the sense that each person is a limited being unable to grasp the revelation of the divine or the ultimate truth except in so far as this or these are refracted in terms of his or her own situation. Every constitutive element in a given religious pattern is ambiguous, one might say, in that it has a meaning at one and the same time both in the general situation of the man to whom it is meaningful and in the symbolic context which bears the revelation of the religion in question. However, while the nature of syncretism is clearly to be found in the nature of religion in general and the nature of religion in the nature of man, I would prefer to continue to speak more specifically about ambiguity as the keynote of syncretism, that is, in connection with the relationship between elements originally foreign to each other and (to accept Kamstra's theory of syncretism from within) elements becoming foreign to each other, in religious situations.

If ambiguity may be taken as the keynote of syncretism of all kinds, it is necessary now to emphasize that this is to be understood dynamically.

Syncretism, as the coexistence of elements of diverse origin interacting ambiguously, is a natural *moving* aspect of major religious traditions such as Buddhism, Shinto, Christianity, and indeed, I would venture to suggest, of all religious traditions. It is part of the dynamics of religion which works its way along in the ongoing transplantation of these religious traditions from one cultural context to another whether geographically or in time, while their more or less sophisticated adherents are more or less aware of what is going on. But since the traditions are moving all the time, and since the meanings are continually being refashioned, any particular case of syncretism is necessarily *temporary*. The ambiguous clash of meanings demands some resolution and even if this is not forthcoming immediately the demand is still inherent in the relationship. Three resolutions seem to be possible in practice as in logic, apart from a postponement of any resolution. The first is the extension of one meaning to the point of the effective elimination of the other, in which case we may speak of *assimilation*. The second is the fusion of the diverse elements such that while a single coherent pattern of meaning has been attained that pattern is so different from any of the patterns hitherto available that *a new religion* may be deemed to have emerged. The third is the drifting apart of the two meanings, in which case we may speak of *dissolution*. These three forms of resolution are all possible whether we consider syncretism from (or towards) without or syncretism from within; although usually syncretism from without will probably make us think more often of the *assimilation* of an existing religious pattern while syncretism from within will make us think more often of the *dissolution* of an existing religious pattern. It would be interesting to analyse the emergence of a new religion in terms of its dependence on syncretism from without and from within preceding religious traditions respectively. (Kamstra refers briefly to some new religions in the context of the latter.) It should be noted further that there is a certain amount of tension between individuals and groups over all this. An ambiguous syncretistic situation may be resolved in terms of one meaning or other for an individual or even a series of individuals, even though the syncretism persists long after as a wider cultural phenomenon offering its various possibilities to further individuals. This is why syncretistic situations may persist for a long time and even indefinitely, even though they are, as explained above, intrinsically temporary. It would be quite wrong to call them permanent. To describe them as temporary is to indicate that they are situations of tension (whatever the various protagonists may say about harmony, toleration, etc!) and that they are to be understood entirely in terms of the dynamics of religion.

To emphasize tension as I have done should not be taken as an invitation to conclude that syncretism is altogether incoherent. A syncretistic situation is coherent even while demanding resolution in that there are various coherent meanings for the various people involved, and also, for the phenomenologist of religion, in the sense that it is a collection of events in the history of religion which have a recognizably coherent structure. Finally, I would agree with Kamstra that the elements involved in a syncretistic religious situation need not necessarily be themselves all of religious origin, but may include political, philosophical and other secular elements of all kinds.

For the above reasons I would define syncretism as *the temporary ambiguous coexistence of elements from diverse religious and other contexts within a coherent religious pattern.*

Notes

1. Cf. a short notice of this same work by the present writer in *Religion: A Journal of Religion and Religions*, Vol. 1 Part 1, Spring 1971.
2. Cf. van der Leeuw's chapters 93 and 94 (1938).
3. Such a comparative approach to hermeneutics really needs a much wider basis than that offered by an examination of syncretism alone. It would also have to consider at least the manner in which religious traditions reassert themselves in intolerably ambiguous situations (cf. my article referred to above), and further the nature of the criteria applied in various religions in the definition or redefinition of the "essence" (*hridaya*) of their respective traditions. This of course raises hosts of theological problems, and their equivalents!

References

Eliot, Sir George. 1959. *Japanese Buddhism*. London: Routledge and Kegan Paul.

Kamstra, J. H. 1967. *Encounter or Syncretism: The Initial Growth of Japanese Buddhism*. Leiden: E. J. Brill.

—1970. *Synkretisme op de Grens tussen Theologie en Godsdienstfenomenologie*. Leiden: E. J. Brill.

Kraemer, H. 1937. *De Wortelen van het Syncretisme*. 's-Gravenhage: n.p.

Leeuw, G. van der. 1938. *Religions in Essence and Manifestation*. London: George Allen & Unwin.

Maeda, Gorō. 1962. "Nihon no Kirisutokyō." *Shisō* (April): 93 ff.

Matsunaga, Alicia. 1969. *The Buddhist Philosophy of Assimilation: The Historical Development of the Honji-Suijaku Theory*. Tokyo and Rutland, Vermont: Sophia University and Charles E. Tuttle Co.

McCullough, Helen. 1959. *The Taiheiki: A Chronicle of Medieval Japan*. New York: Columbia University Press.

Pye, E. M. 1969. "The Transplantation of Religions." *NUMEN* 16(3), Dec.

Renondeau, G. 1964. *Le Shugendô Histoire: Doctrine et Rites des Anachorètes dits Yamabushi*. Cahiers de la Société Asiatique, 8. Paris: Imprimerie Nationale.

Widengren, Geo. 1969. *Religionsphänomenologie*. Berlin: W. de Gruyter.

SYNCRETISM: FROM THEOLOGICAL INVECTIVE TO A CONCEPT IN THE STUDY OF RELIGION

Kurt Rudolph

The rich vocabulary of the Study of Religion (*Religionswissenschaft*, *RW*) includes a number of generally recognized and employed terms specific to the discipline. While some terms have never ceased to be analysed in a critical fashion (e.g. "religion"), others have only been subjected to scrutiny in recent years ("myth," "development," etc.). This terminological introspection is part of the living nature of a scholarly discipline, forming an aspect of its methodological effort to come to grips with the multifaceted object of study, in the sense of an non-theological philological-historical discipline. The ambiguous concept "syncretism" belongs to the basic inventory of the conceptual terminology of religious history as well as that of *RW*, and urgently requires closer examination, following up on various recent efforts. Firstly, (1) a few remarks on the meaning and etymology must preface (2) the discussion of syncretism in recent *RW*, before (3) attempting to present the start of a "typology" or "phenomenology" of syncretism.[1]

1.

As far as is presently known, the expression "syncretism" can be traced back to Plutarch who introduced it in his piece, *De fratero amore* (περὶ φιλαδελφίας) which was included in the collection of the *Moralia*. The reference (§19 = 490 B. Teubner-Edition Leipzig 1972, 3, 249) is: When brothers and friends who are in conflict, join each other and not the enemy in view of a common danger, they are imitating the inhabitants of Crete "who have frequently risen against each other and waged war, but always reconcile themselves and stand united when an external enemy approached; they called

68

this '*synkretismos*'." It thus means, "to hold together in the Cretan way." Plutarch may have learnt of this political etymology from earlier sources (Aristotle?), and it was maintained in Byzantine literature (Etymologicum magnum; Suda: "*synkretisai*—to think like the Cretans"). Another derivation, from κεράννυμι "to mix" (σύγκρατος "mixed together") cannot be altogether excluded, but likewise lacks references, and is probably based on a secondary tradition—dating to the seventeenth century—after the word had developed the meaning of "mixture" (*scil.* of the incompatible). In modern times, the expression was first revived by Erasmus who understood it in the sense used by Plutarch: proceeding together against a common foe despite differing views.[2] In a letter to Melanchton (April 22, 1519), he wrote: "You see with what hatred certain people conspire against science. It is no more than fair that we also close ranks. Unity is a great good." (*Aequum est nos quoque synkretizein. Ingens praedium est concordia.*) This positive appreciation of syncretism as the community (the humanists) among dissonant voices was also entertained by Zwingli in the context of the Basle Holy Communion debate, Melanchthon and Butzer. At the same time, it can be clearly seen that holding a common ground was not invariably viewed positively, particularly among the Lutherans (Melanchthon, Staphylus) who perceived the procedure as a conspiracy against God and Christ. This negative appraisal of syncretism spread in the seventeenth century, shrouding it in that disreputable character which has not been entirely shed, even today. It has become a theological insult!

Among the Christian confessions, syncretism was viewed as a "false peace" when establishing and elaborating confessions as "pure" teachings, according to the Jesuit Adam Contzen in 1616. This development reached its zenith when the Helmstedt Theologian Calixt (d. 1656) came into the crossfire of orthodox polemics from all sides with his (admirable) efforts at unity and peace. His attempt at a compromise was initially, in 1645, branded as syncretism, by both Lutherans and Catholics and hence labeled "syncretic conflict." In his *Eirenikon Catholicum* from 1645, the Jesuit Veit Erbermann concluded that Calixt's thesis of achieving unity by appealing to the Creed of the Apostoles meant only that differences would be unified in appearance. This would not only sanction the unity of peoples of different religions, but also of different religions. This was thus the first use of syncretism in the sense of a "lumping" together of different religions, that is, the concept is used for "mixing religions," and not as earlier—following Plutarch—for the alliance of those divided by teaching, against a common foe. Henceforth, and particularly through the efforts of Calov, syncretism is understood as derived from "mixing," with the exclusively negative connotations of "fake, incompatible unity," syn-cretists as sin-cretists. In 1648, the Alsatian Lutheran Johannes Konrad Dannhauer accordingly wrote a comprehensive monograph on the history of syncretism as the mixing of things which do not belong together, which began with Eve and the Serpent, Israel in Egypt, and so on, and continues with Melanchthon, Grotius and Calixt (*Mysterium syncretismi detecti, proscripti et symphonismo compensati*, Strasbourg 1648). Dannhauer distinguishes three forms of syncretism, according to a physical or chemical method: the blend of two forms to a new one (*digestio absorpotiva*); the reduction of the joint attributes (*digestio temperativa*); and the combination to a tangle (*colluvies*; *digestio conservativa*). A remarkable precursor of modern typology!

The birth of our concept was thus linked to two different ideas. On the one hand was a political usage, with a positive attitude toward unity, in the face of a common danger to the community, among those who would otherwise be in conflict. On the other was a theological usage introducing a negative approach to such a method, rendering the word an invective opposed to the "blending" of incompatible elements (teachings) in a "hybrid religion." It was the latter which left its mark up to the present day, as—particularly in theological circles—a tool of apologetics for the disparagement of other religions or forms of religion. Not even the growth—from the nineteenth century—of the discipline of comparative religion was able to change this significantly.

2.

The re-evaluation of the concept in the nineteenth century commenced with its application to the cultural and religious landscape of Late Antiquity, as led by Alexander the Great's "Hellenism."[3] It was then the "The History of Religion School" in particular, which opened the way for the widespread use of the term in this sense, and which did not even hesitate to use it for early Christianity, "*Urchristentum*," as did Gunkel, Bousset, Bultmann (Rudolph 1992, 301–20). It was an initial step towards objectivity, but a derogatory tone was still audible. Syncretism or "syncretistic" became the mark of a late stage of a secondary development, combining elements of either ideological or cultural practices, which originally had nothing to do with one another and thus lost their intrinsic "purity" or "integrity" in the "blend." Syncretism became a typical "Late Period Problem" lacking the vigor of youth. As its use was primarily restricted to sect-like movements, especially the Oriental cults of the Roman Empire, such as the mysteries, the word lost coverage, as it acquired a deprecatory character. Syncretism became an attribute of religious formations developing between and alongside the great religions.

The *RW* discussion—which is our primary interest here—concerning the content and essence of syncretism as a specific category in the discipline of the history of religions, only began in the twentieth century. The first scholar to do so was G. van der Leeuw in his "Phenomenology of Religion." In §19 "Powers," he defines the process "which repeatedly leads from polydemonism to polytheism" as Syncretism (1st edn, 153; 2nd edn, 186). For him, syncretism is, therefore, an unavoidable manifestation of religion, a kind of developmental stage necessarily linked to the "progress of culture" (ibid.). Syncretism is even assigned to the "dynamics of religion," treated together with the mission (1st edn §93; 2nd edn §94). Agreeing, van der Leeuw cites Joachim Wach's phrase, that every religion is a syncretism when viewed from its own prehistory. "Every historical religion is not one, but several; of course not in the way that it could be the sum of its different forms, but rather in that the different forms have grown together into this form" (1st edn, 577; 2nd edn, 692). This is especially true for the World Religions such as Islam and Christianity for which van der Leeuw produces references (2nd edn, 690–91). The modern occult tendencies represent a basic (conscious?) syncretism, as they assume the unity of all religions. However, the "modern human" is a syncretist as his/her belief is drawn from different sources: philosophical, religious and "scientific." The spirit of "generalizing Christianity" acted as godfather. Van der Leeuw sees the essence of this syncretism in the sense of a "transposition" (1st edn, 578–79; 2nd edn, 693–94). It is "the change in the meaning of a manifestation in the dynamics of religions, whereby the form remains the same." These appear in reformations and in missions; for example, the Protestant Reformation "transposed" the meaning of Holy Communion, but did not eliminate it; the Prophets interpreted the decalogue in the religious-ethical sense. The actual character of a phenomenon is occasionally completely lost in the process. Van der Leeuw, and, before him, in 1933, Pettazoni, also recognized the link between mission and syncretism (2nd edn, 694 ff. more extensively than 1st edn, 579–80). The mission and spread of a religion necessarily leads to syncretism, as shown in St Paul's Aeropagus Speech (Acts 17). "Assimilation," "Substitution," and "Isolation," Frick's three forms through which a religion or mission spreads, are used as a guide (Frick 1928, 53–54). These are really important manifestations of syncretism of which no religion has been "spared."

Van der Leeuw thus gained significant insights into the essence of syncretism and generalized the term to the extent that its one-sided derogatory meaning was lost. The entire, almost "syncretic," form of the presentation and other weaknesses, which cannot be discussed here, have, however, hitherto prevented a systematic understanding and a fundamental analysis of van der Leeuw's view of syncretism. There is an elementary contradiction between his use of the expression in §19 and §93 (94), which is all I want to mention here.

Following van der Leeuw, another Dutch scholar turned to syncretism, and primarily from the standpoint of the study of the mission: Hendrik Kraemer (1937, 1938, and 1959). He wanted to apply the term to the non-

Christian religions, and above all to those of the Far East, which he specifically distinguished from the Prophetic religions of the Judeo-Christian tradition, including Islam (Kraemer 1959, 349 ff.). The "unconscious," historically conditioned syncretism of all world religions is to be distinguished from those consciously open to the amalgamating syncretism of "paganism" (ibid. 389 ff.).[4] I cannot go into this distinction here, but it revived the old theological usage of syncretism in the service of apologetics.[5] This has since been clearly discussed and criticized in works on syncretism.

In a study published in 1971, Robert D. Baird dismissed syncretism as an "inadequate category" in the study of religion (Baird 1971, 42 ff.). Above all, his work countered Kraemer whose normative and inconsistent use of the concept first demonstrated that it was inappropriate for understanding foreign religions. Treating syncretism as an historical phenomenon, he states that, when viewed historically, the interrelationship of ideas and movements are universal and unavoidable, and they even include Christianity. However, the concept thus loses focus and becomes a mere variation of "historical," applicable to "religious expressions" (146). By contrast, the theological usage, as employed by Kraemer, in the sense of a fusion of different and opposing tendencies of belief and practice, is merely imprecise and pointless when they are not in direct conflict; otherwise, syncretism is a contradiction in itself (148). Baird asserts that this understanding is only rooted in the idea that no believer would describe his or her own religion as syncretistic; it is only perceived to be such from outside. The Christian Kraemer thus views the Eastern religions as syncretism while the Hindu Radhakrishnan classifies Christianity in the same fashion.[6] The representatives of the religion themselves see this differently (149–50). The concept of syncretism as an illegitimate combination cannot aid in understanding, a conclusion which failed to catch on since (here and in the school of Wilfred Cantwell Smith, to which Baird belongs) there is no clear conception of the task of *Religionswissenschaft*, the scholarly study of religion. *Religionswissenschaft* is not bound to treat the believer's attitude as a criterion for the correct understanding in its scientific judgment, but must instead follow its own historical-critical methods. In this case, the theological and *RW* points of view are confused, or used as a cover.

For Baird, the only useful role for the term syncretism is in the context of an historical description of a situation where "conflicting ideas or practices are brought together into a new complex which is devoid of coherence" (151). The pejorative meaning, expressing a lack (of "coherence"), is thus attached to syncretism, when viewed from outside. It is, however, itself part of the encounter with a religion, but from the outside (but *Religionswissenschaft* cannot possibly proceed in any other fashion!). Baird closes by noting that "since Syncretism in its historical sense is universally applicable but its theological meaning is a barrier to an authentic *RW* understanding, its use in

RW research should be avoided" (152). This is the necessary result of the above-mentioned condition that *Religionswissenschaft* is obliged to view the "inside" of a religion in order to be able to grasp it properly, and cannot make any objective statements without the criterion of faith. The pejorative sense of syncretism is only available to those who use the term in the customary theological sense and find themselves unable to get along with the neutral usage in *Religionswissenschaft*. It is incidentally not correct that the faithful are unable to view their own religion as syncretistic; Christian theologians have done so repeatedly and enlightened Hindus will not take offense at the expression.

This position was taken by J. Kamstra, a third Dutch scholar who treated the issue of syncretism at length. In his comprehensive monograph on Japanese Buddhism (1967) and particularly in his inaugural lecture at Amsterdam (as the successor of Bleeker in 1970) on "Syncretism on the Border between Theology and the Phenomenology of Divine Service," Kamstra brought new aspects into the discussion of our theme, profiting from his long stay in Japan (Kamstra 1970). He held the usual theological use of syncretism to be inappropriate, as Kraemer taught (16ff.). Using it in the apologetic sense should therefore be abandoned, as the reproach was as applicable to Christianity as to other religions. Kraemer situates the roots of syncretism in human existence itself as such, and not in some case of "pagan" naturalism, etc. "Man's being is simply syncretic being, often with Cretan laws" (23). There is thus no "pure" religion; not excepting even the prophets. Every revelation pushes against a boundary here: man simply cannot come to grips with it and overcome it completely. Kamstra cites Lévi-Strauss on "savage thought" as a root of syncretism; only domesticated thinking, reflection, can organize it—as in the Prophetic religions. "We are all unconscious syncretists. For me, Syncretism begins unavoidably with understanding Revelation" (24). Therefore, syncretism cannot be repressed; according to Kamstra, it belongs to the nature of humanity. Kamstra sets a phenomenological understanding parallel to his theological one, by linking syncretism with the dynamics of religion, following van der Leeuw's train of thought (25 ff.). His essential criterion is "alienation," tied to van der Leeuw's "transposition" (25). Syncretism is thus the result of alienation within an existing religion. His process is thus two-fold: one leading to a new form through assimilation from outside; the other internal, resulting in a loose and mechanical linkage of elements which were originally entirely foreign. The cause of such manifestations (and Kamstra uses examples from Japan and modern Christianity) lies in the changed structure of society: it is a process leading to "pluriformity" bringing the unconscious hidden syncretism to light (29). Kamstra saw such tendencies active in modern theology, as in Thomas Acquinas. On the one hand, older syncretisms are broken, but at the same time, they form new ones (31).

This interpretation of syncretism as a general human problem is very impressive and the first inspection of its use hardly permits the older derogatory meaning to be recognized, except insofar as humankind itself is now a victim of syncretism, capable only of temporarily escaping from it through reflection. The expression "alienation" hints that even Kamstra is still attached to a crypto-theological tradition (as his conception of revelation has revealed). If syncretism is "alienation," and every man is a syncretist by nature (23), then every man is "alienated" in the Marxist sense—but by what and why? From his true nature, from which he cannot escape except in the form of syncretism? It is apparently history which is given more weight, making humankind the heir of its tradition in the broadest sense. Viewed theologically, every revelation is "alienated" in the form which the (religious) person makes of it. I have the impression that Kamstra has not only crossed the bounds of *RW*, but also treated syncretism ontologically such that an historian must accept an infinite and primeval process of continual syncretization as a stream of transmission. Then all cats would be gray!

Kamstra also attempted a more nuanced or typological approach, in a chapter of "Answers," a popular Phenomenology of Religion, entitled "The Cobweb" (Kamstra 1977, 182). There he understood syncretistic religions of both older and more recent date, which had grown and still grow, amid the main branches of the great religion traditions which are themselves interlinked, precisely like a "spider's web" (with an impressive drawing, 182). In the text, Kamstra distinguishes a "conscious" syncretism from an "unconscious" one (183). Both are the expression of an "encounter" of religions and the consequences can be either accidental or deliberate. The former are "confrontations" which lead to conservative persistence or absolute stances by a culture or religion on the one hand, but also to the acceptance of elements from the other realm—either consciously or unconsciously! Every religion is formed by its environment: it is syncretisitc by nature (183b). A "pure religion" (in the sense of the "pure word of god") is inconceivable; such a claim overestimates one's own position as the absolute truth, crossing the borders of human being. The identity of a religion that does not exclude syncretism as a religion must be understood as a single root, dead at one end, but growing at the other (186). Reordering and dynamism belong to every religion. Kamstra describes (184 ff.) some examples for each form of syncretism. The unconscious include: Christianity (since its origins!), modern Buddhist forms in Burma, and Caodaiism in Vietnam. Conscious syncretisms are present in many nativistic, messianic and millennarian movements, mystics, Rosicrucians, spiritualists, Free Masons, Theosophists, modern Sufi- and Yoga-sects, the Jesus-People; older Asiatic forms are Zen-Buddhism, Lemanism and the Sikh Religion (194 ff.).

The British scholar M. Pye, now professor at Marburg, took a position on Kamstra in an article, ascribing him a theological position (which cannot be

doubted), which was simply an alternative to Kraemer's. Pye held that
Kamstra lacked an analysis of meaning and that the dynamic elements were
not treated adequately. The criterion of "alienation" is insufficient and the
view "from within" exaggerated, suggesting that religions are "declining
things" internally torn and attacked from without. Pye opposes this with the
concept of "ambiguity" as the "key" to understanding the discussion of syncretism (1971b, 90). He used Japanese-Buddhist syncretism to illustrate that
foreign elements can peacefully coexist in a religious context. The Shinto
deities and spirits (*kamis*) are Buddhas and Bodhisattvas at the same time.
This ambiguity of religious appearances is a characteristic of most religions
and their "moving aspects" (92). Pye also understands syncretism as a manifestation of the dynamics of religion, but finds himself thereby temporally
restricted. Three possible solutions are always available in this process: assimilation, fusion, or dissolation (92). The tensions in the meanings of religious phenomena necessarily limit the period of a syncretic form, even if this
can last a long time. Its essence consists in the "temporary and ambiguous
coexistence of elements from diverse religions and other contexts within a
coherent religious pattern" (93). Pye's criticism of Kamstra was certainly
correct, especially concerning his concept "alienation." He was, however, so
heavily influenced by the example of Japanese syncretism that his "ambiguity" criterion could suffice for a general understanding of syncretism.
This criterion only touches one facet of syncretism, that of *Interpretatio*.
Pye is also not free of the "inner view," and fails to take account of the
historical-social character which is the base of syncretism.

I would also like to examine an additional voice in the syncretism discussion. Among the German students of Comparative Religion, C. Colpe investigated this problem intensively. His argument is not directed solely at Late
Antiquity as the traditional home of syncretism, but also concerns all the
modern manifestations of syncretism (Colpe 1974, 441 ff.; 1977, 158 ff.).
Important for our line of inquiry was his contribution to the Syncretism
Symposium in Reinhausen, Göttingen in 1971, published as "The Compatibility of Historical and Structural Determinations of Syncretism."[7] Colpe
briefly accounted for the history of the word and was not opposed to the
"mixing" of culture and religious phenomena in the use of the word syncretism, in contrast to linguistic usage (e.g., "Kasus-Syncretism" by B. Delbrück)
which is inappropriate (17–18). According to him, there are three basic
features which define syncretism or a "syncretic structural law":

1. The components of the syncretic formation must have existed or
   remained independent for a long time, or manifestly aspire to reappear
   within it.
2. These components must balance the preservation and dissolution of
   their own independent identities.

3. Their association "must convey their vital capacity to revive in history" (19).

Colpe then devised a typology, based on types representing "ranks of differing intensity of association to a form": symbioses (mostly impersonal and ethnically limited); acculturation (integration, mostly conscious); and identification (*Interpretatio*, "spiritual imperialism"). There are also three additional types in those syncretisms "emerging from discrete components": (1) the type with overlaying components which does not eliminate the underlying parts so that they can reappear later (e.g., in Hatra); (2) the type where the substrate rules (e.g., Sumerian-Akkadian), (3), those with equality of the components (e.g., Manicheism). "Metamorphosis" forms a special problem, common in modern revolutionary movements (Colpe 1975, 23). Investigating the relationship of the individual demonstrable syncretisms on a linguistic, cultural or religious level, differences and transpositions can be identified, and they cannot invariably be accounted for (25). Colpe perceives three alternatives (25 ff.): a hybrid culture, bringing forth a religious syncretism (e.g., Hellenistic Egypt); one which does not (such as the Prophetic religion of Israel); and a religious syncretism which does not stem from a hybrid culture (Bahai religion, spiritism). The latter means that syncretic religions can be separated from a culture in principle (28).

Drawing on the analytical Philosophy of History (Hempel, Dray), Colpe attaches "productive application" of his insights to this phenomenological-typological view, in order to define, correct and verify them (1975, 28 ff.). I lack the time and space to go into this, but can emphasize that Colpe has rightly recognized a "latent critical tendency" in the concept of syncretism. This tendency opposes the "purity" of culture as an expression of a romantic "aristocracy of the spirit," which has forgotten its own origins and can only understand syncretism as decay, degeneration or dissolution. The ghost of the old tradition of syncretism reappears here!

The universal application of the neutralized concept does not merely result in the abolition of its role as a "category of evaluation," but rather requires a critical revision so that it becomes a "category of historic evaluation" (1975, 30). It thus acquires an eminent heuristic value: it aids in finding the "data on antecedents" lying at the base of an historical-genetic explanation of a (syncretic) manifestation or situation. With these reflections Colpe has gotten himself caught in a deductive-nomological channel. By explaining the lack of data on antecedents as critical for syncretism research, he raises a barrier to historical genesis (32–33). The concept of syncretism is thus transformed from an *Explanandum* to an *Explanans*, meaning that the result of a process designated as a syncretism leads to a syncretism, so that syncretism merely becomes a step in the process itself, insofar as it serves as an "explanatory selection and category" (33). Without trying to interpret the not invariably comprehensible statements any further, it must be confirmed that Colpe has made a sincere effort to maintain the concept of syncretism in its critical role as an historical category, while simultaneously avoiding the inappropriate general usage (e.g., not viewing Early Christianity as a syncretism, 33).

However, Colpe comes into conflict with his own approach, by seeking to unify historical research with analytic reflection methods (mixed with features of neo-Kantian historical methodology), employed as an apologetic means of refuting the reproach that Christianity is syncretistic. He thereby destroyed his own carefully crafted model of syncretism when suddenly operating with exceptions. This act can mean nothing other than introducing syncretism as a category of evaluation through the back door. Just as the Middle Ages are not syncretistic, Christianity is not either: an exception which confirms the rule (34). Colpe's cryptotheological interest is more easily discernable at the close of his discussion, where direct theological concerns appear (37, n. 50).

Preceding these theological issues are, however, a number of important points concerning our issue. Religious syncretism has more complex "antecedent dates" than other syncretisms, whereby the "dimension of heterogony," that is, the "heterogony of religion" always plays a role (35–36). The "reservoir of social and economic antecedents" offers a chance to deliver real explanations and not just "parallelizations" or filiations of religious motifs (36). The readiness to accept syncretism in historical processes moves across a broad spectrum, depending upon whether it is used by an "external" or "internal power" to give traditions new meanings. It can therefore be imperial—as with the Romans—or subversive—as in gnosis. A balance is best achieved where the position proclaimed (by a tradition or group) is sociopsychologically installed. Colpe adds that this process excepts or relativizes the issue of truth, which in my opinion is not a relevant question, historically speaking.

Syncretism was also a topic in the framework of the former "Sonderforschungsbereich 13" of the University of Göttingen, dedicated to the religious and intellectual history of the Near East from the Hellenistic period through the emergence of the Byzantine Empire in the seventh century. Special attention was devoted to the issue of syncretism as an essential feature of this period, as reported in the 1978 volume "Syncretism Research: Theory and Praxis" (Wiessner ed. 1978). U. Berner developed a "heuristic model of syncretism research" as the basis of this work, which had already been discussed elsewhere and will be briefly mentioned here.[8]

Berner understands syncretism as one of the possible reactions to a situation of insecurity brought about by the movement of different religious systems (1978, 12). This insecurity is abolished via syncretism through the elimination of the borders and the "competing character" of the "systems" (12). Syncretism is thus processual, being "established through a process between two religions" (13). Berner's chosen approach of using the "System Concept," on an inspiration from P. L. Berger and Th. Luckmann, permits him to view the process of syncretism "independently on two different levels." One is the level of the systems, understood in terms of contextual meaning (*Sinnzusammenhang*) (62). The other is the level of elements. Using a "consistent metalinguistic terminology," Berner attempts to classify these two levels further, assuming three terminological "levels"—or, perhaps "Descriptive Horizons" would be better (16 ff. and 65 ff.). These are:

1. The actual metalinguistic level as forms of "Systematization" and "Rationalization" (which are still further distinguished as process descriptions).

2. The "System Level" with the categories "Syncretism on the Meta-System-Level" or "Pseudo-Synthesis," "Synthesis," "Evolution," "Relationizing" (which are then again divided into harmonious, hierarchical, evaluative, epistemological, chronological, genetic, inclusive and removed).

3. Finally, the "Elements Level" with the possible (simple) "Relationization" and Syncretism as absorbing, differentiating, additive, equalizing, agglomerating (identification, transformation, remodeling, substitution and legalization are assigned to the latter).

Although Berner is explicitly conscious of the dangers of "playing around with" metalinguistic terminology (1978, 15), he is, in my opinion, actually a victim of this. With the confusing variety (some of which have nothing to do with syncretism!) and the insufficiently balanced linguistic levels ("System" and "Elements" are opposed, without any link), the knife of historical heuristics is dulled and fails to lend any immediate aid to the research on the subject. Instead, this case merely leads to the adjustment of the "model" with post hoc (external) designations of facts confused with terminological components, as the following contributions demonstrate.[9] These discussions give few hints about the success of the "model," and the issue was not even discussed—as could be expected. The application of the inherently static "System-Element-Model," with tones of cybernetics, to the concept of syncretism which Berner himself asserts is "processually conceived," is hardly suitable if "syncretism" exists only on the "Element Level" in its historical diversity. The track is quickly lost with the ahistorical dismantling of the two levels, meaning the suppression of the weight of historical tradition in the framework of the general "contextual meaning" of a religion. At this stage, it is not even a question of the sociological aspects and associations of syncretism.

Berner's efforts are nevertheless a step in the right direction, and above all in another contribution, where he attempts to understand his syncretism model as "an instrument of the Phenomenology of Religion" (27–37), reproach *RW* with having hitherto neglected this aspect of religion (esp. 30 ff., 59 ff.). The search for "descriptive categories" (35) to order the variety of "phenomena susceptible to syncretistic interpretation" (36) should actually lead to a "theory of syncretism as part of the future Theory of Religion" (37), but more strongly influenced by *RW* itself than by borrowed foreign models (which can certainly be stimulating). In any event, I consider the testing of Berner's syncretism model unsuccessful, even in his Origenes-contribution (39–57), since it applied the inadequate terminological means (juxtaposition of synthesis and syncretism!) to an inappropriate object. The general conclusion confirms that the theological evaluation is also present (56): Origenes offers a synthesis, the gnosis of a "Syncretism of Belief and Science" (!?).

I have now introduced and discussed the most important statements on the issue of syncretism in modern *RW*. The material produced in two symposia on the theme—in 1966 at the Donner-Institute in Åbo and in 1971 in Reinhausen, Göttingen[10]—is of less relevance for the direct theoretical discussion, but relevant as a special theme of *RW* research, requiring further development in terms of systematic religion.

3.

The following results can be gleaned from the debate:

1. The concept of syncretism has a role as a universal and relatively neutral designation for a form of cultural or religious contact which can be viewed as a "blend," and from which there are few exceptions in *RW*.

2. This universal usage requires an analytical scheme and typological breakdown into its various manifestations, but the requisite uniform terminology has not yet been established. The following designations will be found: symbiosis, acculturation, identification, theocracy, amalgamation, fusion, assimilation, amelioration, transformation, metamorphosis, substitution, eclecticism, dissolation, isolation, synthesis, relativization.

3. The nature of syncretism is characterized by words such as "transposition" (van der Leeuw), "alienation" (Kamstra) or "ambiguity" (Pye), but here there was no agreement, except that syncretism was the expression of the dynamics of religion.

Syncretism has been generally adopted as a term for a "religious blend." On the other hand, a consistent historical analysis must concede that there are no "pure religions," meaning one which is not influenced by its environment or "foreign" traditions. Syncretism is therefore a paraphrase for a state of affairs where no religion or religious tradition (let alone a culture) can be located beyond its borders (aside, perhaps, from very isolated residual or marginal groups). This applies to Christianity as well, as I have remarked elsewhere (1992, 301 ff.). It is certainly true—as Wach once formulated the idea G. van der Leeuw took up again—that every religion must be a syncretism when viewed from the standpoint of the prehistory of religions. It is, however, not just from its *prehistory*, but from its history itself: the process of its complicated *development* is inconceivable without syncretism. It is merely a question of differing degrees or strengths, which mark any differences. The basis is simply cultural contact, but also humankind's openness and capacity to rearrange differing traditions and concepts, and adopting them directly or indirectly into its (cult) practices. It is the *"Encounter,"* or *"Contact"* even including *"Confrontation,"* which are the universal preconditions and the moving principles of syncretism. Its varieties are inevitably diverse, rendering classifications unavoidable (also in the sense of limitations).

I consider the repeated use of the distinction between *"unconscious"* and *"conscious"* syncretism to be accurate and of basic importance. The former can also be considered "naïve," "spontaneous" or "vegetative" (Colpe 1975a, 21). The process of religious development from its prehistoric origins is the basis of all manifestations of religion. The ethnic or national religions defining ancient *RW* all reveal traces of such syncretism, and have not left their heirs (above all the world religions) untouched (popular beliefs!). In each case, their identity and constitution as an independent tradition and expression of a people or a population group is always maintained—not least through the language, culture, and politics into which the religion was integrated. Not even the "tribal religions" form an exception.[11]

"Founded," "conscious" syncretism, based on reflection, profits from the experience of "unconscious" syncretism of its own age to form a new overarching uniform religion, integrating the essential elements of religious and ideological tradition (the best example being Manicheism, but also the Ryôbu-Shintô of Japan). Most of the spiritual and theosophic sects of modern times are subsumed in this group.

This division is a rather coarse-meshed grid, which can only serve for the first classification. The manifold types of "encounter"[12] and "spread" of culture and religion through historical (political) events and the processual forms also determine the development and history of syncretism, leading to variations which are not so easy to catch—as the discussion shows. Differentiated syncretisms will be found in the regional, local, social and individual macro level of the great religions (Pentikäinen 1976, 11–12). The difficulty of grouping these processes under a systematic concept is increased as religions are precisely not sealed homogeneous uniform entities. This applies, above all, when the social hierarchy with its associated receptiveness and assimilation is taken into consideration.[13]

The familiar image offers a differentiated position to this "vertical" section through a religion and its supports. There are conscious bearers of tradition and thinkers reworking the articles of faith (priests, theologians, mythologists). And there is also the broad mass of lay people and simple believers, but these latter are not all passive receptors and objects of doctrinal teaching: they also form independent forms of religious tradition. Religious popular belief is the broad basis of all religions. The "*greater*" and "*lesser*" traditions have been mentioned (in North American ethnology and in *RW*). These should not be judged by numbers, but rather by the weight they bring to bear on the form of the religion. The former contribute the (written!) tradition of the elite, and the latter that of the people (as exemplified in studies on Ceylonese and rural Indian Buddhism).[14] This "lesser tradition" of popular belief is the hoard of unconscious syncretism, passing through the centuries (and also therefore contributing to the horizontal); even today it provides the "religious underground" of our age. It is always open to old and new kinds of religious conceptions. This is incidentally where *RW* and the ethnology of religion meet most intensively.

The forms of syncretism should therefore be studied and explained not only in terms of the history of religions, but also in terms of the sociology of religion, whereby the socio-psychological is also relevant to the inquiry. Among the various types presented, the following are the most relevant heuristic means of pursuing syncretism research (and Colpe has already basically defined them):

> *Symbiosis*, not merely in the sense of the newly-won unity of two or more traditional components, but also in the "living together" of two externally separate forms of religious expression which the believers consider to be a relative unity. In China and Japan, two or three religions exist side by side and are selectively taken by most, depending upon the exigency (Confucianism, Taoism, Buddhism; Shintoism and Buddhism). India and Java offer equally impressive examples.

> *Amalgamation*, or "fusion" must be understood as a typical form of syncretism (spread since antiquity) with its own specific forms: *acculturation*, *adaptation*, and *assimilation* as frequently seen in old and new forms of the spread of religions and religious movements. *Eclecticism* must probably be placed here, identifying an unsuccessful, restless combination of its various elements. *Theocracy* belongs at least partially in this category.[15]

> *Identification* which belongs above all within the framework of conceptions of god (*Interpretatio*). It can also rise up to *Substitution*[16] and *Transformation*.[17]

Metamorphosis or *Transformation* as a particularly successful result of syncretism reached via a synthesis of *Amalgamation* or *Identification*.[18]

Isolation or also *Dissolation* where the contact of religions and missionary intentions may appear and lead, for example, to forms of religion being overcome and shoved into the underworld, generally experiencing some change (popular religion, superstition).

These types of syncretism (of which I will have to omit illustrative examples) say a great deal about the expressions of syncretism, but still do not completely cover its nature, and thus a few more words are in order. Basically, syncretism belongs to the dynamic character of religious manifestations; it is a special expression or a part taken from the *change* of one or more religions and its forms of appearance. Syncretism must therefore be aligned on a temporal axis with a beginning and an end: the "end" having the sense of a new transformation or radical shift into a new form. The weight assigned to the various individual components of an emerging syncretism differs according to the historical and political constellations of power or the resistance of a substrate (Colpe 1975a, 21 ff., 35–36). A hierarchical arrangement with foreign elements dominant can result from above (political power) or below (substrate); a balance is also possible.

The essence of syncretism can be clearly distinguished here. It is not a mere question of a "transposition" or "alienation" (both of which are possible), but rather of an "*interlock*" of religious and cultural elements of different origins into a situation of contact. A process similar to chemical osmosis leading to an equilibrium or adjustment can follow. The contact can, however, just as easily lead to a confrontation with defined borders and exclusivity (e.g. Islam and Christianity in the Middle Ages). The prerequisite for a vital syncretism is that the features of the religious-cultural tradition and ideas which come into contact lead to a functioning synthesis.[19] The synthetic result of the syncretistic process can become an article of faith so that "from inside," the believer does not perceive the syncretism as offensive or foreign. The problem of syncretism is therefore not that of the faithful, but that of the scholar of religion! The process is often a long and continuous one, of theology both conscious and unconscious. The historical-political and social processes frequently determine its course, but they are, simultaneously, in themselves also ideological expressions of precisely these processes and therefore they affect these reciprocally. Syncretistic change in religion is therefore driven from two sides: practice and theory—a discovery which is valid for all processes of religious development, and the application in practice has frequently been opposed.

Notes

1. A first draft of these reflections, celebrating the respected and esteemed Harold Biezais, was presented and discussed on October 18, 1978 at the annual meeting of the Theological Working Group for Religious Sociology and Religious Folklore in Berlin (then in the GDR).

2. Cf. *Realenzyklopädie für protestantische Theologie und Kirche* 19 (Leipzig, 1907): 240–41, with references for this and the following.

3. The first reference was in *Fraser's Magazine for Town and Country* 47 (London, 1853): 294, according to Colpe 1975b, 1648 f.

4. Kraemer 1959, 389 ff. Kraemer distinguishes (a) absorption or "soaking" as an "unintended result" of the meeting of two different spiritual worlds as a byproduct of cultural contact from (b) real conscious syncretism, in order to oppose the view that Christianity is also a syncretism. Opposing the "spontaneous primitive syncretism" is a "naïve unreflected" product of the mass religiosity of the folk religion (392 ff.), whereas conscious reflected syncretism is a property of the "secret religion of the educated" (394). The former is the fertile soil of the genuine self-conscious syncretism which is native to the Indian and Far Eastern religions.

5. Although Kraemer is conscious of the historically negative meaning of the word (1959, 379 ff.).

6. Radhakrishnan 62, is cited by Kraemer 1959, 126, who examines the idea (115 ff.), but inadequately in my opinion.

7. "Die Vereinbarkeit historischer und struktureller Bestimmungen des Syncretisms," Colpe 1975a, 15 ff.; 1980, 162 ff. (slightly modified). Cf. also Colpe 1975b, 1648 ff.

8. G. Wiessner (ed.) 1978. The volume summarizes the contributions to a colloquium held 28–29 October 1977 in Göttingen. Cf. also Colpe 1980, 300 f. (n. 8). See also the contribution of Berner in this volume.

9. See Wiessner (ed.) 1978, 107, 116 f., 133, where the terminology of the model is suddenly taken up at the close of the thematic contributions and "confirmed." Cf. Berner 1979, 68–85; 1982, 95–114. I will not deal with the later and larger work (Berner 1982), as the basic thoughts were not altered, although in the meantime it has become clear that my criticism is based on a "misunderstanding of the intentions of the 'Syncretism-Model' " (115 f.). I nevertheless still hold to the following claims as I still have reservations about the use of Origenes (Chapter III, 117 f.) and Gnosticism (for which the detailed application is missing!).

10. Dietrich (ed.) 1975. Berner (1982, Chapter I, 5–80) discusses the earlier and more recent literature at length.

11. Cf. Hultkrantz 1969, 15ff.; also the relevant articles by H. Sieger, J. Mbiti, H.-L. Swantz and R. Harjula, in *Temenos* 12 (1976), 93 ff.; 125 ff.; 136 ff.; 149 ff.

12. *Temenos* 12 (1976) was dedicated to this theme, with papers from a symposium of 19–20 Sept. 1975 in Helsinki. These also have the current "interreligious dialogue" in mind, which is only marginally related to syncretism.

13. Emphasized by Robertson 1973, 199 f. and supported by Geertz 1960 with an analysis of the Javanese Religion.

14. Introduced by Obeyesekere 1963, 142 ff.; see also Gothóni 1976, 62 ff. Also critical remarks by H. Bechert in *Jahrbuch für Religionssoziologie* 4 (1968): 270 f.

15. Bonnet 1939, perceives the internal Egyptian "fusion of the gods" to be a characteristic of Egyptian thought, which he considers to be syncretism, attempting to explain it with a theory of dynamism (40 ff., esp. 44 f.; 48). He assigns the Egyptians a basic tendency to syncretism: flowing in their veins (41). It is part of overcoming polytheism and

opens the way to monotheism, preparing the divine for the ethical (48 f.). I assume that the use of syncretism in this instance is inappropriate, even if Bonnet has identified syncretistic features. It is a matter of Egyptian forms of thought and the interpretation of being which are unique in their "relationing" of the divine.

16. Cf. Diehl 1969, 137 ff. On the *Interpreatio Graeca* of Egyptian divinities, cf. Bergman in Hartman (ed.) 1969, 207 ff.; on the *Interpretatio Babylonica* of Sumerian divinities, van Dijk in Hartman (ed.) 1969, 171 ff.; on the *Interpretatio Buddhistica* of Christianity, see Edsman in *Temenos* 12.
17. Cf. Biezais 1975, 5 ff.
18. Cf. Segelberg 1969, 228 ff.; Hartman 1969, 263 ff.; Schenkel 1978, 109 ff.; Wiessner 1978, 119 ff., 133.
19. Wiessner emphasized this in the preface to 1978, 11 f. Robertson 1973, 119, refers to "a relatively coherent doctrine" crystallizing from the various elements.

References

Baird, R. D. 1967. "Syncretism and the History of Religions." *The Journal of Religious Thought* 24.

—1971. *Category Formation and the History of Religions*. The Hague: Mouton.

Berner, U. 1976. "Entwurf eines heuristischen Modells zur Synkretismusforschung." *Göttinger Miszellen* 19.

—1979. "Der Begriff 'Synkretismus'—ein Instrument historischer Erkenntnis?" *Saeculum* 30.

—1982. *Untersuchungen zur Verwendung des Synkretismus-Begriffes.* (*Göttinger Orientforschungen. Grundlagen und Erbegnisse.*) Wiesbaden: Harrassowitz.

Biezais, H. 1975. "Transformation und Identifikation der Götter im Synkretismus." *Temenos* 11.

Bonnet, H. 1939. "Zum Verständnis der Synkretismus." *Zeitschrift für ägyptische Sprache und Altertumskunde* 75.

Colpe, C. 1974. "Synkretismus, Renaissance, Säkularisation und Neubildung von Religionen in der Gegenwart." In *Handbuch der Religionsgeschichte* 3, ed. J. Asmussen, J. Laessoe and C. Colpe. Göttingen: Vandenhoeck & Ruprecht.

—1975a. "Die Vereinbarkeit historischer und struktureller Bestimmungen des Synkretismus." In A. Dietrich, ed. 1975.

—1975b. "Synkretismus." *Der Kleine Pauly* 5. Munich.

—1977. "Syncretism and Secularisation: Complementary and Antithetical Trends in New Religious Movements." *History of Religions* 17.

—1980. *Theologie, Ideologie, Religionswissenschaft*. Munich: Chr. Kaiser Verlag.

Diehl, C. G. 1969. "Replacement or Substitution in the Meeting of Religions." In Hartman, ed. 1969.

Dietrich, A., ed. 1975. *Synkretismus im syrisch-persischen Kulturgebiet*. Göttingen: Vandenhoeck & Ruprecht.

Frick, H. 1928. *Vergleichende Religionswissenschaft*. Berlin: W. de Gruyter.

Geertz, C. 1960. *The Religion of Java*. Chicago: University of Chicago Press.

Gothóni, R. 1976. "Buddhism and Sinhalese Culture. A Macro Analysis." *Temenos* 12.

Hartman, S. 1969. "Les identifications de Gayomart à l'époque islamique." In *idem*, ed. *Syncretism*. Papers from the Symposium on Cultural Contact, Meeting of Religions. Stockholm: Almqvist & Wiksell.

Hultkrantz, Å. 1969. "Pagan and Christian Elements in the Religious Syncretism among the Soshoni Indians of Wyoming." In Hartman, ed. 1969.

Kamstra, J. 1967. *Encounter or Syncretism: The Initial Growth of Japanese Buddhism.* Leiden: Brill.

—1970. *Synkretisme op grens tussen Theologie en Godsdienstphenomenologie.* Leiden: Brill.

—1977. *Antworten. Ein Vergleich der grossen Weltreligionen in Wort und Bild.* Zürich: Sperna-Weiland.

Kraemer, H. 1937. *De Wortelen van het Syncretisms.* Gravenhage.

—1938. *The Christian Message in a Non-Christian World.* London.

—1959. *Religion und christlicher Glaube.* Göttingen: Vandenhoeck & Ruprecht.

Leeuw, G. van der. 1933. *Phänomenologie der Religion.* Tübingen: Mohr (Paul Siebeck).

Obeyesekere, G. 1963. "The Great Tradition and the Little in the Perspective on Sinhalese Buddhism." *The Journal of Asian Studies* 22.

Pentikäinen, J. 1976. "The Encounter of Religions as a Religio-Scientific Problem." *Temenos* 12.

Pye, M. 1971a. "Syncretism and Ambiguity." *NUMEN* 18.

—1971b. Review of Kamstra 1970. *Religion* 1.

Radhakrishnan, S. 1933. *East and West in Religion.* London: G. Allen & Unwin.

Robertson, R. 1973. *Einführung in die Religionssoziologie.* Munich.

Rudolph, K. 1992. *Geschichte und Probleme der Religionswissenschaft.* Leiden: E.J. Brill.

Schenkel, W. 1978. "Kultmythos und Märtyrerlegende." In Wiessner, ed. 1978.

Segelberg, E. 1969. "Old and New Testament Figures in Mandaean Version." In Hartman, ed. 1969.

Wach, J. 1924. *Religionswissenschaft. Prolegomena zu ihrer wissenschaftstheoretischen Grundlegung.* Leipzig: J. C. Hinrichs.

Wiessner, G. 1978. "Die Behnam-Legende." In *idem,* ed. *Synkretismusforschung. Theorie und Praxis.* Wiesbaden: Harrassowitz.

Part III

SYNCRETISM: THE DYNAMICS OF RELIGION

INTRODUCTION TO PART III

In Part II, the main issue was the problem of definition in the light of the incompatibilities in the use of the notion of syncretism in theology and the study of religion respectively. However, the notion also refers to processes of change and innovation in religion. Both Pye and Rudolph characterized syncretism as either a mode of production of religion or simply the "dynamics" of religion. This part contains approaches to syncretism as a dynamic factor of religion.

Herman Gunkel (1862–1932) was a German scholar of biblical studies connected to the German school of history of religion, who did not, as already mentioned in Hans Kippenberg's reading in Part II, discriminate the mingling of religious elements from different traditions as a phenomenon of non-Christian religions only. He recognized the syncretistic influences in both ancient Judaism and early Christianity and stated: "That the religion of the New Testament, in important, and even in some vital points, can be interpreted only in the light of influence of extraneous religions, and that this influence reached the men of the New Testament by way of Judaism" (Gunkel 1903, 398). To Gunkel, the cardinal principle of historical study was to accept historical antecedents and he became one of the prime scholars to use the term syncretism in order to stress the historicity of religions. According to the study of Judaism and Christianity in the Greco-Roman period, he identified the cause of the amalgamation of religions in the disintegration of the political environment and the transplantation of religion. He saw the conditions of the individual in the light of the collapse of stable surroundings to be the dynamic factor of religious change, one which, in comparison with the early Christianity of Paul and John, gave room for the individual to create new religious forms by means of syncretism (449–50). Alas, the notion, even in Gunkel's view, was the consequence of a collapse of stable historico-political structures and therefore remained a phenomenon of degeneration. Moreover, Gunkel recognized the dynamic aspect of the phenomenon and modified it from a theological word of abuse into a genealogical concept useful for tracing religious antecedents in the historical study of religions.

The three contributions in this part represent different aspects of an explanation of the dynamics of syncretism. Foremost is the historian of religion Gerardus van der Leeuw in his definition of syncretism, which marks the difference between the genealogical study and the phenomenological study of religion. Hendrik M. Vroom, philosopher of religion, views the dynamic factor from the logical categorization of the incompatibilities of syncretistic elements, whereas the antropologist Roger Bastide takes a socio-historical stand to explain the dynamics of syncretism.

The Transposition of Religion

The major work of Gerardus van der Leeuw (1890–1950), that is, his phenomenology of religion ([1933] 1938), represents an important step towards defining the phenomenon of syncretism as a main dynamic of religion. He was yet another Dutch scholar, who represented, together with Kraemer, a view of religion in between theology and the study of religion. Contrary to Kraemer, van der Leeuw attempted to understand the phenomenon as a general dynamics of religion without the pejorative connotations. Van der Leeuw is famous for quoting the historian of religions, Joachim Wach, and his claim that every religion is to an extent a "syncretism" because of its previous history as processes of amalgamation. Therefore, he maintains that syncretism belongs to a general dynamics of religions that may be seen as a creative process, and not just as a "summation" of different "transpositions." Rather, he concludes that the cause of history simply explains the fact of syncretism in as much as it refers to a process resulting in a new "whole," which obeys its own law. Van der Leeuw uses the concept of syncretism to balance the discrepancy of historical processes, as leading, on the one hand, to changed meanings of the religious phenomena, against showing, on the other hand, what he claims to be the unchanged essential forms of the phenomena. Therefore, he defines syncretism as a *transposition* with reference to the twofold complexity of a religious phenomenon as consisting of something variable and something stable. Van der Leeuw seems to suggest that there is an essence that remains unchanged although variations of meanings arise through the diffusion of a religious phenomenon. We can only agree with van der Leeuw that some form of a religious phenomenon is always recognizable even when it is transposed to a new context and reinterpreted. Jesus is still identifiable as Jesus of Nazareth whether he is the Son of God as in Christianity or just a prophet as in Islam (although it makes a large difference ontologically speaking). However, his typology of religious phenomena is not a mere descriptive phenomenology. It is experiential, which the following quotation may suggest:

> Phenomenology aims not at things, still less at their mutual relations, and least of all at the "thing-in-itself." It desires to gain access to the facts themselves; and for this it requires a meaning, because it cannot experience the fact just as it pleases. This meaning is purely objective: all violence, either empirical, logical or metaphysical, is excluded. (van der Leeuw 1938, 677)

The Essence of Syncretism

According to van der Leeuw, meaning belongs "in part to reality itself, and in part to the 'someone' who attempts to understand it" (1938, 672). Donald Wiebe remarks: "The 'sphere of meaning', according to van der Leeuw, is a realm that is neither merely subjective nor merely objective. The meaning derives from a 'connection' amongst events/phenomena that is neither an abstraction from the data nor directly empirically experienced; it is rather a structure that is intuited" (Wiebe 1991, 74). Van der Leeuw's understanding of syncretism as transposition connects his phenomenological theory to historical events insofar as he attempts to reveal the double nature of religious phenomena as partly rooted in the history of changing interpretations and partly rooted in an unchangeable essence of the phenomenon itself. For instance, he labels the process leading from polydemonism to polytheism syncretism; but contrary to evolutionary theory where one stage leads to the next, he sees two different structures that are interconnected but never entirely merge (van der Leeuw 1938, 69–170). Thus, according to van der Leeuw, the dynamic aspect of religion, in contrast to evolutionist or developmental theories, reflects an idea of stable religious structures, which are exposed to contextual and interpretative variability in the course of history. Michael Pye remarks:

> In principle we may observe here the beginnings of the idea, for van der Leeuw, that the typological analysis of religion may seek ideal patterns running through religions considered in terms of their dynamics, that is, their emergence, their social-cultural coordination and adaption, their flowering, expansion, experience of crisis, renewal, reformation, stagnation and decline.
>
> The overall question is whether these starting points in van der Leeuw's account of religion are sufficient for the development of a full-scale theory of religion under its dynamic aspect, which might better be named a theory of religious tradition. This designation presupposes that "tradition" means, first and foremost, "handing on" and thus implies process and movement. In effect, van der Leeuw's ideas on this subject may be regarded valuable hints but not yet as a fully coordinated analytical typology of religious tradition. (Pye 1991, 108–109)

We may reconsider the rather complex dichotomy between stability and variability implicit in van der Leeuw's theory as basically ontological. The dynamic aspect lies primarily in the notion of "transposition" which may be divided into three types of processes: *syncretism*, *mission* and *reformation*. They all express different processes in the transmission of various religious phenomena, but as it seems, without changing the basic structures of the phenomena. Furthermore, it appears that the variations of meaning and interpretation are active in forming and reforming tradition. This leaves us with the question of where the essence of a religious phenomenon originates, and on what circumstances it may remain unchanged? Van der Leeuw does not provide a clear answer to this question. Nevertheless, he points to an interaction between two ontologically different phenomena—that is, between history and revelation. This coheres with his definition of religion as partly consisting of experience and partly of revelation. Religious experience is characterized as a human phenomenon and it can be studied as such in the different forms it has taken in the course of history. On the other hand, religious revelation is described as essentially incomprehensible and cannot be studied like other products of human society (Waardenburg 1991, 54–55). However, through the study of the human assertions about the phenomena revealed it is possible to assume their essential structures, which, in the view of van der Leeuw, transcend their cultural context (Leertouwer 1991, 58).

There is a precedence of religious phenomena over cultural phenomena that makes his theory a matter for theology rather than for the study of religion. Save for that, his theory of syncretism does not become less interesting. One must remember that van der Leeuw is a child of his time where (contrary to the study of religion today) the view of religions as the product of human societies presented the alternative rather than the norm. His idea of syncretism is appealing because, in opposition to the earlier developmental theories, which described the unfolding of history or the chain of evolution as gradually predisposed processes of one thing leading to another, he recognized that the complex patterns involved in the processes of change are not just processes of progress. He attempted, rather, to show how these processes include the constant flow of variations, interactions and the coexistence of different phenomena inside any given religious context. In addition, they are never completed in fixed forms. In spite of his religious phenomenological outlook, van der Leeuw recognized the social sphere of human activity in religion. He did not wish to reduce religion to a pre-given thing, neither as "biology" in the Darwinian sense nor as a "holy other" in the Christian sense. His theory of the dynamics of religion reflects his aim of a more multiplex view of religion in the history of human activity. This is what makes his representation of syncretism, even today, an inspirational reading despite some theoretical obscurity.

The Incompatibility of Syncretism

Since the days of Gerardus van der Leeuw and Hendrik Kraemer, the scholarly tradition in the Netherlands has placed the study of syncretism somewhere between the comparative study of religion and theology. Thus, Hendrik Vroom is another Dutch scholar who must be considered anchored in theology by virtue of his relating the notion of incompatibility to syncretism. The notion of incompatibility is another pejorative Christian connotation used to determine the nature of syncretism. Therefore, he comes close to Kraemer's definition of syncretism although it is evidently not his intention to characterize syncretism simply as incompatible foreign beliefs. On the contrary, Vroom focuses on interreligious encounter and exchange as a normal and fluid phenomenon between religions, one which he describes as "multi-faceted beliefs-systems." In his opinion, the notion of incompatibility sums up the main points in the scholarly discussion on the meaning of syncretism. Vroom clearly wants to distance himself from a pejorative identification of syncretism by insisting on a logical analysis.

His analysis of the main points of beliefs in *Christianity* (Religion C), *Islam* (Religion D) and *Amida Buddhism* (Religion C´), fulfils the standards for such a logical and objective analysis. His list of incompatibilities between the three religions, no. 6 versus no. 9, no. 12 versus no. 1 and no. 2, suggests how incompatible beliefs are made compatible through the creation of a "space" within that allows for a new interpretation of foreign beliefs. According to Vroom, this is the basic model for religious innovations and a "continual hermeneutic process." Thus, syncretism is the consequence of the interpretational and re-interpretational processes between foreign beliefs that, he claims, exist at the "boundaries" of the belief-system.

The Hermeneutics of Incompatibility

Vroom's hermeneutical understanding of the syncretistic process gives an indication of how symbolic incompatibilities disappear by constructing a "semiotic room" where meaning is restructured to become symbolic compatible. However, he is not entirely right when he claims that "nobody can believe that the earth is flat and round simultaneously, nor that people live only once and many times." In fact people do! According to cognitive science, the human brain does not always discriminate logically among information that stems from different systems of thought (Boyer 2001; Fauconnier and Turner 2002). We can observe how humans have no problem in selecting simultaneously from scientific and religious worldviews even though they represent matters that are mutually incompatible. The individual mind is not usually logically bound to a system of thought—rather it selects elements of meaning depending on specific situations or sentiment. Religious meaning is generally more attached to particular actions, problems, and emotions than to the strictures of logical thought. Furthermore, it remains unclear what he means by the "boundaries of the belief-system." We may ask: what kind of boundaries? Are they of a theological kind, of a cultural, social, or even of a psychological kind?

Vroom's digital model of syncretism echoes the theological pejoratives that he is trying to avoid by his use of logic. The notion of incompatibility as the sole indicator of syncretism insinuates that a syncretistic process is initiated from a biased position. Nevertheless, compatibility between foreign beliefs is just as good a starting point for syncretism. In the case he mentions, of Amida Buddhism, the elements from Christianity are selected precisely because they are compatible with beliefs of nirvana. There is just as much ground to prove that similarity and compatibility are as much dynamic factors for syncretism as are difference and incompatibility.

There is a contradiction in his argument. First, he claims that a "logical" categorization is not also "psychological" nor "anthropological," and later he states that "incompatibility is not only a matter of inconsistency of beliefs, but also of religious experience." By launching the question about incompatibility onto religious experience, Vroom changes his position from a logical analysis to a psychological one. He fails to recognize what his hermeneutic model actually indicates, that symbolic references are not logically composed in the same way as, for instance, indexical references are. The neuro-scientist and anthropologist Terrence Deacon takes up the subject of symbols in a way that suggests how the mechanisms behind the hermeneutics of syncretism work other than by logic:

> Demonstrating true symbolic reference is analogous to establishing symbolic reference in the first place. Symbols refer to relationships among indices, and are learned by first establishing these indexical associations. Regrounding questionable symbolic reference similarly requires a return to the indices on which it is based ... Unlike symbols, indices are part of what they refer to, and this makes them reliable in ways that symbols are not. (Deacon 1997, 404)

This speaks in favour of relating the logical categorization of incompatibility/compatibility to the general or contextual symbolic system of reference in a given religion. That may enable us to present a more adequate picture of the process of negotiation or legitimation of symbolic changes. Consequently, neither the incompatibility nor compatibility of religious syncretism is just relying on logic, because different symbolic patterns are psychologically or socially put to the test in the process, as Vroom rightly points out, and this according to the role of reinterpretation in view of contextuality. Second, when it comes to his final definition of syncretism: "Syncretism is ... the phenomenon of adopting or wanting to adopt beliefs which are incompatible with beliefs that are logically basic to a belief-system," Vroom cannot fully dissociate himself from a theological background. His analysis by the means of logic seems to depend on an idea of symbolic reference embedded in a Christian worldview. Then again, Vroom's analysis represents an interesting challenge. If the positions we speak of are made clear in the analysis, I believe that his model is useful on a semiotic level where it can demonstrate how humans are able to change the meaning of their symbols from clashing or contrasting beliefs by creating mental or semantic "spaces" for reinterpretation. It is certainly a type of process that is well known to the dynamics of syncretism.

The Interpenetration of Civilization

Inspired by Karl Marx, Roger Bastide employs a conflict theoretical perspective. He uses the power-related notion of interpenetration in his description of the imbalanced wedlock between Christianity and African religions in Brazil. However, the motivation from the French sociologist Emile Durkheim, from psychology and from French structuralism, shines through when Bastide accounts for the cooperation of social structures as well as mental processes in Afro-Brazilian syncretism. Contrary to Nina Rodrigues, whom he refers to (and Herskovits; see Part IV of this volume), Bastide recognizes the dynamic fluidity of syncretism. He accounts for different levels of contact, such as the structural, the cultural and the sociological, in order to avoid "the mechanical juxtaposition" of religions in encounter, and to further explain, in a comprehensive picture, the mechanisms behind the syncretistic process; in his case when referring to the "blending" of Catholic saints with African Orixas.

According to Bastide, the main dynamics of syncretism is spelled out in "the interpenetration of civilizations" by which he refers to a complex process of conflicting interests of power, social differentiation and emotional states of mind. His account of the process comes close to a survival strategy of African religion in the disguise of Catholic garments. However, Bastide makes it clear that encounters may result in changes in both of the involved cultures, because his key idea is to point out the different influences from the social and ecological levels that are resolved in syncretism. His research in Brazilian religion shows parallels between a higher tendency towards "mixed-blood" participants and an increase in the degree of ascending status of Afro-Brazilian religious movements in the social sphere. However, Bastide has no illusion (as that of Herskovits, Part V of this volume) about the neutralization of cultural difference and he recognizes a dualism in Brazilian society. He chooses not to describe syncretism mainly as a way of social integration because, according to his Brazilian research, it operates particularly in the lower strata of society of mixed-bloods or part-whites producing blends of "the superstitious Catholicism of medieval European peasants" and an Africanized magic. Moreover, he is aware that *religious syncretism* is rarely followed by *social syncretism*. In that respect, Bastide was ahead of his time by spelling out the differentiating effects of a multi-cultural society.

Differentiation or Identification of Religion

The two main forces at work in the religious integration-process in Brazil were, according to Bastide, the *Catholic saints* and the *African orixás*; that is, the simultaneous differentiation of African and Christian beliefs and the identification of saints with orixas. In Bastide's version, the dynamics of syncretism become an interplay between *differentiation* and *identification*, which is, I believe, much more fruitful than that between compatibility and incompatibility. This is ably demonstrated in the table of correspondences that discloses a *bricolage* of meanings according to different levels in time and space of the process of acculturation. From the table of correspondences we can observe how the operation of "sameness" is the key to overcoming incompatibilities. The dialectic transformations of saints and orixás are not closed up in a rigid pattern, but variations depend on demographic differences and particular social infrastructures. Neither dogmatic nor systemic contradictions between Catholicism and African religion seem to be relevant to the individual believer, but the social infrastructures and mental processes are.

The benefit of Bastide's multi-level analytical model is that, contrary to Vroom, he avoids defining the syncretistic process as fenced in by the digital codes so typical in the traditional scholarly discourse of syncretism. Rather, he prefers to approach the dialectic relationship between what he refers to as *inward* and *outward* syncretism, by which he means the relationship between the levels of psychological effect and the levels of social reality. His results demonstrate how different social and mental constraints are at work when, for instance, a Catholic altar faces the entrance, thus signifying the official legitimate religion, in contrast to the African altar that is hidden away in a special room, signifying the unofficial and maybe even illegitimate religion.

Laws of Syncretism

I find Bastide's division between *religious syncretism* and *magical syncretism* more problematic. It can be said to have some heuristic advantages. But, then again, the categorical division is suspect in phenomenological terms, in particular because he sticks to a universal and almost "archetypical" explanation of magical symbols for which there is no proof: "This syncretism is facilitated by the relative homogeneity of magical symbols all over the world and throughout the ages—the phallus, the knot, the eye, and the hand ..." Through this distinction, he acknowledges two levels of the dynamic character of syncretism. One which he terms the *law of accumulation*, which is a way of enriching African magic with the use of Catholic techniques, and the other, the *dictionary of correspondences*, which refers to codes of analogy that must be formed alongside the integration process for the sake of cultural coexistence. I find this division very fruitful as a means of portraying how psychological and social phases are differently at work in "syncretism." If we suppose that the "law of accumulation" is most frequent in religious life outside the restrictions of supervising religious institutions or authorities, then we may deduce that the "blending" of religious elements is then a more mentally free enterprise which is primarily structured by the mind in face of the social situation. The "law of dictionary correspondences" refers, on the other hand, to a mental operation, which is restricted, similar to language use, by translation and syntax of the involved religious institutions and/or authorities. Therefore, it is obvious that it is structured by a very different syntax of interpretation than the "law of accumulation," because it seems to be based on a more "emblematic" scale of representation, what for lack of a better word can best be described in the abstract term of "worldview." Subsequently, "worldviews" in encounter may necessarily use codes of analogy as well as digital codes to provide ways to dismiss or accept religious innovations as legitimate elements of the known "worldview."

Multi-levelled Model of Analysis

However, Bastide's use of multiple categories to describe the different forms and levels of syncretism can be confusing. In reference to one of the categories, *collective representation*, he states that the introduction of new elements are not so much a deliberate intellectual manoeuvre as "a means of patching holes in the collective memory." It is not at all clear to me what he means by this use of Durkheim's concept. Nevertheless, his analysis confirms that the different levels of which he speaks do not disclose identical sequences of meaning—spatial closeness between African and Catholic altars does not entail social proximity between Afro-Brazilians and white Catholics. Finally, Bastide's Afro-Brazilian "syncretist" in many ways resembles Lévi-Strauss' "bricoleur." That is, the pragmatic and ethnocentric position of the interpreter when he observes that the transformation of meaning happens because it must fit the values of the civilization of the interpreter. The analysis he represents is "multi-levelled," and for this reason it has its advantages as well as flaws. That is because it combines so many different levels from social theories, hermeneutics, structuralism and psychology that it gives a

a religion of Apollo, and of Zeus or of Dionysus, which maintained their independence as against one another and whose incorporation into the great whole remained theoretical or poetic.[1] But as the "world" gradually became smaller, several religions came into contact, the most impressive example of this being the syncretism of the Hellenistic age, which attracted to itself the religions of the whole inhabited world and interwove and united them either into magical modes of activity, or mysteries, or philosophic speculation. It may indeed be asserted that at the close of the imperial era there were countless religions in existence, since each person had his or her private system of devotions, and many even had several simultaneously; but it may also be said that there was only one sole religion, since all the components, of the most varied origin, had become unified within one single astrological-pantheistically tinged piety, for which the name of Zeus signified a rallying-point rather than any distinctive feature.

Every historic religion, therefore, is not one, but several; not of course as being the sum of different forms, but in the sense that diverse forms had approximated to its own form and had amalgamated with this. This is true of even the great, and so-called world, religions, to a quite specific degree. Restricting ourselves to Christianity and Islam, for example, these are from the dynamic viewpoint syncretisms; and thus in Christianity we find, together with the inheritance of Israel, that of Greece and even a small bequest from Persia; and the scars on the amalgam, especially that of the Greek and Israelite spirit, have not yet completely healed! In Islam, similarly, Christianity, Judaism and primitive religion met and fused together into a unique new form.[2]

In recent times, also, there exists a close parallel to the boundless syncretism of the Roman imperial era, in the various semi-, or completely, occult tendencies which appear under the names of theosophy, anthroposophy, Christian science or (new) *sufism*. These forms all pay homage to syncretism, to some extent in principle, because of their conviction that all religions, at bottom, are only one in different guise; nevertheless they are all mixtures taken from religions and spiritual tendencies occurring everywhere—Oriental, Christian, modern idealistic, natural scientific, and so on. Naturally these medleys often produce a very peculiar and confused impression, which however does not at all disturb their own adherents!

2

But at this point a more precise definition of a concept already repeatedly encountered may be given—the concept of *transposition*. "Transposition," then, is the variation of the significance of any phenomenon, occurring in the dynamic of religions, while its form remains quite unaltered. Thus the sacred word, the myth of Bethel, of the "house of God" (Genesis 28), becomes "transposed" from a fetishist experience to that of a theophany; subsequently to an announcement of the nearness of God, and finally edifying consolation. Quite similarly, the killing of the ox, which was regarded in pre-Zarathustrian Parsiism as a praiseworthy release of life (for Mithra slays the animal not at all maliciously, but simply in order to render life as if it were fluid), becomes "transposed" in Zarathustrianism and diabolized into Ahriman's first destructive deed (Lommel 1930, 183). In Christian worship, again, prayers of incense offering (by transposition) become an *epiclesis* of the eucharistic Lord (Lietzmann 1926).[3]

"Transpositions," to continue, appear at all times, but chiefly during reformations (chap. 94) and missions; and as a rule, the old possessions of religion were superseded by only a slight extent and retained in essentials with, however, an altered significance. Thus almost all Protestant religious communities retained the sacrament of communion but "transposed," with a changed meaning, and this too after the Roman Church itself had already accepted it from the ancient church and had transposed it. Israelitish prophecy, again, took over the Bedouin law of the *Decalogue* and interpreted it in a religio-ethical sense, since when we ourselves have not ceased repeatedly to transpose the Ten Commandments anew, from the Gospel down to Luther. Frequently, also, the actual character of a phenomenon is utterly lost in transposition, as in the previous example of incense prayers. But just as often we receive the impression that the essence of the phenomenon, at bottom, is retained even when its interpretation has been modified, as in the case of the Law.

3

The dynamic of religions, further, is displayed as mission. This may in the first place be completely unconscious, and merely a reciprocal influence of religions which is the outcome of local proximity, cultural interchange, and so on. It is called mission, however, because it is a result of speaking forth, of utterance and of testimony (chap. 58), and is accompanied by all sorts of transpositions in the life of both the influencing and the influenced religion. Frick has given an illuminating description of this effect of religions on one another (1928, 53 ff.). Thus there occurs assimilation of religions by each other, and also substitution of a religious value with more or less changed meaning (transposition); but likewise there arises the isolation of those elements which are, as it were, to be rendered harmless. Catholicism assimilated mysticism, for example, and substituted popular religion, while at the same time it isolated asceticism within monasticism (Frick 1928, 55). This type of mission pertains to every living religion.

But as soon as missionary expansion is understood to be the essential activ-ity of the community, it receives a quite different character. Its influence then becomes a fully conscious propaganda of doctrine and worship, and generally of the specific characteristics of a religion. It is in this sense that Judaism has made its proselytes, but has been frustrated because it has unified the "given" community with that of salvation (chap. 32); for, in general, deliberate mis-sionary movements presuppose the collapse of this equivalence. The great mission religions, accordingly, are the "world religions" of Buddhism, Islam and Christianity. Of these three, again, Islam is at present the typical mis-sionary religion because it takes the dynamic power of its faith to be wholly a matter of course: conquest, then, lies in the very essence of Islam. Conse-quently, it sends out no specially trained missionaries at all; every follower of the prophet being, as such, a missionary who, by his example, advocates an extremely simple worship and an equally elementary creed (chap. 62; Gairdner and Eddy 1928). But also in the essence of the Christian church, *una sancta catholica*, missionary activity is inherently incorporated, although Christians themselves are realizing this afresh only very gradually. Religion, however, lives only by being active; and in Christianity this ceaseless agita-tion is the life movement of the Holy Spirit, on whom no limits whatever are imposed.

Notes

1. Chantepie, 1887, 1:75. To a certain degree, a "pantheon" is always theory or poetry; cf. chap. 19 and Furlani 1929, 154. The Babylonian gods were regarded as the limbs of Nimurta.
2. Shinto, the Japanese national religion, is a religion free from syncretism, and therefore one that lacks a mission! In this instance religion has been wholly absorbed within nationalism (cf. chap. 37); Pettazoni 1932, 5.
3. For liturgical transpositions, cf. Will 1935, 2:112 ff.

References

Chantepie de la Saussaye, P. D. 1887. *Lehrbuch der Religionsgeschichte*, vol. 1. Freiburg: J.C.B. Mohr.

Frick, Heinrich. 1928. *Vergleichende Religionswissenschaft*. Berlin: W. de Gruyter.

Furlani, G. 1929. "The So-Called Monotheism of Babylonia and Assyria." In *Actes du V. Congrès International d'Histoire des Religions à Lund*, 27–29 August 1929, 153–55.

Gairdner, W. H. T., and W. A. Eddy. 1928. *The Christian Life and Message in Relation to Non-Christian Systems: Report of the Jerusalem Meeting of the Int. Miss. Council*, vol. 1, 252 ff.

Kees, H. 1929. In *Zeitschrift für ägyptische Sprach und Altertumskunde* 64.

Kraemer, H. 1938. *The Christian Message in a Non-Christian World*. London: Edinburgh House Press.

Lietzmann, Hans. 1926. *Messe und Herrenmahl. Eine Studie zur Geschichte der Liturgie.* Bonn: A. Marcus and E. Weber's Verlag.

Lommel, Herman. 1930. *Die Religion Zarathustras nach dem Awesta dargestellt.* Tübingen: Mohr.

Pettazoni, R. 1932. *Die Nationalreligion Japans und die Religionspolitik des Japanischen Staates, Orient und Occident 5.*

—Sencretismo e Conversione nella Storia delle Religione (Bull. du Com. Int. des Sciences Hist., 1933).

Wach, J. 1924. *Religionswissenschaft. Prolegomena zu ihrer wissenschaftsteoretischen Grundlegung.* Leipzig: J. C. Hinrichs.

Will, Robert. 1925–35. *Le culte. Étude d'histoire et de philosophie religieuses.* II: *Les formes du culte.* Strasbourg: Librairie Istra.

Syncretism and Dialogue:
A Philosophical Analysis

Hendrik M. Vroom

In this contribution, a conceptual analysis of syncretism and dialogue is presented. In contrast to encounter and mutual action—which can be seen as important preconditions for real dialogue—dialogue is conceived of as deliberate discussion concerning interpretations of humankind, the world, and the transcendent. In this analysis of the logic of religious belief, syncretism is conceived of as the incorporation by a religious tradition of beliefs and practices incompatible with its basic insights. Integration of foreign beliefs requires reinterpretation of old beliefs and a re-configuration (particularly) of basic insights. By such a hermeneutical process a religious tradition can accommodate profound change; it can, however, be changed to the point of losing its original identity. Such processes do indeed occur through religious interpenetration as well as through contact with secular worldviews.

1. Introduction

In this contribution, we will attempt to clarify a little the concept of dialogue, and especially the concept of syncretism, through an analysis of the logic of religious belief.

We will first make a few remarks by way of introduction. One could start by asking: What "is" syncretism? Syncretism would then be portrayed as something present amidst many other religious phenomena. Recall, however, van der Leeuw's consideration of the nature of phenomena—of *was sich zeigt*—and the difficulties facing such a view—reminiscent of

Plato's ideas—of a phenomenon as a kind of reality in and behind concrete appearances (van der Leeuw 1963, 634). The term syncretism could better be used to indicate and analyse a certain aspect of the mutual influence between religious traditions. We therefore prefer a stipulative definition of syncretism. It is clear from Drooger's survey of the discussion of the term syncretism that it involves a process in which beliefs and practices from one religious current or world and life view are adopted by certain people in another religious current, and subsequently assimilated or repudiated. It seems to me that the various authors cited by Droogers have focused on important notions of the process of syncretism. Kamstra rightly interjects the element of *foreign-ness* (Kamstra 1970, 9–10, cf. p. 27). Pye points out the *ambiguity* proper to elements newly to be incorporated in the meaning of beliefs and symbols. Droogers himself defines syncretism as *contested interreligious interpenetration*. As far as I am concerned, all these elements are illuminating for the analysis of the process one has in mind with the term syncretism. I believe that these perspectives can be bundled together within the context of an analysis of *religious belief* by speaking of *incompatible beliefs and practices*. I will define syncretism in the first instance as the incorporation of incompatible beliefs from one religion by another. Being incompatible is not the same as being contested, because non-compatibility is not a psychological or anthropological category, but a logical one. Nobody can believe that the earth is flat *and* round simultaneously, nor that people live only once *and* many times. That is a matter of logic. People may, however, differ on these issues; their approval or repudiation can entail all sorts of psychological and social issues, but that is not the concern of this paper. Some of the elements of the discussion on the meaning of syncretism can be assumed by the notion of incompatibility: foreignness, contradiction, and contesting. The point, however, is the alleged incompatibility of beliefs. I will return to the notion of ambiguity when dealing with religious traditions as historical and hermeneutical processes wherein the beliefs of a tradition are subject to reinterpretation and rearrangement.

I will focus primarily on beliefs. This is not in the least to suggest that practices cannot be incompatible. They certainly can. To give just one example: one can recommend practices that foster an attitude of "unattachment," compassion, and neighbourly love. Such practices are incompatible with actions that stimulate an intransigent and belligerent attitude. Beliefs and practices are in fact intertwined in the religious experience of reality. In our logical analysis, though, our concern is with the (in)compatibility of beliefs.

2. Encounter and Dialogue

One could, concurring with Wilfred Smith, state that religious traditions are in a continual process of interpenetration. Adherents of one religion derive insights and practices from adherents of other religious traditions (Smith 1981, 21 ff.). That applies not only to religious traditions, but also to currents within a certain religion. What are the conditions for the possibility of such mutual interchange?

If person A says that he holds belief p to be true, then his assertion contains an invitation to his conversation partner B to acquaint herself with belief p and to experience the subject under discussion in accordance with p. If, for example, A says to B that "Mohammed was a very special person," then A is claiming to articulate a true insight about Mohammed. B can concur; she can contradict the statement; or she can interpret the assertion differently, in that "very special" obtains a different meaning within her philosophy of life than within that of A. Among the conditions for the possibility of such an exchange of ideas belong the facts that people have certain properties in common, that they can acquire knowledge of matters with which they are initially unacquainted, and that they can converse about various aspects of their experience of life and their interpretation of reality. In our example, people have the property that they can be impressed by what certain people say and do; B can learn something about Mohammed; A and B can converse about their views of Mohammed. More generally, we will mention the following conditions for the possibility of such a dialogue:

1) the existential structure of humans,
2) the possibility that people are concerned with the same matters,
3) the possibility of a discussion about a persuasion.

I add here that the existential structure of man is a point of debate between religions, that some "matters" of which religious traditions speak (e.g. *moksha* and *nirvana*) are not wholly, and certainly not easily, accessible and open to discourse, and finally, that "discursive thought and discourse" about such matters is not simple (Vroom 1988, chs. 8 and 9).

I wish to conceive of the dialogue between adherents of various religious traditions as deliberate discussion of interpretations given by various religious traditions (and persuasions in general) with regard to humankind, the world, and the transcendent. For the remaining human contact between adherents of divergent religions, one can reserve the term *encounter*. Such encounter, as well as mutual action to foster humanitarian goals, can be seen as a great help in coming to real mutual understanding. Not every encounter is a dialogue, however, and it is easy to see that a dialogue without encounter and sympathy is not very fruitful.[1]

3. Syncretism

One of the questions entailed by the theme of this volume, *Dialogue and Syncretism* [see *Sources*, p. xiii], is whether someone from one religion who *learns* something from a person of another religion is thereby being syncretistic, that is, adopting beliefs which are *incompatible* with the insights in his or her own tradition. What applies for beliefs can also be said with reference to practices. After the previous assessment of *dialogue*, I will now pass on to a more elaborate exposition of syncretism. I will first present a few results from a study on the theme of *religion and truth*, which are of importance to our topic.

How one views syncretism, and the relationship between religious traditions, depends to a large extent on one's view of the nature of a religious belief-system. If one regards the content of religions as a coherent entity, then religion A cannot adopt a belief from religion B, unless this belief is isolated from B and adapted (assimilated) to the entire belief-system of A. If adaptation is impossible, then A cannot adopt a belief from B. Hendrik Kraemer has spoken about religion in this manner (Kraemer 1938, 148 f., 172; 1958, 38, 66; cf. 112). He regarded religions as closed cultural units in which the meaning of each element is determined by the whole. In terms of this view, the adoption by one religion of elements from another is religious syncretism: every foreign belief is incompatible.

If one does not view religions as coherent belief-systems, but as multi-faceted belief-systems, in which basic insights are related to one another in a looser fashion, then matters lie differently. I will proceed from the assumption that the religious content of a tradition is a more or less fluid configuration of beliefs. These beliefs are compatible in the sense that a certain coherence exists between them or at least that they are reconciled in some interpretational scheme. By reinterpretation of foreign beliefs, incompatibility between beliefs in a belief-system is avoided. Every religion is immersed in a continual hermeneutic process in which the transmitted religious inheritance is reinterpreted. Every tradition is involved in a process of interchange with the culture in which the adherents live; this is commonly designated by the term contextuality. Certain beliefs are basic within a tradition; the accompanying religious experience is nurtured by rites. Beliefs which are not considered central to a tradition by its adherents are particularly subject to reinterpretation; a relatively broad measure of freedom to incorporate "foreign" beliefs appears to exist at the "boundaries" of the belief-system. This view, which I have elsewhere explicated and defended in detail, implies that interreligious encounter and exchange is a normal phenomenon (Vroom 1988, ch. 9, §3). Suppose that religion C contains beliefs (1) through (8), and religion D beliefs (2), (3), (4), (5), (9), (10) and (11). Examples will follow below. The question arises as to whether C can assimilate belief (9) from D. This question springs from religion C's claim to truth: religion C aspires to as comprehensive a view as possible on all of reality as people experience it; religion D claims that belief (9) is true. In terms of religion C, (9) must be wholly or partially accepted or rejected. Since religion C does not form a strict coherent entity, whose unity is such that assimilation of (9) would disintegrate its unity, the adherents of religion C can consider adopting (9) in their belief-system. One would, of course, expect that a belief from another religious tradition will not be adopted without further ado, but that it will be interpreted in connection with other beliefs, thus producing (9´). If religion C assimilates belief (9) from D, a new configuration emerges, C´: (1) through (8), (9´). The new element, (9´), stands within configuration C´. The meaning of other elements can also be altered by the assimilation of (9´): (7´), (8´), and so on. The order of importance of the various elements can also shift due to the adoption of new beliefs. Suppose that (6) and (7) are essential to C, and that (9) is in some tension with (6); then the equilibrium in religion C can shift, so that (6) is explained differently (6´) in (C´), and possibly receives a position of less importance in the whole, in order to integrate (9´).

I will now supply an example in which the issues of incompatibility, coherence, and contradiction play a role. Suppose that religions C and D contain the following beliefs:

Religion C
(1) Eternal salvation is received only through grace.
(2) People must effectuate their blessedness in this life.
(3) God has created the world, and has placed humankind above plants and animals; a human being is, if all is well, a reasonable, loving, and responsible being.
(4) God is transcendent.
(5) Evil is a reality in a world full of sin.
(6) God has revealed himself in the history of Israel and especially in Jesus Christ.
(7) The Bible is the source and norm of Christian tradition.
(8) In the ecclesiastical tradition, the Bible is explained and articulated with the guidance of the Holy Spirit.

Religion D
(2) People must effectuate their blessedness in this life.
(3) God has created the world, and has placed humankind above plants and animals; a human being is, if all is well, a reasonable, loving, and responsible being.
(4) God is transcendent.
(5) Evil is a reality in a world full of sin.
(9) Mohammed is a prophet.

(10) The Koran is the perfect revelation of God.
(11) The Islamic community explicates the Koran.

The question is what will now transpire if religion C incorporates belief (9). One must not say too easily that this is entirely impossible, because in the course of the ages, religious traditions have incorporated many ideas of a foreign provenance. It is therefore sometimes said that every religion is a syncretic entity. But if religion C would adopt belief (9), then both (6) and (9) would have to be reinterpreted to retain a certain amount of coherence between the beliefs. Room would have to be created within (6) for a history of God with people outside one's own tradition; (9) would have to be reinterpreted so that (9´) is compatible with (6´). And the existence of a partial contradiction between (9) and (9´) cannot be excluded, as appears from a further elaboration:

> (9A) Mohammed is the greatest prophet, whose word is purer than that of all previous prophets (at least insofar as they have been passed on).
> (9A´) Mohammed has prophesied fundamental truths about God, and is a prophet through whom God has reached many people.

By incorporating 'foreign' beliefs and reinterpreting old ones, a religious tradition can thus accommodate profound change. I will present another example (for a more extensive consideration, refer to the contribution by Kranenborg[2]); it is also conceivable that religion C assimilates a belief from *religion E*:

> (12) One must acquire 'blessedness' in a long series of rebirths.

This belief would be incompatible with (1) and (2), which speak of salvation through grace alone and of a single existence. One cannot believe (1) together with (12). (12) would therefore come in (2)'s stead. (1) would also have to be reinterpreted, like this, for instance:

> (1´) Man needs grace in order to attain eternal salvation.

In this way (1´) becomes compatible with the beliefs of Jodo-shin-shu Buddhism in which (13) is accepted next to (12):

> (13) By the grace of Amida—on which one concentrates by recitation of the words "Namu Amida Butsu"—one can be reborn in the Western paradise regardless of one's *karma*, whence one can "attain" *nirvana*.

The next question to arise, then, is the question as to the relationship between faith in Amida Buddha and Jesus Christ, (13) and (6) respectively.

In this analytical consideration, I will not delve into the question which could be asked in the theology of the various traditions, that is, whether a certain synthesis with beliefs of other traditions is legitimate, and which criteria are valid within a religious tradition. I merely ascertain that such processes of assimilation do in fact take place. Foreign beliefs, which were previously held to be incompatible, are incorporated. The incompatibility is overcome by a (radical) reinterpretation of old and new beliefs. It is precisely the reinterpretation to which one is brought in incorporating foreign beliefs which gives evidence of the tension which people feel between the old and the new beliefs. Such tension is a matter of logic.

In addition to the reinterpretation of old beliefs, yet another factor plays a role in the assimilation process, viz. the modification of the configuration of beliefs. By the configuration of beliefs, we understand to mean the relations which exist between the various beliefs, and the central or less central position of beliefs within the multi-faceted belief-system. The example of religion C has been derived from Christianity. There has been discussion in the entire history of Christianity about the relationship between (1) and (2). The Protestant churches made (1) central within their belief-system (and in their religious experience). Alongside of that, (2) was given a place. In classical Roman Catholic theology, (2) stands central, although the necessity of grace is not denied. Accordingly, classical Protestant and Catholic theology each presented an interpretation of Christian faith. Neither denied the importance of grace and works, but they were ascribed a different relative weight, and divergent interpretations emerged, leading to vehement conflicts. The difference in belief-system (and religious experience) between one tradition and the other within Christianity was not slight. The cluster of beliefs (including a view on the relation between the different religions) is determinative for the possibility of the integration of beliefs from other traditions. In the example given, (12) is incompatible with (1). Only by reinterpretation of (1) can (12) be incorporated. As far as I can see, a current which regards (2) as more central than (1) will more easily admit of accepting (12) instead of (2).

The reinterpretation of (1) as (1′) allows more room for the acceptance of the teaching of reincarnation and the life of grace, as this is given form by the Jodo-shin-shu, but runs into other incompatibilities, particularly in respect of the relationship between *nirvana* and belief in God, and between faith in Amida Buddha and Jesus Christ.

Since religious traditions include many currents with divergent emphases, one may not place them over against one another as closed units. There is room for learning from other traditions. Since people aspire to an interpretation of the whole of the reality they experience, they will be inclined to integrate as many insights from elsewhere as possible. Which insights they consider important to integrate depends on various factors, including what is held to be true and what is considered to be of value (for better or for worse) in the culture in which one lives, and on what is impressive in other persuasions, impressive in the sense that justice is done to essential aspects of being human. Interpenetration of religious traditions will be more common in a religiously pluralistic society than in a society with a single common worldview.

Syncretism is, we can now say, the phenomenon of adopting or wanting to adopt beliefs which are incompatible with beliefs that are logically basic to a belief-system. Due to syncretism, basic beliefs are reinterpreted in such a way that they are (a) radically modified in their meaning and (b) no longer basic to the configuration of the belief-system. The original identity of such a configuration is thereby changed.

I believe in this way to have done justice to the discussion of syncretism as Droogers has presented it. The notion of "foreignness" is expressed in the assimilation of beliefs from another provenance, necessitating a thorough re-interpretation. The notion of reinterpretation is entailed by the ambiguity which Pye describes. Droogers himself speaks of "religious interpenetration, either taken for granted, or subject to debate." The analysis given here illumines the reasons for debate and contradiction; these lie in the incompatibility. This incompatibility is not only a matter of inconsistency of beliefs, but also of religious experience. The religious experience, for example, of "being sustained by grace" and "not having to do it oneself," is in conflict with the feeling that one must obtain salvation for oneself by observing the *Shari'ah*, for example, or by doing good works. Incompatibility can also surface in the rites and liturgies of a religion, since different practices evoke and nurture diverse religious experiences.

Finally, I must examine the incompatibilities that lie in religious traditions themselves. Since religious beliefs stand in close connection to fundamental human experiences, tension can exist between the various basic beliefs. An example which has already been mentioned of belief is (5): the existence of evil. The question of how one can relate the goodness of God or the Divinity to such awful misery surfaces in all kinds of religions. Religious belief-systems contain within themselves tensions between insights which are recognized to be true. These tensions, however, are interpreted in such a way as not to issue in direct contradiction. The well-known example of a contradiction is (a) God is good; (b) God is all-powerful and has made all things; (c) much misery exists. A classical manner of reconciling these three insights with each other is the assumption of (d) that the suffering governed by God has a purpose (unfathomable for human thought). Nowadays the tension between these perceptions is often mitigated by reinterpreting the "omnipotence" of God, in the sense that God must countenance affliction for reasons too deep for human comprehension, or by denying that God actually desires suffering. In this way people reconcile the basic beliefs that God is the powerful Creator and that God is full of love, with the reality of suffering in the world. Religious belief-systems thus incorporate their own incompatibilities; they have tempered these by placing certain relations between the beliefs which are experienced as incompatible, and by ascribing some beliefs priority (e.g., God is good). These beliefs are closely related to those aspects of human experience which are fundamental to a certain religious tradition; the conscious experience of this is evoked and "nurtured" by those traditions.

Syncretic processes display a different kind of incompatibility, since they disturb the balance which has grown between the basic beliefs of a belief-system and necessitate a new configuration of beliefs. What distinguishes syncretism, viewed in this manner, from the normal hermeneutic process which religious traditions undergo, is that the new insights are incompatible with basic beliefs of a tradition, as it has grown at a certain stage, or with basic beliefs that are essential to the identity of a religious tradition (e.g., Sinai or the enlightenment of the Buddha). Syncretism denotes the adoption of beliefs that alter the essential experience and the central beliefs of a tradition. A legitimate reason can therefore exist for contesting syncretism, that is, this incompatibility and the aspiration to keep certain beliefs pure, both in reflection as well as in experience. It is plain that abuse of power can play a role in repudiating the incorporation of other beliefs; abuse of power, however, has also often played a role in the syntheses which religions have entered into with each other and with secularized life.[3]

In summary, by dialogue, we understand discussion with followers of other persuasions. In this dialogue, one can learn from others. One then adopts elements from another persuasion or religious tradition and assimilates them into one's own belief-system. One can speak of syncretism if beliefs from one tradition are transferred to another, with whose basic beliefs they are felt to be in serious tension.

Notes

1. On dialogue as encounter and as lifestyle, see the *Guidelines on Dialogue with People of Living Faiths and Ideologies*, 2nd edn. WCC: Geneva, 1982, 10. See also "Rules for Dialogue," drawn up by R. MacAfee Brown and originally published ca. 1960 in connection with Catholic-Protestant ecumenical discussion, but "recognized as embodying sound general principles for any form of bridge-building encounter," according to the editors of *Study Encounter*, vol. 1. 1965, 133 f.
2. Reender Kranenborg, "Christianity and Reincarnation." In Gort *et al.*, eds. 1989, 175–87.
3. It should be kept in mind that the original context of the critique of syncretism and "religion" in dialectical theology was the era of German fascism with its appeal to the laity, as well as to theologians and philosophers. I am afraid that there is no reason to idealize the religion of the laity and the masses, nor for that matter, the religion of popes, bishops and synods. True religious life and insight seem rare.

References

Gort, J. 1989. *Dialogue and Syncretism: An Interdisciplinary Approach*. Amsterdam: Editions Rodopi.

Kamstra, J. H. 1970. *Synkretisme: Op de Grens tussen Theologie en Godsdienstfenomenologie*. Leiden: Brill.

Kraemer, H. 1938. *The Christian Message in a Non-Christian World*. London: Edinburgh House Press.

—1958. *Godsdienst Godsdiensten en het Christelijk Geloof*. Nijkerk.

Leeuw, G. van der. 1963. *Phänomenologie der Religion*. Tübingen: Mohr (Paul Siebeck).

Smith, Wilfred C. 1981. *Towards a World Theology*. London: Macmillan.

Vroom, H. M. 1988. *Truth and Religions: Currents in Encounter*, vol. 2. Amsterdam: Rodopi; Grand Rapids: Eerdmans.

Problems of Religious Syncretism

Roger Bastide

As we have seen, throughout the period of slavery the black gods were forced to hide behind the statue of the Virgin or a Catholic saint. This was the beginning of a marriage between Christianity and the African religions in the course of which, as in all marriages, the two partners would change more or less radically as they adjusted to each other. Long before the scholars began to talk about the phenomena and processes of acculturation, Nina Rodrigues drew attention to this syncretism between the cross of Christ and the stone of the *orixás*. Distinguishing between the Africans, who in his day still existed, and the Creoles, who were beginning to establish their own *candomblés*, he noted that the Africans simply juxtaposed the saints and their own deities, considering them to belong to the same category though completely separate. Among the Creoles, however, Catholicism was already infiltrating the African faith and transforming it into an idolatrous cult of statues conceived as images of the *orixás*. "In the mind of the African Negro the religious ideas instilled by Catholicism have always coexisted—and still coexist—with the fetishist ideas and beliefs brought over from Africa. The Creoles and mulattoes, however, show a manifest and unrestrainable tendency to identify the two teachings" (Rodrigues 1935, 171).

Rodrigues quite rightly sensed that syncretism was an ongoing process and that its degrees should be distinguished, but he failed to recognize a phenomenon that was to counteract it. This was the African sects' resistance to assimilation—the "back to Africa" movement that I have already mentioned. Present-day observers are always struck by the priests' careful differentiation of their beliefs from those of Catholicism and spiritism—at any rate in cities like Bahia where there is no police persecution. (An immediate consequence of police persecution is that to avoid prison sentences devotees of African religious sects swear that they are "good Catholics.")[1]

113

One *candomblé* priest told me that Catholicism and the African religions are alike in believing that everyone has their guardian angel, but, while the Catholic is simply aware of this as a fact, the African knows the specific name of the angel: it is that of the *orixá* who "protects his head." Another similarity between the two religions is that both the *orixás* and the saints once lived on earth. Thus the two cults share a common point of departure in what might be described as euhemerism. But, added this priest, the Catholic canonizes his saints, while the African knows nothing of canonization. The *orixás* manifest themselves—that is, they descend into the bodies of their votaries, causing them to fall into an ecstatic trance—whereas the priests forbid the materialization of saints.[2] So far as spiritism is concerned, it is a cult of the dead, who enter into the medium in order to communicate with their devotees. In the African religion the *eguns* (the souls of the dead) do not manifest themselves in trance. "They do not descend, they appear," and they do so in the form of masked individuals who impersonate them. Or they may "speak from without," and then the voice of the dead on the island of Itaperica is heard. To put it briefly, in the sects we are concerned with, the *orixás* manifest themselves inwardly, the *eguns* outwardly. We are a long way from spiritism. Moreover, spiritism is a somber religion. The room is dimly lit and lugubrious. The believers sit on benches, eyes closed, heads bowed in concentration. The only sound is an occasional sniff or gulp, a breath caught and held like the breathing of a woman in labor straining to deliver the spirit. The African religion is a joyous one, celebrated in an atmosphere of music, singing and dancing, festivity; faces reflect sheer gladness. These descriptions are accurate. But other priests, less afraid of offending their presumably Christian questioner, go much further in analyzing the differences. One even exclaimed: "I don't want anything to do with the saints. They're dead—*eguns*. But the *orixás* now, they're *encantados*!"—a remark that brings out the profound difference between a cult commemorating people who have died and been canonized and African polytheism, which worships the forces of nature—the sea, the storm, the sky.

Rodrigues's distinction between African and Creole *candomblés* must therefore be modified if it is to hold good today. As we shall see, it is now meaningful only if the distinction is drawn instead between the traditional Ketu or Gêgê *candomblés* and the Bantu, Angola, Congo, or *caboclo* sects.

Nevertheless, both types closely equate the gods, *voduns* or *orixás*, with the Catholic saints. The colonial mask remains firmly affixed to the black god, even when the two are not identified in any way. This so-called syncretist phenomenon is not particularly Brazilian and actually predates the slave trade. The evangelization of blacks began in Africa a couple of centuries before the settlement of Brazil, and certain Dahoman gods and some of the Congo Negroes' spirits had already been identified with Catholic saints (Honorat 1955, 105). And in Cuba and Haiti, in Louisiana voodoo, and in the *xangôs* of Trinidad, we find correspondences between saints and African deities transplanted to America that are analogous to those found in Brazil.[3]

The prevalence of this phenomenon can be explained only by the structural, cultural, and sociological parallels (to the extent that we have seen them in action) that facilitated the infiltration of Catholicism into the African sects and its reinterpretation in African terms. Briefly summarized, they are:

1. The structural parallel between the Catholic theology of the saints' intercession with the Virgin Mary, the Virgin's intercession with Jesus, and the intercession of Jesus with God the Father and the African cosmology of the *orixás* as mediators between man and Olorun.

2. The cultural parallel between the functional conception of the saints, each of whom presides over a certain human activity or is responsible for healing a certain disease, and the equally functional conception of the *voduns* and *orixás*, each of whom is in charge of a certain sector of nature and who, like the saints, are the patrons of trades and occupations, protecting the hunter, the smith, the healer, and so on.

3. The sociological parallel between the Brazilian "nations" or the Cuban *cabildos* and the Catholic fraternities.

But these parallels, which facilitated the approximate equation of saints and gods, were complemented by more specific parallels between individual saints and gods. Obviously Omolú, the god of smallpox, could be identified only with Saint Lazarus, whose body is covered with sores and who cures skin diseases, or with Saint Roch, whose dog licks wounds, or with Saint Sebastian, of whom popular prints show bound to a tree, his flesh bleeding from arrow wounds. Oxóssi, god of hunting, could be linked only to warrior saints like Saint George and Saint Michael, whose statues show them impaling dragons with their lances or crushing some other monster under foot. Yansan is identified with Saint Barbara because she ate the "magic" of her husband Shangô and therefore spits lightning, while Saint Barbara is the patron of artillerymen and offers protection against thunder and fire. (According to legend, her father was struck by lightning when, enraged at her refusal to abjure Christianity, he tried to decapitate her.)[4] Ribeiro also suggests another reason. Chromolithographs often depict Saint Barbara "standing before a tower with three windows, holding a martyr's palm branch and often a chalice and the Eucharist," and Ribeiro believes that this symbolic reminder of her role as comforter of the dying may have helped to link her with Yansan, the only goddess who does not fear death, participates in the *achêchê*, and watches over the dead in the "*balé* room" (Ribeiro 1952, 65–67). Saint Francis is linked with Irôkô because he is the saint of nature and pictures show him talking to the little birds under a leafy tree. The Beji, the divine twins, naturally seek out other twins like Saints Cosmas and Damian in the Catholic hagiography.

The importance of popular lithographs and statues is undeniable, and many writers have called attention to it.[5] Nor should we forget the stories of the Golden Legend or the superstitions of rural Catholicism, even though the latter were not recognized by the church. Shangô is identified with Saint Jerome because, according to unofficial tradition, Saint Jerome is the husband of Saint Barbara, while Shangô is the husband of Yansan (Saint Barbara). Nanamburucú is identified with Saint Anne because Saint Anne is the mother of Mary and the grandmother of Jesus, while Nanamburucú is the "oldest" deity of the Afro-Brazilians and the ancestor of all the *orixás*. As Ribeiro says: "This suggests that the mythological kinship between the various deities of the African pantheon and their position in the hierarchy must be taken into account in analyzing the identification of these deities with the Catholic saints," as must their specific functions and the way they are depicted in popular prints (Ribeiro 1952, 56).

But with a little good will correspondences are not hard to find, which is why a certain *orixá* may be identified with different saints at different times or in different places, as the table below clearly shows. Exú, for instance, may be the Devil because he is one of the masters of black magic; Saint Anthony because he leads people into temptation, is given to evil thoughts, and disturbs ceremonies (Saint Anthony was tormented by demons); Saint Peter because he opens or closes the ways and is the gatekeeper of the *candomblé*, having his *pegi* at the entrance to the houses, as Saint Peter keeps the gates of Heaven, opening and closing them with his great bunch of keys; or Saint Bartholomew because of the saying that on this saint's feast day, August 24, "all the devils are turned loose." Conversely, one saint may be identified with various *orixás*. Our Lady of Pleasures is sometimes identified with Obá because in Africa Obá is the patron of prostitutes; sometimes with Oxun because she is the goddess of sensual love.[6] Saint George, astride his white horse, his lance couched, may be either Ogun, god of war, or Oxóssi, god of the hunt.

All the same, the richness and complexity of our table of correspondences—this jumble in which several *orixás* represent the same saint and several saints represent the same *orixá*—is somewhat disquieting. We need a guideline to help introduce some order into this chaos of contradictions. To begin with, it should be noted that the table gives all identifications known for Brazil without any indication of the date of the research on which they are based. Yet syncretism is fluid and dynamic, not rigid and crystallized. In Nina Rodrigues's day, for instance, Shangô was identified with Saint Barbara, patron of lightning.

The identification of the protectors in the mind was strong enough to overcome sex discrepancies. Whenever I pressed fetishist believers to explain this physically absurd ambivalence, they would always come back with the question: "Isn't Saint Barbara the patron of lightning?" Among some blacks a still more curious inversion is found. Shangô's wife is Oxun; Saint Barbara's partner in protecting people from lightning is Saint Jerome. They simply turned this relationship around and made Oxun, Shangô's wife, the husband of Saint Barbara and hence Saint Jerome. (Rodrigues 1935, 56)

Logic, however, proved stronger than functional analogies, and today the *orixás* are associated with saints of their own sex. Shangô has become Saint Jerome and Yansan Saint Barbara. Similarly, when Gonçalves Fernandes made his study of syncretism in the *terreiros* of Recife, he found certain equivalences that have now completely disappeared. Ogun, for example, was identified with Saint Paul, Oxun with Our Lady of Pleasures, but the latter has been replaced by Our Lady of Carmel, who, being the patron saint of the city, is very popular in Catholic circles. (For the same reason Oxun became the most popular female *orixá* in Recife.) Yemanjá was identified with Our Lady of Sorrows or Our Lady of the Immaculate Conception, probably by analogy with Bahia (Fernandes 1937, 25, 128; Valente 1955, 134, 142–44).

Correspondences are born and die with every age. But when we study them in space rather than time, we find even wider variations. Some of them are the same everywhere—Yansan and Saint Barbara, the Beji and Saints Cosmas and Damian. Generally, however, they change from Bahia to Alagoas, from Maranhão to Recife, from Rio to Pôrto Alegre. This is because Brazil grew out of independent settlements separated by veritable deserts, with no channel of communication except the sea. Thus every African center had to invent its own table of correspondences. Of course the same factors were at work everywhere, so that despite the chaos the correspondences are always comparable (Herskovits 1969, 328), but local circumstances naturally affected their operation. In Bahia, for example, Yemanjá is still identified primarily with Our Lady of the Immaculate Conception of the Beach because she is the beloved protector of sailors and because every year the Virgin of the Immaculate Conception emerges from her church to bless the sea. In Pôrto Alegre, however, the procession of fishermen and sailors is dedicated to Our Lady of Navigators, so it is she, not Our Lady of the Immaculate Conception, who is identified with Yemanjá (Laytano 1955). In Bahia, Ogun is identified with Saint Anthony because Bahia was the capital of Brazil during the colonial period, and Saint Anthony, who had victoriously defended the city against foreign invasion and been rewarded with the title

God	Bahia	Recife	Alagoas	Pôrto Alegre
Oxalá	St.Anne (a) N.S. of Bomfim (abcde) The Christ Child (e)	The Holy Spirit (o) N.S. of Bomfim (m) The Eternal Father (n) St. Anne (l) The Holy Trinity (n)	The Eternal Father (c) N.S. of Bomfim (r)	The Holy Spirit (stu) Sacred Heart of Jesus (u)
Exú-Legba	The Devil (abcde)	The Devil (lm) St. Bartholomew (hp) The Rebel Angel (o) St. Gabriel (i)	The Devil (r)	St. Anthony (tu) St. Peter (htu)
Shangó	St. Barbara (a) St. Jerome (bc) St. Peter (e) St. John as a Child (e)	St. John the Baptist (Ani-Shangó) (imo) St. Anthony (l) St. Jerome (ho)	St. John (c) (Dada) (r) St. Barbara (Bonin) (r) St. Jerome (r) St. Anthony (Kilo) (r)	St. Jerome (Ogoda) (s) St. Michael the Archangel (t) St. Barbara (t) St. John (Dada) (h) St. Mark (Osseinha) (u)
Ogun	St. Anthony (a) St. Jerome	St. George (lmo) St. Paul (l) St. John (h)	St. Roch (c) St. George (Ogun Meji) (r)	St. George (stu)
Oxóssi-Odé	St. George (abcdgi) Archangel Michael (e)	St. George (il) St. Michael (ilo) St. Expedit (imo) St. Anthony (h)	St. George (r)	St. Michael and the Souls (t) St. Onophrius (t) St. Sebastian (su) O.L. of the Rosary (u) St. Roch (u) St. Iphigenia (u)
Omulu-Obaluayê	St. Benedict (bc) St. Roch (bcdef) St. Lazarus (cdef)	St. Sebastian (lo)	St. Sebastian (cr) St. Benedict (c)	N.S. of Bomfim (r) N.S. of the Passion (u) St. Jerome (u) St. Anthony (u)
Ifá-Orunmila	Holy Sacrement (cdg) St. Francis (cd)			St. Joseph (s) St. Catherine (u) N.S. of Bomfim (u) St. Louisa (Orunmila) (u)
Oxun-marê	St. Bartholomew (d)			O.L. of the Immaculate Conception (tu) O.L. of the Rosary (u)
Irôkô-Lôkô Katende-Time	St. Francis (b) St. Sebastian (d) St. Lawrence (e) St. Gaetano (Time) (e) O.L. of Navigators (Time) (e) St. John (Katende) (d)			St. Lazarus (u) The Holy Spirit (u)
Nanamburucú	St. Anne (be) O.L. of Candlemas (d)	St. Anne (hi) O.L. of Candlemas (h) O.L. of the Good Death (e) St. Barbara (l)		St. Peter and St. Catherine (Dahoman houses) (u) O.L. of Montserrat O.L. of the Rosary O.L. of Navigators St. Anne and St. Peter (Nagô houses) (u)

Rio de Janeiro	Pará	Maranhão	Cuba	Haiti
God (j) St. Anne (c) N.S. of Bomfim (c) St. Barbara (k)			Virgen de las Mercedes The Holy Sacrament Christ Crucified	
The Devil (cj) St. Anthony (c)		"The Dog" (i.e. The Devil) (v)	The Souls in Purgatory *Anima Sola* St. Anthony The Devil	St. Anthony the Hermit St. Peter
St. Michael the Archangel (c) St. Jerome (bc)		St. Peter (Nagô house) (v)	St. Barbara	St. John as a Child
St. George (jc)		St. John (Nagô house) (v)	St. Peter	St. James St. Joseph
St. Sebastian (c)			St. Albert St. Humbert	
The Holy Sacrament (j) St. Lazarus (c)	St. Sebastian (i)	St. Sebastian (Nagô house) (v)	St. John the Batist St. Lazarus	
St. Francis				
				St. Patrick
	St. Barbara (i)	St. Rita (Nagô house) (v)		

God	Bahia	Recife	Alagoas	Pôrto Alegre
Yemanjá	The Virgin Mary (a) O.L. of the Rosary (abc) O.L. of Compasion (dg) O.L. of the Immaculate Conception of the Beach (c) O.L. of Lourdes and O.L. of Candlemas (h) (Bantu Houses) O.L. of Candlemas (Yemanjá-Saba)	O.L. of Sorrows (l) O.L. of the Immaculate Conception (lo) O.L. of the Rosary (l)	O.L. of the Rosary (r)	O.L. of Navigators (h) O.L. of the Good Journey (u)
Yansan-Oiâ	St. Barbara (bcf)	St. Barbara (lmo)	St. Barbara (r)	St. Barbara
Oxun	The Virgin Mary (a) O.L. of Candlemas (cdf) O.L. of the Immaculate Conception (bc) The Infant St. Mary in the arms of St. Anne (e) O.L. of Lourdes (Bantu houses) (d)	Mary Magdalene (hq) O.L. of Pleasures (l) O.L. of Carmel (hio) O.L. of the Immaculate Conception (o)	Mary Magdalene (c)	O.L. of the Rosary (tu) O.L of the Immaculate Conception (s) O.L. of Sorrows (Nagô houses) (u)
Obá	St. Joan of Arc (d)	O.L. of Pleasures (ln) O.L. of Perpetual Help (o) St. Joan of Arc (o) St. Martha (io)	O.L. of Pleasures (r)	St. Catherine (st)
The Beji (the twins)	Sts. Cosmas and Damian (cd) St. Crispin and St. Crispinian (cd)	Sts. Cosmas and Damian (l)	Sts. Cosmas and Damian (c)	Sts. Cosmas and Damian (stu)
Ossain				St. Manuel (h) St. Onuphrius (s)
Aniflakete Verekete		St. Anthony		
Sakpatan				
Lisa				
Sobô				
Dosu				
Badé				

Rio de Janeiro	Pará	Maranhão	Cuba	Haiti
O.L. of the Immaculate Conception (b) O.L. of Sorrows (c)	O.L. of the Immaculate Conception (i)	O.L. of Good Childbirth (Nagô house) (v)	Virgen de la Regla	The Immaculate Conception O.L. of Grace
	St. Barbara (i)	St. Barbara (v)		
			Virgin of Charity	
			O.L. of Candlemas	
Sts. Cosmas and Damian (j)		Sts. Cosmas and Damian (Tosa and Tose) (v)	Sts. Cosmas and Damian	Sts. Cosmas and Damian (Marassa)
		St. Francis of Assisi (Nagô house) (v)		
St. Anthony (j)		St. Benedict the Moor (v)		
		St. Lazarus (Dahoman house) (v)		
		St. Paul (Nagô house) (v)		
		St. Barbara (vw)		St. Peter (x)
		St. George (v)		
		St. Jerome (w)		St. Paul (x)

Sources: (a) = Nina Rodrigues; (b) = Manoel Querino; (c) = Arthur Ramos; (d) = Edison Carneiro; (e) = Thomas Kockmeyer; (f) = Pierre Verger; (g) = Donald Pierson; (h) = Roger Bastide; (i) = Oneyda Alvarenga; (j) = Jean de Rio; (k) = Magalhães Corrêa; (l) = Goncalves Fernandes; (m) = Vicente Lima; (n) = René Ribeiro; (o) = Waldemar Valente; (p) = Pierre Cavalcanti; (q) = Jacques Raimundo; (r) = Abelardo Duarte; (s) = Leopold Bethiol; (t) = M. J. Herskovits; (u) = Dante de Laytano; (v) = Octavio de Costa Eduardo; (w) = Nunes Pereira; (x) = Milo Marcelin.

of lieutenant, was an appropriate symbol of the warrior spirit. In Rio, however, where the blacks have always been more resentful of the whites and where Saint George used to take part in the Corpus Christi processions mounted on a real horse and acclaimed by the crowd, the Negroes wanted their own black Saint George, protector of murderers, *capoeiras*, and upholders of the black cause, so Ogun was linked with him rather than Saint Anthony.

Sometimes variability is so great that the correspondences change from one cult center to another. In Recife, for example, in the time of Gonçalves Fernandes and when I was there, Oxun was identified with Our Lady of Pleasures in Joana Batista's house, with Our Lady of Carmel in Master Apolinário's, and with Mary Magdalene in the African Center of Saint George. In Joana Batista's house Shangô was identified with Saint Jerome, in Master Apolinário's with Saint Anthony (probably because of the color prints showing demons tormenting Saint Anthony as he emerges from the *fires* of Hell), and in the Saint George center with Saint John the Baptist (because of Saint John's Eve bonfires). In Joana's house, Ogun, who was usually equated with Saint George, was called "Saint Paul in the Portuguese language." In the Eloy *terreiro* Saint Anne, generally the Catholic equivalent of Nanamburucú, was the counterpart of Oxalá (apparently a vestigial survival of the androgynous character of that African deity).[7] It seems that originally every priest followed his own judgment in his intent to disarm the whites by masking his deities and labeling them with the names of Catholic saints.

The apparent confusion in the table of correspondences may also be due to the researchers' failure in some cases to indicate the ethnic origin of the sects they studied. It is possible that the Dahomans do not react to the Catholic hagiography in exactly the same way as the Yoruba. In fact two phenomena that ought to be clearly distinguished are often confused by the Africanists: regional syncretism and ethnic syncretism. My attention was called to this by the fact that in Pôrto Alegre, Herskovits found identifications different from those previously reported by Arthur Ramos for Exú and Shangô and for Saint Onophrius, whom Ramos linked with Osain, Herskovits with Odé (a form of Oxóssi). Herskovits states that the "nation" he visited was Oyo; Ramos does not cite the source of his information. When I visited Pôrto Alegre, however, I found that the Gêgê table of correspondences differed slightly from that of the Oyo "nation." Obviously geographic isolation is a factor in regional variations, but so is the isolation of the "nations," which are kept apart by rivalry. This isolation, to which I have already called attention, still persists in the form of competition and rivalry between *candomblés*. It has produced the same results as geographic isolation: variations in *orixá*-saint correspondences. As of now Dante de Laytano is the only scholar to have made a systematic study of these divergences between "nations." Unfortunately his findings have been published only in part, but they are sufficient to show the importance of the cultural affiliations of the *terreiros*.

Four Gêgê Houses		One Nagô House	
Oxalá	The Holy Spirit	The Sacred Heart of Jesus	
Yansan	Saint Barbara	The young Yansan	St. Catherine
		The old Yansan	St. Barbara
Oxóssi	St. Sebastian	St. Roch	
The young Yemanjá	O.L. of Navigators	The young Yemanjá	O.L. of the Good Journey
The young Omolú	St. Jerome or St. Anthony	The young Omolú	N.S. of Bomfim
Oxun-marê	O.L. of the Rosary	O.L. of the Immaculate Conception	

(Laytano 1955, 59)

It would be useful to conduct a similar study in other regions of Brazil before drawing any final conclusions.

But it seems to me that the most important lead to follow in introducing a little logic into our table of mixed-up correspondences is the protean character of every deity. *Orixás* are not confined to a single form. There are at least twenty-one Exús, not just one. There are twelve different forms of Shangô, sixteen different forms of Oxun. It is therefore likely that each form (or at least the principal ones) will have its Catholic equivalent. Hence it comes as no surprise to find one *orixá* corresponding in our table to several saints or Virgins. What at first seemed capricious now appears as a more harmonious arrangement. Nina Rodrigues identified Yemanjá with Our Lady of the Rosary, whereas today she is identified with the Virgin of the Immaculate Conception. The explanation is that we are dealing with two different Yemanjás, since there is one Yemanjá who is always identified with Our Lady of the Rosary. Again, Oxalá is said to be the Eternal Father, although most scholars equate him with Nosso Senhor de Bomfim, but the difficulty disappears when one remembers that Oxalá is split into Oxaguiam and Oxalufan. Kockmeyer's table of correspondences for Bahia allows for this to some extent by carefully distinguishing an old and a young form of each god. Dante de Laytano does the same for Pôrto Alegre (Laytano 1955, 59; Kockmeyer 1936, 32). But we still need to go beyond this dualism and envisage the totality of the divine forms. Then we would see that Saint Jerome is not the counterpart of Shangô in general but of Shangô Ogodo, so that this correspondence does not prevent or contradict the identification of Shangô with Saint Anthony, Saint John, or even Saint Barbara, these saints being linked with other forms of the same god (Saint John the Baptist with Sangô Dada, Saint Mark with Osseinha, Saint Anthony with Shangô Nile, and Saint Barbara with Shangô Bonin). I believe that a study of this sort would simplify the problem of syncretism, especially in the case of Exú, Shangô, and

Ogun, although it would not completely eliminate the contradictions in our table of correspondences.

So far we have tried to define syncretism from the outside. We must now try to comprehend it from within—that is, to discover the emotional or mental attitudes at work in the black psyche when it identifies its *vodun* or *orixá* with a Catholic saint. We must try to find out what inner feelings or images underlie this syncretism. I devoted almost the whole of one of my stays in Bahia and Recife to this problem, yet, as my studies progressed, I found that so far as the Negro was concerned it was nonexistent; it was a pseudoproblem. I had been reasoning according to the logic of Western thought, which is based on the principle of identity and noncontradiction. I had imagined that all outward syncretism must have its psychic counterpart, whereas the black did not see the contradictions that I saw; and psychic syncretism, if it exists, takes quite different forms from the outward syncretism with which I had assumed it to be linked. It is true that the endless questions I put to African cult members forced some of my informants to rationalize their faith, but on the whole I felt that their replies were largely dictated by the form in which I stated my questions and that I had forced my black friends to step outside their own mentality for a moment and assume mine. A spiritist who attended *candomblés* saw the *orixás* purely as effluents of the astral world—benign (guardian angels) or malevolent (Exú). Hence the names by which they are called, whether African or Catholic, are of no importance since these are purely spiritual forces. The *mãe pequena* of a former Gêgê house that had been taken over by an Angola sect told me that there are two hierarchized heavens. The first contains God, Christ, and the Virgin, and immediately below it is the heaven of the *orixás*. This was an admission of the superiority of Catholicism and of white to African civilization, but she hastened to add that it represented only her personal belief, not that of her colleagues. An *obá* of Shangô, and a Recife *babalorixá* gave me the most logical replies, based on euhemerism. According to them, in the beginning there were only the *orixás* and they accepted the bloody sacrifices. But *orixás*, like mortals, die and reincarnate themselves, and in the course of their posthumous evolution their souls were reincarnated in the bodies of white Europeans. Yet since they were still the same all-powerful *orixás* the people recognized them as gods, despite their changed physical appearance, and canonized them, and these are the Catholic saints. This explains the belief that the spirit of the *orixá* and the saint are one and the same and that the saint's name is the Portuguese translation of the *orixá*'s (Bastide 1973, 12, 27–33). These rationalizations drawn from my own experience may be supplemented by one made to René Ribeiro by a Recife priest: "The saint we worship is a saint who never died ... There are the saints of Heaven (those of the Catholic church), but ours too have the power to speak with God ... When Jesus Christ ascended to Heaven, some of the apostles and some of

His followers accompanied Him to the celestial court ... Others remained in the world where animals can speak ... Those other saints live in the *ayê*—in space" (Ribeiro 1952, 134).

In general, however, the priests do not confuse saints and *orixás*, although they attend church and call themselves good Catholics. "We are no longer Africans," they like to say. "We are Brazilians, and as Brazilians we are obliged to worship the saints of the church too—especially as they are the same spirits under different names." This notion of a purely linguistic difference is the one that recurs most frequently in answers to questions. The saint is the *orixá* under a Portuguese name. For most daughters of the gods the problem I am posing is therefore no problem at all. If you ask a child what the wind is, he will reply with a simple tautology: the wind is the wind. The *filhas* give the same kind of answer. Why is Yansan Saint Barbara? Because she's the same. Tradition weighs so heavily on the beliefs of the faithful that they become oblivious to the contradiction between Catholicism and the African religion. As I said just now, the problem is a pseudoproblem. But this is true only of certain strata of the population or certain "nations." Thus our study has led us to take social structures into account and to open up the question of inward and outward syncretism—that is, to reexamine it in the light of relationships between the levels of psychic life and the levels of society. In fact there are almost as many forms of syncretism as there are social strata. We need to reexamine the question as a whole.

* * *

First there is syncretism on the ecological level, which is quite understandable because the whites had to be given the impression that the members of the "nations" were good Catholics. It was therefore only natural that an altar with statues of the saints should occupy a conspicuous place in the *candomblé*, one immediately visible to any outsiders who might drop in. The defining characteristic of the ecological space is juxtaposition. Material objects, being rigid, cannot merge; they are located side by side within the same framework. Consequently the degree of syncretism is denoted here by the relative closeness or separation of what might be termed the Catholic and the African areas of the sacred space. Both in Bahia and in Pôrto Alegre every traditional *terreiro* has a Catholic altar and one or more *pegis* for the *orixás* (in Recife, so far as I know, only the *terreiro* of Father Adão conforms to this norm). The Catholic altar is located in the dancing room and often faces the entrance to make it more visible to visitors. The indoor *pegi* for Oxalá, Shangô, and so on, is hidden away in the obscurity of a special room, where the stones of the gods repose in dishes and receive offerings of blood and food from their daughters. The outdoor *pegis* for the "open air" gods—Exú, Ogun, and Omolú—are scattered about the grounds in the form of small closed houses. Sometimes one finds both a cross and Exú's little hut at the entrance to the *candomblé*, but the cross stands neither on nor immediately beside the hut. Here again the two spaces, the Catholic and the African one, do not impinge on each other. Moreover the Catholic altar has no functional role in the ceremonies honoring the *orixás*. The daughters of the gods do not salute the statues of the saints as they do the *pegi*, by prostrating themselves, or as they salute the drums that evolve the gods and cause them to descend, by kneeling before them and touching the leather drumhead. Indeed, when they dance they turn their backs on the saints. One feels that this altar is just an extraneous decoration lacking any deeper meaning. It is true that the choice of statues to be displayed is dictated by the symbolism of the *orixá*-saint correspondences, but that is as far as it goes. Here both spatial and social distance between the objects are at their maximum.

In the Bantu *terreiros*, where as we have seen the collective memory is less well organized, the objects are closer together, though still separate. The esthetic needs of the blacks, which here are not counterbalanced by the desire to respect a mythology not entirely their own, compel the *babalorixás* to decorate their *pegis* to make them look more appealing and thus attract larger congregations. With this in mind, they adopt features they have admired in Catholic churches and chapels. For instance, they may cover the dishes in which the stones rest, immersed in blood or oil, with immaculate cloths, or drape the ceiling with a canopy that falls in graceful folds. In what we have referred to as "proletarian" *candomblés* the very smallness of the house makes it necessary to bring the Catholic and African spatial areas closer together. Since it is difficult to find room for a Catholic altar, statues are replaced by colored prints hung on the walls, and since there is not room for all of them in the tiny dancing room, many are hung in the *pegi*. Thus the two theoretically separate spaces tend to impinge on each other. In the Recife *terreiros* such closeness is the general rule (Valente 1955, 116, 124–25).

In every case it is spatial rather than social distance that is abolished. That is to say, morphological syncretism cannot be taken as an identification of divinities with saints, although it certainly promotes it.[8] Finally, in *catimbó* (which, it is true, is more Indian than African, but which blacks have penetrated) the bowl of *jurema* lies next to the Christian rosary on the rustic table that serves as the altar, the *caboclo*'s cigar next to the Catholic candle. In Rio *macumba*, and still more in Umbanda spiritism, the Catholic and African areas are completely merged, and the *orixás* are totally identified with the statues of their Catholic counterparts.[9] The substitution of the statue or print for the stone in the *pegi* means that the two spaces have become one, so that the *orixá* and the saint can totally fuse in the affective awareness or the imagination of the votaries. The degree of psychic syncretism thus keeps pace with the degree of ecological syncretism so closely that it is impossible to tell cause from effect.

group that does not follow the same structural laws. In fact religion constitutes a relatively closed traditional system linked to the total social and cultural life, confined within the boundaries of the tribe or "nation." Hence when two religions come into contact, the result will be either religious stratification, with one of them being considered the only true religion and the other relegated to the realm of mysterious cults or black magic, or an attempt to establish equivalences between the gods and place them on a common value level. But the two religions will always tend to persist as entities. The law of magic is the exact opposite and always has been, from classical antiquity to the present day, from the land of the Eskimos to the South Sea islands. Magic is associated with the omnipotence of desire and retains all the excited illogicality, all the unyielding passion, of desire, which never gives up hope. Specialized sorcerers certainly exist who practice only certain types of rites, who have their own formulae and procedures. But if these procedures fail, they have to take stronger measures and find more powerful techniques. Beliefs that originate in the emotions are not willing to recognize defeat. Failure does not arouse skepticism toward magical practices; it just forces them to become more complicated. In order to succeed, the sorcerer takes more precautions. He goes through every name of the god or spirit he is invoking because if he omitted one he would draw a blank. He invokes him in all languages, for if he did not use the most mysterious and archaic tongues, the spirit would not hear his call. He piles action upon action, words upon words. In this respect magic is rather like some experimental science based purely on "experiments to see what will happen." The sorcerer tries out everything he knows or can think up in the hope of achieving his goal. This law of accumulation, which is characteristic of magical (in contrast to religious) thinking precisely because it is bound up with individual or collective desires, actually sets in motion the process of syncretism.

Newly arrived in Brazil, the blacks found themselves exposed to a popular Catholicism that was familiar with and treasured the "potent prayers" of medieval Europe against various diseases, sterility in women, and the accidents of life,[12] and that in the colonial or imperial chapels amassed *ex votos* testifying to miracles performed by the Virgin or the saints in response to desperate prayers or promises (Saia 1944, 202–204; Neves n.d., 399). With such "experimental" proof before their eyes, the blacks could not fail to recognize that the whites, like the Negroes, were the masters of benign or formidable powers. Some connection may even have formed in his unconscious mind between the stronger *mana* of the Catholic religion and the whites' higher place on the social ladder. This explains why they grafted the Catholic tradition onto their own—but not before they had rethought and reinterpeted it in terms of magic. They then fortified and enriched it with procedures drawn from their own tradition, mixing Christian and African rites to make them more efficacious. And it must be stressed that they did

131

not borrow from Catholicism alone. Since the law of magical thought is the law of accumulation and ever-increasing complication, the blacks looked everywhere for ways to intensify magical dynamism. This explains why Mussulman magic survived although the Mussulman religion died out. Non-Moslem blacks unhesitatingly accepted it to enrich and fortify their own magic, adding the *mandingas* of the Malê to their own spells. This is why blacks were not afraid to use Indian techniques during the colonial period or to pore over the books of Cyprian of Antioch or Albert le Grand in the nineteenth century and even over Tibetan or Rosicrucian books of magic in the present day. Far from promoting skepticism, the spread of education and literacy widened the scope for potential syncretism.

Nevertheless, these borrowed elements introduced into African magic changed in character and function. Magical syncretism is not the automatic result of contact between civilizations or of the pressure of the Luso-Brazilian civilization on the civilization of slaves or their descendants. Strictly speaking, magical elements were not combined with Catholic ones. African magic was supplemented, enriched, and intensified by the use of Catholic techniques that in this newly-created complex immediately acquired a magical character. The black does not see the priest saying mass as a priest but as a formidable magician who would like to reserve all his secrets for whites and withhold them from blacks, so as to maintain white supremacy. Father Ildefonso was asked by a *babalorixá* named Chico: "Where do you hide the key for opening and closing the body?" Catholic rites are not seen as religious rites but as magic ones, efficacious in themselves. To quote another dialogue reported by Father Ildefonso:

> "Father, I've been ill for six months and getting worse for the last two. But if I confess I could get well."
>
> "My friend, confession does not benefit the health of the body but that of the soul."
>
> "Father, you don't know. [Obviously he was afraid to say: "You don't want to know."] If you confess me, I'll be cured. My neighbor had a spirit tormenting him. When Father Gaspar came to see him, he confessed and was cured. My mother has consulted the *feiticeiro* but he couldn't do anything for me ... Now there's nothing for it but confession." (Ildefonso 1938, 11)

We may note that Chico's *candomblé* shows the highest possible degree of syncretism in all the magical expedients I have mentioned: African deities in the form of saints, Oxun in the form of Our Lady of Lourdes (because of the spring), magic herbs, toads, snakes, lizards, dolls, molasses—the whole lot, even down to the fortune-teller's crystal ball. "The small change is for summoning the saint. The string helps. The crystal ball tells who cast the evil spell. The person appears in it. The ball changes color; it turns black or blue. Sometimes a knot forms in it. When the white ball turns black, there's nothing to be done. The person will die" (Ildefonso 1937, 64–65).

Magic always tends to be quantitative. The *balangandan* worn by Bahian women is a silver frame hung with the *figa* of the ancient Romans, the Jewish Star of David, the symbolic fish and dove of Christianity, African horns to protect against the evil eye, *candomblé* drums, keys, the four-leafed clover of European sorcery—a touching conglomeration of worldwide magic.[13] This syncretism is facilitated by the relative homogeneity of magical symbols all over the world and throughout the ages—the phallus, the knot, the eye, and the hand—and by the monotony and poverty of the substances used—excrement, nail clippings, hair, strongly scented herbs, strangely shaped roots. Thus syncretism assumes different forms in religion and in magic according to the different laws that govern the structuring of the various types of collective representations.

But the divergence between religious syncretism (through correspondences) and magical syncretism (through the piling up of elements) should not make us forget that the differences between Africa and Catholicism diminish (a) as we move downward from the supreme priests to the sons and daughters of the gods, then to the *candomblé* members still tenuously attached to the sect though operating on its periphery rather than at its center, and (b) as we move from the traditional to the Bantu sects more or less complicated by *caboclos* and from there to the *macumba* of Rio.

This evolution is easy to understand. In the first case, moving downward from the priests or priestesses, we come first to highly Africanized individuals on a lower intellectual level who are less interested in myth than in rites, less concerned with collective representations than with practices, because of the favorable effect these may have on their lives in general. Next come people who belong to the Brazilian rather than the African society and who in their hyphenated allegiance to two different mental worlds derive reassurance from identification with the *orixás* and the saints. In brief, the intensity of the syncretism varies with the degree of participation in institutionalized groups.

In the second case several factors tend to bring the African religion and Catholicism closer together. First, the Bantu assign a more important place to magic in the activities of the *candomblé* than do the Yoruba. Anyone privileged to spend a few days in both types of *candomblé* and observe the type of caller received by the *babalorixás* or *yalorixás* and the advice given to them will recognize this essential difference. As for *macumba*, it openly crosses the line separating religion from magic, particularly black magic. The *macumbeiros* are constantly being asked to make *despachos* against football clubs, politicians, or rivals in love. Thus the law of magical syncretism, which brings Catholicism and Africanism together, tends to replace the law of religious syncretism, which confines itself to compiling a dictionary of correspondences or analogies. Another factor is that the Bantu songs, like those of *macumba*, are generally in Portuguese, and their composers indiscriminately use the god's African name and the other name by which he is known—that of the Catholic saint. By calling the *orixás* by their Portuguese names, they identify the two in the minds of the singers or listeners. A last point to remember is that the color of the participants grows lighter as one passes from the traditional *terreiros* to the Bantu ones and then to *macumba*, which has as many white as mulatto devotees—and far fewer pure black ones. Interracial marriage finds a parallel in the marriage between civilizations. "Mulattoism" is a cultural as well as a biological phenomenon. *Macumba* is a mulatto or rather a mixed-blood religion (since it combines Indian elements with African and white ones). But this cultural mulattoism can only be explained by, and always occurs together with, mulattoism in the form of the mixing of races or blood through marriage or concubinage.

While the ecological and ceremonial levels led us in a rising dialectic to the level of collective representations, our study of the latter has led us, in an inverse dialectic, to a lower level, that of social structures.

* * *

Civilizations may meet and live side by side without mutual penetration. Contrary to what one might expect, this does not happen because they shut one another out in mutual hostility. A state of war is not prejudicial to cultural fusion. It brings the civilizations together as much as it separates them, because to win a war it is necessary to learn from experience and borrow the victor's most effective weapons. We have seen how, in Brazilian *quilombos* such as Palmares, the saints made their way into the chapels of the runaway slaves fighting against the white planters. So-called counter-acculturation movements begin to operate only after a more or less prolonged exploitation of one ethnic group by another, so that the civilization to which one returns is not the authentic one of former times but a mythical version of it, and the counteracculturation always bears in its wake some of the characteristics of the rejected civilization. Cultural exchange seems to be at its lowest in times of peace, not war, as the example of India shows. In peacetime, civilizations in contact are mutually complementary—cattle raisers or crop raisers, pure agriculturists or craft workers.[14] This state of complementary though hierarchized activities was typical of Brazil in the days of slavery. Under this system of labor the blacks and whites could not get along without one another. The black was his master's "hands and feet"; he supplied the indispensable labor force without which the white would never have been able to establish himself and prosper in Brazil. On the other hand the white provided the minimal security his slaves needed, protecting them against raids by wild Indians and the hazards of disease, infirmity, or old age. As I have shown, before the "nations" came into being, the great plantations replaced the African village with the slaves, providing them with a cooperative environment in which security made up for the loss of liberty. The two worlds, the world of the blacks laboring in the fields and that of the whites living in the *casa grande*, did not interpenetrate. Africa simply coexisted with Europe.

But in addition to these rural slaves there were the house servants, maids and black nurses, and the mistresses selected by the master for his sexual pleasure. Two courses were open to the blacks who could not bear this subjection: to revolt or to seek integration into the dominant group, even in a subordinate position, for the sake of the advantages this would bring them. This integration, however, entailed the de-Africanization of the blacks in their new environment and a parallel though less profound Africanization of the whites. In any case, from the colonial era on, the two systems existed side by side—the encystment of the different races and the integration of individuals into one community. These two phenomena are constantly at work in the network of interpersonal or interracial relations in Brazil. The social class has of course replaced the closed caste. But class barriers, especially when their hierarchy coincides with a color hierarchy of some sort, still confront the blacks with the same dilemma as before: encystment or participation. The degree of syncretism or assimilation depends upon the degree of encystment or integration of individuals into the global society. To be more precise, both cases actually constitute integration (since individual isolation, far from promoting the preservation of some kind of culture, tends to turn human beings into animals interested only in survival), but in one case it is integration into a partial community, in the other into society as a whole. In the conclusion to Part I of this book [see *Sources*, p. xiii] we saw that the abolition of slave labor completely disorganized the black group, leaving it without any institutional frameworks—even deleterious ones—to support it. In this situation we found that the *candomblés* provided one of the rare community niches within which uprooted men deprived of all social ties could re-create communion.

Yet today *candomblé* members too are caught up in the movement of integration into Brazilian society as a whole, and as a result of economic competition in the labor market (which arouses or revives color prejudice and racial discrimination), are forced back upon themselves and compelled to form encysted communities.[15] Today one should perhaps distinguish between cultural encystment, which would reach its highest point in the *candomblé*, though without leading to racial encystment; and racial encystment, which would be strongest in the southern part of the country, though without leading to cultural encystment. However well justified this distinction may be, it should not distract us from the first correlation we established: the correlation between the degree of participation and the degree of syncretism, especially since, as we have seen, the principle of compartmentalization enables the blacks to participate in the economic or political activity of the region they live in while remaining loyal to their African norms and values. We must always view the facts of syncretism in the dualist context of Brazilian society. Even Pierson, who, in *Negroes in Brazil*, places so much stress on miscegenation and racial democracy, is forced to admit that when one moves from the lower to the upper class one finds oneself in a totally different world (Pierson 1942, xviii). Hence encystment and integration or integration into a community and integration into the global society always operate in tandem, and we may safely follow this lead in seeking to understand the phenomena of syncretism.

In Bahia, multiracial integration occurs within the framework of cultural encystment. Whites and mulattoes are linked with *candomblé* life primarily in the capacity of *ogans*, the patrons and protectors of the *terreiro*, or as its political friends. The godparent relationship, which links the various levels in the hierarchy of color, takes the form of godparenthood *de santo*—that is, the godfather pays all or part of the expenses of an initiation. The most prestigious members of the Negro group belong both to the world of the *candomblé*, where they often hold important offices, and to the Luso-Brazilian world, where they may be businessmen, property owners, or members of Catholic fraternities. Consequently syncretism, which was originally merely a mask, a means of distracting the white man's attention and evading his watchful eye, is transformed into the system of equivalences, of correspondences between saints and *orixás*, that I have described in some detail. The saints and *orixás* are not confused; they are not identified—or at any rate not completely. In fact in Ketu, Jesha, or Nagô *terreiros* they are quite sharply distinguished. But they are linked, as the blacks are linked with the whites without completely merging with them. In Pôrto Alegre, as we have seen, the survival of the *batuques* varied even more clearly with the social distance between the black masses and the middle- and upper-class whites. Yet the blacks are Catholics too; they were integrated into Brazil primarily through Christianization. So here too correspondences were established, facilitated by the blacks' participation in the festivals of the Rosary, although never to the point where saints and *orixás* were merged. To put it briefly, the more closely integration adheres to the community type, or the greater the social or cultural encystment within which it occurs, the less profound the syncretism. What I have said about the Yoruba religion also applies exactly to the Dahoman religion of Maranhão. It may be noted that in the *Casa das Minas* most of the *voduns* have never found a Catholic counterpart.[16] Here the syncretism is primarily between the calendar of African festivals and the Brazilian calendar, civil as well as religious: Christmas, Carnival, the feasts of Saint John and Saint Sebastian (Pereira 1947, 38; Eduardo 1948, 53–54).

In the areas of *pagelança* and *catimbó*, however, the blacks are much more thoroughly integrated into the surrounding society, as is reflected in the acceptance of *caboclo* spirits. The same is true of Rio, where the surrounding society is white and preponderantly Catholic rather than of mixed blood. Syncretism occurs as the saints are accepted and gradually replace the *orixás*. But the black is never integrated directly into society as a whole; his integration always proceeds by way of the social class system and—as has been true from the outset—by way of the dualism of Brazilian society. It is certainly integration, but with what? With the lower-class masses of mixed-bloods or part-whites. That is, with a Catholicism that is not the official one but the superstitious Catholicism of medieval European peasants. With a society in which miscegenation Africanizes the whites as much as it de-Africanizes the blacks. Hence integration with a class (the form that black integration into the global society assumes) does not do away with the African religions altogether but, by pushing syncretism to its limits, denatures and corrupts them. The corruption takes different forms in rural areas and in big cities—that is, according to whether the black is integrated into the lower peasant class or into the urban proletariat.

Notes

1. Arthur Ramos effectively exposed the importance of these two movements: counter-acculturation, which promotes separation; and police persecution, which promotes assimilation. He mentions the former in discussing Nina Rodrigues's thesis (Ramos 1942, 8) and the latter later in the same book (223–24). Cf. Valente (1955, 114).

2. I would add that Christian mysticism is always defined as a merging with God. But it should be noted that even though the saints do not inspire mystic trance, phenomena do occur which suggest a type of trance closer to the African type than the classical rapture of oneness with God. I am referring to those that mime the passion of Christ or the suckling of Jesus by the Virgin. In these cases mysticism appears as an "imitation of sacred history" recalling, *mutatis mutandis*, the link between myth and ecstatic rite in the *candomblés*. See Bastide 1931, 177–83.

3. For Cuba, see the books of Fernando Ortiz and Lydia Cabrera; for Haiti, those of Milo Marcelin, Alfred Métraux, Louis Maximilien, Jean Price-Mars, M. J. Herskovits, etc. For Louisiana, see Newbell Niles Puckett, *Folk Beliefs of the Southern Negro* (Chapel Hill: University of North Carolina Press, 1926), ch. 3. For Trinidad, see M. J. and F. S. Herskovits, *Trinidad Village* (New York: Knopf, 1947), appendix. For America as a whole, see M. J. Herskovits, *The Myth of the Negro Past* (New York: Harper & Brothers, 1941).

4. On these parallels see Bastide 1973.

5. See (especially for Haiti) Leiris 1953, 201–208.

6. Ribeiro, it is true, gives another reason. "Local variations in the prestige of certain saints, so common in Catholic countries, explain the differing identifications of the African deities. Obá presents a typical case. In Recife this warrior god is equated with Our Lady of Pleasures, who is said to have been responsible for the Portuguese victory

over the Dutch in the Guararapes mountains, while in Bahia he is identified with Joan of Arc" (1952, 57).

7. Fernandes 1937, 25–26 (Joana Batista's Santana sect) and 27 (Eloy *terreiro*); Bastide 1973, 19 (Master Apolinário's *terreiro*); P. Cavalcanti 1935, 252 (African Center of Saint Barbara, where Obaluayê is identified with the Savior, not with Saint Sebastian as in the other centers); and 254–55 (African Center of Saint George).
8. Ribeiro's study of the same *xangôs* during the same period confirms this (1952, 134).
9. See, for example, the photographs of *pegis* in Bantu *candomblés* in Ramos 1934, 20, 22, 39.
10. A description of the ceremony, signed by Ribeiro and with photographs by Pierre Verger, was published in *O Cruzeiro*, November 19, 1949, 50–59.
11. See the description by Carvalho (1915, 50 ff.), cited by Ramos (1934, 153–55).
12. Ramos 1942, 253–71; Cesar 1941, 143–67; Campos 1955, 139–81; Teixeiro 1941, 413–19; Neves n.d., 49–57, 87–91.
13. On the *balagandan* and the *penca* see F. Oliveira Neto, "A Penca e o Balangandan," *Dom Casmurro*, May 16, 1942, 8; E. Tourinho, *Alma e Corpo da Bahia* (Rio de Janeiro: J. Olympio, 1950), 306 ff.; Afranio Peixoto, *Breviário da Bahia* (Rio de Janeiro: Livraria Agir, Editôra, 1946), 318–21. Some of the charms are controversial. What some interpret as African drums others see as the wood blocks in which blacks used to cut a notch to record payment of their monthly dues to a society for slave emancipation. On the *figa* and its origins see Vasconcellos 1925.
14. Mandelbaum, quoted by M. J. Herskovits in 1952, 249. Other cases could be cited, including those of the Guaycuru and Guaná Indians (see Guido Baldus, *Os Caduveo*, São Paulo: Martins, 1945, and the introduction by H. Baldus).
15. I myself was deeply struck by this phenomenon, to which Victor Vianna had already called attention in his reply to an inquiry about the feasibility of Negro immigration to Brazil as proposed by the Society for Agriculture (*Sociedade Nacional de Agricultura: Imigração*, 300–301).
16. The table of correspondences presented here shows the only existing equivalents for some forty *voduns* worshiped in Maranhão.

References

Bastide, Roger. 1931. *Les problèmes de la Vie Mystique*. Paris: A. Colin.
—1958. *Le Candomblé de Bahia (Rite Nagô)*. Paris: Mouton & Co.
—1973. "Contribuição ao Estudo do Sincretismo Católico-Fetichista." In *Estudos Afro-Brasileiros*. São Paulo: Editora Perspectiva.
Campos, Eduardo. 1955. *Medicina Popular: Superstições, Crendices e Meizehnas*. Rio de Janeiro: Livraria-Editôra da Sasa do Estudante do Brasil.
Carvalho, Carlos Alberto de. 1915. *Tradições e Milagres de Bomfim*. Bahia.
Cascudo, Luis da Câmara Cascudo. 1954. *Dicionário do Folclore Brasileiro*. Rio de Janeiro: Ministério de Educação e Culturo, Instituto Nacional do Livro.
Cavalcanti, P. 1935. *Estudos Afro-Brasileiros*, p. 252.
Cesar, Getulio. 1941. *Crendices do Nordeste*. Rio de Janeiro: Irmãos Pongetti.
Eduardo, Octavio da Costa Eduardo. 1948. *The Negro in Northern Brazil*. Seattle: University of Washington Press.
Fernandes, Albino Gonçalves. 1937. *Xangôs do Nordeste*. Rio de Janeiro: Civilização Brasileira.
Frobenius, Leo. 1926. *Die Atlantische Götterlehre*. Jena.

Herskovits, Melville J. 1952. *Les Bases de l'Anthropologie Culturelle*. Trans. F. Vaudou. Paris: Payot. [*Man and His Works*. New York: A. Knopf, 1947].

—1969. "African Gods and Catholic Saints." In *The New World Negro*. Bloomington, IN: Minerva Press.

Honorat, M. Lamartinière. 1955. *Les Danses Folkloriques Haïtiennes*. Port-au-Prince: Imprimerie de l'État.

Ildefonso, P. 1938. "Candomblé." *Santo Antonio*, p. 11.

Kockmeyer, Thomas. 1936. "Candomblé." *Santo Antonio*.

Laytano, Dante de. 1955. *Festa de Nossa Senhora dos Navigantes*. Pôrto Alegre.

Leiris, Michel. 1953. "Note sur l'Usage des Chromolithographies Catholiques par les Vodouisants d'Haïti." In *Les Afro-Américains*, 201–208. Mémoires de l'Institut Francais d'Afrique Noire, 27. Dakar.

Neves, G. Santos. n.d. *Alto Está e Alto Mora*, pp. 49–57.

Ortiz, Fernando. 1917. *Hampa Afro-Cubana: Los Negros Brujos*. Madrid: Editorial-América.

—n.d. "A Poesia Mulata." *Estudos Afro-Cubanos* 1(6).

Pereira, Nunes. 1947. *A Casa das Minas*. Rio de Janeiro: Publ. da Sociedade Brasileira de Antropologia e Etnologia.

Pierson, Donald. 1942. *Negroes in Brazil*. Chicago: University of Chicago Press.

Ramos, Arthur. 1934. *O Negro Brasileiro*. Rio de Janeiro: Civilização Brasileira.

—1942. *A Aculturação Negro no Brasil*. São Paulo: Cia. Editora Nacional.

Ribeiro, René. 1952. *Cultos Afro-Brasileiros do Recife*. Recife: Boletim do Instituto Joaquim Nabuco de Pesquisa Social.

—1976. "Novos Aspectos do Processo de Reinterpretação nos Cultos Afro-Brasileiros de Recife." *Proceedings and Selected Papers of the Thirty-first International Congress of Americanists*. Nendeln, Lichtenstein: Kraus Reprints.

Rodrigues, Nina. 1935. *O Animismo Fetichista dos Negros Bahianos*. Rio de Janeiro: Civilização Brasileira.

Saia, Luiz. 1944. *Escultura Popular Brasileira*. São Paulo: Edições Gaveta.

Teixeiro, José A. 1941. *Folclore Goiano: Cançioneiro Lendas, Superstições*. São Paulo: Cia. Editora Nacional.

Valente, Waldemar. 1955. *Sincretismo Religioso Afro-Brasileiro*. São Paulo: Cia. Editora Nacional.

Vasconcellos, Leite de. 1925. *A Figa*. Pôrto Alegre.

Part IV

RELIGIONS IN CONTACT:
POWER, SYNCRETISM AND CREOLIZATION

INTRODUCTION TO PART IV

All throughout history, the encounters of cultures and religions have caused conflicts that have changed peoples' traditional forms of life. We do not need to look far into history to find that the consequences of contact can be either war, oppression or enslavement; sometimes even resulting in the extinction of peoples and their cultures. In reference to European colonialism, we must be concerned with the history of Christian mission together with the tragic history of the enslavement and deportation of Africans to the New World to understand how the concept of power is linked to the discourse of syncretism. However, it is a misunderstanding to see a direct connection between the abuse of power and religious innovations. Syncretistic formations happen with or without the application of power. Yet, for some reason the outcomes from particular historical encounters involving Christianity at the one end of the contact relation have been especially imposed with power. This part of the book will therefore discuss the historical motives for the scholarly discourse connecting power with syncretism.

Colonization and the Anthropological View

The issue of defining the category of syncretism has mostly been a problem for historians of religions who were occupied with interpreting heterogenous or innovative historical data primarily from Late Antiquity. However, the discourse of syncretism has entered the field of anthropology through the correspondences between colonization, Christian mission and anthropological studies. Thus, it was in the wake of European colonization that modern ethnography was born, often carried out by eager missionaries or colonizers that at best collected valuable data, which later served as information for professional scholars of ethnography. Unfortunately, the predisposed colonialist ideas of races and cultures were carried into the scholarly field in the wake of colonization. As a result, the old anthropological view of the oppressor came to influence interracial studies and acculturation processes. Consequently, the notion of syncretism has become a problematic term in current anthropological and cultural studies, because it is embedded in the misconceptions of racial theories of former days. The idea that cultures and religions exist in essentially pure forms still adhered to the term.

In the days of the American anthropologist Melville Herskovits and his contemporaries, the field of anthropology was particularly attentive to studies of acculturation processes. The main interest of these anthropologists was to learn about isolated cases of acculturation, in reference to ethnic minorities situated in new and dominant cultures, and to induce from these singular studies how stages of change evolve in civilizations in general. The approach to syncretism was largely a search for "cultural survivals" of ethnic minorities as a way of keeping track of the project of reformulating old customs in contact with newer ones. Essentially syncretism referred to the innovations following the process of the mixing of opposed cultural forms. In the end, the notion kept its bad reputation from theology by continuously implying the incomplete and impure products of culture.

The history of colonization involved racial issues, which collided with the emergence of new Creole identities in the New World; identities that met the discrimination with counter-cultural force. This gave rise to several racial misunderstandings that are now entering the already problematic paradigm of syncretism. Roger Bastide's example of Brazilian creolization, in this volume (Part III), echoes the consequences of power abuse, wherein the act of syncretizing is described as similar to a "defence mechanism" for saving a minority's ethnic and religious identity. In this perspective, the notion of syncretism goes hand in hand with the notion of power.

Cultural Survivals

From the works of the American anthropologist Melville Herskovits we get an idea of the psychological effects of syncretism as, at least partly, a defence against change in the acculturation process. He defined this defence as *survivals*. Herskovits's work will be thoroughly dealt with in the essays of Andrew Apter and Charles Stewart (below, Parts IV and V). However, since the term syncretism was introduced in anthropology through the works of Herskovits we will introduce some of his focal points of interest and influence. Contrary to most of his contemporaries, Herskovits recognized a strong influence of what he named *Africanism* in the Afro-American culture of his time. This was the main subject of his book *The Myth of the Negro Past* (1941) which was strongly in opposition to the prevailing racist misconception of Afro-Americans as peoples without a past. Herskovits was aware of the current racist theories that suggested that biological and innate properties were the reason for the differences between the races and cultures. For that reason his achievement must not be underestimated; he replaced biological and racist ideas with cultural genealogies. He found the answers in the observation of the processes of acculturation. It was in these studies that he introduced the notion of syncretism.

The Influence from Boas

The anthropologists André Droogers (see below in this part) and Sydney M. Greenfield mention, in a more recent work (Droogers and Greenfield 2001), the influence of the work of the German-American ethnographer Franz Boas on Herskovits. Droogers particularly points to the way in which Boas envisioned culture (especially "primitive" people), contrary to earlier evolutionist thinkers such as E. B. Tylor and other late nineteenth-century scholars, as distinct and self-contained groups of people, each a separate society that has its own language, institutions and way of life (25). In this type of society, change is an abnormality that only occurs under the combination of "specific internal and exogenous forces" (25). The idea was that cultures exist in pure forms until they come into contact with other groups of people, or are absorbed into the greater civilization. This view of national identity owes much to the legacy of German romanticism as well as to the theories of the then-prominent *Kulturkreislehre*.

Therefore, in the 1930s, Herskovits saw it as an immense opportunity to study the acculturation process of the descendants of the African slave population in the New World because he believed that they were fairly close to their origin. The idea was, that because cultures exist in pure forms, so do the elements of culture, and this makes it possible to trace them in the new religious forms. Droogers remarks, concerning Herskovits's elaboration of a syncretistic paradigm, that the Boasian influence shines through in the light of the post-World War I situation in the United States with more immigrants entering the country. The assimilation and integration of ethnic and racial minorities became part of the agenda for American anthropology. In this program syncretism became a means to achieve the national plan of a new way of life (Droogers and Greenfield 2001, 27).

Herskovits's main contribution was that he made it apparent how the impact of the cultural "luggage" works with people. A group never becomes devoid of culture, not even under such pressures to abstain from their traditions as the African slaves had suffered in America. With the notion of survivals, Herskovits marked out the process of transformation, that is, the process of syncretism, that he believed had reinforced the old traditions. He was not blind to the fact that the process of acculturation motivated mutual influences of black and white America. Especially prominent was the Afro-American influence on Christianity. Most significantly, according to current studies of multicultural societies, Herskovits observed, in his studies of Afro-Americans and Caribbeans, that a person could be the carrier of several cultural traits at the same time. (This is what is included in the concept of creolization to be discussed in the chapter below.) However, the Boasian dilemma of cultural *sui generis* identities versus cultural diversity is without doubt the main problem in his work. Herskovits asked many fundamental questions about inter-cultural mechanisms, but he was not aware of the static way in which he looked at culture, so that he, subsequently, maintained the idea of syncretism as being a dubious and incomplete stage in the acculturation process towards a new form of life, in this case, the American. Despite the fact that this view later became offensive to the Afro-American and Caribbean population, he never tired of pointing out that what was then considered racial differences were fundamentally cultural differences.

"Borrowing" and "Survivals"—Herskovits's Paradigm of Syncretism

Herskovits generally considered the dynamics of syncretism as being one of borrowing. "A borrowing," he claimed, "will always result in a new form being created with a distinctive quality of its own because additional changes which originated in the new habitat are incorporated" (1941, 225). He recognized, somewhat in contrast with his otherwise static view of culture, the unpredictable forms of new cultural artefacts. That cultural or religious "mixing" is not just present as given, as if it were a chemical recipe. He acknowledged in terms of borrowing the "experiment" of a new way of life before it settles down in a new structure. His example of the Baptist *shouters* gives us an idea of how he perceived the interaction of "borrowing" and "survivals":

> ... the outstanding thing about their ritual being the devotion of the communicants to the "Sankeys," as they term songs from the Sankey and Moody hymnal, which they know in enormous numbers, with every verse to each song memorized. Yet even at first sight certain aspects of their humble meeting places are apparent that, differing from what is found in more conventional Christian churches, at once strike the eye of the Africanist. Markings in white chalk on the floor, at the doors, and around the center pole are reminiscent of so-called "vever" designs found in Haitian *vodun* rituals ... the manner in which baptismal rituals, begun as decorous Baptist meetings, turn into "shouts" is not at all European ... The song begins in its conventional form, sung, if anything, with accent on the lugubrious measured quality that marks hymns of this type. After two or three repetitions, however, the tempo quickens, the rhythm changes, and the tune is converted into a song typically African in its accompaniment of clapping hands and foot-patting, and in its singing style. (Herskovits 1941, 223)

Herskovits's understanding of the concepts of "borrowing" and "survivals" is both a problem and a challenge in his theory of syncretism, because it is embedded in the Boasian paradigm of "pure" culture. If we care to keep those concept as markers of syncretism it is a challenge to rethink them in accordance with a new theoretical paradigm that is more perceptive to the constant mutations of borrowed or surviving symbols. We need to look behind the curtains of the acquisition of religion to find an explanation of the new emergent structures evolving from syncretism.

Creolization in Language

The linguist Derek Bickerton presented a theory about linguistic *creolization* that says something about how we acquire language. Then again, it may also say something of how we acquire religion. His research is based on a more recent historical event from Hawaiian sugar plantations around the turn of the twentieth century where demands for labour brought in workers from various places such as China, Japan, the Philippines and Portugal. His theory offers a demonstration of how pidgin can develop into *Creole* as a full and complex language (Pinker 1994, 33) if just one generation of children is exposed to the pidgin at the age when they acquire their mother tongue. The intriguing part of his theory is the demonstration of how Creole develops into a new language with a complex grammar of its own, in marked contrast to a pidgin language, which only consists of fragmentary word strings (Pinker 1994, 33; Bickerton 1981; 1999). Bickerton's main concern is to present evidence on how children are able to format a new language. His second concern is, of course, to shed light on the acquisition process of language in general (Bickerton 1999, 1–2).

The Theory of Creolization

In the study of syncretism, we are concerned with an understanding of the concept of creolization in the context of religions in contact. This depends on whether we can use a theory from linguistics in the analysis of cultural and religious acquisition, and on how we may look upon the fundamental mechanisms of cognition and language. First, there is no unanimous agreement in the study of linguistics concerning Bickerton's theory, but that is not important for our discussion for the time being (DeGraff 1999). The main idea, the one that most linguists can agree upon, is that the theory of creolization proves that language acquisition is also language creation. We may then ask if a similar pattern is present in religion. This also concerns the question about the influence from children on religious formations, if we, similar to Pinker's suggestion about children as the main inventors of language (Pinker 1994, 35–36), shall consider children's acquisition of a new religion or culture as a factor of change. A study on how children acquire religion in particular and culture in general would be highly conducive to our grasp of the processes of innovation in intercultural or multicultural studies. Although it may seem a bit far-fetched to apply linguistic theories about the acquisition of the Creole language to religion that usually has complicated rules of regulation of faith, which constrain the process of acquisition, the theory may still give us an idea about the link between change and tradition. This would also help redefine such notions as survival and syncretism in the light of the cognitive processes of acquisition.

Universal Grammar or General Cognition

Before we link assumptions from one theory to another there are some important and much debated issues about language acquisition and general cognition that we must consider. Derek Bickerton (and the other linguists Steven Pinker and Michel DeGraff referred to here) agrees, more or less, with the theory of the linguist Noam Chomsky about the existence of a *Universal Grammar*, which locates language in a specific innate module or program in the brain, one that is distinct from our general cognition. In short, he based his theory on the fact that children develop complex grammars rapidly and without formal instruction, not withstanding the fact that neither children nor adults have any problem in constructing new sentences in an unlimited number (Pinker 1994, 22). If Chomsky and other linguists are right in assuming that there is a special module for language in the brain, then we must take the precaution of identifying patterns of similarity in what we may term *cultural creolization* with language creolization. Recently, however, a division in the cognitive sciences has voiced criticism against Chomsky's hypothesis concerning the innate language module.

Some of the more prominent critics are Gilles Fauconnier and Mark Turner. They have produced a cognitive theory, which contradicts the idea of a language module as set apart from our general cognition. They refer, among others, to Terrence Deacon who argues that today's languages are systems of linguistic forms that have survived a long process of selection in the evolutionary process. And he further argues that "Language ... is not an instinct and there is no genetically installed linguistic black box in our brains; language arose slowly through cognitive and cultural inventiveness" (Fauconnier and Turner 2002, 173). Fauconnier and Turner's theory, which disputes the universal grammarians, is a theory of conceptual blending. They argue, against Chomsky, that "the everyday capacities of the well-evolved human mind are the best candidates for complexity and promise the most interesting universal generalization" (Fauconnier and Turner 2002, 33). According to their theory, language is only the tip of the iceberg of invisible meaning constructions (Fauconnier 1997, 1). This is an important step towards seeing the same mechanism at work in the process of "creolization," whether it is happening in language, culture or religion.

Conceptual Blending

Fauconnier and Turner propose, instead of Chomsky's universal grammar, that the architecture of acquisition proceeds from the cognitive inference of conceptual blending. In brief, this theory refers to mental operations that largely operate behind the scene of language. We are not consciously aware of how we blend. It is a mental operation of meaning-construction, consisting of "mental spaces," which Fauconnier and Turner characterize as small conceptual packets. These are constructed when we think and talk for purposes of local understanding and action. According to Fauconnier and Turner, that is how we think, and, in addition, blending is what we do when we associate. The theory of "blending" is an all-encompassing theory of what is claimed to be the simple everyday action of the brain that exists in grammar, in mathematics, in poetry, in religion; in fact, in all of our cultural expressions. There are, however, constraints similar to those in language when it comes to how we blend and what we blend. This becomes exceptionally striking in religion. Therefore, if the theory of conceptual blending proves to be useful in theories about religion and syncretism we must look for the social rules and group interplays that constrain the endless, in principle, possibility of conceptual blending in the individual mind. Tradition in general (religious as well as cultural) suggests one type of constraint whereas politics and ethics would suggest other types, but they all play a part in summarizing the issues about syncretism. While the theory of blending may imply that syncretism is a phenomenon close to conceptual blending, it is still a phenomenon restricted by rules from the social sphere of human action. There are limits as to what makes sense in a given context, for example it is difficult for a speaker to blend entities that are unknown to the hearer.

Creolization in Culture

The notion of cultural creolization can be understood as a particular result or form of syncretism in as much as it refers to a particular culture with a particular background in history. Therefore, this notion relates to questions about power-relations in the encounter of religions. In reality, creolization may seem to be a more justifying notion because it refers directly to the peoples it signifies, that is, as a particular property of a language as well as of a culture. Syncretism is a general notion and therefore a more abstract one that does not necessarily refer to any real-life encounters; one that can just as well be appointed to discourses wherein different religious or ideological elements are fused. However, whether we speak of "syncretism" or "creolization" the words of Edouard Glissant, a Martinican critic, confirm that we may have to look for the interaction between the mechanisms of blending and social constraint in order to explain the ongoing formation of, for instance, Creole societies in the Caribbean. He writes:

> Creolization's most manifest symbol is the Creole language. Its genius rests on its being always open; that is, maybe, its becoming fixed only within some systems of variables that we have to imagine as well as define. Thus, creolization carries in itself the adventure of multilingualism along with the extraordinary explosion of cultures. But this explosion of cultures does not mean their scattering nor their mutual dilution. It is the violent manifestation of their assented, free sharing. (quoted in Balutansky and Sourieau 1998, 1)

The words of Glissant also remind us that culture is never a finished product. Hence, the challenge of creolization, in spite of the very painful history of enslavement and colonization, is to define the current human spirit as one of adaptability and growth, which the making of new languages, cultures and religions proves. Albeit both the concepts syncretism and creolization refer back to the situation of an abuse of power, there is nevertheless a positive sound to them—the inclination to propagate cross-cultural imagination.

The Study of Religion and Religions in Contact

The five essays in this part represent different fieldwork studies of religions in contact. They all locate the problem of syncretism in relation to power and social or hegemonic paradigms. The anthropologist Andrew Apter sees the syncretistic paradigm of Melville Herskovits as the main problem with the concept in today's anthropology, whereas the Caribbean writer Carlos Guillermo Wilson describes the notion "creolization" as an all-encompassing concept of the Afro-Caribbean syncretism in light of racial degradations and de-nationalization of the "Chombos" in Panama. Gustavo Benavides, who is a historian of religions, defines the interaction between religion, power and the processes of syncretism as a way of granting legitimacy or illegitimacy to new cultural products in Latin America. The anthropologist André Droogers presents an analytical model of the three levels—syncretism, power and play—to illustrate how syncretism is connected to the struggle of possessing and controlling the symbolic production of society. Finally, the historian of religions Armin W. Geertz describes the situation of cultures in collusion/collision between different groups of Hopi-Indians and Euro-Americans, wherein syncretism is used for the purpose of social strategies.

The Discursive Character of Syncretism

Andrew Apter discusses Herskovits's syncretistic paradigm with reference to his questionable concept of *Africanism*. He further questions the relevance of the notion "Africa" that in the Africanists' studies still adheres to Herskovits's paradigm of syncretism in anthropology today. The solution to that problem, as Apter sees it, consists in addressing it and possibly rethinking it in a new and critical way. It is the syncretistic principle of identification that Apter criticizes for being "a model of cultural and theological fragmentation," a principle of which Herskovits's table (as represented in Apter's essay) of correspondences between African gods and Catholic saints is a demonstration. He is particularly observant of the assumptions of aboriginal purity and ethno-history in Herskovits's paradigm. The idea of uniformity, for example that there ever was a theological Golden Age in the West African tribes, Fon and Yoruba, is confronted. In fact, he argues, there never were any discrete cults of Yoruba orisas in the first place. Apter disputes, from the base of Herskovits's data and the supplement of his own data from Nigeria, that these cults and religious pantheons were syncretistic formations already in the African context. Consequently, he rejects the classical view of syncretism, that was inherent to Herskovits's Boasian paradigm with its view of stable self-contained societies, and instead he emphasizes the presence of general syncretistic processes as part of the religious systems of New World cults as well as in Nigeria.

Cultural Hermeneutics

In his reformulation of Herskovits's static syncretistic paradigm into a dynamic model of "cultural hermeneutics," Apter directs particular attention to the discursive impact on the issue of syncretism. This is important for an understanding of Apter's own use of the concept. By concentrating on Herskovits's paradigm problems and by deconstructing them, Apter obtains a possibility of defining a new paradigm that allows him to describe his own empirical data from Nigeria in terms of syncretism. As a result, and well aware of the problematic politically incorrect and racist discourse embedded in the concept, he must deconstruct the previously problematic discourse in order to form a new one that is not racially offensive. He does that brilliantly, by recasting the syncretistic system into a system of "cultural hermeneutics" that has the advantage of signifying a non-discriminating intercultural and

...escribing the African/New World-syncretism
..." From that view of the concept of syncre-
...its paradigm within the context of cultural
...sing Herskovits's description of passive
... syncretism so as to form a hermeneutical
... defines as *modalities of revision and*

...tism is rescued from a troublesome dis-
...dies concerning Herskovits's understanding
... notion that ought to be abandoned. Apter's
... the discussion on syncretism is, beside his realiza-
...n phenomena in religion are best described as syncretistic, his
...owledgment of the discursive predicament of the category.

The Ambiguous Ways of Creolization

With the keywords "marvelous cradle-hammock and painful cornucopia" in the title of his essay, Carlos Guillermo Wilson illustrates, in his contradictory wordplay, the historical as well as psychological ambivalences of creolization: African children stolen away from their cradles to enslavement has fostered the fantastic enrichment of new languages and cultures in the Caribbean. The Garifuna-culture, indigenous to St. Vincent, is an example of this ambivalence *per se*. Wilson's work indicates how the bloody history of invasion, revolt, enslavement and deportation has engendered these people.

To Wilson, creolization is an all-encompassing concept of the Afro-Caribbean syncretism, one that refers to language, religion, music and food. With the Garifuna-peoples as the eloquent example of syncretism, *cultural creolization* can be compared to a linguistic counterpart since it is the bearer of a new branch of culture. However, the ambivalence of the historical beginnings remains a fact. Wilson explicitly directs the negative side of creolization to the separation and national hatred amongst colonial Blacks and the Black West-Indians in Panama. With this, he illustrates the sad consequences of an "Africanism," which, similar to Apter's suggestion, is rooted in discrimination, psychologically as well as politically, and one that resulted in social as well as in racial degradations of a people. The story of the denationalization of the *Chombos* in Panama echoes Nazi-Germany's racial politics. The nationalist political program in Panama of ethnic "whitening" in order to "better the race" lacks Apter's positive counter-hegemonic strategy of the "Africanist" syncretism. On the other hand, it confirms Gustavo Benavides' portrait of the many shifting and power-related syncretistic processes in Latin America.

Syncretism and Power

With reference to Latin American history, and with a spec[...]
the Spanish conquest of the Andes, Gustavo Benavides delimi[...]
tion between religion, power and the processes of syncretism a[...]
granting legitimacy or illegitimacy to new cultural products. In h[...]
the interaction of religion and power, religion plays a prominent par[...]
hands of power as a way of establishing transcendental sources that[...]
legitimation and sanction to particular power-relations. This becomes p[...]
ticularly poignant in the conquest and government of peoples in Lati[...]
America, which have brought about the encounters of different cultures,
languages as well as religions. Benavides stresses, concerning the history of
the Andes, that we can use the concept of syncretism in tracing the formative history of new cultural elements of mixed origins, but not just in the
neutral sense of the purely descriptive and imprecise.

Benavides touches upon one of the dilemmas of the subject, which we are
dealing with in this book—that is, the complexity, even ambiguity, between
the making of a good and objectively workable definition; not too loaded
with the specificities of particular empirical data, because, at the same time,
such a definition must be concurrent with all kinds of data. Perhaps this is
not possible. The solution to the problem of definition may not be found in
an all-encompassing definition. Instead, we will have to make up our minds
whether we need to work out a model that clarifies different levels of reality
that we find in the subject of syncretism. Relating it to political power is
one of them.

The Boundaries of Syncretism

Benavides observes that it is difficult to use the notion of syncretism about
religions that have become fully functional, and therefore the notion is best
identified as a temporary formation. He questions, as does Apter, the problematic connotations of the term syncretism and the traditional view of
religion having imagined "cores" and "surfaces" that we can distinguish
(Benavides 2001). Like Apter, he observes that the traditional paradigm of
syncretism is useless, also according to "Latin American syncretism," because
it is connected to a Christian and colonialist self-understanding.

As an alternative, Benavides adjusts to social and socio-linguistic theories
to find a more workable theory to back up the definition of syncretism. He
draws on Michael Mann's conflict-theory of society and culture as power
networks and partly to the linguistic theory of creolization propagated by
socio-linguists (e.g. Bickerton). In this manner, he finds explanations more
applicable to the specific problem of defining the religious syncretism in the

Andes region. By using an organic definition on society and religion, and thereby defining society as a constantly reconstituted entity, Benavides defines syncretism in such a way that it does not contradict his data or the idea of the influence of power on the legitimating of new religious elements. Syncretistic formations are then, according to Benavides, the natural outcome of a repertoire of elements from which a believer of a faith can choose. In addition, if I understand Benavides correctly, then these formations, often contradicting in nature, can become dangerous and powerful means, depending on the political and historical situation, in the reconstruction of society. Supported by socio-linguistic theories about the functioning of pidgin and Creole languages, Benavides adds the extra dimension of power and sees, in the developmental aspect of language-formation, a similar structure in the syncretistic formations in culture. In short, he fuses a linguistic model with a model of power in order to focus on the developmental scheme of religion in the Andes region. The religious equivalent to pidgin becomes the Indians' distortion of Christian rituals that Benavides claims are the short-lived and fragmented elements of religion used by the conquered people as a means to communicate and survive. In this process, power relates to the more or less psychological urge to acquire prestigious elements from the conquering group. Although it seems like a plausible suggestion, I do not agree that those "pidgin" forms of religion are necessarily short-lived. I have seen burlesque *and* long-lived customs, similar to those that Benavides describes, in Caribbean carnivals. We may reply that there is, after all, a difference between developmental patterns of language and religion, because a religious form, pidgin or Creole, tends to become tradition when first it has "entered" a particular context. On the other hand, he describes a cultural equivalent to Creole language when a new system of meaning is born, which is not identical with the mother group. Túpac Amaru and his followers demonstrate this point. According to Benavides, it is also a complex pattern intertwined with power structures and the problem of the legitimacy of Creole religion. What makes Túpac Amaru and his followers Creole, says Benavides, is their self-definition as Christians, which involves the aspect of power and "mastery of a symbolic code." In a more recent work Benavides remarks:

> The equivalent of Creoles can be found in those situations in which an accommodation of sorts has been reached and a new system of meanings has been born, related but not identical with the mother group. In any event, it is not justified to assume that the grammatical structure of Creoles (or the symbolism of new religious formations) is intrinsically less complex than the source language, or less able to make communication possible: the only criteria that can be used to place Creoles and source languages in a hierarchy depend upon the social and ultimately

political prestige and power of the source language. (Benavides 2001, 492)

Similar to Apter, Benavides recognizes the hermeneutical aspects in South American "syncretism," as refers to the line of definition and self-definition that is coupled with powerful discourses of legitimacy and illegitimacy.

Returning to an organic theory of society, Benavides answers the perpetual dilemma of the concept of syncretism as relating either to the process or to the result of the process. In an organic view of society, change does not contradict the structure of society itself; therefore, syncretism may denote both the process as well as the resulting formations. Much more could be said about Benavides' use of the concept of power to explain the progress of cultural innovations and the coupling to the linguistic theory of pidgin and Creole. This combination makes it an interesting topic to work from, as long as we remain cautious about the comparison with developmental structures. They may not be the same in religion as in language, because there is the difference of innate structures of cognition and the social structures of power to consider. However, it would be interesting to know more about just how cognitive structures of knowledge acquisition work together with social structures of power. Benavides' concluding comments in a more recent work resonate this issue: "the emergence of boundaries—whether these are placed around languages or religions—is not merely the result of the exercise of power, as naïve constructivists claim nowadays, but one also having to do with mutual intelligibility" (Benavides 2001, 498).

The Semiotics of Power and Syncretism

The issue of power is also part of Droogers' theory of syncretism. He, too, criticizes the approach from the study of comparative religion that ignores the dimension of power, and he suggests that we add the perspective of power to the definition of syncretism. Droogers is also indebted to linguistic anthropology and he gives the concept of power a more semiotic turn that explains its influence upon syncretism and "meaning-making" in general. Droogers presents a model of three levels: *syncretism*, *power* and *play* that form the dynamic constellation that generates meaning in society. Accordingly, he sees changes in the symbolic inventory of culture as appearing from the dialectics between actors and the stock of social and symbolic structure in society. Consequently, power plays an important role in controlling the access to meaning making. Syncretism is for that reason used as a means by competing religions, precisely because it has access to a double stock of meanings. And, as Droogers continues, because it satisfies "the thirst for clarification." Although there is a touch of naïve functionalism to this last idea,

Droogers does not simply reduce syncretism to a notion of conflict. Through the use of linguistic and social theories inherent in his analytical model he represents, as Benavides, layers of power structures in society that impose different modes of religious constructions. It is a great advantage of Droogers' theory of power that it goes hand in hand with a semiotic view of syncretism. He appropriately emphasizes the symbolic production of religion. In that respect, we may compare it to the struggle of possessing, controlling and transforming symbolic meaning. Droogers sees a dichotomy between the ruling social structures and their relatively slow ability to change and the subjectivist influences that are more open towards change. Accordingly, it is spelled out as a difference between leading authorities and individual actors of religion, which explains why "anti-syncretism" is an inevitable consequence of "syncretism." It is not "the religious intermingling as such," he states, but "the way the concept itself is applied" that provokes power partly because of the determination of religious leaders to control the production of religion.

Then again, to follow up on Droogers' claim, we must ask whether it is in the "nature" of syncretism itself (i.e. the phenomenon of "blending religion") to provoke this dual state of incompatibility? Alternatively, is it the discourse about the *concept* of syncretism that maintains the conflict between patterns of authority and subjective invention in certain types of society? Droogers seems to presuppose that society is fundamentally anti-syncretistic. At least, he sees a tension between the socio-structural mechanisms and the individual's fondness of "play." His sketch of society particularly resembles a Christian society, wherein the maintenance of dogma constrains the innovation of religion of its individual members. Consequently, Droogers' concept of power in relation to syncretism is more relevant for societies with dominant scriptural traditions.

The Dynamics of Religious Transformation

However, Droogers does suggest a reconciliation of the dual nature of syncretism. He refers to a basic linguistic rule for showing how a semiotic gap between ideas from two different worlds is bridged by metaphor and finally become one: a *pars pro toto* (a part of the whole) in both the mind of the individual as well as at the "mechanical" level of society. His proposal of using a metaphor analogous to syncretism, in particular regarding the encounter of two different cultures such as the African and Christian in Brazil, functions much better than concepts such as "borrowing" and "survival" used by Herskovits, because "metaphor" emphasizes the transformative nature of syncretism. By implying the analogous structures of metaphor and syncretism, Droogers gives us an illustration of how we deal cognitively with a "double stock of meaning" that comes close to what the cognitive scientists Gilles Fauconnier and Mark Turner call *conceptual blending* (see p. 148). Conceptual blending is associated with a general cognitive process, wherein structures from two input spaces are projected onto a separate space, the "blend." The blend inherits partial structure from the input spaces, and has an emergent structure of its own (Fauconnier and Turner 1996, 113).

Droogers' demonstration of the Afro-Brazilian case proves that humans are reluctant to give up their cultural or ethnic luggage even when facing such oppression as slavery. However, no human mind contains full information about its own culture or the cultures of others. In fact, the mind discriminates and selects among information and it will reconstruct the information communicated by others to fit its own form; that is a basic hermeneutic view. Droogers' implication of the interaction of subjectivity and play according to the actors of syncretism may well confirm how our mind works by selective dynamics.

The Discourse of Power

There is no doubt that the selective dynamics of syncretism is constrained by the mechanism of power, particularly in societies where Christianity (or Islam) has been dominant. This is the fact of all the examples represented in this part. I agree with Droogers and the other writers that power does play a large role in the encounters of cultures and religions. I do not see an inherent link between "syncretism" and "power," but I agree that "syncretistic blends" provide space for manipulation as well as for negotiation of power. To call attention to the "original" cultural or religious inputs they do not disappear just because they find new structures. So, indeed there is space for constantly generating variability as well as tension of variability in the progression of culture and religion in general. Syncretism can be compared to the trial and error processes of history; the notion either refers to the successful innovations of history or the anti-structures that pollute the known structures of society. Which way it goes depends on the combination of the mode of the blend and the type of society.

Worlds in Collusion

Armin Geertz observes that "syncretism" is used for different interests by different groups for social-strategic purposes within traditions engaged in reformulating their religion and culture. The reformulation of Hopi prophecy to make it fit messianic expectations, oriented to various religious "Euro-

American" worldviews, is, according to Geertz, supported by the Traditionalist Movement as a means to claim authority among other Hopi groups. This way of syncretism is defined as *transculturalization*. It refers to the mutual reinforcement of the political interests of different groups in manipulating their religious symbols. This "collusion" of different interests, Geertz tells us, results in both misrepresentations and misinterpretations.

The advantage of the notion of "transculturalization" to illustrate this case of syncretistic transmission is that it does not insinuate any incompatibility in the blending of religious elements from different traditions, so often suggested to be the nature of syncretism. In Geertz's understanding, the transmission of inter-religious elements rather illustrates a vehicle for the comparability of religious ideas. In fact, he shows, as do both Gustavo Benavides and André Droogers, that there is as much a good reason to identify particular religious practices and beliefs as similar despite obvious cultural differences in the realm of power relations.

Misrepresentations/New Religious Formations

In my opinion, Geertz's focus on *misrepresentation* does better justice to what we might call the "essence of syncretism" than does the concept of power because it illustrates more aptly how we transmit our ideas. If we accept the suggestion from linguistics, with the slight transcription that "culture acquisition is also culture creation," then ideas transform already in the process of acquisition because minds are not empty containers into which experience and teaching is poured as unaltered information. According to the anthropologist Pascal Boyer: "A mind needs and generally has some way of organizing information to make sense of what is observed and learned. This allows the mind to go beyond the information given, or in the jargon, to produce *inferences* on the basis of information given" (Boyer 2001, 42). As a result of our cognitive limitation it is easy to see how misrepresentation becomes a keyword in the inter-religious dialogue, such as the case of the shared messianic expectations, because of its associations with significant religious reality in both cultures. Geertz's concept of *symbolic syncretism* illustrates the quality that some symbols have to trigger associations of identity such as the "white brother" of the Hopis. Boyer states that the mind "is not a free-for-all of random associations," and Geertz's study of the Hopi case of syncretism confirms that we are mentally disposed to arranging conceptual material in certain ways rather than others because of our cultural luggage—an idea which is also a common point in hermeneutics. Besides his recognition of the transmission of the religious elements through "the meetings of minds," Geertz points to literacy as a vehicle for syncretism because it has "frozen prophetic tradition into texts," and, therefore, it is carried beyond the control of its bearers. This is an important detail for an understanding of why religious traditions that become "universal," such as Christianity, must exercise more control than small-scale religions in order not to become a totally fragmented belief-system.

Syncretism as Mechanism of Cultures in Collision

Geertz is critical of the category of syncretism, especially if it is used to characterize a specific type of religion. However, he finds it useful in a study of the "mechanisms that are brought to play in the collision of cultures." Analogous to Droogers and Benavides, he accentuates syncretistic courses of action as catalysts for power-struggles, but not without emphasizing the creative mechanism within. In Geertz's definition, "syncretism" involves individuals and groups who construct worldviews out of bits and pieces of other worldviews. I wish to support his claim with reference to the works of the human mind and the ways in which we acquire information about other worlds through a "false" comparability, or strings of intellectual "misrepresentations."

References

Balutansky, K. M., and M. Sourieau. 1998. "Introduction." In *Caribbean Creolization: Reflections on the Cultural Dynamics of Language, Literature, and Identity*, ed. K. M. Balutansky and M. A. Sourieau, 1–12. Gainesville: University Press of Florida.

Benavides, Gustavo. 2001. "Power, Intelligibility and the Boundaries of Religions." *Historical Reflections/Réflexions Historiques* 27(3): 481–98.

Bickerton, Derek. 1981. *Roots of Language*. Ann Arbor, MI: Karoma.

—1999. "How to Acquire Language Without Positive Evidence: What Acquisitionists Can Learn from Creoles." In DeGraff, ed. 1999, 49–74.

Boyer, Pascal. 2001. *Religion Explained: The Evolutionary Origins of Religious Thought*. New York: Basic Books.

DeGraff, Michel. 1999. "Creolization, Language Change, and Language Acquisition: A Prolegomenon." In DeGraff, ed. 1999, 1–46.

—ed. 1999. *Language Creation and Language Change: Creolization, Diachrony, and Development*. Cambridge, MA: Massachusetts Institute of Technology.

Droogers, André, and Sydney M. Greenfield. 2001. "Recovering and Reconstructing Syncretism." In *Reinventing Religions: Syncretism and Transformation in Africa and the Americas*, ed. Sydney M. Greenfield and André Droogers, 21–42. Lanham/Oxford: Rowman & Littlefield.

Fauconnier, Gilles. 1997. *Mappings in Thought and Language*. Cambridge: Cambridge University Press.

Fauconnier, Gilles, and Mark Turner. 1996. "Blending as a Central Process of Grammar." In *Conceptual Structure, Discourse, and Language*, ed. Adele Goldberg, 113–29. Stanford: Center for the Study of Language and Information (CSLI) [distributed by Cambridge University Press].

—2002. *The Way We Think: Conceptual Blending and the Mind's Hidden Complexities*. New York: Basic Books.

Herskovits, Melville. 1958 [1941]. *The Myth of the Negro Past*. 2nd ed. Boston: Beacon Press.

Pinker, Steven. 1994. *The Language Instinct: The New Science of Language and Mind*. London: Penguin.

HERSKOVITS'S HERITAGE: RETHINKING SYNCRETISM IN THE AFRICAN DIASPORA[*]

Andrew Apter

It is customary, if not mandatory, in contemporary African diaspora studies to invoke the pioneering spirit of Melville J. Herskovits (1895–1963), whose life's work was dedicated to the repossession of Africa's heritage in the New World.[1] Not that Herskovits was the first to engage in such research. Others before him included W. E. B. Du Bois and Carter G. Woodson, as well as Jean Price-Mars of Haiti, Fernando Ortiz of Cuba, and—more his contemporaries than his predecessors—Zora Neale Hurston and the Brazilian ethnologists René Ribeiro, Arthur Ramos, and Gilberto Freyre.[2] But Herskovits more than any other scholar posed the African-American connection as a theoretical problem that, in the service of a progressive if intellectually circumscribed political agenda, demanded systematic research into an unprecedented range of West African and New World cultures. It is not my aim to praise a great ancestor, whose flaws and limitations are as legendary as his virtues, but to assess the relevance of his theoretical program to contemporary African-American research. In particular, I will focus on his syncretic paradigm, which continues—even among those who disavow it as crudely essentialist or unwittingly racist—to inform the current renaissance in studies of the African diaspora.

There is much that seems wrong, misconceived, and simply outdated in Herskovits's syncretic paradigm when it is evaluated against the current standards of a more critical anthropology. It is not difficult to see how Herskovits essentialized tribal origins in Africa, perpetuated myths of cultural purity in the New World, overlooked class formation, and developed passive notions of acculturation and cultural resistance, all of which distorted the ethnographic record under the guise of an imputed scientific objectivity. But there is also something elusively tenacious about the concept of syncretism. Even when critically deconstructed, it somehow slips back into any meaningful discussion of Africanity in the New World. And even as we recognize that "Africa" has been ideologically constructed to create imagined communities in the black Americas—as Guinée in Haitian *Vodoun*, or the nations of Cuban *Santería* and Brazilian *Candomblé*—such invented identities cannot be totally severed from their cultural analogues (dare we say origins?) in West Africa. The objective of this essay is to rethink syncretism in a way that does justice to both sides of this methodological divide: to the invented-ness (and inventiveness) of New World African identities as well as to their cultural and historical associations with West African peoples. This resolution requires greater clarity about just what it is we are comparing, contextualizing, and historicizing on both sides of the Atlantic, an exercise that gives a new twist to Herskovits's ethnohistorical method and owes its revisionary strategy to some critical lessons that I learned from the Yoruba in Nigeria.[3]

It is perhaps noteworthy that recent studies of "Africanisms" in the Americas, focusing on particular deities such as Ogun, on religions such as Santería and Vodoun, or even on transatlantic aesthetic and philosophical complexes, have effectively erased syncretism from their lexicons.[4] These excellent studies indeed reveal that there is much more to such New World cultural forms than a blending of two distinct traditions into a hybrid form. Scholarly emphasis has shifted to disclose the nuanced complexities of the historical conditions in which African identities are remembered and forgotten, fractured and fused, invoked, possessed, repossessed, transposed, and reconfigured within rural peasantries, urban centers, immigrant communities, national arenas, even at transnational conferences on, for example, the Yoruba-based *Òrisa* tradition.[5] Consistent with this move is a shift away from cultural form toward cultural performance and practice, to traditions in the making rather than those already made, preserved, or retained. These developments are welcome as part of the positive trend in cultural studies, but it is equally clear that nothing as powerful as the syncretic paradigm has arisen from its ashes, resulting in a compelling crisis of representation. In brief, what is Africa's place in the New World? Indeed, what is "Africa"?[6]

Rather than address this rapidly growing literature, I will return to the essentials of Herskovits's syncretic paradigm in order to extract the interpretive kernel from its scientistic shell. This involves a pilgrimage to the classic shrines of New World syncretism where, in Brazilian Candomblé, Cuban Santería, and Haitian Vodoun, African gods embrace Catholic saints to promote new religious empires. I honor these sites not only because, for Herskovits, they represented the clearest cases of syncretism as such, but because for us, they provide the clearest examples of how African critical practices in the Americas can inform our own research.

161

1. The Syncretic Paradigm

Herskovits (1958, xxii) credited Arthur Ramos as one of the first to employ the concept of syncretism to account for the identification of African deities with Catholic saints in Brazilian Candomblé. Syncretism suggested, for Herskovits, "a pattern of first importance" in the study of Afro-American culture contact and change, the dynamics of which he continued to document and theorize while refining his method over the years. If the scientificity of this method appears contrived today, we should appreciate that Herskovits posed a radical challenge to the sociological interpretations of American and New World "Negro" institutions and practices which, according to E. Franklin Frazier and Robert E. Park (among others), represented functional adaptations to socioeconomic conditions rather than African cultural holdovers or survivals (see Frazier 1939; Park 1919; and Smith 1957). Herskovits called for greater sensitivity to history and culture in the acculturative process, arguing effectively that synchronic sociological reductionism not only violated the ethnographic record, but worse, supported the racist myth that the Negro had no meaningful African history or heritage. It is with this spirit and strategy in mind that his syncretic paradigm must be understood.

Under the rubric of "ethnohistorical method," Herskovits meant simply that ethnology and history should be combined "to recover the predominant regional and tribal origins of the New World Negroes" and "to establish the cultural base-lines from which the processes of change began" (1966, 49). This baseline, he argued, was restricted to the West African coastal and rainforest belts, running from Senegal to Angola, since the smaller and later shipments of slaves from East Africa, Mozambique, and Madagascar had minimal cultural impact on previously established West African patterns in the New World. While this claim is debatable, although probably true, it is not my aim to evaluate its empirical plausibility in light of new evidence (e.g., Curtin), but to clarify its underlying logic. In this view, West African cultures are figured as discrete, coherent wholes, which, with varying degrees of purity and in different spheres of social life, left their impress on the black Americas. To assess the relative purity of African retentions and to specify their social domains, Herskovits developed a number of related concepts which together can be glossed as the syncretic paradigm.[7] In addition to the ethnohistorical method, these concepts are: (1) scale of intensity, (2) cultural focus, (3) syncretism proper, (4) reinterpretation, and (5) cultural imponderables. I will review these concepts not only to point out their profound limitations, but also to draw out their theoretical relevance to contemporary diaspora studies.

If Herskovits regarded his scale of intensities as one of his greatest methodological achievements, with hindsight it seems to parody the epistemology of liberal social science. In an effort to quantify New World Africanisms, albeit for heuristic rather than statistical purposes, Herskovits developed a logical continuum from most to least African, segmented into (a) very African, (b) quite African, (c) somewhat African, (d) a little African, (e) trace of African customs, or none, and (?) no report. These relative values were placed in a two-dimensional array, with New World regions and communities such as Guiana (bush and Paramaribo), Haiti (peasant and urban), and the United States (Gullah Islands, rural South, urban North) along a vertical axis, and with specific sociocultural domains (technology, economics, social organization, religion, art, music, etc.) segmented along a horizontal axis to represent variable degrees of African intensity within each region or community. Despite internal variations, the resulting table (Table 1, overleaf) reveals that "the progression of Guiana, Haiti, Brazil, Jamaica, Trinidad, Cuba, Virgin Islands, the Gullah Islands, and southern and northern United States comprise a series wherein a decreasing intensity of Africanisms is manifest" (Herskovits 1966, 54). Today, the empirical conclusions can be revised. For example, we know from the Prices' work in Surinam that Guiana is much more creolized than Herskovits ever imagined (see R. Price 1976, 1983; S. Price 1984; and S. and R. Price 1980; 1991). But the conceptual problems of this schema are more serious. Clearly the intensities themselves (such as "very," "quite," and "somewhat African") are highly relative and subjective. Also, the sociocultural domains (social organization, religion, art) are in no way discrete and ignore class divisions, while the regional and community designations are inconsistent with each other. For example, only Haiti is divided into "urban" and "peasant," even though this is a distinction which Bastide has shown to be highly salient in Brazil.

As a form of knowledge, the scale of intensities resembles the anthropometric measures of physical anthropology, which Herskovits deployed in his postdoctoral research on the phenotypical effects of miscegenation in North America (1928). Although he was always explicit—following his mentor, Franz Boas—about separating race from culture and language, his scale of intensities echoes a blood-based logic by transposing notions of purity and dilution from racial stocks to cultural genealogies. Thus he could claim that "the Bush Negroes of the Guiana forests manifest African culture *in purer form* than is to be encountered anywhere else outside Africa" (Herskovits 1958, 124) and that "rural and urban Negro cultures took on *somewhat different shadings*" (135) (emphasis added), with the darker peasants more African than their lighter, more acculturated urban brothers and sisters. I do not mean to suggest that Herskovits was a closet racist—a rather cheap shot against a scholar whose progressive views were so ahead of his time.[8] But it should remain clear how easily the language of race entered into the discourse of syncretism in the New World, particularly when the rhetoric of science was wedded to essentialized concepts of African culture in comparative studies funded by the Carnegie Corporation.[9]

	Technology	Economic	Social organization	Non-kinship institutions	Religion	Magic	Art	Folklore	Music	Language
Guiana (bush)	b	b	a	a	a	a	b	a	a	b
Guiana (Paramaribo)	c	c	b	c	a	a	e	a	a	c
Haiti (peasant)	c	b	b	c	a	a	d	a	a	c
Haiti (urban)	e	d	c	c	b	a	e	a	a	c
Brazil (Bahia-Recife)	d	d	b	d	a	a	b	a	a	a
Brazil (Pôrto Alegre)	e	e	e	d	a	a	e	a	a	c
Brazil (Maranhao-rural)	c	c	b	e	c	b	e	b	b	d
Brazil (Maranhao-urban)	e	d	c	e	a	b	e	d	b	b
Cuba	e	d	c	b	a	a	b	b	a	a
Jamaica (Maroons)	c	c	b	b	b	a	e	a	a	c
Jamaica (Morant Bay)	e	c	b	b	a	a	e	a	a	a
Jamaica (general)	e	c	d	d	b	b	e	a	b	c
Honduras (Black Caribs)	c	c	b	b	b	a	e	b	c	e
Trinidad (Port of Spain)	e	d	c	b	a	a	e	b	a	e
Trinidad (Toco)	e	d	c	c	c	b	e	b	b	d
Mexico (Guerrero)	d	e	b	b	c	b	e	b	?	e
Colombia (Choco)	d	d	c	c	c	b	e	b	e	e
Virgin Islands	e	d	c	d	e	b	e	b	e	d
US (Gullah Islands)	c	c	c	d	c	b	e	a	b	b
US (rural South)	d	e	c	d	c	b	e	b	b	e
US (urban North)	e	e	c	d	c	b	e	d	b	e

a: very African, b: quite African, c: somewhat African, d: a little African, e: trace of African, or none, ?: no report

Table 1. *Scale of Intensities of New World Africanisms*

Source: Adapted from Herskovits 1966, 53.

If the scale of intensities represented variable degrees and domains of African retention—high for religion, low for economics and art—it offered no explanations. To understand why some practices thrived when and where they did while others went underground or disappeared, Herskovits developed his general theory of syncretism, supplemented by concepts of reinterpretation, cultural focus, and what he called (no doubt echoing Malinowski 1961, 20–211) "cultural imponderables." Narrowly defined, syncretism is produced in situations of contact between cultures from "the tendency to identify those elements in the new culture with similar elements in the old one, enabling the persons experiencing the contact to move from one to the other, and back again, with psychological ease" (Herskovits 1966, 57). Thus, he notes, in the Catholic New World, African gods are identified with saints of the Church, whereas in Protestant areas the religious associations are more subtle, and African cultural retentions (e.g., mourning and shouting) less intense. We can perceive in this notion a strong psychological emphasis on the individual as syncretic agent, on identification as the syncretic process, and on adaptation and integration ("psychological ease") as syncretic functions, which extend secondarily to groups in their new cultural contexts. The same process occurs, according to Herskovits, "in substance rather than form, in psychological value rather than in name" (1966, 57) when the resemblance between cultural elements is too weak to afford a fully syncretic relationship but is strong enough to allow a reinterpretation of the new by the old. Herskovits's favorite example of reinterpretation is his claim that African polygyny was retained under monogamous constraints, with his arguing that polygyny was reinterpreted in diachronic terms by the practice of serial unions. This example reveals Herskovits's sociological naïveté in downplaying contemporaneous social conditions in favor of imputed cultural continuities, but the principle itself, I will argue, is extremely salient when recast as a revisionary strategy.

If syncretism and reinterpretation are mainly psychological concepts that explain how the new culture is adopted within the framework of the old, the concept of cultural focus shifts the analysis to culture *sui generis*. To explain why African religious beliefs and practices in the New World are retained with greater clarity and vigor than, for example, kinship, economic, and political institutions, Herskovits argues that religion itself constitutes the cultural focus of African peoples—their "particular emphasis," "distinguishing flavor," and "essential orientation" (1966, 59). That which is given highest cultural priority by a people will offer the greatest "resistance" to change, he argues, and will thus rank high on the scale of New World Africanisms. Therefore culture, by way of its distinguishing focus, plays a determinative role in the selective process of what is and is not retained, in what form, with what degree of intensity, and in what sphere of social life. Thus for Herskovits:

More elements which lie in the area of focus of a receiving culture will be retained than those appertaining to other aspects of the culture, acceptance being greater in those phases of culture further removed from the focal area. When a culture is under pressure by a dominant group who seek to induce acceptance of its traditions, elements lying in the focal area will be retained longer than those outside it ... (1966, 59)

We have no clearer commitment to (a relativized) cultural determinism than in this passage, which provides a rather strange take on the initial socioeconomic context of African culture contact—that of slavery in the New World. Elsewhere Herskovits was clearly aware of the different forms of plantation slavery and the modes of passive and active resistance that the slaves deployed, including foot-dragging, suicide, escape, *maronnage*, and organized revolt (1958, 86–109). But here we are led to believe that religion—more than kinship, politics, or economics—persisted in a world that turned Africans into laboring chattel and destroyed their families because it served as the dominant cultural focus. Such a position seems to defy rational argument if not common political sense, displaying what Jackson identifies, in another context, as Herskovits's "curious naivete about the relationship between culture and power" (Jackson 1986b, 144). But even here, I will argue, lies the germ of an idea that helps to explain the power of syncretic practices in real and effective terms. I will argue that the hermeneutical principles of West African religions—particularly Yoruba religion, which has thrived in various New World guises—have provided salient forms of popular resistance in a variety of oppressive conditions.

The final concept in Herskovits's syncretic paradigm—that of cultural imponderables—introduces the variable dimension of consciousness in African diaspora research and prefigures the study of practical and embodied knowledge in current anthropology. For, in addition to consciously retained Africanisms emanating from the cultural core, Herskovits discerned a range of "retentions" that "are carried below the level of consciousness" (1966, 59) and persist in everyday practices. These include the linguistic patterns of accents, dialects, and creoles; the musical styles of, for instance, Son, Rumba, Mambo, and Blues; the "motor habits" of expressive gestures and dance; and the "codes of etiquette" which inform greetings and politeness formulae. At a time when such phenomena were often explained in racist terms, as transmitted through blood, Herskovits took great pains to emphasize their cultural character, as acquired by successive generations. More interesting for us, however, was his understanding that such culturally embodied imponderables persisted as retentions because they resisted change. Clearly, this notion of resistance is passive, attributed elsewhere to "the force of cultural conservatism" (57), and is conceived negatively as the absence of assimilation. But as we shall see, when "updated," this notion foreshadows theories of active resistance that identify bodily practices as contested sites of symbolic and ideological struggle (Comaroff and Comaroff 1991, 24–25).

Thus reduced to its essentials, Herskovits's syncretic paradigm highlights the limitations of American liberal scholarship. In retrospect, its major features—the racist overtones of the scale of intensities; the psychologistic orientation of syncretism and reinterpretation, which privilege adaptation and accommodation over opposition and contradiction; the absence of any sustained class analysis; the emphasis on an inertial cultural focus over and above the dialectics of power and identity construction; and finally, the essentially conservative vision of cultural retention as that which resists change—all seem to relegate Herskovits to a dubious past. Having dissected the syncretic paradigm to critique its component parts, highlighting their limitations while flagging their redeeming features for later discussion, I will now turn to the paradigm as a whole in its more substantive applications, in order to interrogate the notion of cultural origins that informs the syncretic process.

2. Deconstructing Origins

In Herskovits's "African Gods and Catholic Saints in New World Negro Belief," first published in *American Anthropologist* (1937), we find the official liberal blueprint of the science of New World syncretisms, based on fieldwork in Haiti as well as on published Cuban and Brazilian data. To be sure, Herskovits was one of the first North American anthropologists to recognize the validity—indeed the privileged status—of Caribbean societies as objects of ethnographic study, at a time when the discipline preferred "pristine" primitives in "natural" habitats to cultures reconstituted in "diluted" forms through slavery or other coercive dislocations. Such settings, he argued, provided "laboratory situations" (1966, 46) for investigating the dynamics of acculturation—of what is lost, modified, or retained through culture contact, and the mechanisms that govern the process.

In this respect, Herskovits perceived the universal significance of New World syncretisms for the "science of man," in that they provided the clearest cases, given adequate data, of more general principles of culture contact and change the world over. In this view, New World cultures moved from a marginal ethnographic status to center stage, and if the assumptions that guided his study appear simplistic and naïve, distorting (as I shall now illustrate) the very data themselves, the larger conceptual revolution that he inspired linked empirical studies of the African diaspora to a general theory of culture.

According to Herskovits, the syncretic identification of African gods with Catholic saints was shaped by two primary factors in the New World: by slavery as the dominant institution of social life (or, for Orlando Patterson, "social death") and by Catholicism as the official religion of the masters. These two factors together account for the distinctive patterns of syncretism found in Haitian Vodoun, Cuban Santería and Brazilian Candomblé, in that the slaves were summarily baptized as they came off the ships and were thrust into sugar mills and plantations, where they secretly continued to worship their gods under the cloak of official Catholicism. Banned by the authorities, the African cults were forced underground, where they provided a focus for sporadic slave revolts, were uneasily tolerated during Catholic holidays, and fragmented into local groups that were mainly shaped and dominated by the personalities of their leaders (Herskovits 1966, 322). I do not have space in this limited review to discuss the complex social, political, and religious variations that historically unfolded, except to mention the most general cultural consequence identified by Herskovits. This is the profound fragmentation of aboriginal African unities, a forced fusion of different African cultures and the dismemberment of religious cult hierarchies into shattered splinter groups, "reflected in a resulting confusion of theological concept" (1966, 322–23).

It is this model of cultural and theological fragmentation that I will challenge, focusing first on Herskovits's tropes of aboriginal unity. Despite his call for rigor in identifying the numerous cultural origins of New World slaves, Herskovits reduces African influences to two principal sources—Fon and Yoruba.[10] The deities identified with Catholic saints are limited—at least upon first inspection—to the pantheons of these two great West African cultures, such that Fon gods such as the trickster Legba, the rainbow-serpent Damballa, and the Marassa twins were syncretized with Saint Anthony, Saint Patrick, and the twin saints Cosmas and Damien; while Yoruba gods such as the trickster Eshu, the thunder-god Shango, and the watergoddess Yemoja (Yemanja) were similarly identified with the Devil, Saint Barbara, and the Virgen de Regla. The correspondences are based, we may recall, on the similarities of religious elements, such that the saintly icons depicted on Catholic chromolithographs exhibit symbolic features of African counterparts; thus, the serpents on Saint Patrick's image invoke the Fon serpent-deity Damballa, whereas the twin saints Cosmas and Damien resemble the Fon Marassa or Yoruba Ibeji twins. Under repressive conditions of official opprobrium, the slaves—so the argument goes—were able to worship in two worlds at once; outwardly Catholic, inwardly they honored their African gods.

Following this syncretic principle of identification, Herskovits constructed a table of correspondences between African gods and Catholic saints in Brazil, Cuba, and Haiti, listing African deities in a vertical left-hand column with their saintly counterparts to the right (Table 2, below). Again, it is not the specific correspondences that I will challenge (since as Herskovits perceived, these vary both regionally and over time), but the table itself as a form of knowledge and the assumptions embedded within it. For these amount to a specific discursive modality, a way of constructing African identities and differences, of figuring (or as Mudimbe might say, conjugating) Africanity in the New World as an acculturative process. And it is this discourse that can be fruitfully deconstructed, not abstractly from the lofty heights of postmodern criticism, but concretely, on the basis of internal evidence supplemented by empirical data from Nigeria.

First, I would call attention to a subtle but powerful slippage subsumed by the category of the left-hand column—that of "African deities," wherein several significant contrasts are neutralized. Following the logic of the syncretic paradigm, "Africa" refers to a West African baseline, an ethnohistorical reality circumscribed by space and time and identified as the source of African influence in the New World. Here the Fon and Yoruba figure as dominant cultural origins (with Congo receiving a passing reference associated with Haitian Simbi deities), since either Fon or Yoruba deities can be identified with Catholic saints. But here is where the cultural waters get muddied, for apart from a few central deities like the Fon Damballa and the Yoruba Ibeji, it is impossible to distinguish the two religious pantheons as culturally discrete. I will not recount the complex history of Dahomean-Yoruba political relations, except to mention that from at least the sixteenth century (and probably earlier) through the mid-nineteenth century, warfare, slave-raiding, migration, and ritual reciprocity between the kingdoms of Dahomey, Ketu, and Old Oyo persisted, with much cultural mixing of religious deities and institutions (see Akinjogbin 1967; Law 1977; Parrinder 1956). There is a general historiographic tendency to see Yoruba gods like Ogun (of war and iron) and Ifa (of divination) recoded in Dahomey as Gu and Fa, suggesting a regional Yoruba diaspora to the west. But one equally finds the Yoruba trickster Eshu referred to as Eshu-Elegba as far east as the Ekiti region of Yorubaland, suggesting a complementary infusion of Fon deities into Yoruba pantheons. My point is not to argue which gods came from where—a possible and quite valuable regional exercise within limited terms—but to challenge the aboriginal purity of Herskovits's tribal baseline. In brief, Fon and Yoruba are not pure cultural categories. Indeed, the very notion of a singular Yoruba people was a missionary invention of the mid-nineteenth century, subsuming Egba, Egbado, Ijebu, Ijesha, and Ekiti peoples, among others, to a standardized Oyo-Yoruba linguistic and cultural model.

Whether wittingly or not, Herskovits avoids this problem of interposed origins by lumping them under the general category of African. His table of correspondences erases the difference between Fon and Yoruba, which remains implicit in the names of certain deities, but which also remains highly ambiguous. The baseline is thus occluded by the trope of aboriginal Africa, grounding a primordial cultural genealogy that quickly vanishes into an unknown past. Nor does systematic slippage stop here. If we examine the left-hand column further, we find "African" deities such as la Sirène, *loa* Christalline, *loa* St. Pierre, *loa* Kpanyol (the Spaniard), Maitresse Erzulie, and 'Ti Jean Petro (little John Petro), deities that never did or could exist in pre-contact West Africa because they represent European mythic and historical allusions and social stereotypes.

Part of this problem lies with Herskovits's failure to distinguish what he as an external observer and trained anthropologist calls African from what Haitians, Brazilians, and Cubans call African. The table of correspondences confuses both perspectives under "Africa," merging the "etic" with the "emic." Thus Herskovits notes:

> The Haitian ... does not merely stop at identifying the saints with African gods, for saints are occasionally themselves conceived as *loa* ... thus St. Louis, the patron of the town of Mirebalais where this field work was carried on, is a *loa* in his own right. Similarly two of the kings who figure in the *image* that depicts the Adoration of the Christ Child, Balthazar and Gaspar, are also held to be *vodun* deities. (1966, 325)

Before proposing a more critical solution to this problem, it is enough to point out that Herskovits has failed, in the terms established by his syncretic paradigm and table of correspondences, to clearly distinguish cultural origins and African deities from their reconstructed and syncretic forms. The ethnohistorical baseline remains a myth of African origins, not a documented or even documentable point of empirical departure. This myth is significant not only as a foundational fiction, but because it was elaborated by Herskovits in substantive claims that have continued to misguide much New World research.

This brings me to the second tropic function of aboriginal unity, that of coherent, unified, and standardized theologies and pantheons in West Africa that were uprooted and fragmented through the slave trade to be reconstituted in locally variable and confused forms in the Catholic New World. I call this elaboration tropic because it establishes a nostalgic topos of a theological Golden Age that never existed in West Africa and should be abandoned as a comparative standard for studying New World religions. The general idea derives from Herskovits's discovery that *Vodoun* theology is highly inconsistent. He found differences of opinion not only from region to region, but within a given region even between members of the same group concerning such details of cult belief and practice as the names of deities, modes of ritual procedure, or the genealogies of the gods, to say nothing of concepts regarding the powers and attributes of the African spirits in relation to one another and to the total pantheon (1966, 323).

Eliciting lists of deities from a single Haitian valley, he discovered that "the differences between these lists were much greater than the resemblances; and ... in identifying deities with Catholic saints, an even greater divergence of opinion was found" (1966, 323). The same indeterminacies and patterns of variation apply, on a larger scale, to the African pantheons and their syncretic manifestations in Brazilian Candomblé and Cuban Santería, summarized by the table of correspondences.

It is not the indeterminate character of Herskovits's data that I would challenge but his inference that a greater uniformity ever existed in West Africa. It is in fact the very idea of listing African deities as discrete mystical entities, in fixed relations within pantheons associated with stable sociological correlates on the ground, that my own research on Yoruba òrìṣà worship undermines. Yoruba deities are not only vested in lineages (what Bascom, following Herskovits, called "sib-based" cults), but articulate with more inclusive corporate groups (Bascom's "multi-sib cults"), such as quarters (àdúgbò) each ruled by a town chief, or in the case of royal cults, the town or kingdom as a whole (ìlú). Thus, in a crude sense, the ritual configuration of òrìṣà cults within any kingdom represents its dominant relations of political segmentation, the patterns of which vary spatially, from one kingdom to another, and within kingdoms over time, accommodating (and on important occasions, precipitating) political fission, fusion, or the reranking of civil chiefs (see Bascom 1944; Barber 1981; Apter 1992, chs. 2, 3). The methodological implication of this politico-ritual complementarity—a very gross reduction of a complex dialectic—is that no two Yoruba kingdoms arrange their pantheon of òrìṣà in the same way. The situation is further complicated by the fact that within kingdoms, the òrìṣà cults of different town quarters organize their pantheons around their own principal deities, so that if, officially, a civil chief pays ritual obeisance to the superior òrìṣà of the town king, secretly, within the confines of his own quarter's cult, the chief and his followers recognize the hidden paramountcy of their òrìṣà around which their pantheon revolves (Apter 1992, ch. 6).

The cosmological principles that render such polyvocalities possible and intelligible are grounded in Yoruba notions of "deep knowledge" (imọ jinlè) referring to the privileged access of powerful priests and priestesses to hidden truths and secrets. I will return to the power of such knowledge in due course. For now, it is enough to point out that within this ritually safeguarded space of interpretive possibilities, official dynasties and genealogies are revised, deities are repositioned to express rival political claims, and the deities themselves are fragmented and fused into multiple and singular identities. Small wonder that Herskovits had trouble with his lists, since even in Nigeria, no òrìṣà cult, community, or Yoruba kingdom (let alone two individuals) would produce the same list or pantheon of òrìṣà.

African deities as found in:	Brazil	Cuba	Haiti
Obatala		Virgen de las Mercedes; the Most Sacred Sacrament; Christ on the Cross	
Obatala; Orisala; Orixala (Oxala)	'Nosso Senhor do Bomfim' at Bahia; St. Anne; 'Senhor do Bomfim' at Rio (because of the influence of Bahia).		
Grande Mambo / Batala / Shango	St. Barbara at Bahia; St. Michael the Archangel at Rio; St. Jerome (the husband of St. Barbara) at Bahia		St. Anne
Elegbara, Elegua, Alegu / Legba / Exu	the Devil St. George at Rio; St. Jerome; St. Anthony at Bahia	'Animas benditas del Purgatorio'; 'Anima Sola'	St. Anthony; St. Peter
Ogun / Ogun Balandjo / Ogun Ferraille / Oxun / Yemanja	Virgin Mary; N. D. de Candeias / Virgin Mary; N. S. de Rosario (at Bahia); N. D. De Conceicao (Rio)	St. Peter / Virgin de la Caridad del Cobre / Virgin de Regla	St. James the Elder; St. Joseph / St. James
Maitresse Erzulie; Erzilie; Erzilie Freda Dahomey			Holy Virgin (of the Nativity); Santa Barbara; Mater Dolorosa
Saponam / Osa-Ose (Oxossi)	The Sacred Sacrament; St. George at Bahia; St. Sebastian at Rio	St. Alberto; St. Hubert	
Ololu; Omulu	St. Bento	St. John the Baptist	

African deities as found in:	Brazil	Cuba	Haiti
Agomme Tonnere			St. John the Baptist
Ibeji (Brazil and Cuba); Marassa (Haiti)	St. Cosmas and Damien		St. Cosmas and Damien
Father of the Marassa			St. Nicholas
Orunbila (Orunmila)			
Loco	St. Francisco	St. Francisco	
Babayu Ayi		St. Lazarus	
Ifa	The Most Sacred Sacrament		
Yansan (wife of Shango)	St Barbara (wife of St. Jerome)		
Damballa			St. Patrick
Father of Damballa			Moses
Pierre d'Ambala			St. Peter
loa St. Pierre			St. Peter
Agwe			St. Expeditius
Roi d'Agoueseau			St. Louis (King of France)
Daguy Bologuay			St. Joseph
la Sirene			the Assumption; N.D. de Grace
loa Christalline			St. Philomena
Adamisu Wedo			St. Anne
loa Kpanyol			N.D. de Alta Gracia
Aizan			Christ (?)
Simbi			St. Andrew
Simbi en Deaux Eaux			St. Anthony the Hermit
Azaka Meda			St. Andrew (?)
'Ti Jean Petro			St. Anthony the Hermit

Table 2. *Correspondence between African Gods and Catholic Saints in Brazil, Cuba, and Haiti.*

Source: Adapted from Herskovits 1966.

From this stems a second dominant misconception—that òrìsà cults in West Africa represent discrete deities, with one cult worshipping Shango, another Yemoja, a third Obatala, and so on. In fact, all òrìsà cults house clusters of deities that are represented by specific priests and priestesses, altars, and sacrifices, and are grafted onto an apical deity.[11] Within these microarenas, the configuration of these clustered deities also shifts with changes in the status of their associated lineages and titled representatives and according to contesting claims from within. Under these conditions, no definitive list of deities is possible. More significant for syncretic models is the mistaken claim—and here Bastide and Verger keep company with Herskovits—that formerly discrete cults in Africa were restructured, in the New World, to house a multiplicity of African deities and Catholic saints. The ethnohistorical record reveals that Yoruba òrìsà cults were never discrete in the first place.

Zora Neale Hurston was one of the first to grasp the elusive polymorphism of the Haitian *loa* in her more personal (and in many ways proto-experimental) ethnography of Vodoun, understanding that "*No one* knows the name of every *loa* because every major section of Haiti has its own variation" (1938, 114), and that the *loa* themselves are both multiple and singular. My point has been to extend this indeterminacy back to southwest Nigeria where the Yoruba religion reveals much greater continuity with its syncretic manifestations than Herskovits ever imagined. The theological confusion in New World cults and pantheons which for Herskovits resulted from the upheavals of slavery is actually endemic to òrìsà worship (and I suspect to Fon religion as well) and resolves into a critical hermeneutics of power, once its relevant dimensions are grasped. In thus reformulating Herskovits's ideas, we will see that he was onto something very important. He concluded his seminal comparison of Brazilian, Cuban, and Haitian syncretisms with the observation that despite the confusion surrounding African deities and their Catholic correspondences, a general syncretic process was at work:

> Considered as a whole ... the data show quite clearly to what extent *the inner logic* of the aboriginal African cultures of the Negroes, when brought in contact with foreign traditions, worked out to achieve an end that, despite the handicaps of slavery, has been relatively the same wherever the forces for making change have been comparable. (1966, 328) (emphasis added)

It is this inner logic, recast as a cultural hermeneutics, that provides the key to understanding the West African contribution to New World syncretic forms and does so without recourse to foundational fictions of essentialized aboriginal unity.

3. From Syncretic to Critical Practice

Thus far I have deconstructed Herskovits's myth of African origins—its figures of cultural purity, theological unity, lineage-based cult organization, and cult singularity (i.e., one deity per ritual collectivity)—in order to extract the interpretive kernel from its ideological shell. If Herskovits distorted the West African baseline with misconceptions that can be scrapped or readjusted, he also established the ground of a cultural argument that can be further developed. The goal of this argument, as I mentioned earlier, is to determine what is African in the African diaspora, focusing on religious syncretism as a clear case of Africanity in order to theorize its subtler forms of influence in the New World.

First, however, we must acknowledge that the trope of "Africa" has served as a dominant ideological category in the service of empire, a category that has naturalized, as Mudimbe (1988) so cogently demonstrates, the normative and territorial dominions of Europe's "civilizing mission" (see also Comaroff and Comaroff 1991, 86–125). But it must also be emphasized that a deconstruction of this master trope, as Mudimbe's radical project demands, does not do justice to the other side, to that which lies beyond the ideological limits of an Africa produced by missionary-colonial discourse. This other side of Africa must not be taken to refer to the fiction of pristine cultures stipulated by Herskovits, but neither is it reducible to some unknowable Other in a move that annihilates the very histories of peoples who have come to define themselves as Africans with specific national and ethnic identities. If African worlds are as much the constructs of Africanist discourses as the objects of their inquiry, then it is within this dialectic of invention and observation that the concept of syncretism performs a double synthesis. In brief, Africa is assimilated to the New World through culture contact if and only if an invented Africa is assimilated to an Africa observed. We are caught in a double bind. Either we essentialize Africa or renounce it.

One way out of this ideological dilemma is to focus on the inner logic of syncretic practices as strategies of appropriation and empowerment. What Haitian Vodoun, Brazilian Candomblé and Cuban Santería have in common is a history of accommodation and resistance, not merely in the cultural terms of allying uneasily with Catholicism but also in the political contexts of class division and the state. It is precisely this relation between implicit social knowledge and political economy—what in my Yoruba research has emerged as a hermeneutics of power—that defines the horizon of Africanity in the New World: not as core values or cultural templates but as dynamic and critical practices.

Nowhere is this critical relation between forms of knowledge and relations of domination more evident than in the history of Haitian Vodoun. The conventional historiography traces a grand development from the late eighteenth century to the regime of Francois Duvalier ("Papa Doc"), over the course of which Vodoun's original revolutionary impulse was gradually co-opted by the state. Thus in 1791, rites conducted by the famous *houngan* (priest) Boukman inspired the first organized blow against the French plantocracy (see Courlander 1966). According to Haitian historical memory, it was in a clearing of the Bois Caiman that, "under a raging tropical downpour accompanied by lightning and the cracking of giant trees, [Boukman] performed a Petro ceremony" in which "a pig was sacrificed and its blood, mixed with gunpowder, was distributed among participants to strengthen their will to win" (Bastien 1966, 42).[12] The revolutionary triumvirate of Toussaint L'Ouverture, Jean-Jacques Dessalines, and Henri Christophe were quick to capitalize on Vodoun's popular appeal and its secret channels of communication in mobilizing the masses. Hence it is generally accepted that Vodoun played a strategic role in achieving Haitian independence. After the revolution's success in 1804, however, Vodoun played into the hands of both the center and the opposition. In his efforts to stabilize the new government, Dessalines allied with the mulatto elite and tried to foster Catholicism. He was murdered in 1806 and then resurrected as a *loa*, thereby incorporated into the very pantheon of deities that as official leader he had grown to oppose. His successor, Christophe, suffered a similar reversal. As king of northern Haiti until his suicide in 1820, he encouraged Catholicism as the official religion of state administration and alienated himself from the peasantry. Subsequent Haitian leaders, such as the self-proclaimed Emperor Faustin Soulouque (1847–59), cultivated alliances and reputations among the houngan (priest) and their followers while paying official lip-service to Catholicism. Under Antoine Simon (1906–11), for example, the National Palace was recognized as a sacred site of Vodoun activities.

Thus in the first century of Haitian independence, Vodoun articulated with a complex set of emerging political and class divisions. Centralized government favored Catholicism as the official religion of administration, based in the urban centers of Cap Haitien, the northern seat of black elite power, and in Port-au-Prince, the southern seat of the mulattos. Vodoun remained a predominantly rural religion of the black peasantry, providing a powerful political resource for black leaders such as Soulouque, who could play the peasantry against the mulatto elite by invoking the popular religion of the people. In this postcolonial context, the religious syncretism of Vodoun and Catholicism played into the dialectics of class and color stratification. As Catholicism spread into the countryside and merged with Vodoun, the latter seeped, as it were, into the palace, providing unofficial access to leadership and state power. This trend was not constant, since Vodoun was periodically attacked by mulatto leaders who allied, after 1860, with the Vatican and waged at times brutal campaigns against the houngan. But these campaigns only reinforced the black opposition, which eventually united under Duvalier into a deadly combination of Vodoun, noirisme, nationalism, and state power.

The stage for Duvalier's appropriation was prepared by the American occupation of Haiti (1915–43), which inspired Haitian intellectuals such as Jean Price-Mars to rediscover within Vodoun the "genius" of the Haitian people in his celebration of *negritude*. Formerly disdained by the educated elites, Vodoun was suddenly elevated in the respectable language of poetry and folklore to the status of national heritage and identity (Derby 1992). Leftist intellectuals allied with the peasantry to demand an authentic and truly autonomous Haiti. It was in such an atmosphere that Papa Doc appropriated Vodoun to consolidate dictatorial control. As a peasant religion, Vodoun mobilized enough popular support to counterbalance mulatto and church opposition; as a symbol of Haitian nationalism, it appealed to leftist intellectuals and noiristes; and with its underground network of secret Bizongo and Secte Rouge societies (Davis 1988, 241–84), it provided an ideal channel for administering state power and terror while effectively dividing all organized opposition to the self-proclaimed President-For-Life.

It appears that the history of Haitian Vodoun is a history of popular resistance and state appropriation—of the high and official appropriating the low and popular—in that the religion which originally inspired revolution came to uphold a dictatorial state. In a basic sense this is true, but what is lost in such an instrumental interpretation is how Vodoun and its associated notions of Africanity (Guinée) have mediated the complex dialectics of political competition and class division. To be sure, Vodoun remained a powerful resource in the hands of revolutionary leaders and shrewd politicians and has clearly made a difference to Haitian history. But what has made Vodoun so powerful? Strategic explanations that it mobilized collective action only beg the question of how this was done.

At this point, I would like to tie the various threads of this discussion together, rethinking syncretism in the African diaspora as a critical and revisionary practice, one that reconfigures dominant discourses with variable, and at times quite significant, consequences. Haiti provides the clearest illustration that resistance waged through syncretic struggle—through the appropriation by African powers of Catholic saints, post-revolutionary kings, and nationalist rhetoric—was more than symbolic wish fulfillment. But it also illustrates the other side of syncretism, in that the dominant categories which were semantically revised were also, in more formal terms, reproduced and perpetuated.[13] If Vodoun took possession of Catholic hierarchies through the very gods that possessed their devotees, it also reproduced the authoritative structure of God the Father and his saintly messengers, disseminating popular Catholicism throughout the countryside. It was this double aspect of syncretism that Herskovits identified as an acculturative process, as the uneasy adaptation of cultures in collision. What Herskovits missed was the critical relation between cultural form and hegemony, although he intuited the variable modalities that this relation could take.

Returning to the classic syncretism of African gods and Catholic saints, we can recast its historical genesis as a grand counter-hegemonic strategy. What Herskovits perceived as a psychological mechanism of cultural integration, allowing blacks to move between African and colonial orders with relative conceptual and emotional ease, was in fact a much more powerful process of discursive appropriation. If in Haiti, as in Cuba and Brazil, the dominant discourse of Catholicism baptized Africans into slavery, it was also Africanized through syncretic associations to establish black nations, identities, and idioms of resistance. The role of Vodoun in the Haitian revolution may stand out for its outstanding impact, but parallel developments occurred throughout the New World. Thus in Brazil, the *quilombos* and *mocambos*, or black republics of escaped slaves, began as religious protest movements which Africanized Portuguese Catholicism along various ethnic lines. Palmares, the largest and most famous of the *quilombos*, recreated Bantu models of social organization and government, combining African effigies with Catholic icons in its shrines as early as 1645 (Bastide 1978, 83–90). And in Cuba, the 1844 slave revolt called *La Escalera*—so named to commemorate the ladders to which the vanquished slaves were tied and tortured—grew out of "an elaborate conspiracy in Matanzas, organized through the *cabildos* and drum dances of the sugar estates, the 'king' and 'queen' of the weekly dance being the agents of conspiracy" (Thomas 1971, 205). I mention these famous uprisings not merely to illustrate a strategic relationship between slave religion and organized revolt but to argue that the power of syncretic revision was real and that when conditions were right, the African communities thus imagined and organized asserted themselves with considerable impact.

The syncretic revision of dominant discourses sought to transform the authority that these discourses upheld. To be sure, radical ruptures were exceptional and stand out in Caribbean history as memorable flashpoints in the perduring black struggle. But the general point I wish to emphasize is that the power and violence mobilized by slave revolts and revolution were built into the logic of New World syncretism itself. The Catholicism of Vodoun, Candomblé and Santería was not an ecumenical screen, hiding the worship of African deities from official persecution. It was the religion of the masters, revised, transformed, and appropriated by slaves to harness its power within their universes of discourse. In this way the slaves took possession of Catholicism and thereby repossessed themselves as active spiritual subjects. Nor was this revisionary strategy specific to slavery; it developed also under subsequent conditions of class and color stratification, among black rural peasantries and urban proletariats (Bastide 1978). The political dimensions of such syncretic revision began not with social protest and calls to arms but with the unmaking of hegemony itself. As carnival and possession rituals so clearly illustrate, this is accomplished by reversing high and low categories with blacks above whites in the Africanized streets and shrines, by recentering Catholic hierarchies around African gods, by reinscribing ritual space with palm fronds, crossroads, and kingly thrones, by marking time to different drum rhythms and ritual calendars, and by liberating the body from its disciplined constraints (see DaMatta 1991; Parker 1991; Alonso 1990). Possession by spirits—which include Catholic saints as well as African deities, for even these two orders ritually collapse—involves sexual transgression and gender crossing because it transcends and transforms the most fundamental categories of the natural and social worlds.

But if hegemony is unmade through syncretic ritual, it is also remade, and it would be wrong to equate its religious impulse with proto-revolutionary struggle pure and simple. As noted earlier, the ritual revision of dominant discourses also reproduces their grammar and syntax, which it reconstructs from below. In Vodoun, this unmaking and remaking of hegemony corresponds to two sets of spiritual powers: the cool Rada deities of the right hand (often traced back to Allada in Dahomey), who sanction authority, and the hot Petro deities of the left hand (identified as chthonic), who lampoon and decenter the status quo. In Brazilian Candomblé and Cuban Santería, as in Yoruba òrìṣà worship, both types of power inhabit one general pantheon and associate with cool and hot deities such as Obatala and Shango. One can trace the permutations of this basic opposition through innumerable examples, but the point I wish to highlight is that syncretism necessarily involves both the unmaking and remaking of hegemony and thus is intrinsically political.

Returning to Herskovits's syncretic paradigm and locating it within a context of cultural hegemony, we can reduce its basic concepts to a more general dialectic of revision and reproduction. Those things Herskovits reified into categorical distinctions—between syncretism proper, reinterpretation, cultural focus, and embodied forms of expressive culture—reflect variable modalities of cultural resistance, not in his passive sense of resisting change, but actively, as counter-hegemonic strategy. By appropriating the categories of the dominant classes, ranging from official Catholicism to more nuanced markers of social status and cultural style and by resisting the dominant disciplines of bodily reform through the "hysterical fits" (Larose 1977, 86) of spiritual possession, New World blacks empowered their bodies and souls to remake their place within Caribbean societies. As we have seen, the material consequences of these revisionary strategies range from negligible to revolutionary, from the spiritual nationalism asserted, for example, by Vodoun sword-flags brandished before the National Palace, to the self-conscious nationalism of Jean Price-Mars, reclaiming Vodoun as the model of negritude, to the Haitian revolution itself. And, as we have also noted, the power of revisionary challenges from below could be reappropriated by the elites in the academic folklore of Fernando Ortiz and Gilberto Freyre, or in the Machiavellian statecraft of Duvalier. There is no single trajectory of exalted class struggle built into syncretic forms of revision and resistance, or vice versa (as has been suggested for Haiti). What concerns us is the hermeneutics of revision as such and the interpretive conditions of its possibility.

This final concern brings us back to our initial inquiry into what is properly African in the African diaspora. I have deconstructed Herskovits's essentialized cultural baseline, its trope of an aboriginal Golden Age, and its attendant reifications of cultural purity and dilution, without renouncing the logic of cultural genealogies. I will conclude by making my position explicit, by establishing the historically critical relationship between West Africa and the New World.

Boldly stated, the revisionary power of the syncretic religions derives from West African hermeneutical traditions which disseminated through the slave trade and took shape in black communities to remake the New World in the idioms of the old. It is not the elements of Old and New World cultures that should be meaningfully juxtaposed in the concept of syncretism—as Herskovits maintained—but the orthodox and heterodox discourses in which such elements have been deployed and the tropic operations that they have performed. I have dwelt perhaps excessively on refiguration and revision because these are the strategies that have made, and continue to make, a difference—rhetorical, pragmatic, and, in key moments, political—among blacks, mulattos, and whites in the Americas (see Gates 1998). These are also the discursive strategies that characterize West African religions, particularly Yoruba religion, which has had a long history of reconfiguring hegemony, documentable from the rise and fall of the Old Oyo empire (1600–1836), through the nineteenth-century Yoruba wars, to the appropriation of Christian and colonial rhetoric in Nigeria's long march to independence. Thus West Africa's contribution to the African diaspora lies not merely in specific ritual symbols and forms, but also in the interpretive practices that generate their meanings. In Yoruba cosmology, for example, deep knowledge (*imọ jinlè*) has no determinate content but rather safeguards a space for opposing hegemony. Sanctioned by ritual and safeguarded by secrecy, deep knowledge claims are invoked to revise dynastic genealogies, the rankings of civil chiefs, and even the relative positions of deities within official pantheons. Deep knowledge by definition opposes public discourse, and the authoritative taxonomies that it upholds—whatever they may be. If this is what has made West African religions powerful in relation to local, colonial, and postcolonial hegemonies, it has also informed syncretic revisions of dominant hierarchies in the New World, incorporating them within more popular pantheons and cosmological fields of command.

The concepts of syncretism, reinterpretation, and cultural imponderables, which for Herskovits distinguished different types of African retentions, are recast in my argument as modalities of revision and resistance. I have traced them back not to a pristine cultural baseline but to a dynamic variety of West African interpretive strategies, thereby revising Herskovits's concept of cultural focus into a more critical concept of cultural hermeneutics. If I seem to have succumbed to the indeed substantial hegemony of Yoruba chauvinism in black diaspora debates, it is not to assert that Yoruba cosmology has had the greatest impact in the New World, although its impact has been and remains profound, but because its hermeneutical principles of refiguration and revision are so clearly at work in the classic syncretic religions and illuminate their power. I have restricted my discussion to Herskovits's ethnohistorical project (which, if groundbreaking in its time, appears narrow next to current research on colonial mimesis, public culture, and transnational identity) because within this more global set of issues, it reminds us that even after they are deconstructed, the Old World origins of the African diaspora can be recovered and their heritage explored in endless depth.

Notes

* This essay was first presented at the African Studies Public Lecture Series, Northwestern University, 28 October 1991. I would like to thank David Cohen, Ivan Karp, Karin Hansen, Bill Murphy, and Teju Olaniyan for their challenging and insightful comments.
1. The term "New World," which denotes the post-Columbus Americas, is full of ideological problems all the more pressing in this quincentennial year. I retain the term uneasily for the sake of historiographic continuity, with the qualification that invisible quotes surround each of my usages to bracket its pejorative connotations.
2. See, for example, Du Bois 1939; Woodson 1936; Price-Mars 1983; Ortiz 1916; Hurston 1938; Ribeiro 1952; Ramos 1937; Freyre 1956.
3. The Nigerian fieldwork on which this argument is based took place from October 1982 to December 1984 and during three months of summer 1990. I gratefully acknowledge funding from Fulbright-Hays, the Social Science Research Council, the American Council of Learned Societies, and the American Philosophical Society.
4. See, for example, Barnes 1989; D. Brown 1989; Murphy 1988; K. Brown 1991; Thompson 1984. Of these, only Murphy (1988, 120–24) discusses syncretism.
5. These conferences have been held in such cities as Ife (Nigeria), Bahia (Brazil), Miami, and New York City. They mark the self-conscious transnationalism of the òrìsà tradition, and deserve a special study.
6. For a sustained and rigorous critique of the rhetoric and ideology of Africanist discourse, see Mudimbe 1988.

7. I use the term *syncretic paradigm* to identify the larger model (and its additional concepts) within which the more specific meaning of syncretism proper is located.
8. In his essay "Tolerance," Fernandez recounts Herskovits's affiliation with the NAACP after expressing an initial reluctance (1990, 150–51).
9. For a glimpse of the ideological conflict that Herskovits experienced with the Carnegie Corporation, as well as the corporation's colonial epistemology, see Jackson 1986b, 117–18, and 1986a.
10. The "Fon" (also called Dahomeans by Herskovits) and the "Yoruba" are missionary-colonial ethnic designations that emerged in the nineteenth century to refer to peoples of what is today the southern half of the Republic of Benin and southwest Nigeria. The infamous slave port of embarkation was at Ouidah, controlled for a long time by the Portuguese.
11. Thus in Ayede, the Yemoja cult houses the additional deities Orisha Oko, Shango, Ogun, Oshun, Oya, and Olokun.
12. For a more detailed version of this story, see Metraux 1972, 42–43.
13. In her discussion of Tshidi Zionists, Jean Comaroff notes how the intent "to deconstruct existing syntagmatic chains to disrupt paradigmatic associations and therefore to undermine the very coherence of the system they contest" inevitably reproduces, on a formal level, aspects of the symbolic order which it reconfigures, so that "subversive *bricolages* always perpetuate as they change" (Comaroff 1985, 198). It is her association of "syncretistic movements" with subversive bricolages that I am calling "critical practice."

References

Akinjogbin, I. A. 1967. *Dahomey and Its Neighbours, 1708–1818*. Cambridge: Cambridge University Press.

Alonso, Ana M. 1990. "Men in 'Rage' and the Devil on the Throne: A Study of Protest and Inversion in the Carnival of Post-Emancipation Trinidad." *Plantation Society in the Americas* 3: 73–120.

Apter, Andrew. 1992. *Black Critics and Kings: The Hermeneutics of Power in Yoruba Society*. Chicago: University of Chicago Press.

Barber, Karin. 1981. "How Man Makes God in West Africa: Yoruba Attitudes Toward the òrìṣà." *Africa* 51(3): 724–45.

Barnes, Sandra T., ed. 1989. *Africa's Ogun: Old World and New*. Bloomington: Indiana University Press.

Bascom, William. 1944. "The Sociological Role of the Yoruba Cult Group." *American Anthropologist* NS (46) 1.2 (Memoirs, 63): 1–75.

Bastide, Roger. 1978 [1960]. *The African Religions of Brazil: Toward a Sociology of Interpenetration of Civilizations*. Trans. H. Sebba. Baltimore: Johns Hopkins University Press.

Bastien, Remy. "Vodoun and Politics in Haiti." In *Religion and Politics in Haiti*, ed. H. Courlander and R. Bastien. Washington, DC: Institute for Cross-Cultural Research.

Brown, David H. 1989. "The Garden in the Machine: Afro-Cuban Sacred Art and Performance in Urban New Jersey and New York." Diss. New Haven: Yale University.

Brown, Karen McCarthy. 1991. *Mama Lola: A Vodou Priestess in Brooklyn*. Berkeley: University of California Press.

Comaroff, Jean. 1985. *Body of Power, Spirit of Resistance: The Culture and History of a South African People*. Chicago: University of Chicago Press.

Comaroff, Jean, and John Comaroff. 1991. *Of Revelation and Revolution: Christianity, Colonialism and Consciousness in South Africa*, vol. 1. Chicago: University of Chicago Press.

Courlander, H. 1966. "Vodoun in Haitian Culture." In *Religion and Politics in Haiti*, ed. H. Courlander and R. Bastien. Washington, DC: Institute for Cross-Cultural Research.

Curtin, Philip. 1969. *The Atlantic Slave Trade: A Census*. Madison: University of Wisconsin Press.

DaMatta, Roberto. 1991 [1979]. *Carnivals, Rogues, and Heroes: An Interpretation of the Brazilian Dilemma*. Trans. J. Drury. Notre Dame: University of Notre Dame Press.

Davis, Wade. 1988. *Passage of Darkness: The Ethnobiology of the Haitian Zombie*. Chapel Hill: University of North Carolina Press.

Derby, Lauren. 1992. "Caribbean Nationalism and the Science of Folklore in the Early Twentieth Century." Unpublished essay.

Du Bois, W. E. B. 1939. *Black Folk: Then and Now: An Essay in the History and Sociology of the Negro Race*. New York: H. Holt and Co.

Fernandez, James W. 1990. "Tolerance in a Repugnant World and Other Dilemmas in the Cultural Relativism of Melville J. Herskovits." *Ethos* 18(2): 140–64.

Frazier, E. Franklin. 1939. *The Negro Family in the United States*. Chicago: University of Chicago Press.

Freyre, Gilberto. 1956. *The Masters and the Slaves: A Study in the Development of Brazilian Civilization*. New York: Knopf.

Gates, Henry Louis. 1988. *The Signifying Monkey: A Theory of Afro-American Literary Criticism*. New York: Oxford University Press.

Herskovits, Melville J. 1928. *The American Negro: A Study of Racial Crossing*. New York: Knopf.

—1937. "African Gods and Catholic Saints in New World Negro Belief." *American Anthropologist* NS 39: 635–43.

—1958. *The Myth of the Negro Past*. Boston: Beacon Press.

—1966. *The New World Negro: Selected Papers in Afroamerican Studies*. Bloomington: Indiana University Press.

Hurston, Zora Neale. 1978 [1935]. *Mules and Men*. Bloomington: Indiana University Press.

—1938. *Tell My Horse*. Philadelphia: Lippincott.

Jackson, Walter. 1986a. "The Making of a Social Science Classic: Gunnar Myrdal's *An American Dilemma*." *Perspectives in American History* 2: 43–61.

—1986b. "Melville Herskovits and the Search for Afro-American Culture." In *Malinowski, Rivers, Benedict and Others: Essays on Culture and Personality*, ed. George Stocking Jr., 95–126. Madison: Universsty of Wisconsin Press.

Larose, Serge. 1977. "The Meaning of Africa in Haitian Vodu." In *Symbols and Sentiments: Cross-Cultural Studies in Symbolism*, ed. Ioan Lewis, 85–116. London: Academic Press.

Law, Robin. 1977. *The Oyo Empire, c.1600–c.1836*. Oxford: Clarendon Press.

Malinowski, Bronislaw. 1961 [1922]. *Argonauts of the Western Pacific*. New York: Dutton.

Métraux, Alfred. 1972 [1959]. *Voodoo in Haiti*. Trans. H. Charteris. New York: Schocken.

Mudimbe, Valentin Y. 1988. *The Invention of Africa: Gnosis, Philosophy and the Order of Knowledge*. Bloomington: Indiana University Press.

—1990. "Which Idea of Africa? Herskovits's Cultural Relativism." *October* 55: 93–104.

Murphy, Joseph. 1988. *Santería: An African Religion in America*. Boston: Beacon Press.

Ortiz, Fernando. 1916. *Hampa Afro-Cubana: Los Negros Esclavos, Estudio de Sociologica y Derecho Publica*. La Habana: Revista Bimestre Cubana.

Park, Robert E. 1919. "The Conflict and Fusion of Cultures with Special Reference to the Negro." *Journal of Negro History* 4: 111–33.

Parker, Richard G. 1991. *Bodies, Pleasures and Passions: Sexual Culture in Contemporary Brazil*. Boston: Beacon Press.

Parrinder, E. G. 1956. *The Story of Ketu: An Ancient Yoruba Kingdom*. 2nd ed. Ibadan: Ibadan University Press.

Patterson, Orlando. 1982. *Slavery and Social Death: A Comparative Study*. Cambridge, MA: Harvard University Press.

Price, Richard. 1976. *The Guiana Maroons: A Historical and Bibliographic Introduction*. Baltimore: Johns Hopkins University Press.

—1983. *First Time: The Historical Vision of an Afro-American People*. Baltimore: Johns Hopkins University Press.

Price, Sally. 1984. *Co-Wives and Calabashes*. Ann Arbor: University of Michigan Press.

Price, Sally, and Richard Price. 1980. *Afro-American Arts of the Surinam Rain Forest*. Berkeley: University of California Press.

—1991. *Two Evenings in Saramaka*. Chicago: University of Chicago Press.

Price-Mars, Jean. 1983 [1928]. *So Spoke the Uncle*. Trans. M. Shannon. Washington, DC: Three Continents.

Ramos, Arthur. 1937. *As Culturas Negras no Novo Mundo*. Rio de Janeiro.

Ribeiro, René. 1952. *Cultos Afrobrasileiros de Recife: Urn Estudo de Ajustemento Social*. Special issue of *Boletim do Instituto Joaquim Nabuco*.

Smith, M. G. 1957. "The African Heritage in the Caribbean." In *Caribbean Studies: A Symposium*, ed. Vera Rubin, 34–46. Jamaica: Institute of Social and Economic Research, University College of the West Indies.

Thomas, Hugh. 1971. *Cuba: The Pursuit of Freedom*. New York: Harper & Row.

Thompson, Robert F. 1984. *Flash of the Spirit: African and Afro-American Art and Philosophy*. New York: Vintage.

Verger, Pierre F. 1982. *Orisha: Les Dieux Yorouba en Afrique et au Nouveau Monde*. Paris: A. M. Metailie.

Woodson, Carter G. 1936. *The African Background Outlined*. Washington, DC: Association for the Study of Negro Life and History.

THE CARIBBEAN: MARVELOUS CRADLE-HAMMOCK AND PAINFUL CORNUCOPIA

Carlos Guillermo Wilson

Translated by Elba D. Birmingham-Pokorny and Luis A. Jiménez

In 1492, the three caravels—the *Santa María*, the *Pinta*, and the *Niña*—landed on the coast of the island of Quisqueya, where later Santo Domingo, the oldest Spanish colony in the New World, was founded. This event was the beginning of an impressive historical Caribbean phenomenon: a marvelous cradle-hammock and painful cornucopia.

The ceremonies of the quincentennial (1492–1992) of that historic October 12, jubilantly celebrated the marvel born in that cradle, or better yet, Caribbean "cradle-hammock." In the fifteenth century, the legends of El Dorado and the Fountain of Youth called attention to the marvelous and obsessive search which started in the Caribbean, and consequently caused much interest in Spain in the news about Tenochtitlán, the great center of the Aztecs; Chichen Itza, a great center of the Mayas; Darién and the Pacific Ocean (then known as the South Sea); and Cuzco, the great center of the Incas. One of the most important legacies of the marvelous cradle-hammock is the Spanish spoken in the Caribbean.

In 1492 Antonio de Nebrija published the *Castilian Grammar*, the first grammar of any European language. Curiously, Nebrija's *Grammar* was published in the same year as the Catholic monarchs' soldiers finally took the Alhambra, the last Moorish fortress, thus ending almost eight centuries of Moorish domination of the Iberian Peninsula—a domination initiated in the year 711 by the African general Tarik in Gibraltar and later supported by another African general, Júsuf.

The Moorish conquest had enriched the Spanish language with Arabic words, but it was in the Caribbean that Spanish quickly accumulated indigenous Caribbean and African words. Referring to the enrichment of the Spanish language in the Caribbean, Jorge E. Porras writes:

> Spanish is believed not to exhibit significant substractal influence from Indoamerican or African languages in its phonological, morphological, or syntactic components but it certainly exhibits much of an influence in its lexicon. Just as in Medieval times, when Castilian [borrowed] words from other languages Latin American Spanish enriched its lexical stock with Native American languages such as Arawak (Taíno), Nahuatl, Mayan, Quechua, Tupí-Guaraní, Mapuche, and from African languages such as Kikongo, Kishigongo, Kimbundu, Ewe, and Yoruba. (1993, 181)

Some Arawakan, like canoe, hammock, cacique, bohio, tebooron, barbacoah, batata, hurricane, and maize, are now part of Latin American Spanish, as the result of linguistic syncretism, or mixing. Equally important are some examples of Africanisms: bomba, babalao, bilongo, bongó, conga, cumbia, chéchere, gahngah, guandú, geenay, lucumí, malembe, mambí, marimba, motete, ñame, ñinga, samba, tumba (see Mosonyi 1993; also see Megenny 1993).

The mixing of indigenous, European, and African languages in Caribbean Spanish, and other developments such as the Palenquero spoken in San Basilio de Palenque in Colombia, the Palenquero spoken among the descendants of maroon runaway Congo slaves of Portobelo in Panama, and the Papiamento spoken in Curaçao, are very much like the religious syncretisms of Santería, Regla, Abakuá, Palo Mayombé, Ñañiguismo, Baquiné, Voodoo, Macumba, Candomblé, as well as the musical syncretisms of Rumba, Samba, Plena, Bomba, Mambo, Bamba, Huapango, Bamboula, Cumacos, Chibángueles, Quichimba, Carángano, Quitiplás, Tango, Milonga, Beguine, Merengue, Cumbia, and Tamborito. They are also like the mixing that takes place in food: rice with chick peas, ajiaco, mondongo with lima beans.

This important syncretism or mixing of languages, religions, music, and cuisine are all original developments of the marvelous Caribbean cradle-hammock, but one of the most extraordinary telluric developments of Caribbean syncretism is the Garifuna culture. According to the research of direct descendants of the Garifuna people, this culture dates back to the mid-seventeenth century, when a hurricane in the Caribbean Sea caused slave ships coming from Africa to crash on the coast of the island of Yurumei, known today as Saint Vincent, near the coast of Venezuela. The shipwrecked Africans' odyssey had started with the abduction of children stolen from their cradles and forced to board the slave ships anchored off the Atlantic coast of Africa. Those who survived this odyssey shared food and huts with the Arawakans and Caribs when they alighted on the island of Yurumei.

There, the African children learned to communicate with their neighbors in a language that was a curious mixture of two indigenous languages: Arawakan and Carib. This Arawakan-Carib syncretism was born when the bellicose Caribs invaded the Caribbean islands and sentenced to death the Arawakan men on the island of Yurumei. The descendants of Carib fathers and Arawakan mothers taught Carib to their male offspring and Arawakan to their female offspring. In the manner of their Arawakan Carib neighbors, the shipwrecked Africans progressively became Garifunas in an interesting process of syncretism, in which they not only adopted the basic staples of the Indians on the island of Yurumei—yucca and cassava bread—but also contributed to the Arawakan-Carib language with French, English, and Spanish words (the result of their contact with Africans and slave traders, pirates, corsairs, and *flibustiers*). Above all, the intonation of African languages also influenced the Arawakan-Carib language, which later became the Garifuna language.

Scholars of Garifuna culture have pointed out that the British settlers in Yurumei—in an attempt to match the prosperity that the French settlers of Haiti gained from their fruitful sugar cane fields—tried to enslave the Garifunas who had, thanks to their shipwreck, escaped the yoke of slavery. When these settlers tried to capture the Garifunas—as free labor for the sugar cane fields, and mills for the production of highly coveted sugar, the Garifunas launched a revolt under the leadership of Satuyé—the greatest Garifuna hero. When the Garifuna warriors—armed primarily with machetes—were defeated by the firearms of the British, as punishment for defending their dignity and rejecting the yoke of slavery, Satuyé was executed on March 14, 1795. Five thousand Garifuna followers of Satuyé were captured in the Palenques (Indian ranches) of the island of Yurumei. Two years later, on March 11, 1797, the Garifunas who didn't accept enslavement were deported in eleven ships headed for Jamaica. More than a thousand of them died aboard the British ships, and after painful sailing in the Caribbean, the surviving Garifunas were abandoned by the captains on April 12, 1797, on the island of Roatán near the coast of Honduras. In Honduras the Arawakan-Carib-African syncretism or mixing continued, and there the Garifunas established their capital in Trujillo. Later they established Garifuna settlements in the Caribbean coast of Honduras: Ciriboya, Carozal, Sambuco, San Juan, Tornabé, Triunfo de la Cruz, Saraguaina, Masca, and other communities. Garifuna communities were also established in Livingston, Guatemala; in Orinoco and La Fe in Nicaragua; and in Stann Creek, Hopkins, Dangriga, and Punta Gorda in Belize.[1]

The Garifuna language is the main patrimony of the Garifuna culture. And this Arawakan-Carib-African linguistic syncretism demands attention because although the phonetics of the language are African, unlike other Palenquero languages (such as the Palenquero spoken in San Basilio de

Palenque in Colombia or the Lucumí which is sung in the ceremonies of Santería in Cuba and Candomblé in Brazil), the base of its vocabulary is not African. According to Professor Salvador Suazo,

> The linguistic structure of the Garifuna language is made up of 45 percent Arawakan words, 25 percent Kallina or Carib words, 15 percent French words, and 10 percent English words. The remaining 5 percent is made up of technical Spanish words [for the Garifunas-speakers in Honduras, Guatemala, and Nicaragua] and of English [in the Garifunas communities of Belize and among residents of the United States of America]. (Suazo 1991, 6)

Suazo offers some examples of the Carib contributions to the Garifuna language: wuguri (man), wuri (woman), arutubu (hammock), yagana (canoe), fágayu (oar); Gallicisms: weru (verre), músue (mouchoir), gulíeri (cuiller), búnedu (bonnet), mariei (maríe); Anglicisms: súgara (sugar), wachi (watch), machi (matches), haiwata (high water), giali (girl).

Garifuna culture is an important development of Caribbean syncretism which can counter both the images generated through a colonial educational system and—more devastatingly—through the popular images that we, in some nations of Central America and the Caribbean, have of Africa and of Africans in the New World. These popular images are still those of the films of Tarzan, King of the Jungle and Great Savior, who in Africa constantly defeats the dangerous Africans (the majority of whom are Pygmies and cannibals) who supposedly were the ancestors of the slaves in the Caribbean. Unfortunately, our public-school textbooks continue to present the African aspects of our culture and history through an emphasis on the African slaves who were happy because Christianity saved or delivered them from pagan and dangerous Africa. Emphasis is also placed on the "ungrateful" African slaves, who, instead of loving their masters for the salvation of their souls, dedicated themselves to marooning activities or to fighting the yoke of slavery, rescuing their human dignity, and obtaining their freedom. Thus, our students never learn from their textbooks that Africans participated in the great Pharaonic civilization in Egypt, as well as in other rich and powerful kingdoms in Nubia, Ethiopia, Mali, Shongay, Ghana, and Zimbabwe. Nor do they learn from official textbooks about the heroic deeds of conquistadors, explorers, and maroon chiefs of African ancestry such as Juan Garrido, Nuflo Olano, Juan Valiente, Estebanico, Yanga, Bayano, Ganga Zumba, Benkos, Satuyé, Fillipa Maria Aranha, Fabulé, Chirinos, Coba, Felipillo, and José Antonio Aponte (see Rout 1976).

Garifuna culture is indeed an outstandingly positive example of Caribbean syncretism, underscoring the pride and courage of Africans in the New World who rejected the yoke of slavery (and, when necessary, defended their dignity with their lives), but this syncretism has also been a painful cornucopia.

Painful are the almost four centuries of African slavery in the New World. The yoke of African slavery in the Caribbean began in 1517, when Bartolomé de las Casas petitioned Carlos V to concede licenses to Spanish settlers to import to Santo Domingo black slaves directly from Africa, a solution to the genocide of the Indians, and as a substitute for Indian slave labor.[2]

The unquestionable and undeniably important African contributions to the Creole cultures of the Spanish Caribbean stand out in Santería, in Ñañiguismo, in Merengue, in Bembé, in Bongó, in Rumba, in Ajiaco, and in the Garifunas, amongst others. However, as far as a Hispanic Caribbean identity is concerned, the African heritage is not only rejected (as in the obsessive preoccupation with racist sayings such as: "the race must be improved" and "your grandmother, where is she?"), it is also denied. Aside from being a fanatic illusion, this obsession is also an example of the profound and hateful racism that many Cubans show when they affirm that the "true Cuban" is white; that many Puerto Ricans exhibit when they proudly proclaim that Puerto Rico is "the whitest island" of the Antilles; that many Dominicans demonstrate when they swear to be "Dark Indians" and not black like the Haitians; and that many Panamanians manifest in their passionate hatred of Chombos.

In Panama the best example of the negative consequence of creolization is the separation and national hatred that exists among the so-called colonial blacks (descendants of African slaves dating back to Vasco Núñez de Balboa) and the black West Indians (disrespectfully called "Chombos"). This latter group is composed of the descendants of two waves of English- and French-speaking West Indian workers from Barbados, Haiti, Grenada, Jamaica, Martinique, St. Lucia, and other islands. The first wave emigrated in 1850 to participate in the construction of the trans-Atlantic railroad—a project financed by the North Americans during the California gold rush. The second wave of West Indian workers emigrated to participate in the construction of the failed sea-level canal (under the direction of the French), as well as in the construction of the lock-canal, 1904–1914 (under the direction of the North Americans).

Many Panamanians hate the Chombos because they are not all Catholics (since their grandparents were originally from the West Indies, many of them practice other religions); because they prefer to speak French and English in their homes; and finally because, according to racist Panamanians, too many Chombos have failed to participate sufficiently in the process of ethnic whitening in order to "better the race"—or to put it more frankly, to erase all that is African. As a result, all traces of an African gene or phenotype is hated and rejected: the woolen hair; the flat, broad nose; the thick lips; and above all, the black skin of the Chombos.[3]

The Cuban poet Gabriel de la Concepción Valdés, Plácido, was one of the first in the Caribbean to denounce the racist obsession with whitening the race:

> Don Longuino always claims
> With a passion stronger than bacon skin,
> and with his sallow complexion
> which African lineage betrays,
> "I come from pure and noble blood."
> Deluded, he proclaims to be
> from sublime kinship!
> Let him tell it to his grandmother!
>
> (Castellanos 1984, 48)

On the island where many are proud to be natives of "the whitest island" of the Caribbean, the Puerto Rican writer José Luis González has stated:

> As far as the African roots of Puerto Rico popular culture are concerned, I am convinced that the essential racism of the island's ruling class has done everything possible—at times in brutal ways and at times with subtlety worthy of a better cause—to avoid, to conceal, and to distort its importance. (1989, 74)

This Cuban, Puerto Rican, and Dominican obsession with whitening has been synthesized and has become in Panama the cornerstone of both the "Panameñista" concept and the Constitution of 1941. The latter solely welcomes those immigrants who are "capable of contributing to the improvement of the race" and calls for the denationalization of the Panamanian [Chombos] descendants of grandparents and parents of illegal immigration who are "members of the black race whose original language was not Spanish" (*Constitucion de la Republica de Panama*, 5–7).

In my own essays, poems, short stories, and novels, I have denounced and condemned the aspects of creolization that have as their sole goal and intention to erase the African heritage in Caribbean culture and identity.[4] In other words, I denounce the rejection of the African in the process of creolization which initially began with the rape of young African slave girls and which still persists today in the hatred concealed in the edict: "It is necessary to better or improve the race." For example, in *Chombo*, I display that rejection:

> Abena Mansa Adesimbo vehemently opposed the name that had been given to her child. She argued that they should forget the African traditions because it was important to keep in mind that they weren't in Haiti, Jamaica, Barbados, and even less, in Africa. She recalled that during the short time that she was able to attend public school, the

teacher severely criticized her name for being so African and asked her daily why West-Indian blacks did not adopt Panamanian last names such as Chiari, Wong, Heurtemate, Ghandi, Tagaropoulos. (1981, 59)

In a poem entitled "In Exilium" (1977, 8), I protest against any form of syncretism that has as its only intent the erasure and destruction of the heritage and pride of my African ancestors:

How disgraceful!
I am ASHANTI
and they address me as
Carlos
How insulting!
I am a CONGOLESE
and they call me
Guillermo
How base!
I am YORUBA
and they name me
Wilson.

Another poem, "Desarraigado" (or "Uprooted") articulates the psychological conflict produced by the erasure of the African heritage in the Caribbean identity:

African grandmother,
Do you not recognize me?
My language is Gongoric.
My litany is Nazarene.
My dance is Andalusian.
African grandmother,
why don't you recognize me?

Finally, in the novel *Los nietos de Felicidad Dolores* (1991) I also portray characters of African descent who absurdly surrender to and become accomplices of the ideology of whitening:

Blaaaaack woman of the devil. I have already told you a thousand times not to get involved in my business. If I want to give my telephone number to all the American soldiers, of course, to the whitest with blue eyes, it's my business and au contraire, it should not matter to you nor to anyone else. And don't remind me that I have five illegitimate petits enfants because I don't feel ashamed of it. In fact, I am very happy and, yes, very proud that there were five blond soldiers, yes, very blond with blue eyes, the ones that made me pregnant. All of them white.

Well, I did as my Godmother Karafula Barrescoba advised me: "Look for a white husband in order to improve the race." Fortunately, my five children don't have woolen hair like those chombo boys with so much African blood. Neither are they thick lipped. Nor snub nosed. Neither are they ... (75)

Creolization was indeed the inevitable result of the initial violent clash among the Indians who lived in such places as Quisqueya, Xaymaca, Borinquén, and Cuba; the European conquistadors who invaded these territories of the Caribbean Sea; and the African slaves brought to the New World to excavate gold mines, cultivate sugar cane fields, work in sugar mills, and build fortresses and ports. The ensuing mixing of the languages, religions, music, and food was indeed positive and admirable. Sadly, this creolization has not defeated the absurd, repugnant, and above all, insulting attitude that is an affront to the pride and dignity of the African heritage of our Caribbean cultures.

Notes

1. This information is gleaned from the following works of scholars of Garifuna culture: Lopez Garcia, Suazo, Savaranga, Avila; I also refer to the papers of Melecio R. Gonzales and Jorge Bernardez in the Primero and Segundo Encuentro Cumbre Garifuna, held in New York in 1991 and Los Angeles in 1992, respectively.
2. As a Sevillian soldier, Las Casas had participated in the killings and conquests of the Indians in Quisqueya and Cuba; he later became the first ordained Dominican Catholic priest in the New World, the Apostle of the Indians, and later the Bishop of Chiapas (see Sauer 1984).
3. For more details of this practice, see Jackson 1988 and Birmingham-Pokorny 1993.
4. The works I refer to here are my novels *Chombo* (1981) and *Los nietos de Felicidad Dolores* (1991) and my poems "In Exilium," and "'Desarraigado" (*Pensamientos* 1977).

References

Avila, José Francisco, ed. 1991. *U.S.A. Garifuna*. Allen, TX: Avila.

Birmingham-Pokorny, Elba, ed. 1993. *Denouncement and Reaffirmation of Afro-Hispanic Identity in Carlos Guillermo Wilson's Works*. Miami: Ediciones Universal.

Castellanos, Jorge. 1984. *Placido, Poeta Social y Politico*. Miami: Edicìones Universal.

González, José Luis. 1989. *El Pais de quatro pisos y otros ensayos*. Rio Piedras, Puerto Rico: Ediciones Huracan.

Jackson, Richard L. 1988. *Black Literature and Humanism in Latin America*. Athens: University of Georgia Press.

Lopez Garcia, Victor Virgilio. 1991. *Lamumehan Garifuna: Clamoo Garifuna*. Tela, Honduras: Tornabé.

Megenny, William W. 1993. "Common Words of African Origin Used in Latin America." *Hispania* 66 (March): 1–10.

Mosonyi, Esteban Emilio. 1993. "Nuestro legado Linguistico Africano." *Africamérica* 1(1) (January): 22–26.

Porras, Jorge E. 1993. "The Spanish Language in the Americas 500 Years After: Unity within Diversity." *Diaspora: Journal of the Annual Afro-Hispanic Literature and Culture Conference* 2(2) (Spring).

Rout, Leslie B. Jr. 1976. *The African Experience in Spanish America*. Cambridge: Cambridge University Press.

Sauer, Carlos Ortwin. 1984. *Descubrimiento y dominacion Espanola de la Caribe*. Trans. S. Mastrangelo. Mexico: Fondo de Cultura Economica.

Savaranga, Crisanto Uayujuru. 1992. "Conferencia de la cosmovision historica, cultural del pueblo kaliponan (garifuna) kalinagus (garinagus) de Honduras." Tegucigalpa, Honduras.

Suazo, Salvador. 1991. *Conversemos en Garifuna*. Tegucigalpa, Honduras: Editorial Guaymuras.

Wilson, Carlos G. 1977. *Pensamientos*. Los Angeles.

—1981. *Chombo*. Miami, FL: Ediciones Universal.

—1991. *Los nietos de Felicidad Dolores*. Miami, FL: Ediciones Universal.

SYNCRETISM AND LEGITIMACY IN LATIN AMERICAN RELIGION

Gustavo Benavides

The issue of cultural legitimacy is inseparable from that of political legitimacy. How is power to be exercised in a society, how will goods be produced and consumed by a population, how will the boundaries and the internal divisions of that population be determined? The phenomenon of religion is present in all these issues: present from the very beginning of Latin American history, from the moment indigenous societies came into disastrous contact with Latin Europe; for, as it is well known, the colonial enterprise was carried out in a manner that precludes making an easy differentiation among military, political, cultural, economic and religious realms.[1] If to conquer is to erase certain external boundaries in order to establish new internal ones, religion was ready to fulfill the mission it has usually fulfilled, that of establishing differences based on transcendental sources of power. What was to happen then to the systems of difference and power prevalent in the Andes at the time of the Spanish conquest: would they be destroyed, or entirely absorbed by the more powerful Christianity, or would a compromise of sorts be reached in which European and Andean systems would be combined?[2] In order to study possible cases of accommodation, a solution could be to resort to concepts such as syncretism, and employ them to trace the history of the emergence and transformation of mixed cultural formations in the Andes beginning in the sixteenth century.

To engage in such study, however, one has to assume that it is possible to distinguish between cores and surfaces, between centers and boundaries of religions, and more generally of cultural formations. But since this assumption is by no means unproblematic, one will have to consider whether religions can be regarded not as systems with cores and boundaries, but rather as networks of representations, as symbolic repertories, whose margins—and possibly centers as well—are ultimately nowhere to be found. Employing, in a very tentative manner admittedly, sociolinguistic concepts which bring into the discussion of linguistic categories the issue of power relations, and the related issue of cultural and political legitimacy, we will explore the parallels between linguistic and cultural-religious formations with a special focus upon the Andes. It should be stressed, however, that despite the central role played by power in this essay, power will not be approached in the tautological manner fashionable these days, according to which, power is exercised for its own sake; rather, its exercise will be understood in terms of needs, needs that generally arise in a context of material scarcity.[3]

I

In the study of the cultural changes that began to take place in the Andean world in the sixteenth century, as well as in discussions about contemporary Latin American culture, it is frequent to encounter terms whose function is shamelessly ideological, along with others whose purely analytical or even descriptive functions would seem unimpeachable. Among the first, the most common is that of *mestizaje*: a concept that attempts to erase political, economic and social differences by postulating a oneness, halfway between the biological and the mystical, according to which, for example, the fact that soon after the Spanish conquest both the Indian and the *encomendero* ate potatoes and maize would erase the fact that the labor that made that consumption possible was the responsibility of the Indian, while the *encomendero*'s only work had to do with eating. Although it is not possible to discuss here the functions of the *mestizaje* ideology, nor of concepts such as *Nación*, *Pueblo*, spiritual community, and the like, which because of their utopian content may create a sense of organic solidarity but which deflects attention from issues of class,[4] it is instructive to stress the central role played by religion in most of these formulations. As a relatively recent example, one could refer to the following passage by Victor Andrés Belaúnde, one of the ideologists of *Peruanidad*:

> As an expression of a spiritual community, the sense of nationhood (*nacionalidad*) has had its origin and has been maintained by the force of religious feeling ... Economic disparities, political struggles, class rivalries, conspire against that unity. It is only the rootedness and the force of religious sentiment that guarantee cohesion and unity. (1951–52, 109)

Among the second type of concept, we find a variety of terms—syncretism, popular religion, superstition, magic, witchcraft, heresy—all related to what is non-official and having to do, ultimately, with religious illegitimacy.[5] Of all these concepts, that of syncretism seems to be the least ideologically charged—the one that is purely descriptive or analytical. In the study of religion the term "syncretism" is employed in a more or less imprecise manner to refer in general to situations in which elements from more than one religion are combined, but in such a way that it is still possible to recognize the foreign and adventitious nature of those elements.[6] Given its uncertain content, it has been suggested that the term should be abandoned altogether (Baird 1971, 146), a proposal that is not likely to be widely accepted. In any event, it seems clear that it is difficult to use the term when the supposedly syncretistic religion has become fully functional (Ringgren 1969, 13; Rudolph 1979, 210), in which case syncretism, besides serving as an example of the dynamic nature of religion, would have to be understood as referring to a temporary formation (Pye 1971, 92–93). However, this last characteristic in itself is ultimately not illuminating, as most cultural formations are limited by temporality.

Although part of the vocabulary of the study of other regions and periods,[7] the term syncretism is almost synonymous with the religions and other cultural formations in the Mediterranean world during late antiquity. Students of late Greco-Roman, early Christian, Iranian, Syrian and Gnostic (including Manichaean and Mandean) religions, confronting the frequently self-conscious manner in which elements taken from various traditions found in the religions of late antiquity were combined, defend the non-theologically determined use of the term and have proposed various typologies of syncretism. Thus, Carsten Colpe, recognizing that one cannot find living religions that are pure, recommends that the term syncretism not be used as a value category (1975/1980, 176–77), and proposes instead a refined typology (1975/1980, 166–76). Dealing with the political aspects of syncretism, he suggests that a readiness to develop syncretistic formations can be seen as forming a continuum: at one end one finds the imperial motivation, exemplified by the Romans; at the other, the subversive, represented by the Gnostics. In the middle, one finds skepticism, the attitude that is most likely to produce the most complete forms of syncretism (1975/1980, 184). One of the most insightful discussions of syncretism is to be found in Kurt Rudolph's "Synkretismus—vom theologischen Scheltwort zum religionwissenschaftlichen Begriff" (1979). In this article, Rudolph reviews the literature, provides a critique of Colpe's ultimately theological position (1979, 204), and contributes a typology, related to Colpe's, that involves symbiosis, amalgamation or fusion, identification, metamorphosis and isolation (1979, 209–10). Rudolph emphasizes the importance of the difference between conscious and unconscious syncretistic formations (1979, 207–208), and in general approaches syncretism as an example of the dynamic character of religious formations, dialectically related to historical, political and social processes (1979, 210).

In a number of publications, Ulrich Berner, making use of the concept of system as developed by Niklas Luhmann, regards syncretism as a response to a situation of insecurity resulting from the encounter of different systems, this goal being achieved through the abolition of the boundaries of the system (Berner 1978b, 12). More recently he has expanded his use of systems theory (1982, 83–114), and provided an extensive review of the literature (1982, 5–80). Among the most interesting recent contributions is that of Droogers, an author who, while opposing the abandonment of the term, stresses the role played by power and contestation in syncretistic developments.[8] Droogers reminds us that the use of the term syncretism to refer to certain ambiguous historical developments presupposes that ambiguity is the exception whereas cohesion and integration are normal; he also emphasizes the need to pay attention to the social location not just of those who generate syncretistic movements, but also of those who think that syncretism is a problem.[9] Considering the frequent coincidence of clerical and academic foci, he writes: "one wonders if students of religion might ever have spoken of syncretism without the clergy being worried about the phenomenon, just as one may wonder whether syncretism would exist if there were no clergy" (1989, 15, 20).

In the Andean context, a syncretistic Christianity[10] would be one in which, for example, the Christian god incorporates, although without fully assimilating, elements of Andean gods, especially of Andean creator gods, such as Wirakocha or Pachacamac. Another example would be that of Illapa, the divinity of lightning, syncretized with the apostle Santiago, patron of the Spanish armies. As stated earlier, unlike the transparent ideological functions of the concept of *mestizaje*, the concept of syncretism seems to fulfill a purely descriptive or analytical function: that of describing cultural encounters, explaining fusions or quasi-functions, studying the articulation among gods and other supernatural beings. However, the ideological content of this concept becomes clear once we start examining our presuppositions about the realms of the "religious" and the "cultural." In effect, to talk about an Andean, a Haitian, or a Latin American syncretism means to assume that the "syncretized" religion—Christianity—has, on the one hand, clearly delimited boundaries, and, on the other, a fixed center inhabited by the imperturbable contents of faith and revelation. It is clear that if one thinks in terms of boundaries and cores, however one may imagine such centers and limits, any situation in which Christians come in contact with non-Christians can give birth to syncretistic formations. But one should ask whether religions, as well as other cultural formations, have fixed boundaries and motionless cores:[11] is it not true that all the elements that regular believers—although not necessarily theologians—accept as the building blocks of Christianity are the result of complex historical developments, none of which reached its conclusion during the life of Jesus of Nazareth? This includes the Christologies of the first centuries, as much as the doctrine of the trinity, not to mention the changing fortunes of Mary, the fluctuations in the understanding of what constitutes the realm of the "supernatural," or the debates about the status of the bishop of Rome.

To speak, therefore, of an Andean or a Latin American syncretism may make sense to those who take their religion as a given, but it does not from the viewpoint of a historian or an anthropologist (and not necessarily either from the point of view of a modern or "postmodern" theologian). To speak of an Andean syncretism means ultimately to have accepted quite uncritically the self-understanding of the colonial clerics, especially those in charge of the extirpation of idolatries, and of their contemporary counterparts. Such clerical approach is present today, when some missionaries continue to take for granted that "archaic superstitious practices ... interfere with the Christian faith" (Debarge 1984, 159); on the other hand, these *"mesquines superstitions"* (ibid., 168) can be considered, according to more enlightened missionaries, as a kind of Old Testament that can be used profitably in the catechetical enterprise[12] (Marzal 1985, 219). In any event, whether in an enlightened or non-enlightened manner, the issue is still one of perspective: a matter of choosing between the self-understanding of the conquerors and that of the conquered. The problem of syncretism—an innocuous or even inexistent problem at first sight—forces us to confront the issue of power and legitimacy: the power to determine not only who works and who makes use of the fruits of labor, but also the power to design the structures of the supernatural. Considering the role played by the supernatural realm in the legitimation of cultural and political structures, one can see that to postulate a definition given from outside results in depriving certain groups, and frequently also oneself, of cultural and political legitimacy.

If, however, besides not assuming a theological position, however implicit, one abandons certain preconceptions about what constitutes a society, and leaving aside approaches that reify what is "social," one rather understand societies, borrowing Michael Mann's expression, as power networks,[13] the problem of syncretism dissolves, and the same happens with the problem of what constitutes the realm of the religious. If one understands societies as networks that are constantly being reconstituted, the realm of the religious appears as an analytical category which may have a more or less identifiable referent (as is the case in the modern world since the Enlightenment), or as a realm which can be rather understood, in the sixteenth century for instance, both in the Andes as in Europe, less as a discrete element than as a coloration—or as a pitch—of the practices that make possible social reproduction. It was therefore unavoidable that the coloration we call "religion" would play a role in the reproduction of the Andean and the Iberian power networks. Once those networks intersected at the end of the fifteenth century with Columbus, and then in the sixteenth with Cortés in Mexico, and with Pizarro in the Andes, religion, as much as the technology available at the time, had to be used on both sides in the struggle for supremacy. From the point of view of the Spaniards, the Christian idea of Crusade and the Iberian notion of reconquest (both still alive in this century, both during the Spanish Civil War, and in the failed invasion of Cuba on 17 April 1961), had to play a central role during the conquest, organization of forced labor, indoctrination and "extirpation of idolatries." From the opposite angle, Andean practices which had the purpose of maintaining and expanding, often violently, social relations of a hierarchical type were also activated in response to the genocidal European attack. Now, if one assumes that societies function as more or less organic entities, it is almost inevitable to consider that the religious components of these organisms, besides functioning as elements in the confrontations referred to above, can eventually die in the event the societies to which they belong are defeated by more powerful groups. According to this point of view, and to some of the theories reviewed above, syncretistic formations would have a merely episodic and ultimately illegitimate character, since syncretistic developments would have to be understood as compromises that would ultimately end up betraying both religions. On the other hand, if we consider societies as formations that are constantly being reconstituted, lacking in many cases a dominant ideology (Abercrombie *et al.* 1980), the religious realm would appear as something that can be appropriated and reformulated, in much the same way as members of a conquered society are able in a very short time to make use of the language and the technology of the conqueror.

Another implication of the careless use of the term "syncretism" is the disproportionate importance given to the role played by "faith" and "belief" in the constitution of the social imaginary. In effect, if it is necessary to remember that religions do not necessarily have fixed limits, functioning actually as fuzzy sets, it is equally necessary to consider that the contents of most individuals' faiths are unstable and subject to constant reinterpretation and negotiation. This means that the "faith" of a "believer"—Christian or not, Andean or not—is constituted by a repertory of elements, often of a contradictory nature, which generally coexist in a state of tension, and which can be activated and reformulated according to what circumstances require. This behavior, which would not be improperly labeled as opportunistic, has its counterpart in everyday communication where each monolingual speaker choses from a verbal repertoire or perhaps even dialects;[14] a situation which becomes much more complex, but also potentially more dangerous, when there is the possibility of using more than one language. Therefore, it would be worthwhile to reconsider the role that linguistics can play in the study of religion. By this it is not meant the facile application of the formalistic linguistic categories employed uncritically during the days of French structuralism[15] (replaced nowadays by the no less uncritical acceptance of so-called poststructuralism), when one referred triumphantly and vacuously to those binary oppositions that could be found everywhere (just as one triumphantly talks today about discourses, reflexivity, narrative and textuality).[16] On the contrary, what is meant is the use of sociolinguistic categories which can help us reconceptualize the role of accommodation and conflict and more generally of change in social formations.

In the case of sociolinguistics, the discussion about the formation and function of pidgins and creoles—that is, linguistic formations born out of the need to communicate in situations of cultural contact brought about in many case by situations of colonialism—can be employed profitably to try to reconceptualize situations labeled as syncretistic. Pidgins,[17] ad hoc, short lived, and possibly simplified languages which are improvised in order to cope with situations in which communication would be otherwise impossible—and creoles[18]—languages into which one is born—function in the same way in which religious representations do in colonial situations. The religious equivalents of pidgins would be some of the cases to be discussed later, in which certain words, segments of rituals, random images, liturgical vestments, and so on, are adopted by members of a conquered people in order to communicate and then to survive the onslaught of the conquering group. The role played by power and prestige is central in these cases, as elements from the foreign group are perceived, not unjustly, as able to deliver what one's own culture cannot provide. The equivalent of creoles can be found in those situations in which an accommodation of sorts has been reached and a new system of meaning has been born, related to, but is not identical to the mother group. In any event, there is nothing in the grammatical structure of the creoles (or in the symbolism of new religious formations) that can be considered as intrinsically less complex than the source language, or as less able to make communication possible. The only criteria that can be used to place creoles and source languages in a hierarchy depends upon the social and ultimately political prestige and power of the source language. Legitimacy or the lack of it now becomes the central issue, to the extent that often it is not simply a matter of establishing a hierarchy of linguistic or religious practices, but rather of members of the dominant group recognizing the legitimacy of a creole as a language *tout court*, or of a set of practices as religion rather than as witchcraft or sorcery.[19]

The fundamental ambiguity of cultural goods, including religious ones, makes possible the survival both of religions and of their practitioners because this ambiguity facilitates the assimilation of new elements and the consequent accommodation to circumstances which otherwise would have destroyed a totally centered and rigid world of meanings. If one considers how the pivotal role played by the Inca in the Andean world led, once he was captured by the Spaniards, to the collapse of the political system of which he was the axis, one should also consider that despite the political the Indians access to the sacraments, it was not considered proper to ordain Indians as priests (Spalding 1984, 251, 254); if it was necessary to use candles and oil in the churches, it was necessary to insist, as did the Council of Lima, that the wax and the olive oil be imported from Spain (MacCormack 1985, 450 n. 26). Attempts, such as those by Francisco Tito Yupanqui, had to be resisted, because it is one thing to be a Christian, and quite another to want, concretely or metaphorically, to take Christianity in one's hands, as a sculptor or as a practitioner.

Santiago, Apostle of Spain, whose name served as the battlecry during the *reconquista*, was also identified with Andean representations and ended up being used both by Indians and by Spaniards. In this case, besides the unavoidable identification between Santiago and the Spanish *arcabuces* on the one hand, and the semantic field of Illapa, the Andean divinity of lightning,[24] on the other, what is significant is the adoption on the part of the defeated of the most bellicose member of the Spanish pantheon. The history of the transformation of Santiago *Matamoros*—Santiago-Killer-of-Moors—into Santiago *Mataindios*—Santiago-Killer-of-Indians—and the subsequent transformation of the apostle into an Andean divinity, a history that is only superficially paradoxical, shows again the intimate connection between mythological representations and the struggle for power, as well as the peculiar ambivalence that characterizes every colonial situation.[25] Rather than a Freudian identification with the aggressor, the identification Santiago-Illapa is one more proof of the use of symbols, of the symbolic *guerrilla* one has to engage in, necessary in order to rebuild defense lines. That this is so is proved by the prohibition of the use of the names Illapa, Rayo and Santiago by Indian children, issued by Spanish colonial authorities: having demonstrated his prowess in the battlefield, Santiago was now part of the Andean arsenal (Silverblatt 1988, 184). In non-military terms, on the other hand, the transference of the cult of saints from Spain to America was also successfully accomplished, as the functions of the European saints as advocates and as protectors of material well-being, especially health and crops, were welcomed by Indians, even if the relationship between saint and Mayan ancestor or Andean divinity was, and is, one fraught with the same ambiguity that characterizes the relationship between dominant and subaltern groups.[26]

III

If leaving aside saints and divinities one considers movements such as the Taki Onqoy,[27] in the sixth decade of the sixteenth century, one finds an apparently nativist movement,[28] centered around the region of Huamanga, whose followers proclaimed the resurrection of the Andean *huacas*, although not necessarily those linked to the Incas of Cuzco. These *huacas*, it

and, more importantly, demographic collapse of the sixteenth century, Andean social organization, ritual practices, and means of ecological control did not disappear entirely due precisely to the built-in ambiguity of all cultural, as opposed to purely political, systems. It is also important to put in perspective the role played by the beliefs with which theologians and historians of theology deal, and consider also the importance of the readjustments that take place through less exalted verbal means, such as myths and songs, as well as through non-verbal means, including iconography and ritual activity. Now that the study of the conquest and colonization of Latin America has ceased to be the exclusive province of those who work with the methods of traditional historiography, it is possible to discover the multiple responses of the conquered to the horror of the conquest, with its massacres and rapes, forced labor and massive suicides—that history, which, after five hundred years, some are attempting to rewrite, replacing the concrete brutality expressed by "conquest" with the shameful blandness of "encounter."

II

After the first terror caused by the horses and the arcabuces, the Andean armies began to make use of the horses, the spears and the firearms of the Spaniards.[20] Should one talk of a syncretistic use of power or gunpowder? If the answer is negative, negative must also be the answer to the question about the syncretistic nature of, for instance, the Taki Onqoy, Santiago-Illapa, the Virgin Mary, and Inkarrí. After all, both Spaniards and Andeans employed gunpowder for military purposes; and regarding the ritual use of gunpowder, it should be remembered that it is used in firecrackers and in elaborate fireworks as much in Andean as in European religious celebrations.[21] The only reason why one would be inclined to talk of an Andean religious syncretism would be due to the explicit or implicit acceptance of the self-evaluation of European clerics as the final interpreters of a Christianity whose dogmatic contents and ritual practices would have found its state of final perfection in the official—but not "local"—Christianity of sixteenth-century Spain. From a non-confessional viewpoint, the Christianity that began to emerge in the Andes in the sixteenth century is one of the dialects of Christianity, related to the versions found in the Mediterranean, Celtic and Germanic worlds, and probably as related to the Mediterranean as it is to the Catholicism of the Philippines and to the growing Christian Churches of sub-Saharan Africa. The dogmatic fidelity of Andean or Latin American Christianity matters little to a corpus that is always and everywhere being reinterpreted: what is important is to discover the causes of these specific religious transformations. These causes can be found in the conquered groups' capacity to rearrange their symbolic world, incorporating on the one hand, elements whose brute force had been demonstrated: the god of the Christians, the cross, the apostle Santiago. On the other hand, conquered or oppressed peoples also use elements of a more benign nature as utopian horizons, which provide the basis for moral judgment and condemnation of the oppressors. This way, both aspects of the struggle for power are protected: the assimilation of powerful and victorious gods reinforces the pantheon and makes access to the ideological goods of the invader possible. In a parallel manner, the incorporation of benign divinities makes it possible to confront the exploiter with the mirror of his own ideology and, thus, to judge him with his own laws, as it would happen at the end of the eighteenth century with Túpac Amaru.

It is instructive to begin with the idea of god. Without stopping to consider the conciliar debates about the Christian Trinity, or the Christological controversies of the first centuries, let us compare the decision taken by Constantine in the year 312 with the multiple decisions taken by Andean lords beginning already in the sixteenth century to adopt the god who had proved his power participating in the destruction brought about by Spanish forces. In Constantine's case, the Christian god functioned initially as a typical Roman god of victory: one of those divinities ritually acclaimed before the battle and then honored after victory (Wardman 1982, 137–39). We must also remember that as a result of the ambiguous relationship between the god of the Christians and the *Sol invictus*, when the Christian god finally emerged as the official god of the state, the new divinity has already incorporated some of the characteristics of the god worshipped by Heliogabalus and the priests of Emessa.[22] Analogous processes took place during the expansion of Christianity among the barbarians, as well as among Andean, Mayan and Aztec populations. There are differences to be sure: in the case of Constantine, the one who adopted the new god was the victor, a victor who would preside over the inaugural session of the council of Nicea in May of 325, and who would therefore contribute to the definition of triumphant Christianity; in the Andes, those who gradually adopted Christianity primarily as a kind of ritual pidgin imposed by necessity were the defeated ones, and thus, their definitions of Christianity were, in the best of cases, considered as exotic and syncretistic, and in the worst, as witchcraft and consequently subject to torture and persecution. What is important, however, is to keep in mind the process of emergence, transformation and disappearance of divinities, and to remember that the apparent dogmatic closure of the Christian god is as much an *a posteriori* construct, as it is an ongoing process. If such closure does not exist, it is futile to talk about syncretism, but rather of the continuous transformation of an uncertain net of representations whose semantic content comes less from the inside—from an assumed core—than from the opposition between one god and its counterpart.

Something similar happened with the Christian god's mother. Although the Virgin Mary does not play as important a role in the Andean countries as she does in Mexico, she, nevertheless, has a long history in which she appears as a military deity, helping the Spaniards defend Cuzco against the armies of Manco Inca during the siege of 1536, as well as being the protector of defenseless Indians. Mary, as patron to the military, is particularly interesting not only because of the history of the Virgin as "La Conquistadora," protecting the Spaniards in Mexico (Taylor 1987, 10), and later as *Mariscala* of Latin American armies, or because of consecrations of entire countries to her, as it happened when Argentina was consecrated to the Virgin of Luján during the Onganía dictatorship (Benavides 1987, 124). Mary, in her military avatara during the first years of the conquest, is relevant in the context of a discussion of the relationship between power and syncretism (and in more general terms in the relationship between religion and violence), because if we accept the reconstruction of events proposed by Sabine MacCormack, the Incas of Copacabana accepted the Virgin in 1582 after she demonstrated her power defeating the Indian armies and showing, therefore, the impotence of the Sun, protector of the Cuzco dynasty.[23] This means that some Andean aristocratic groups took a military-religious initiative appropriating key elements of Spanish Christianity, barely half a century after the capture of Atahualpa in Cajamarca. Another significant contemporary episode related to Mary is one involving a statue made by an Indian sculptor, Francisco Tito Yupanqui. This statue, which had been placed with the permission of the Copacabana priest, had to be removed once a new priest, Montoro, took charge of the church. Tito Yupanqui complained to the bishop of Chuquisaca, but the prelate confirmed the prohibition and recommended that Tito Yupanqui paint monkeys. What is significant in this case is the desire on the part of Andean lords to identify themselves with certain aspects of triumphant Christianity, an identification that appears quite clearly when the belief becomes widespread that the Virgin of Chuquisaca, besides performing miracles, would talk with some Indians, but never with Spaniards (MacCormack 1984, 51–53).

The other side of the coin, the Spanish one, seems to have oscillated between the evangelizing obsession and the desire to keep the new and the potential converts in a subordinate position. This was nothing new for Spanish ecclesiastical and civil authorities, since in the Iberian peninsula these were in charge of controlling popular access to the realm of the supernatural, punishing those who deviated from the approved norms. In America, however, this control had to fulfill the two functions required by the colonial situation: the supernatural realm had to include the conquered, as the conversion of these idolaters was in the last instance the justification of the conquest, but at the same time the supernatural realm had to be identified with the political power of Spain. Therefore, although it was necessary to allow

was believed, would destroy the European invader and erase their memory for ever. According to the testimony of Diego Gavilán, the first of twenty-five witnesses presented by the priest Cristóbal de Albornoz in his "Información" of 1570:

> Cristóbal de Albornoz made a great service to God Our Lord, because through his zealousness in the service of Lord Our God, he discovered among the native of these provinces the sect and apostasy of the Taqui Ongo, known also as Aira. Those who preached this doctrine said that one should not believe in God nor in his holy commandments, nor should one worship crosses or images, or enter churches, or take confession, but should rather seek confession with the leaders of the movement, and should also fast certain days according to the usage of Inca times, and these leaders preached in the name of the *huacas* which they had and worshipped.[29]

But according to the testimony of Pedro de Contreras, the sixth witness presented by Albornoz, among the participants in the movement there were women "who called themselves Santamaría and Santa Maria Magdalena and other names of saints which they had given to themselves in order to be revered as saints ..."[30]

Recently, Bruce Mannheim has tried to show that the Taki Onqoy—the Quechua terms translated not "dance disease" but as "Song of the Pleiades"—may be related to attempts to associate the Andean celebration of the Pleiades to the feast of Pentecost.[31] What kind of nativism is this then? An attempt to provide an answer brings us back to our general considerations about power and religious representations: Andean power networks attacked by violent and successful Christians began to be readjusted and to adopt, in a manner not too different from that employed more than a thousand years earlier by Roman emperors and barbarian kings, superstructural elements of the victorious enemies. Andean nativism (as it probably happens with every movement considered as nativist or revivalist) is one which looks not just to the past but also to the present, and above all to the future: to the past seen through the eyes of a present invaded by Spaniards so avid for gold, that Guamán Poma depicts them eating the precious metal. As Hobsbawm has shown persuasively, the present creates the past, traditions are invented,[32] but within the limits imposed by necessity, and not as the result of ludic textual dispersion or as the infinite play of intertextual echoes, as those postmodern anthropologists enamored of tautological culturalist explanations and local histories would have it.[33] In the Taki Onqoy rebellion, three decades after the Cajamarca massacre, Christianity is a feared presence, but precisely because of that it is a presence that has to be taken into account and which must be appropriated.

But it is necessary to remember that assimilation and appropriation, and even opportunism, do not necessarily imply the cynical and purely instrumental use of representations perceived as foreign. The fundamentally ambiguous nature of religious beliefs, and of the religious realm in general, forces us to use with caution comfortable labels such as dissimulation. Therefore, without forgetting cases in which dissimulation is consciously resorted to—among the Shi'ites and *Marranos*, for example—it is exaggerated to maintain that behavior is belief and that participation in certain ritual activities is what determines one's belonging to a religious community. Using a linguistic analogy, one could say that just as being able to affect somebody's behavior by making an utterance in a hitherto foreign language means that one is in some way a speaker of that language, so being able to function in a ritual context means that one is a member of that religious—or cultural—community. It could be argued that merely to act, perform, or utter can be regarded as functioning at a surface level, at the fringes of a system of signification, while to inhabit the core of a religion would involve truly believing that, for example, Jesus is the Christ. But the nature of belief, or more precisely of believing, is so hopelessly problematic and depends so much on an almost reified understanding of subjectivity, that it may be advisable to concentrate on the apparent surfaces constituted by those bodily practices we call rituals.[34] Is language the house of being, as those who find discourse everywhere inform us in solemn tones from time to time? Maybe so. But perhaps the true house is the body—less a source of fashionable desire than of need—and its many dwellings are provided by its movements, by its genuflections or by the refusal to perform those genuflections. If this is so, the surfaces and not the cores are the givers of meaning, and the surfaces are also the places of encounter, of assimilation, of accommodation and of rejection. Pidgin rituals would involve the fragmented acceptance of certain objects, costumes and bodily practices of another group, as seen in one of the cases studied by Manuel Burga, in which an Indian used a stick as if it were a horse, and covered its hind parts with the robe of a statue of the Virgin, thus parodying Christian rituals (Burga 1988, 191). Creole rituals would involve the masses celebrated for instance in the San Juan de Chamula church, not far from San Cristóbal de las Casas in Mexico: a creole of Christianity, to be sure, but keeping in mind that European Christianity is a language only in the sense in which a language is a dialect with an army.

The great revolt of Andean colonial history was the one led by Túpac Amaru, the Andean lord whose profile in black and white would become almost two hundred years later the icon of Velasco's quasi-revolution in Peru. Alberto Flores Galindo and Manuel Burga have talked of multiple Andean utopias, not just during the colonial period but also currently.[35] The *tupamarista* utopia—to use the title of Jan Szeminski's book (1984)—would have been one of the aristocratic and learned forms of utopia, created in part by Garcilaso's mythification of the Inca past (Flores Galindo and Burga 1982, 88 ff.). Besides these utopias, dreamed up by dispossessed aristocrats, we find popular ones, kept alive through myths and especially through ritual activity (Burga 1988). Were these Andean, Joachinist, or syncretistic utopias? What is the relative importance of the cyclical conception of time and of the idea of *pachacuti*,[36] the cosmic upheaval, in their genesis and unfolding? A possible, although hasty answer would say that the tupamarista utopia was totally Andean, in the sense in which the Taki Onqoy rebellion appears as purely Andean. Let us consider, in support of this position, edicts like the one proclaimed by an envoy of Túpac Catari on 19 March 1781, in which one finds some of the elements already encountered in the testimonies presented by Albornoz:

> The sovereign Inca orders that all *corregidores*, and their caciques, tax collectors and other dependents be killed; likewise all Spaniards, creoles, women and children, and all persons who are or appear to be Spanish, or who are dressed in the Spanish manner ... likewise he ordered that Indians should not have their meetings in places other than mountains, that they should eat no bread nor drink water from fountains, but should rather keep away from all Spanish customs. (Quoted in Szeminski 1984, 45)

To this we should add that on some occasions, those killed included priests, and that these acts involved sacrileges, as we find in a letter dated 7 May 1781 from Arequipa:

> In the village of Toracari and San Pedro de Buena Vista not even priests were spared. The rebel who committed these atrocities was an Indian named Simón Castillo, who ordered more than a thousand people to be killed inside the church, including more than six priests, one of whom was Dr. Ysidro Herrera, who had raised Simón Castillo.

According to the letter, the priest asked Castillo:

> Is it possible son, that you will deprive me of my life, me who raised you, who made you know God, who gave you food? To which the Indian responded: Do not tire yourself father, because for those reasons you will die ... after the death of the priest an Indian woman took the monstrance, filled it with coca, and spitting at God said that it was a lie, that he was not there, because it was just filthy flour she had brought from the valley. (Quoted in Szeminski 1984, 175)

We know that the rebels not only used firearms and horses, and ate beef, food of European origin, but also attempted to produce firearms, cannons and gunpowder (Szeminski 1984, 197–98). Something similar happened with Christianity: despite the death of many priests at the hands of the rebels, Christianity and the Church as an institution were not the target of rebel attacks. On the contrary, Túpac Amaru visited churches, attended mass, and at the end of his life, while being tortured, cried out the names of Jesus and the Virgin Mary (Szeminski 1987, 178; 1989, 41). Moreover, in a letter dated 5 March 1781, the rebel leader placed his rebellion within Old Testament mythology, particularly that key political text, Exodus, and made use of the images that have served to legitimize revolutionary (and counter-revolutionary) movements throughout the history of Christendom. In this letter, Túpac Amaru refers to the myth of the flight from Egypt in search of the promised land, interpreted now as the search for justice and peace. We find also the references to David, to Goliath and pharaoh, that will reappear two hundred years later, along with Marxist vocabulary, in Gustavo Gutiérrez's *Theology of Liberation*:

> A humble youth with a stick and a sling, and a rustic shepherd, because of divine providence liberated the people of Israel from the power of Goliath and Pharaoh: and the reason for this is that the tears of these poor captives claimed to heaven for justice, and so in few years they left their martyrdom and torment for the promised land ... but we, poor Indians, with more tears and sighs than they, in so many centuries have not been able to find any consolation ... (Quoted in Klaiber 1982, 179)

The absolutist logic of a religion with universal claims appears finally with all clarity in an argument apparently paradoxical and ahistorical but formally irrefutable and historically inevitable, since it emerged in the Andes as among the Maya: the Indians who live according to their rites and ceremonies are the true Christians; the Spaniards are the heretics: that is why they must die.[37]

IV

Definitions are acts of power. For Túpac Amaru, to be able to define himself and his followers as the true Christians requires having achieved the mastery of a symbolic code, the creation of a religious creole that could claim for itself the status of language. Such self-definition was the culmination of a process that began in the sixteenth century when some of the leaders of the Taki Onqoy named themselves Santamaría and Santa María Magdalena. With the Taki Onqoy, we witness a pidgin-like case of learning words perhaps without having mastered a syntax: that is, the uncertain and perhaps clumsy attempts at making use of central elements of the Christian symbolic universe—names, a god, rituals—as discrete sources of power which could be used against the Spaniards in combination with non-Christian Andean sources, rather than in terms of a comprehensive symbolic system within which actions could be meaningful. In the eighteenth century, on the other hand, both vocabulary and syntax have been mastered and recreated and we find that Christianity provides the general framework within which action of all type, including military, can take place. As a central element in Andean self-definition, Christianity can now be used against the colonial Christian—or from the Indian point of view, anti-Christian—power. But that self-definition had to be defended with weapons against those who using essentially the same means—weapons blessed by self-definition, self-definition defended by weapons—were seeking to maintain control of the subject population. This competition between circularities, which was neither about logic nor about doctrine, had to be solved in military terms and at the end Túpac Amaru was defeated, captured and killed.[38] Having become Christians, the Andean peoples were condemned to continue their struggle in Christian terms, even though this spiritual aroma would be labeled in the best of cases as syncretistic. In the last decades of the twentieth century one could even regard the Theology of Liberation as perhaps the last attempt to articulate a quest for political protest in terms of Christian mythology. With the Theology of Liberation the issue of syncretism resurfaces, because it would not be difficult to conceive opposition to it presented as opposition against the illegitimate combination of Marxism and Christianity (as opposed to the supposedly legitimate combination of Christianity and capitalism, or earlier social formations). Whether it be dispossessed peasants forced into *encomiendas* or mines in the sixteenth century, or eighteenth-century ones forced into the *repartimiento* economy, or twentieth-century ex-peasants sucked into the market system, the dreams constructed to validate their actions will be considered as illegitimate. The concept of syncretism can be regarded, then, as fulfilling now the same role fulfilled in previous centuries by witchcraft, for just as in earlier centuries clerics could define Andean transformations of European Christianity as illegitimate and dangerous, in the twentieth century anthropologists, some of them still acting as missionaries, would define it as perhaps colorful, but nevertheless, illegitimate.[39] In either case, definition and self-definition, legitimacy and illegitimacy are inextricably bound to one's unspoken point of reference and ultimately to one's political and material concerns.

*Editor's Note: Benavides has continued to work in this field and has expanded the scope of his investigations. In response to our invitation, he provided the following comments:

As is to be expected, my views regarding the connection between religion and power have changed to some extent. Already in the essay reprinted in this volume I made a point of distancing my approach from certain modish views concerning the omnipresence of a power understood tautologically as the source of life itself, as well as from the bundle of incantations that go under the name of "postmodernism." Likewise, I made reference to the related issues of continuity and intelligibility, having written that "the issue of continuity and mutual intelligibility, crucial in the study of dialects, pidgins and Creoles, is no less relevant for the study of religious beliefs and practices, particularly when one is interested in discovering the elusive and perhaps ultimately inexistent boundaries of communities of belief." These concerns resulted in a new essay, "Power, Intelligibility and the Boundaries of Religions," published in an issue of *Historical Reflections/Réflexions historiques* devoted to the concept of syncretism (vol. 27, 2001, 481–98). In the new essay I explore whether it is only *pouvoir*, in its meaningless Foucaultian sense, that creates boundaries or whether it is the changes sedimented in generation after generation that lead to the cessation of intelligibility and thus to the emergence of boundaries, whether these be placed around languages or around religions. Still using linguistic analogies I ask whether one can still speak of different dialects of a given language once the speakers of those dialects cease to understand each other, or whether one must consider that a new language has emerged. In terms of religious formations, that means that one cannot simply maintain, as I do in the essay above, that "little matters the dogmatic fidelity of Andean or Latin American Christianity to a corpus that is always and everywhere being reinterpreted." On the contrary, however tenuous, that dogmatic or ritual continuity matters insofar as its disappearance would necessarily result in certain individuals or groups no longer being considered by others as sharing a ritual or symbolic space. By "others" I mean primarily ordinary practitioners, rather than priests or theologians, for in many cases the speculations of theologians are utterly alien to the religious self-understanding of ordinary people.

The issues explored in "Power, Intelligibility and the Boundaries of Religions," that is, the interplay between intelligibility and power, are related to the concern with studying the interplay between identity and difference, naturalness and construction, cognition and ideology, rather than with just assuming, as is fashionable these days, that everything is construction, difference and the like.

Notes

1. On the inseparability of religion and politics in Latin American history, see Benavides 1987, 107 f.; on the political role of ritual and etiquette, see Trexler 1982.
2. On religion, difference and power see Benavides 1989a; on the role of space, Benavides 1992b. For European parallels involving triumphant Christianity and pagan practices see Flint 1991.

3. Despite the concern with surfaces and distrust of objectified subjectivity found in this paper, we will not assume a "postmodern" perspective, since the devotees of this ideology, lost in their peculiar combination of self-absorption and ludic pantextuality have lost sight of what representations represent.

4. On the ideological functions of the concept of *mestizaje* in Latin America, see Stutzman 1981. For a discussion of this issue in the context of fascist ideology, see Benavides, "Giuseppe Tucci, or, Buddhology in the Age of Fascism," in *Curators of the Buddha: Orientalism and the Study of Buddhism*, ed. Donald S. Lopez, Chicago: University of Chicago Press, 1995. This should be compared with the frequency of the use of the term *mestizaje* among Latino theologians in the United States, along with terms such as "latino," "Hispanic," or "pueblo." When the terms are used in an all-encompassing or celebratory manner to refer to people of Latin American origin who live in the United States, focusing on a supposed oneness understood partially in biological terms, issues of class are often obscured. Discussions of these dangers can be found in Antonio M. Stevens Arroyo, *Prophets Denied Honor*, Maryknoll: Orbis Books, 1980, 4–5, 32–33.

5. On magic as a category of religious illegitimacy see Benavides 1992a. On popular religion as a category, see Vrijhof and Waardenburg, eds. 1979; in a Latin American context, the concept is examined in Kselman 1986; for Spanish parallels, see Christian 1981; modern European developments are studied in Badone, ed. 1990.

6. On syncretism in general, see Edmonson 1960; Ringgren 1969; Pye 1971; Baird 1971; Colpe 1975/1980; Berner 1978a, 1978b, 1982; Rudolph 1979; Werblowsky 1987; Droogers 1989.

7. See, for example, Bechert, ed. 1978; Lanciotti, ed. 1984; Heissig and Klimkeit, eds. 1987.

8. Droogers 1989, 20–21, defines syncretism as "religious interpenetration, either taken for granted or subject to debate."

9. See also Werblowsky 1987, 7.

10. On Andean syncretism see Debarge 1984; MacCormack 1984, 1988; Marzal 1985; Benavides 1991.

11. See Rudolph 1979, 208; and in more general terms, Abercrombie *et al.* 1980.

12. In the Aztec world, a case of syncretism would be that of the Virgin of Guadalupe, whose apparition took place, conveniently, in Tepeyac, the place where the goddess Tonantzin may have been worshipped; it should be kept in mind, however, that this case of Marian devotion was one in which Spanish missionary efforts played an important role, the devotees being more frequently non-Indians rather than Indians (see Taylor 1987, 15; Uchmany 1982, 111–13; and the classic study by Wolf 1958/1979).

13. Mann 1986: "Societies are constituted of multiple overlapping and intersecting sociospatial networks of power."

14. On dialects, see Haugen 1966/1972.

15. See Mounin 1970, 199–214; Merquior 1986.

16. See Merquior 1986, esp. ch. 5. On pan-discursive absurdities Palmer 1990 is indispensable.

17. On pidgins and creoles: DeCamp 1971a, 15; Hoenigswald 1971, esp. 475 ff.; Hall 1972.

18. On creoles: DeCamp 1971a, 16 and *passim*; 1971b. The issue of continuity and mutual intelligibility, crucial in the study of dialects, pidgins and creoles, is no less relevant for the study of religious beliefs and practices, particularly when one is interested in discovering the elusive and perhaps ultimately inexistent boundaries of communities of belief.

19. The situation is essentially ambiguous; for situations, in Mexico, in which conquerors did recognize the status of certain practices, see Trexler 1982.
20. See Spalding 1984, 123. The Spaniards attempted to keep Indians from having access to horses and firearms (213).
21. See, however, the absurd statement found in Debarge 1984, 165.
22. Wardman 1982, 120–21; on the confusion between Christ and the *Sol invictus*, 137–38. It should be remembered that 25 December, originally the "dies natalis invicti solis," acquired its current meaning only in the fourth century, either in 336 or 354; cf. Andresen 1971, 363.
23. MacCormack 1984, 48–49; on Aztec attitudes towards Mary, see Trexler 1982, 185; on Maya revolts in the eighteenth century protected by the Virgin, see Thompson 1960, 20–21; and Wasserstrom 1982.
24. On lightning in the Andes and on Illapa, see Gade 1983; Silverblatt 1988.
25. On Santiago among the Maya examples, see Watanabe 1990, 134–35; on Santiago as mediator, ibid. 142.
26. Watanabe 1990, 135–37; on ambiguity see 140–41. On saints as sources of power, see Thompson 1960, 25; Madsen 1982, 155–56.
27. On the Taki Onqoy, consult the literature cited in Benavides 1989b: 173 n. 4, to which one should add Stern 1982, 51–71. Cristóbal de Albornoz's "Informaciones" (1569, 1570, 1577, 1584) have been edited in Millones 1990; this book also includes several studies, the most valuable of which is Varón Gabai 1990; psychoanalytically inclined readers may want to consult the article by Lemlij *et al.*
28. Linton 1943/1979 defines "nativism" as "any conscious organized attempt on the part of a society's members to revive or perpetuate selected aspects of its culture." Wallace 1956/1979 regards nativism as a type of revitalization movement.
29. "Información" of 1570, f. 7v/8r: Millones, ed. 1990, 70–71.
30. "Información" of 1570, f. 18r: Millones, ed. 1990, 89; cf. Stern 1982, 66; Spalding 1984, 248.
31. Bruce Mannheim, Cornell University, 18 July 1990; see also MacCormack 1988, 983 n. 42.
32. See the articles collected in Hobsbawm and Ranger, eds. 1983, esp. Hobsbawm 1983. But see also note 34, below.
33. For a lucid critique of the contemporary infatuation with textuality see Palmer 1990.
34. On the importance of the body in ritual and in the constitution and maintenance of societies see Connerton 1989, a book that should be read as the counterpart to the volume ed. Hobsbawm and Ranger (note 32, above).
35. Flores Galindo and Burga 1982; Flores Galindo 1986a, 1986b, 1988.
36. On the concept of *pachacuti*, see the literature cited in Benavides 1989b: 174 n. 15; MacCormack 1988.
37. On Maya parallels, see Thompson 1960, 23; Madsen 1982, 163; Wasserstrom 1982, 55.
38. On Maya parallels, see Thompson 1960, 16–19.
39. See, however, Thompson 1960, 32; and Madsen 1960, 152, 170, 172.

References

Abercrombie, N., S. Hill and B. S. Turner, eds. 1980. *The Dominant Ideology Thesis*. London: Allen & Unwin.

Andresen, Carl. 1971. *Die Kirchen der alten Christenheit*. Die Religionen der Menschheit 29, 1/2. Stuttgart: W. Kohlhammer.

Ansión, Juan, ed. 1989. *Pishtacos, de verdugos a sacaojos*. Lima: Tarea.

Archer, Margaret. 1988. *Culture and Agency: The Place of Culture in Social Theory*. Cambridge: Cambridge University Press.

Badone, Ellen, ed. 1990. *Religious Orthodoxy and Popular Faith in European Society*. Princeton: Princeton University Press.

Baird, Robert, D. 1971. *Category Formation and the History of Religions*. The Hague: Mouton.

Bechert, Heinz, ed. 1978. *Buddhism in Ceylon and Studies in Religious Syncretism in Buddhist Countries*. Symposien zur Buddhismusforschung, 11. Göttingen: Vandenhoeck & Ruprecht.

Belaúnde, Victor Andrés. 1951–52. "La evangelización y la formación de la conciencia nacional en el Perú." *Boletín del Instituto Riva Agüero* 1: 45–109.

Benavides, Gustavo. 1987. "Religion and Politics in Latin America." In *Movements and Issues in World Religions: A Sourcebook and Analysis of Developments since 1945*, ed. Charles Wei-hsun Fu and Gerhard F. Spiegler, 107–42. Westport, CT: Greenwood Press.

—1989a. "Religious Articulations of Power." In Benavides and Daly, eds. 1989, 1–12, 197–202.

—1989b. "Millennian Politics in Contemporary Peru." In Benavides and Daly, eds. 1989, 173–96, 219–32.

—1991. "Sincretismo religioso o resistencia política en los Andes?" *Humanitas* 20: 5–19.

—1992a. "The Invention of Magic." *Excursus* 5: 10–15.

—1992b. "Spatial Hierarchies and Sacred Order." Paper presented at the Annual Meeting of the Society for the Scientific Study of Religion, Washington, DC, 17 November 1992.

Benavides, G., and M. W. Daly, eds. 1989. *Religion and Political Power*. Albany: State University of New York Press.

Berner, U. 1978a. "Heuristisches Modell der Synkretismusforschung (Stand August 1977)." In Wiessner, ed. 1978, 11–26.

—1978b. "Das 'Synkretismus-Modell' als Instrument einer historischen Religionsphänomenologie." In Wiessner, ed. 1978, 27–37.

—1982. *Untersuchungen zur Verwendung des Synkretismus-Begriffes*. Göttinger Orientforschungen, 21. Wiesbaden: Harrassowitz.

Bourdieu, Pierre. 1977. "Sur le pouvoir symbolique." *Annales* 32: 405–11.

Burga, Manuel. 1988. *Nacimiento de una utopia. Muerte y resurrección de los Incas*. Lima: Instituto de Apoyo Agrario.

Christian Jr., William A. 1981. *Local Religion in Sixteenth-Century Spain*. Princeton: Princeton University Press.

—1984. "Religious Apparitions and the Cold War in Southern Europe." In Wolf, ed. 1984, 239–66.

Colpe, Carsten. 1975. "Die Vereinbarkeit historischer und struktureller Bestimmungen des Synkretismus." In Dietrich, ed. 1975, 5–37; rpd. in Colpe 1980, 162–85.

—1980. *Theologie, Ideologie, Religionswissenschaft*. München: Chr. Kaiser Verlag.

Connerton, Paul. 1989. *How Societies Remember*. Cambridge: Cambridge University Press.

Debarge, Louis. 1984. "Conservatisme et syncrétisme religieux au pays des Incas." *Mélanges de science religieuse* 41: 159–69.

DeCamp, David. 1971a. "The Study of Pidgin and Creole Languages." In Hymes, ed. 1971, 13–39.

—1971b. "Toward a Generative Analysis of a Post-Creole Speech Continuum." In Hymes, ed. 1971.

Diehl, Carl Gustav. 1969. "Replacement or Substitution in the Meeting of Religions." In Hartman, ed. 1969, 137–61.

Dietrich, Albert, ed. 1975. *Synkretismus im syrisch-persischen Kulturgebiet*. Abhandlungen der Akademie der Wissenschaften in Göttingen, Philologish-historische Klasse, 3. Folge, Nr. 961. Göttingen: Vandenhoeck & Ruprecht.

Droogers, André. 1989. "Syncretism: The Problem of Definition, the Definition of the Problem." In Gort *et al.*, eds. 1989, 7–25.

Duviols, Pierre. 1972. "Religions et répression dans les Andes aux XVIe et XVIIe siécles." In Jaulin, ed. 1972.

Edmonson, Munro S. 1960. "Nativism, Syncretism and Anthropological Science." In *Nativism and Syncretism*, ed. Munro S. Edmonson *et al.*

—*et al.*, eds. 1960. *Nativism and Syncretism*. Middle American Research Institute, Publication 19. New Orleans: Middle American Research Institute, Tulane University.

Flint, Valerie J. 1991. *The Rise of Magic in Early Medieval Europe*. Princeton: Princeton University Press.

Flores Galindo, Alberto. 1986a. *La utopia andina: Europa y elpais de los Incas*. Lima.

—1986b. "Es posible la utopia?" *El caballo rojo*. 28 September.

—1988. *Buscando un Inca*. Lima: Editorial Horizonte.

Flores Galindo, A., and M. Burga. 1982. "La utopia andina." *Allpanchis* 20: 85–101.

Gade, Daniel. 1983. "Lightning in the Folklife and Religion of the Central Andes." *Anthropos* 78: 770–88.

Gort, Jerald D. *et al.*, eds. 1989. *Dialogue and Syncretism: An Interdisciplinary Approach*. Grand Rapids: Eerdmans.

Gow, David D. 1980. "The Roles of Christ and Inkarrí in Andean Religion." *Journal of Latin American Lore* 6: 279–88.

Hall, R. A. 1972. "Pidgins and Creoles as Standard Languages." In Pride and Holmes, eds. 1972, 142–53.

Hartman, Sven S., ed. 1969. *Syncretism*. Scripta Instituti Donneriani Aboensis, 3. Stockholm: Almqvist & Wiksell.

Haugen, Einar. 1966. "Dialect, Language, Dialect." *American Anthropologist* 68: 922–35; rpd. in Pride and Holmes, eds. 1972, 97–111.

Heissig, Walther, and Hans-Joachim Klimkeit, eds. 1987. *Synkretismus in den Religionen Zentralasiens*. Studies in Oriental Religions, 131. 1–7. Wiesbaden: Harrassowitz.

Hill, Jonathan D., ed. 1988. *Rethinking History and Myth: Indigenous South American Perspectives on the Past*. Urbana: University of Illinois Press.

Hobsbawm, Eric. 1983. "Inventing Traditions." In Hobsbawm and Ranger, eds. 1983, 1–14.

Hobsbawm, Eric, and Terence Ranger, eds. 1983. *The Invention of Tradition*. Cambridge: Cambridge University Press.

Hoenigswald, Henry M. 1971. "Language History and Creole Studies." In Hymes, ed. 1971, 473–80.

Hymes, Dell, ed. 1971. *Pidginization and Creolization in Language*. Cambridge: Cambridge University Press.

Jaulin, Robert, ed. 1972. *L'Ethnocide à travers les Amériques*. Paris: Fayard.

Klaiber, Jeffrey. 1982. "Religión y justicia en Túpac Amaru." *Allpanchis* 19: 173–86.

Kselman, Thomas A. 1986. "Ambivalence and Assumption in the Concept of Popular Religion." In Levine, ed. 1986, 24–41.

Lanciotti, Lionello, ed. 1984. *Incontro di religioni in Asia tra il III e il X secolo d. C.* Firenze: L. S. Olschki.

Lessa, William A., and Egon Z. Vogt, eds. 1979. *Reader in Comparative Religion.* 4th ed. New York: Harper & Row.

Levine, Daniel H., ed. 1986. *Religion and Political Conflict in Latin America.* Chapel Hill: University of North Carolina Press.

Linton, Ralph. 1943. "Nativistic Movements." *American Anthropologist* 45: 230–40; repr. in Lessa and Vogt, eds. 1979, 415–21.

Lorenzen, David, ed. 1982. *Cambio religioso y dominación cultural: el impacto del islam y del cristianismo sobre otras sociedades.* Mexico.

MacCormack, Sabine. 1984. "From the Sun of the Incas to the Virgin of Copacabana." *Representations* 8: 30–60.

—1985. "'The Heart has its Reasons': Predicaments of Missionary Christianity in Early Colonial Peru." *Hispanic American Historical Review* 65: 443–66.

—1988. "Pachacuti: Miracles, Punishments and Last Judgment: Visionary Past and Prophetic Future in Early Colonial Peru." *American Historical Review* 93: 960–1006.

Madsen, William. 1960. "Christo-Paganism." In Edmonson *et al.*, eds. 1960, 105–79.

—1982. "Sincretismo religioso en Mexico." In Lorenzen, ed. 1982, 139–68.

Mann, Michael. 1986. *The Sources of Social Power*, vol. 1. Cambridge: Cambridge University Press.

Marzal S.J., Manuel. 1977. "Una hipótesis sobre la aculturación religiosa andina." *Revista de la Universidad Católican* s.2: 95–131.

—1985. *El sincretismo latinoamericano. Un estudio comparativo sobre los quechuas (Cusco), los mayas (Chiapas) y los africanos (Bahía).* Lima: Pontificia Universidad Católica del Purú.

Merquior, J. G. 1986. *From Prague to Paris: A Critique of Structuralist and Post Structuralist Thought.* London: Verso.

Millones, Luis, ed. 1990. *El retorno de las Huacas, estudios y documentos sobre el Taki Onqoy, siglo XVI.* Lima: Instituto de Estudios Peruanos.

Mondloch, James. 1982. "Sincretismo religioso maya-cristiano en la tradición oral de una comunidad quiché." *Mesoamérica* 3: 107–23.

Morandé, Pedro. 1982. "Synkretismus und offizielles Christentum in Lateinamerika. Ein Beitrag zur Analyse der Beziehungen zwischen 'Wort' und 'Ritus' in der nachkolonialen Zeit." *Beiträge zur Soziologie und Sozialkunde Lateinamerikas* 81.

Mounin, Georges. 1970. *Introduction à la sémiologie.* Paris: Editions de Minuit.

Palmer, Bryan D. 1990. *The Descent into Discourse: The Reification of Language and the Writing of Social History.* Philadelphia: Temple University Press.

Pride, J. B., and Janet Holmes, eds. 1972. *Sociolinguistics.* Harmondsworth: Penguin.

Pye, Michael. 1971. "Syncretism and Ambiguity." *NUMEN* 18: 83–93.

Ringgren, Helmer. 1969. "The Problem of Syncretism." In Hartman, ed. 1969, 7–14.

Rudolph, Kurt. 1979. "Synkretismus—vom theologischen Scheltwort zum religionswissenschaftlichen Begriff." In *Humanitas religiosa.* Festschrift für Haralds Biezais zu seinem 70. Geburtstag, 194–212. Stockholm: Almqvist & Wiksell.

Silverblatt, Irene. 1988. "Political Memories and Colonizing Symbols: Santiago and the Mountain Gods of Colonial Peru." In Hill, ed. 1988, 174–94.

Spalding, Karen. 1984. *Huarochirí: An Andean Society under Inca and Spanish Rule.* Stanford: Stanford University Press.

Steger, Hanns-Albert. 1970. "Revolutionäre Hintergründe des kreolischen Synkretismus. Soziale Aspekte der geheimen Religionsumwälzung im kolonialen (und nach- kolonialen) AfroAmerika." *Internationales Jahrbuch für Religionssoziologie* 6: 99–141.

Stern, Steve J. 1982. *Peru's Indian Peoples and the Challenge of Spanish Conquest: Huamanga to 1640*. Madison: University of Wisconsin Press.

—(ed.) 1987. *Resistance Rebellion and Consciousness in the Andean Peasant World, 18th to 20th Centuries*. Madison: University of Wisconsin Press.

Stutzman, Ronald. 1981. "El Mestizaje: An All Inclusive Ideology of Exclusion." In Whitten, ed. 1981, 45–94.

Szeminski, Jan. 1984. *La utopia tupamarista*. Lima: Pontificia Universidad Católica del Purú.

—1987. "Why Kill the Spaniard?" In Stern, ed. 1987, 166–92.

—1989. "El único español bueno es el español muerto: maten a los españoles." In Ansión, ed. 1989, 19–60.

Taylor, William B. 1987. "The Virgin of Guadalupe in New Spain: An Inquiry into the Social History of Marian Devotion." *American Ethnologist* 14: 9–33.

Thompson, Donald E. 1960. "Maya Paganism and Christianity." In Edmonson *et al.*, eds. 1960, 1–35.

Trexler, Richard C. 1982. "Aztec Priests for Christian Altars: The Theory and Practice of Reverence in New Spain." In *Scienze, credenze occulte, livelli di cultura*, 175–96. Firenze: L.S. Olschki.

Uchmany, Eva Alexandra. 1982. "Cambios religiosos en la conquista de Mexico." In Lorenzen, ed. 1982, 81–124.

Varón Gabai, Rafael. 1990. "EI Taki Onqoy: Las raíces andinas de un fenómeno colonial." In Millones, ed. 1990, 331–405.

Vrijhof, P. H., and J. Waardenburg, eds. 1979. *Official and Popular Religion*. The Hague: Mouton.

Wallace, A. F. C. 1956. "Revitalization Movements." *American Anthropologist* 58: 264–81; rpd. in Lessa and Vogt, eds. 1979, 421–29.

Wardman, Alan. 1982. *Religion and Statecraft among the Romans*. London: Granada.

Wasserstrom, Robert. 1982. "Indian Uprisings under Spanish Colonialism: Southern Mexico in 1712." In Weller and Guggenheim, eds. 1982, 42–56.

Watanabe, John M. 1990. "From Saints to Shibboleths: Image, Structure, and Identity in Maya Religious Syncretism." *American Ethnologist* 17: 131–50.

Weller Robert P., and Scott E. Guggenheim, eds. 1982. *Power and Protest in the Countryside: Studies of Rural Unrest in Asia, Europe, and Latin America*. Durham: Duke University Press.

Werblowsky, R. J. Z. 1987. "Synkretismus in der Religionsgeschichte." In Heissig and Klimkeit, eds. 1987, 1–7.

Whitten, Norman E., ed. 1981. *Cultural Transformations and Ethnicity in Modern Ecuador*. Urbana: University of Illinois Press.

Wiessner, Gernot, ed. 1978. *Synkretismusforschung. Theorie und Praxis*. Göttinger Orientforschungen, 1. Wiesbaden: Harrassowitz.

Wolf, Eric. 1958. "The Virgin of Guadalupe: A Mexican National Symbol." *Journal of American Folklore* 71: 34–39; repd. in Lessa and Vogt, eds. 1979, 112–15.

—ed. 1984. *Power and Protest in Local Communities: The Northern Shore of the Mediterranean*. Berlin: Mouton.

SYNCRETISM, POWER, PLAY

André Droogers

Introduction

In this contribution an effort will be made to explore the interrelationship between the three terms mentioned in the title.[1] The most logical way of proceeding is to discuss each of these terms in turn and then relate them to each other. But since my views on these themes are connected with those on culture and metaphor, I prefer to start with some remarks on the latter concepts, in the second section. In the third section, I then proceed to discuss power, a notion that is fundamental to my understanding of the concept of syncretism. A discussion of syncretism follows in section four. In discussing play, in section five, I intend to add an extra argument to my discussion of power and syncretism. Section six offers an illustrative case, taken from Afro-Brazilian religions. In the final section, a conclusion will be drawn.

Culture and Metaphor

Culture has been defined in many ways, but most often with reference to customs, traditions, ways of life; in short, as the concrete local result of some universal human capacity. In other words, culture has been used in two senses, first with a plural referring to the diversity of specific concrete cultures, but secondly in an exclusively singular sense, referring to a universal human capacity called culture. In the latter sense, human beings are contrasted with animals and are defined by their capacity to produce a concrete culture and cultures. Though perhaps somewhat confusing, it can be

217

said that the implication is that thanks to the universal culture (the exclusive singular) specific culture and cultures (the singular *and* the plural) can be produced.

Symbolic anthropology has focused on culture as a universal human capacity, understanding human beings as meaning-makers (Crick 1976). Culture can then be defined as the capacity to generate meaning. For the purpose of the study of religion and—more specifically—syncretism, this approach seems appropriate, since meaning is bestowed upon an invisible, not empirically verifiable, supernatural reality. As I intend to show, such a view concerning human beings is also promising when discussing power and play. In fact, the relationship between the three terms mentioned in the title can best be understood by reference to culture as the human capacity to generate meaning.

I hasten to add that I do not propose a purely actor-centred approach, as if each individual can start attributing meaning from scratch and on his or her own. There is of course a dialectic between actors on the one hand and the stock of social and symbolic structures of their society on the other hand. With J. C. Alexander (1990), I find a combination of mechanistic and subjectivistic approaches most promising: structural mechanisms and strategically operating actors together produce social and cultural reality. It is almost three decades since Berger and Luckmann launched their programmatic triptych: "Society is a human product. Society is an objective reality. Man is a social product" (1971, 79). Since then, several authors have suggested elaborations on the basis of this programme. The best known proposals are generally referred to as praxeological, praxis or practice theories (for an overview see Ortner 1984). When discussing syncretisms, I opt for such an approach.

To me, the dialectics suggested by this approach seem extremely relevant to the topic of this book [cf. *Sources*, p. xiv above]. From social and symbolic structures, imposing themselves through socialization, actors derive means and meanings to interpret events, but also to provoke them. This stock of symbolic and social structures is not static. Though a source of meanings, it is in turn subject to meaning-making activity. Especially when new events cannot be interpreted within the familiar framework, changes will occur.

In thus constructing and reconstructing their culture, people build and transform their identities. In this context, "reproduction" is an interesting term, since it points to static and faithful imitation as well as to reproduction with social and cultural structures being produced again. Schematically, this process can be represented by the "triangle of signification" (Figure 1).

There is one aspect of the human capacity to generate meaning that needs special reference. Meaning is produced by using tropes, among which metaphors are the most important. A metaphor pertains to two domains; what is evident in one domain clarifies what is unclear, "inchoate" (Fernandez 1986, *passim*) in the other. If social scientists depict society as an organism, or as a

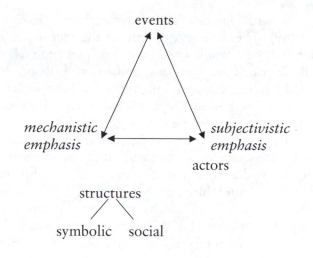

events

*mechanistic
emphasis*

*subjectivistic
emphasis*

actors

structures

symbolic   social

Figure 1.

pyramid, they are using metaphors—presenting clear images in order to clarify how that huge, complicated and abstract phenomenon "society" is structured. Meaning is derived from the clear image and applied in the interpretation of the new and unfamiliar. This is not a matter of just one meaning, but generally metaphors offer a plethora of meanings and can be reinterpreted so that new meanings are continually added. The metaphors "organism" and "pyramid" have proved a mine—and a mine field—of meanings, and therefore have contributed to our understanding, as well as misunderstanding: no comparison is perfect.

Metaphors are crucial to the field of religion—and to syncretism in particular. The possibility to develop metaphors is a condition for religious discourse. They serve two objectives. First, the very different experience of a strange, supernatural reality can be expressed through familiar secular metaphors: God is a father, and so on. Once established and defined, that same reality can itself serve as a stock of metaphors. In that case, religion's supernatural reality offers a more or less clear domain, including its corresponding meanings, as instruments that help to solve the ultimate questions human beings pose. Thus it is said: "You have to carry your own cross." Believers adopt this reality, populated by God, gods, spirits, saints, and so on, who give meaning to affliction and providence, to good and evil. The clear supernatural world contains a countless number of realities that in order to exist only need to be thought. They are not subject to empirical verification: they may be invisible, future or absent. In the case of syncretism, two or more sets of religious metaphors are available to the believers, who then can combine them in various ways.

However, some amending observations should be added. Next to metaphors, metonyms are widely used tropes. The difference between the two is that metonyms do with one domain what metaphors do with two (Leach 1976; Poewe 1989). The clearest example of the metonym is the *pars pro toto*, in which a part of a whole is taken to represent the whole: the crown has decided, the fleet counted five sails, and so on. In connection with religion, a striking difference between etic and emic viewpoints can be noted with regard to metaphor and metonym. What to the observer seems a case of metaphoric language may not be recognized by the believer, who instead would suggest—if she or he has knowledge of the terms—that a metonym is involved. This is a consequence of the fact that to the scientific observer, the supernatural reality is different from the observable reality, or is not even considered "real," and therefore another domain whereas to the believer there may be only one reality in which the observable and the supernatural coexist. If a Christian believes that the Holy Spirit is wind, the outside observer may understand and interpret this statement as an example of a metaphor, whereas to some believers the Spirit *is* wind and manifests itself as such. Similarly, in another Christian example, the cross may represent metaphorically Christ's death and the salvation he offers, whereas metonymically the cross *is* the reality of Christ's sufferings.

Power and Religion

Power has been defined in rather vague but also in very specific terms. A minimal definition of power focuses on the capacity to bring something about (van Baal 1981, 114; Morriss 1987, 46). Within the social sciences, this 'something' that is brought about is defined as a form of behaviour. Power then refers to the capacity of certain people to control the behaviour of others (Clegg 1989; Lukes 1986). This may seem to be a one-way street, an exclusive property of one person; but usually power is viewed as a bilateral relationship, a give-and-take, a push-and-pull, even though in most cases one side is in a dominant position.

In more specific definitions of power, a reference is made to the control of resources as an instrument of power. Though what is meant is often economic resources, for the study of religion and of syncretism it might make sense to think of religious resources, represented by God, gods, spirits, saints, and so on. Within religions, human power may be exercised through the management and control of these resources. Much of the division of labour within a religion has to do with the access to the ritual control of these supernatural resources. Moreover, meaning-making with regard to reality is often reserved for those in power. Syncretism implies access to a double stock of meanings, more often than not jealously guarded by competing religious elites who do not appreciate such mingling, and who will use their power to prevent it from happening.

Following this train of thought, a model can be developed for the study of religion—and, by implication, of syncretism—in which meaning-making and power come together. I do realize that reality is too complex to be translated into models. Yet what has been said above about metaphor has made us realize its bounties and boundaries. Therefore, I use models more as heuristic devices than as instruments for the explanation of phenomena. Since culture was defined above as the capacity to generate meaning, an interpretation of power presents itself that emphasizes the control of the access to meaning-making.

In any religious context, three dimensions can be distinguished: an internal, an external and a supernatural dimension. In two ways mechanistic and subjectivistic approaches are combined in such a distinction. First, it can be said that the internal and external dimensions are primarily social structural in nature, with their own mechanisms and regularities. The supernatural dimension can be viewed as primarily symbolic structural, with an emphasis on the actors' capacity to generate meaning through metaphors. However, this would be too simple a representation of a complex process. In dealing with internal and external social structures, actors use their capacity for meaning-making to deal with the roles these structures imply. Similarly, the supernatural dimension is approached by means of social structural metaphors, in order to organize the signification process with regard to the supernatural. So, in each dimension a mixture of mechanistic and subjectivistic elements is at work.

This will now be illustrated for each of the three dimensions, representing a second way in which mechanistic and subjective approaches are combined. In each dimension, two modes of religious construction will be distinguished, as the extremes of a whole spectrum of possibilities. These extremes must not be thought of as mutually exclusive: they may represent trends within a religion even though going in contrasting directions. They will be shown to correspond to the distinction between mechanistic and subjectivistic foci.

Thus, the *internal* dimension of a religion must be understood in the light of what has just been said about power and the division of labour. Certain people, considered religious specialists of some sort, have a right—legitimated by an appeal to—or a gift from, the supernatural, to occupy a leading position in the internal social structure and to represent it symbolically. They are, for example, supposed to produce and protect the right metaphor, the central image. The power at stake in such an internal social structure reinforces its continuation. Religions differ with regard to the degree in which religious specialists have a monopoly on the religious production. Elsewhere (Droogers and Siebers 1991, 15) I have distinguished between the extremes of a *hierarchical* and an *inclusivist* mode of religious construction, the latter allowing much space for the laity to behave as actors with a certain freedom, despite social structural constraints. Within Christianity, the Roman Catholic Church, with the Pope as its leader, is an example of the hierarchical mode, whereas the Quakers represent an inclusivist mode of religious construction. In addition, relationships between believers, as well as those between religious specialists, can be integrated into this dimension.

In the *external* dimension, let us first look at the case in which a religious group regards itself as exclusive. It is critical of its social and cultural context, including other religious groups, and may strive to impose itself on the surrounding society and thus seek expansion. Such a development can also be interpreted in terms of control of the access to meaning-making. The kind of meaning-making that is characteristic for that religion is presented as the only true one, in contrast to that of wider society. Because of its attitude towards society, I have called this (Droogers and Siebers 1991, 15) the *hostile* or transforming mode of religious construction. There is a subjectivist emphasis in this mode, believers acting in a transforming way. Within Christianity, Pentecostalism and minority groups, referred to as sects, present examples of this mode (Yinger 1970, 259–62). At the other extreme one finds a *sympathizing* or cooptative mode. In that case, no criticism is made, but instead approbation takes place. Religious and secular forms of power legitimate each other. Here the social structure of society imposes itself. Within Christianity, state churches provide an example.

One might also think of power in the third religious dimension, that of the relationship with the supernatural. Though different from the relationships in internal and external dimensions, this *supernatural* dimension also contains relationships in which power is exercised. These relationships are primarily metaphorical, but are modelled after the social structure of either the internal or external dimension: God is, for instance, pictured as a king. Consequentially, the Durkheimian view on religion emphasizes the social structural origin of religious experience. As was the case in the two earlier dimensions, within this dimension too the extreme forms of religious construction can be defined. At one end of the continuum, when believers experience a revelation, it means to them that God, gods or spirits powerfully transmit a form of meaning-making, thereby controlling the religious behaviour of the faithful in a supra-individual way. This might be called a *revelatory* mode of construction. Religious founders may experience such revelations; Moses and Mohammed are examples of this. Since power is a bilateral relationship, the corresponding contrasting mode is that people impose their meanings on God, gods and spirits and make them behave according to their will. Instead of mechanistic, there are subjectivistic overtones. This pole could be called the *explorative* mode of religious construction (Droogers and Siebers 1991, 15). The discussion on the presumed difference between religion and magic has focused on this distinction between revelation and manipulation. Interestingly, this explorative mode of religious construction has sometimes been treated pejoratively, especially where a distinction is made between a great and a little tradition, or between official and popular religion. This treatment of the explorative mode is a symptom of a hierarchical trend, a feature mentioned earlier when the internal dimension was discussed.

What has been said so far can be summarized in a table:

DIMENSION	categories *modes of religious construction*	
INTERNAL	religious specialists *hierarchical*	lay believers *inclusivist*
EXTERNAL	believers *hostile*	society *sympathizing*
SUPERNATURAL	God, gods, spirits *revelatory*	believers *explorative*

Table 1. *Modes of Religious Construction*

In each concrete religion, it is the constellation of the three dimensions, in combination with the six modes of religious construction, and the interrelationship between these components, that will determine that religion's particular profile. There need not be a consistent connection between the options in the three dimensions. The result may even contain contradictions, as a consequence of the complicated interplay between mechanistic and subjectivistic tendencies. It is the dynamics between the three dimensions, as well as between the extremes represented by the modes of religious construction in each dimension, that are part of the specificity of each case. In cases of syncretism this becomes even more complicated, since two or more religious constellations are in contact. The constellation of one particular religion can be graphically represented by a cube (Figure 2).[2] The model could substitute church-sect typologies that seem too restrictive and too much inspired by Christianity to be applicable to other religions.

Having discussed culture and metaphor, as well as power and religion, we are now in a position to consider syncretism. The term itself comes from a metaphor (Rudolph 1979, 194–96): Plutarch used the term to refer to the inhabitants of Crete who, when facing a common enemy, forgot their conflicts and joined forces. So syncretism appears to represent a process in which seemingly contrasting tendencies merge into a new consensus. In this sense, it has especially been used with reference to religious contact.

For a long time, the term has had a negative connotation, representing false religion over and against pure, uncontaminated and therefore true, religion. In fact, this depreciative view on syncretism is one of four types of interpretation (see Rudolph 1979 for a useful overview). This first type has mainly been used by Christian theologians, in defence of the pureness of their religion.

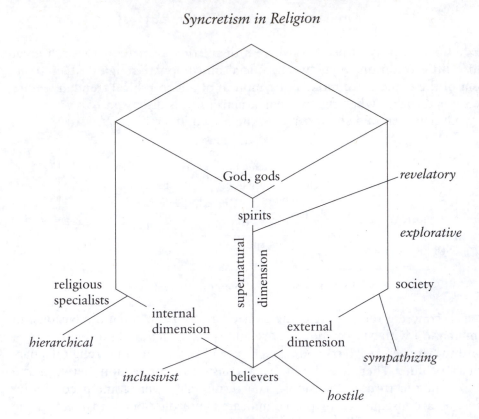

Figure 2.

Syncretism

The second interpretation of the term is meant to be more objective and neutral, and is common among phenomenologists and students of comparative religion. Its proponents want to avoid a value judgment; they limit themselves to the study of the mixing of different religious traditions into a new one (for instance, Berner 1978; Ringgren 1969). A number of distinctions have been made in interpreting the phenomenon. Thus:

- The emphasis may be either on the process or on the result. Some prefer to speak of syncretization when emphasizing the process. When dealing with the result, various degrees of integration and synthesis have been distinguished, such as symbiosis, amalgamation, acculturation, metamorphosis, identification, dissolution and some other forms (Colpe 1975, 21–23; Rudolph 1979, 207–10).
- Another emphasis depends on whether the two religions in contact have a symmetrical or an asymmetrical relationship, that is, whether one of the religions dominates the other even though influenced by the other.
- One also distinguishes between a receiving and a visiting religion.

- Another distinction made is between conscious, purposeful, constructed syncretism on the one hand and unconscious, implicit, spontaneous, popular, almost natural—though that may also be called cultural—mixing of religious traditions on the other.
- A final distinction one might make is that between a functional and a substantial approach to syncretism. The first asks what syncretism *does*, the second what syncretism *is*.

Then there is a third option, which will only be mentioned here for completeness, namely to see syncretism as a positive phenomenon. Some of the new religions represent such a view.

In the fourth place, there is the option to abolish the term throughout (for instance, Baird 1970, 142–52). The main reason suggested is that the phenomenon of the mixing of traditions is so widespread that the term is not specific enough to be of any use. Besides, the supposed syncretists themselves do not use the term.

My suggestion, and that would represent option number five, has been not to abandon the term (Droogers 1989), but to add to it the perspective of power (cf. Bourdieu 1971). As has been pointed out, when the model of the three dimensions in religion was presented, power is essential to the internal, external, and supernatural dimension.

- With regard to the internal dimension, the first option, the negative judgment on syncretism, is illustrative. It points to a struggle between official and so-called illegitimate producers of religion.
- As to the external dimension, because syncretism implies the influence of another religion, it is also relevant.
- The supernatural dimension has influence because it can be used either to legitimate or to condemn the intermingling of religions. Once the gods or Gods of different religions are said to be the same, and religious experience seems to confirm this, mixing is justified. However, if the God of a religion is presented as exclusive or even "jealous," syncretism is heresy.

Considering the constellation of power as represented by the combined dimensions, legitimate producers of religion will normally defend their monopoly against trespassers, either from within their religious organization (the internal dimension) or from without (the external dimension), and will call them syncretists, meaning to pass a very negative judgment on them, justified by an appeal to notions from the supernatural powers. This is the main reason why syncretists rarely identify themselves by that name.

So it seems that it is not just the coexistence of disparate religious influences that is typical of syncretism, but much more the fact that this coexistence may be subject to debate and strife, or even persecution. The power aspect that is present in each of the three dimensions will play a role in this process. In this way the emphasis is not only on the religious intermingling as such, but much more on the way the concept itself is applied.

My intention on adding the dimension of power to the definition of syncretism is not to adopt the negative connotation, but to include the possibility that syncretism is an expression of a power struggle. My criticism of the more neutral approach of comparative religion, as represented by the second interpretation, is that it seems to ignore this power dimension, focusing predominantly on the mixing of religious influences itself.

However, I must admit that in some cases the power aspect seems to be absent. Even official producers of religion may take a very tolerant stance and integrate whatever they find worthwhile. Yet, in that case they are also using their power. But in other cases, when religious leaders are critical of syncretism, their views may be highly selective, concentrating on certain obvious points, and leaving others unobserved. So in the end, amending a more objective definition of syncretism, I have proposed the following definition of syncretism: "religious interpenetration, either taken for granted or subject to debate" (Droogers 1989, 20 f.).

It may seem superfluous, yet I would like to add that syncretism is not a process that is marginal to the world religions, only occasionally happening to and between them but, as it were, without them, as if they themselves were immune to the penetration of foreign religious ideas. At the origin of a religion, syncretist processes are often essential to the formation of that religion, as has happened most clearly in Islam, but also in Buddhism and Christianity. Once a religion is established and religious founders have completed its codification, these syncretist origins are often forgotten. Yet, syncretism may occur also after the foundational phase. Popular religion is of course a field in which syncretism is very much present, but even in official religion it can be found, despite the pureness professed by its proponents. It is not uncommon that official religion adopts ideas from popular religion. In terms of power relations, this may be part of a process in which the power balance changes to a certain degree.

Metaphors have a central role in the syncretic process. If they serve to clarify events that occur to believers, the thirst for clarification brings people to drink from various sources. The possibilities available to the interpreter of events are especially numerous in situations characterized by religious pluralism. The need to use them may correspond to feelings of crisis and affliction, as happens in Afro-Brazilian religions, but it may also be stimulated by a purely religious or even intellectual interest, as happens in New Age movements.

Metaphors may exist by themselves and be used as autonomous data, but most often are part of a pattern and represent a way of thinking. It would therefore be misleading to present syncretism, as sometimes happens, merely as a borrowing or exchange of elements, since these elements, more often than not, are part of a structure. Their adoption may mean that they become part of another structural context. This may even change their meaning. Since metaphors have a rich potential of meanings, change will be common. On the other hand, syncretic processes may be stimulated by similarity in metaphors, meanings and patterns. Types of syncretism could be distinguished according to the degree of change in metaphors, meanings and patterns, as compared to the contributing religious traditions. Some of the terms Colpe and Rudolph suggest, as mentioned above, could be applied to these types.

An approach through metaphors, meanings and patterns should be accompanied by a focus on the people using them, even though structural constraints are always present to some degree. These actors are the architects of the new symbolic and social structures that emerge from the syncretic process. The context in which they act orients them in their choices. As was observed above, what presents itself as a metaphor to the outsider may have the characteristics of a metonym to the believer. This involves a reduction of two domains to a single one, a process and way of thinking not unlike what is happening in syncretism.

Power relations are part of the context, in the internal religious dimension (as just mentioned when I presented my definition) but also in the external and supernatural dimensions. My hypothesis is that each of the six modes of religious construction presented above can be said to have consequences for the chances that syncretic processes will take place. This can be verified in each of the three dimensions, either in one of the religions involved, or in both, or with regard to the result of the process: a syncretic religion. All depends on the case that one studies.

In the internal dimension the *hierarchical* mode represents a situation of strong control of the production of religion. This means that non-specialists have few chances to contribute to the process of religious construction. On the other hand, it is possible that exactly the hierarchical climate provokes a reaction in which people seek to produce their own interpretations. Popular Catholicism has in that way accompanied official Catholicism. When, in the same internal dimension, we look at the other extreme—at the *inclusivist* mode—it is obvious that here syncretism may be very much present. Popular religion will predominate and will produce its own new versions (Rostas and Droogers 1993).

In the external dimension, the *hostile* exclusive mode will not allow much room for syncretism, as happens with Pentecostalism and with evangelical churches, even though from the internal viewpoint they are of the inclusivist type. This is opposed to the *sympathizing* mode where the embrace between religion and society opens many chances for syncretism to occur—as happens for example in Islam in sub-Saharan Africa—despite its revelatory emphasis on the supernatural dimension.

When we take a look at the supernatural dimension, a *revelatory* mode of religious production may prevent syncretism because of the emphasis on the given religion. An *explorative* mode will represent the opposite side, because it will stimulate syncretism as people seek assistance from God, gods and spirits, wherever they come from. This latter attitude will be common where there is a need for solutions in cases of affliction.

Interestingly, this means that the modes of religious construction that reveal more subjectivistic than mechanistic characteristics are more open to syncretism. The space allowed to actors, despite ever-present social structural constraints, makes for initiatives that lead in the direction of syncretism. Where a mechanistic emphasis predominates, with social structural constraints limiting actors' space, syncretism will have less chances to come about.

Turner's distinction (1969) between structure and anti-structure comes to mind. Structure is meant by him as social structure, whereas anti-structure represents an abundance of symbolic structure. The marginal or liminal context allows for experiments in symbolism since the social structural constraints are temporarily ineffective. Syncretism flourishes in such a climate.

Similarly, Moore's distinction (1975, 234 f.) between processes of regularization and processes of situational adjustment can be helpful in interpreting the occurrence of syncretism. Both processes respond to situations of indeterminacy, or the inchoate as Fernandez (1986) would put it. Regularization is the effort "to fix social reality, to harden it; to give it form and order and predictability" (Moore 1975, 234). Few things remain for real negotiation because most events are easily classifiable. In the case of situational adjustment, people react by "exploiting the indeterminacies in the situation, or by generating such indeterminacies, or by reinterpreting or redefining the rules or relationships. They use whatever areas there are of inconsistency, contradiction, conflict, ambiguity ..." (1975, 234). Obviously, syncretism has the best chances in the case of situational adjustment. Contradiction and ambiguity are no problem at all—on the contrary, they stimulate syncretic processes. When regularization is opted for, social structural constraints will prevent syncretic deviation. A religion's leaders will more readily opt for regularization; common believers may follow them, but may also opt for situational adjustment, including the syncretic possibility.

Play

The notion of play does not add structurally to the model that has been developed so far in this paper. Yet it draws attention to dimensions of syncretism that seem relevant. It emphasizes the human capacity to generate meaning and the role actors fulfil, thereby reinforcing the conclusion reached at the end of the preceding section. Besides, through play, an over-reductionist view on religion and syncretism can be avoided. Before elaborating on these two points, some general remarks on the concept of play should be made.

Play is a rather anarchistic term. It is ambiguous and vague. It is used for such diverse activities as sports, children's play, animals' play, political power games, theatre, and so on. Since it is so diversely used in discussions about play's characteristics and its definition, categories are blurred and boundaries become relative. Ironically, that is exactly what syncretism seems to be about. Therefore some kinship exists between the two concepts. It is worthwhile to elaborate on these kin terms.

One source of the diversity in opinions about play is the circumstance that authors from a variety of disciplines have written about it, including historians (e.g. Huizinga 1952), ethologists (e.g. Bateson 1973), theologians (e.g. Pannenberg 1984), psychologists (e.g. F. Alexander 1958; Erikson 1977; Winnicott 1971), philosophers (e.g. Gadamer 1975), social scientists (e.g. Elias 1971; Handelman 1987; Turner 1982, 1988; van Baal 1972) and others, all giving their own interpretations.

It is impossible to do justice to all these different phenomena and approaches. One solution might be to propose an ideal-type or a family-resemblance description, indicating at least some of the potential defining characteristics. Thus it can be said that play is a way of exploring the unknown, of trial and error, of *bricolage*. It includes the possibility of the impossible, the surprise of the unexpected, the hunch of the unthinkable, the liberty of the intuition. Turner (1988, 25, 169) has called this the "subjunctive" in play, the "as if," as opposed to the "indicative," the "as is." In Moore's terms, play presupposes situational adjustment, much more than regularization. Though play is viewed as an activity that lacks a purpose, as a subjunctive process, it must be practised in a serious manner, as if it were a normal indicative. Play therefore moves between the poles of playing-just-for-fun and playing fanatically. In the latter case it may be necessary to remind the player: "it is only a game." Despite the "as if," play has its own obliging frame of reference, its own rules, even when these are invented on the spot, developed in the course of the game, as children love to do. Because of this obliging force, it is an instrument in power relations, as when we say that somebody plays with another person. Inversely, it can also obtain an anti-authoritarian, anarchic trait, as when fun is made of authorities (carnival, rituals of rebellion). Play allows for the creation of a separate reality, as in games, outside normal reality, but real to those who play along. This is of course what happens in religions too. Yet, in religion the subjunctivity of play seems to have disappeared behind the indicative, because normally the "other" reality is taken so seriously that all play seems to have been forgotten. This tendency also occurs in the use of metaphors, which may explain religion's seriousness, since metaphors are essential to religion. Play is present in metaphorical language, especially in the arbitrariness of the link between two separate domains. Here too the indicative may impose itself. The fiction of an identity between the two domains is taken seriously as long as it helps to clarify things. But at a certain moment the metonymic indicative seems to take over from the metaphoric subjunctive. The two realities involved in play then turn into one. This corresponds with the delicate mix of serious play. In summary: play is the capacity to deal simultaneously and subjunctively with two or more ways of classifying reality.

When play is defined in this way, the kinship with syncretism becomes even more visible. It is in giving attention to the playful dimension of syncretism—including its relatedness to power, religion and metaphor—that the process of human meaning-making may become more visible. The attitude that play represents can be discerned in syncretic processes. In them religious boundaries are explored and crossed. This quest is executed in a serious manner, but also with *Entdeckersfreude*. Syncretism often is a way of playing with metaphors, their levels of meaning and their patterns. Since play cannot occur on its own, it includes the actor's role in the production of syncretism.

Though metonym has been described as pertaining to one domain instead of two, as was the case with metaphor, a similar duality is present, allowing for play to occur. Since in the metonym a part or aspect represents the whole, here too a double perspective is used. Play, as the capacity to deal with two perspectives at the same time, makes use of metonyms as well.

As Fernandez (1986, 188–213) has made clear, tropes such as metaphor and metonym help to create the sensation of wholeness, despite the fragmentation of experience in reality. Thus the two domains metaphor deals with are combined through the bridge of metaphor. Similarly, metonym reunites part of a domain with the domain as a whole. Syncretism is one way of combining disparate domains in order to give at least an illusion of belonging and togetherness. The claims from opposed sides are reconciled in a new synthesis that combines the best of both worlds, at least to the believer.

This approach implies caution against over-zealous reductionist approaches to syncretism and—by extension—to religion. Even though contextual factors of a structural nature can and must be shown to have influenced syncretic and other religious processes, the dialectic between structural mechanisms on the one hand and the actors' subjectivisms on the other should not be forgotten. The concept of play can be helpful in this context, because it confirms the conclusion that syncretism flourishes when the emphasis is on subjectivist creative space, rather than on mechanistic constraints. The attention given in this paper to power relations should on the other hand compensate the opposite procedure: an over-zealous actor approach. Though such an approach—more than a mechanistic structural approach—would reveal the playfulness in religion and syncretism, a reliable picture of religious reality can only be attained when both approaches join forces in a dialectical view.

An Illustrative Case

In Afro-Brazilian religions, spirit possession occupies a central place. These religions have often been presented as clear cases of syncretism (for instance, Bastide 1978). In their rise, at least two and sometimes four religions may have been involved, providing the sources, depending on the case. African religions and Catholicism have been important origins, but Amerindian religions and French spiritism have also had widespread influence. The various types of Afro-Brazilian religion that came about in the course of the last two centuries differ as to the mixture they have realized. Thus the Candomblé of Bahia, one of the eldest forms, is much more African than the later Macumba of Rio de Janeiro, which in turn is more African than the more recent Umbanda (Birman 1983; Brown 1985; Droogers 1985; Luz and Lapassade 1972; Turner 1988, 33–71).

Historically speaking, the descendants of the African slaves, brought to Brazil, were for a long time the principal actors in this syncretic process. Though slaves seem to represent the most extreme case of subjection to structural constraints, it was exactly this limitation of freedom that stimulated the search for strategic compensation, and thereby was an incentive to the religious imagination. By imposing Catholicism, the powers-that-were at that time have contributed indirectly to the rise of the Afro-Brazilian religions. Rupture and continuity were to go hand in hand, also after slavery was abolished. In fact, Brazilians from all strands in the population can be said to have contributed to the syncretic process that produced and reproduced these religions. Local forms were developed, each reflecting the particular context. The currently most popular wing among Afro-Brazilian religions, Umbanda, emerged only in this century. Though it has been characterized as "the white death of the black magician" (Ortiz 1978), its de-Africanization made it acceptable to Brazilians of non-African descent, especially the white middle-class that was already interested in French spiritism. Its rise is an indication of the ongoing process of syncretic signification in a country where, in a complex manner, a variety of cultures come together and interact.

The aspects of syncretism that have been presented in this paper can be illustrated with reference to Afro-Brazilian religions. When the slaves were brought to Brazil, they were subjected to their masters' power and were supposed to behave as converted Catholics. Yet, at the same time the African religious representations and rituals had not been left behind and could serve as a counter-power. The outward behaviour of the slaves may have satisfied their masters, but behind the cult to saints, West African gods, especially those from the Yoruba pantheon, were being venerated. Some of these were used against the slave masters. Besides, a strategic syncretism was developed. This was possible because certain characteristics of these gods were similar to those of popular Catholic saints. In this way, Yemanjá, the goddess of the sea, could be identified with the Virgin Mary, especially in her role as Stella Maris, or as Our Lady of the Sailors (*Nossa Senhora dos Navegantes*). Ogum, god of warfare and of the blacksmiths, became identified with St. George, who with his sword killed the dragon. Nowadays, in the temples of the Afro-Brazilian religions, an altar with statuettes of saints, with incense and candles, occupies a central place.

Through an imaginative play with metaphors and metonyms, people of African descent could take part in the events that characterized the colonial society, but at the same time defend and maintain their identity. From the margins of that society, they succeeded in dealing simultaneously with two realities. What is more, from these two realities they constructed a new reality of their own. This new reality was incorporated literally through spirit possession. The metaphoric supernatural reality became metonymic by means of spirit mediumship, the medium representing the gods and spirits.

The Brazilians of African descent dealt with double realities in a very playful manner. The indeterminacy that was so imposingly present in their life was put to use in order to find a satisfying situational adjustment. Thus, even though within the power context slaves had to obey, they nevertheless succeeded in conquering a space of their own. Sometimes this space was already available, because of racial segregation, as happened in Catholic lay brotherhoods of the so-called third order. Sometimes it had to be conquered, as happened in the *quilombos*, the small states founded by fugitive slaves. Once the *terreiros*, the Afro-Brazilian temples, were tolerated in the public sphere, as happened from the end of the eighteenth century, the believers could operate within their own ambience.

Because meaning-making and power were closely related, the syncretic process can be analysed by means of the three dimensions and the six modes of religious construction developed earlier. This can be illustrated, first by discussing the dimensions in Catholicism, then those in the Afro-Brazilian, religions. As it is not possible, within the limited context of this article, to analyse this syncretism from the point of view of each of the contributing four religions, I will limit myself to one of the four, and to the view from within the result of this syncretic process: the Afro-Brazilian religions themselves.

The rise of Afro-Brazilian religions has long been criticized in the internal dimension of the Roman Catholic Church, where a hierarchical mode of religious production was common. This hierarchical way of constructing religion protected the official version of the Catholic faith, with its emphasis on supernatural revelation. With regard to the external dimension, the Catholic Church was much more sympathizing than hostile to civil society. As a consequence, Brazilian civil authorities have co-operated in combating the groups that held Afro-Brazilian sessions. These religions were viewed as a form of unauthorized religious production. Social structural constraints were strong and until recently persecution was considered normal by Brazilian authorities.

From the point of view of the adepts of Afro-Brazilian religions, the external dimension represented to them a lot of affliction, which called for a religious expression and remedy. Afro-Brazilian syncretism has also been interpreted as a form of resistance. The masters of the slaves feared the "black" magic directed against them. So also with regard to the external dimension, power relations are important. In the supernatural dimension, the African gods gave to the believers the religious power that was expressed in spirit possession. The identification with the Catholic saints reinforced this effect. This power from spirit possession stimulated syncretism, since every spirit medium is a legitimate producer of religion. Within the groups, the mode of religious production is much more inclusivist than hierarchical, though the leader—often a woman—may occupy a central place in the power relations.

Even today, these groups are rarely allowed to use Catholic churches for their celebrations. Though individual parish priests, especially black Brazilians, sometimes take a sympathizing position, the hierarchy does not seek dialogue with the groups. In compensation, the civil authorities have recently become much more tolerant in their attitude and it is common that politicians seek support from Afro-Brazilian groups, not only at the polls, but also in a spiritual way. In that sense, the power relation has been inverted in the course of time and civil rehabilitation is currently taking place.

This has even led to the beginnings of a desyncretization process, initiated by militants from black consciousness movements. Now that the Afro-Brazilian religions have gradually been rehabilitated, these militants no longer see the strategic need for syncretism. They defend an Afro-Brazilian religion that is devoid of Catholic elements and influences. A return to the African roots has been adopted as a program. This trend illustrates the ongoing process of meaning-making within a context in which relations of power play a decisive role. It also shows the dialectics between social structural conditions and actors' initiatives. Where before syncretism was a strategic necessity, now purism is felt as inevitable.

Conclusion

In this contribution, an effort has been made to produce a model for the anthropological study of syncretism. Accordingly, special attention has been given to syncretism as a cultural phenomenon. This has led to a focus on meaning and metaphor: more specifically, following a praxis-type approach (Ortner 1984), on the way actors deal with them within a context of power relations. In order to specify this latter aspect, relations of power have been identified within a religious context, distinguishing between an internal, external and a supernatural dimension. In each of these dimensions two modes of religious construction have been distinguished. The chances that syncretic processes will take place have been studied in a tentative manner. It was suggested that syncretism flourishes where playfulness gets a chance, that is, where social structural constraints are less imposing and where actors' subjectivity and subjunctivity are offered space. Though the internal dimension is the most important in the case of syncretism, the two other levels are also relevant, since the three levels form one dynamic constellation in which power relations are important. The value of this exercise should be established through further tests within the ethnographic experience.

Notes

1. Special thanks to the organizers of the IASSA Gothenburg Anthropological Summer Festival, June 7–9, 1993, for their invitation; to the participants for their comments, particularly Göran Aijmer and Gerd Baumann.
2. I am grateful to Gerd Baumann for his suggestion to represent the three dimensions as a cube.

References

Alexander, F. 1958. "A Contribution to the Theory of Play." *Psychoanalytic Quarterly* 27: 175–93.

Alexander, J. C. 1990. "Analytic Debates: Understanding the Relative Autonomy of Culture." In *Culture and Society: Contemporary Debates*, ed. J. C. Alexander and S. Seidman. Cambridge: Cambridge University Press.

Baal, Jan van. 1972. *De boodschap der drie illusies: Overdenkingen over religie, kunst en spel*. Assen: van Gorcum.

—1981. *Man's Quest for Partnership: The Anthropological Foundations of Ethics and Religion*. Assen: van Gorcum.

Baird, R. D. 1970. *Category Formation and the History of Religions*. Den Haag: Mouton de Gruyter.

Bastide, Roger. 1978. *The African Religions of Brazil: Towards a Sociology of the Interpenetrations of Civilizations*. Baltimore and London: Johns Hopkins University Press.

Bateson, Gregory. 1973. *Steps to an Ecology of Mind: Collected Essays in Anthropology, Psychiatry, Evolution and Epistemology.* Baltimore and London: Johns Hopkins University Press.

Berger, Peter L., and Thomas Luckmann. 1971. *The Social Construction of Reality: A Treatise in the Sociology of Knowledge.* Harmondsworth: Penguin.

Berner, Ulrich. 1978. "Heuristisches Modell der Synkretismus-Forschung (Stand August 1977). Das 'Synkretismus-Modell' als Instrument einer historischen Religionsphänomenologie." In *Synkretismusforschung: Theorie und Praxis*, ed. G. Wiessner, 11–26. Wiesbaden: Harrassowitz.

Birman, P. 1983. *O que é umbanda.* São Paulo: Brasiliense.

Bourdieu, Pierre. 1971. "Genèse et structure du champ religieux." *Revue Francaise de Sociologie* 12: 295–334.

Brown, D. 1985. "Uma história da umbanda no Rio." In *Umbanda e Política*, ed. D. Brown *et al.* Rio de Janeiro: Marco Zero.

Clegg, S. R. 1989. *Frameworks of Power.* London: Sage.

Colpe, C. 1975. "Synkretismus, Renaissance, Säkularisation und Neubildung von Religionen in der Gegenwart." In *Handbuch der Religionsgeschichte*, vol. 3, ed. J. Asmussen, J. Laessøe and C. Colpe. Göttingen: Vandenhoeck & Ruprecht.

Crick, Malcolm. 1976. *Explorations in Language and Meaning: Towards a Semantic Anthropology.* London: Malaby Press.

Droogers, A. 1985. *É a umbanda?* São Leopoldo: Sinodal.

—1989. "Syncretism: The Problem of Definition, the Definition of the Problem." In *Dialogue and Syncretism: An Interdisciplinary Approach*, ed. J. Gort, H. Vroom, R. Fernhout and A. Wessels, 7–25. Amsterdam: Editions Rodopi.

Droogers, A., and H. Siebers. 1991. "Popular Religion and Power in Latin America." In *Popular Power in Latin American Religions*, ed. A. Droogers *et al.* Saarbrücken: Breitenbach.

Elias, Norbert. 1971. *Wat is sociologie?* Utrecht: Spectrum.

Erikson, Erik H. 1977. *Toys and Reasons: Stages in the Ritualization of Experience.* New York: W.W. Norton.

Fernandez, J. W. 1986. *Persuasions and Performances: The Play of Tropes in Culture.* Bloomington: Indiana University Press.

Gadamer, Hans-Georg. 1975. *Truth and Method.* New York: Seabury Press.

Handelman, D. 1987. "Play." In *The Encyclopedia of Religion*, vol. 11, ed. M. Eliade. New York: Macmillan.

Huizinga, J. 1952. *Homo Ludens: Proeve eener bepaling van het spel-element der cultuur.* Haarlem: Tjeenk Willink.

Leach, Edmund R. 1976. *Culture and Communication: The Logic by which Symbols are Connected.* Cambridge: Cambridge University Press.

Lukes, S., ed. 1986. *Power.* Oxford: Basil Blackwell.

Luz, M.A., and G. Lapassade. 1972. *O Segredo da Macumba.* Rio de Janeiro: Paz e Terra.

Moore, Sally F. 1975. "Epilogue: Uncertainties in Situations, Indeterminacies in Culture." In *Symbol and Politics in Communal Ideology: Cases and Questions*, ed. Sally F. Moore and B. G. Myerhoff. Ithaca, NY: Cornell University Press.

Morriss, P. 1987. *Power: A Philosophical Analysis.* Manchester: Manchester University Press.

Ortiz, R. 1978. *A morte brance do feticeiro Negro, Umbanda: Integracão de uma religião numa sociedade de classes.* Petrópolis: Vozes.

Ortner, Sherry B. 1984. "Theory in Anthropology Since the Sixties." *Comparative Studies in Society and History* 10: 121–41.

Pannenberg, W. 1984. *Anthropologie in theologischer Perspektive.* Göttingen: Vanderhoeck & Ruprecht.

Poewe, K. 1989. "On the Metonymic Structure of Religious Experiences: The Example of Charismatic Christianity." *Cultural Dynamics* 2: 361–80.

Ringgren, Helmer. 1969. "The Problem of Syncretism." In *Syncretism*, ed. Sven Hartman, 7–14. Stockholm: Almqvist & Wiksell.

Rostas, S., and A. Droogers, eds. 1993. *Popular Use of Popular Religion in Latin America*. Amsterdam: Centre for Latin American Research and Documentation (CEDLA).

Rudolph, Kurt. 1979. "Synkretismus—von theologischen Scheltwort zum Religionswissen-schaftlichen Begriff." In *Humanitas Religiosa: Festschrift für Haralds Biezais zu seinem 70. Geburtstag*, 193–212. Stockholm: Almqvist & Wiksell.

Turner, Victor W. 1969. *The Ritual Process: Structure and Anti-Structure*. Ithaca, NY: Cornell University Press.

—1982. *From Ritual to Theatre: The Human Seriousness of Play*. New York: PAJ Publications.

—1988. *The Anthropology of Performance*. New York: PAJ Publications.

Winnicott, D. W. 1971. *Playing and Reality*. London: Tavistock.

Yinger, J. M. 1970. *The Scientific Study of Religion*. New York and London: Macmillan.

WORLDS IN COLLUSION: ON SOCIAL STRATEGIES AND MISREPRESENTATIONS AS FORCES OF SYNCRETISM IN EURO-AMERICAN AND NATIVE AMERICAN AFFAIRS

Armin W. Geertz

A long-time study of Hopi millennial prophecy has led me to the conclusion that Hopi prophecies are fluid in nature primarily due to political intrigue and strategy.[1] I found that prophecy is a kind of intellectual currency which some people own and others try to get in order to achieve social and political goals. Prophecy is clearly a mechanism for incorporating contemporary affairs into the framework of traditional religious values, for evaluating those affairs in terms of conceived tradition, and for interpreting and judging those affairs on the authority of conceived tradition. Seen in this light, prophecy is primarily a rhetorical device and is pivotal to social and political strategies.

I found it useful to characterize the ways in which prophecies are used, identify interest groups who manipulate the cosmological mythology, and identify the themes which are meaningful to these groups. The strategic use of religious narrative seems to fall into the following functional categories:

1. Myth as a strategy to establish (or maintain) ethnic identity and/or internal socio-political structures;
2. Myth as a strategy to resist the dominant White society;
3. Myth as a strategy to attract subversive interest groups in the dominant White society;
4. The use of Hopi myths by White interest groups as a strategy to search for an identity;

5. The use of Hopi myths by White interest groups as a strategy to resist their own society; and

6. Myth as a strategy to re-create psycho-social stability and meaning.

The categories reflect a historical progression where categories 1–3 and 6 are employed by Hopis, category 6 representing a recent conscious reflection and regeneration, whereas categories 4 and 5 are strategies employed by Whites.

I hope to show in this paper how a symbolic syncretism, shared by separate cultures and based on mutual misrepresentation due to differing social strategies, has left a lasting impact on the cultures involved. I will also attempt to explain how and why this type of syncretism occurs.

The term syncretism has all too often functioned as a derogative term. Historian of religions Robert D. Baird argued against the implications of the term syncretism because it is based on a search for origins that runs counter to the historical method (Baird 1971, 145). His argument was that "such borrowing, blending, and influencing on the plane of history is part of the whole historical process and is both inevitable and universal," and, therefore, no real purpose is served by using the term. As he wrote: "Historically speaking, to say that 'Christianity' or the 'mystery religions' or 'Hinduism' are syncretistic is not to say anything that distinguishes them from anything else" (146). To insist on using the term to characterize certain religions implies that they have brought together elements that are conflicting and illegitimate. Besides the implicit theological and ethnocentric value judgment, the term diverts attention from one of the central aspects of religion, namely, that it serves as a creative mechanism for producing and reproducing unity, meaning, and meaningful relationships even in the face of inconsistencies.

With these caveats in mind, it is still useful for us to study the elements that are brought together and the mechanisms that are brought to play in the collision of cultures. More specifically, I am primarily interested in what happens when cultures in collision become cultures in collusion.

The Prophetic Core

Hopi prophecies about the end of the world are usually narrated as integrated portions of the emergence mythology. Emergence mythology deals with prior cycles of existence that humanity has gone through in three subterranean worlds. Each world begins as a type of paradise but ends in cataclysmic destruction due to the evil propensities of humanity. No less so in the world before this one when the faithful were forced to climb through a giant reed that pierced the floor of this world in order to escape the terrors of a primordial catastrophe. It is therefore evident that the central narrative in Hopi cosmology is apocryphal in its very framework.

The prophetic element appeared when the survivors met with the tutelary of the fourth world, Maasaw. The people asked him for land and they became lease-holders on the condition that one day in the future they would surrender the land in good shape to Maasaw. They asked him to become their leader, but he refused and pointed out that they had brought evil ambitions and intentions with them so he would one day have to return to punish and cleanse them. How Maasaw is to return and what the signs of his coming may be are subject to lively debate among the Hopis today, as in the past.

The Hopis had an older White brother who holds a stone tablet or a piece of a stone tablet identical to the one held by his Hopi brother. The end of the world, called Nuutungk, Talöngvaqa, "The Last Day," will be heralded by the return of the White brother with his tablet and will be carried out by Maasaw as the *powataniqa*, "the one who will purify." Some stories are not very specific, but others speak of his weapon *qöötsaptanga*, "container of ashes," and others speak of beheadings. All are in agreement that the purification will result in a new paradise.

This basic narrative constitutes the framework for the various myths, legends, and historical narratives about each individual matriclan. The emergence myth is emphasized both individually and collectively in hundreds of ways in social praxis. In fact, it can be shown that every ceremonial and social drama either refers explicitly to this narrative or assumes it. The narrative provides powerful instruments for the creation and maintenance of meaning and significance. It especially provides continuity through mythological coherence, structural coherence in social and religious domains, and a coherent frame of reference for each individual.

Until the rise of the Traditionalist Movement during the 1940s, the knowledge attached to the clan myths and to the narratives of the secret brotherhoods were kept secret. Peter Whiteley noted in his 1987 paper on Hopi politics that a primary source of power in Hopi society lies in *esoteric* ritual knowledge. Drawing on recent anthropological discussions of the political effects of secret knowledge, Whiteley indicated that "through secrecy, knowledge takes on the character of property" (1987, 703). Seen in this perspective, "secret knowledge can be used ... as a medium of social value and a calculus of social differentiation" (704). This knowledge is gained through gradual initiation throughout the life of an individual, but even in the upper echelons of knowledge, the hierarchy pervades so that the most knowledgeable are the oldest members of the clan elite—the *kiikyam* or *pavansinom*.

The Traditionalist Movement as an integral part of their political strategy attempted to change this hegemony through the exposure of supposed esoteric knowledge to non-Hopi audiences. I will return to this problem below.

Mistaken Identities: Part One

The entrance of Europeans on the historical horizon provoked a search for an explanation and interpretation of such a world-shattering event. From the curious behaviour that the Hopis have evinced during actual historical contacts with White people, it is clear that each White visitor is appraised in terms of Hopi apocryphal expectations. Their reactions often indicate a collective misrepresentation of the Other. Homer Cooyama from Kykotsmovi told folklorist Harold Courlander in 1970:

> There were two main things the Hopis were looking for in the old days, a promised land and a promised person. These things were prophesied. Religious Hopis are still looking for the promised place where they are supposed to settle. We've discussed these things many times in the kiva.[2] The person they are expecting is said to be a bahana, a white man, who will arrive in great glory. Everybody knows this belief. (Courlander 1982, 125 f.)

The Hopis have nurtured a messianic expectation which measures each and every White person who happens to show up on the Reservation. The highly agglomerate gathering of diverse peoples and interests at Hopiland—a sort of international congestion—is an unfortunately common occurrence. Living on the borders of imperialistic neighbours since before the rise of the Aztecs, the Hopis have had their share of strange visitors.

The Hopis have been waiting for centuries, first accepting and then rejecting one White group after another as the White brother. But with each passing European or American, they became disappointed and disgusted. From missionaries to government officials and on to the many American movements that have visited the Hopis, speculation increased, debate became heated, and families and villages have been split.

Some Hopis are convinced that the Americans are the White brother and that the new era has already begun. Others reject the idea and find more meaning in clinging to their eschatological hopes and dreams.

During a series of hearings conducted by a Bureau of Indian Affairs (BIA) team on the reservation in 1955, Earl Murrizewa at Walpi believed them to be the White brother. His speech depicted the primordial bonds between the BIA team and himself:

> My people, I am glad that you have found us. You want to know what we have to offer. I believe that is the purpose of us meeting here. I am only existing. I am taking care of what subects I have under me, because they are subject to me. I remember how we are to greet each other, and also what we are to do. I realise now at this age you know our plight. We had an agreement to fulfil. This agreement, if you have any record,

was made at the place in our language called "Bapchiva," or a rugged place. How we talked over things with one another and how we are to proceed on the way of an agreement. We have agreed on certain things, and before parting, after making the agreement, we shook hands as brothers before we separated. We went our way with the common understanding that some day we might meet one another and greet ourselves again the way we have separated. You told me, because you are intelligent you know how to cope with life by acquiring the true experience, and because of that there would be a different phase after we meet each other again in the future. We are to prepare, then, and you told me if I was burdened with many things that are a detriment to me you ask me to leave it behind. I did so afterwards. You said to me that when we separate you will go to the eastward direction, and you said that is where you will abide. I asked if you settle how are you to let me know. You said, "there is to be a sign in the heavens that you can observe. That would be the sign that I am to return." When I saw that sign in the heavens, I had my hopes and was wishing that I would see you again in the near future. If you return we will have things in common again. You instructed me, the younger brother, to lead my people the best that I know how. You said, "If I come back I might come back speaking a different language. Then I will lead you and deal with you accordingly." Then when you started off to the eastward direction, I, the younger brother, asked you to return as soon as you can. We bade each other farewell. Ever since we have separated I have had hard times, and was on my way to a place called Flower Mountain, on my journey after suffering many things. I arrived at a place where I expected to make my home with the people that I have led. We met a group of people and were received cordially. You said that falling stars would be the sign that you were returning, and when I saw that again I felt in the hope that you would come sooner. The agreement that we made is still intact in my memory. I am still in the position that I was in at the time you left me. Your life is good, as I say. We are to treat one another with the best of love. (Bureau of Indian Affairs 1955, 331 f.)

This remarkable speech illustrates with painful clarity that for Murrizewa there was no doubt that primordial times had converged with contemporary times. His monologue is in the present perfect, past perfect, and future perfect tenses simultaneously—in both time and space. For him, his feet were firmly planted both near the place of the Emergence, Sipaapuni (during the primordial dialogue between the two brothers), and at Walpi, in front of a seated panel (reliving the primordial dialogue). In shaking hands with the committee members, mythical heroes were meeting once again in order to begin life anew.

Mistaken Identities: Part Two

On the other side of the dialectics of misrepresentation are countless Europeans and Americans who have been attracted to the myth of the returning White brother and have identified themselves with this myth. In other words, the Hopis have been visited by Euro-Americans who more or less adopt Hopi ideology as their own, enacting, as it were, their own fantasies about the long-lost White brother. It resembles the "Pocahontas perplex," formulated by Rayna Green (1976), but differs in the fact that the White man's self-image is staged within the framework of the Hopi (and therefore a foreign) cosmology. Furthermore, it involves the question of mutual reinforcement, noted by Stewart Brand, in which American Indians have provided the counterculture with a living identity base (1988, 572).

I introduce in my book a series of documents which describe exotic Euro-American individuals and groups within the framework of a typology consisting of explicit identification, symbolization, eclecticism/syncretism, activism, and hobbyism/tourism. Under "explicit identification," I noted the man who thought he had the missing corner of the ancient stone tablet of Hopi legend, the Chinese Buddhist priest who thought he was the awaited apocryphal White brother; the Flying Saucer prophet who believed that the White brother consisted of beings from Venus and that he was their prophet; the Jungian PhD student who thought Carl Gustav Jung was the awaited White brother, and others. Some thought they were the White brother, and others, like Mrs Gates from Pasadena, "went native" during the early years of this century. A. Irving Hallowell (1963) called the phenomenon "transculturalization," whereby individuals temporarily or permanently leave one culture and enter into the web of social relations in another culture.

The category "symbolization" involves individuals and groups who use the Hopis as a symbol or focus of their own particular ideology. The best example is the Flagstaff- and California-based umbrella organization Friends of the Hopi. Here it can be noted how this type of support rests not only on stereotypes of the Hopis but also on stereotypes of our own culture. Gerald Sider (1987) and others saw it as just another form of domination where Europeans wind up parroting their own fantasies of the Other.

"Eclecticism/syncretism" involves individuals and groups who construct worldviews out of the bits and pieces of other worldviews. One of the more intriguing examples is the German occultist Eberhard Kohler who claimed to have spoken to Christ in 1978. He became a missionary for an esoteric kind of universal Christianity. In 1984, he came into contact with the spokesman of the Hopi Traditionalist Movement, Thomas Banancya, through the assistance of the Austrian support group "Aktionskreis Hopi/Österreich." That same year, he flew to the Hopi Reservation together with his closest followers, but was ignored by the Traditionalists. His reaction was that they were naive, ignorant, and degraded, and due to their karma, it was right and proper that they follow the path of Christ and make the grand sacrifice of life and land in order to become fellow citizens in the New Age. He then made a pilgrimage to San Francisco Peaks just west of Hopi territory where he allegedly met the Hopi deities, called Katsinas, and celebrated the Christian sacrament with them. The Katsinas then invested him with the status of "Hopi Mystic in the German-speaking countries," and he became their distinctive missionary (Schweidlenka 1987).

"Activism" concerns people who for one reason or another—usually one or more of the above—actively support the Hostile or Traditionalist campaigns. Here we find Mrs Gates, Friends of the Hopi, action anthropologist Richard Clemmer, activist Craig Carpenter, and others. In my 1987 article I quoted one vociferous Hopi response to what Hopis consider them to be as ignorant "do gooders." Many Hopis have felt disgust for and enmity against the activists, not only because of their influence on the Reservation, but also because of their naïvety.

"Tourism/hobbyism" involves people who come to the Reservation as tourists or who imitate Indian life and customs in their free time as a hobby. Tourism has been a problem ever since the laying of the railroad lines, and the Hopis have made serious efforts to make everybody happy while protecting their ethnic integrity. Hobbyism, on the other hand, is a more difficult problem. Hobbyism has a long history in the US and Europe. Some consider it to be useful in promoting understanding and preserving Indian culture. Others (Indian activists most prominently), however, denounce it as imbecilic, sacrilegious and cultural genocide. It demonstrates, at least, the fulfilment and actualization of stereotypes. The Hopis have tried to cope with and stop a group of Prescott businessmen who call themselves Smokis, and who dress, dance, and propagate thinly-disguised versions of Hopi religion in order to preserve "the ancient ceremonial rites of a vanishing race." While the Smokis believe that they are demonstrating empathy and reverence, the Hopis consider it to be mockery and sacrilege. Tribal Chairman Abbott Sekaquaptewa repeatedly attempted throughout the 1970s to get the organization to stop their imitations of Hopi dances, but the Smokis denied any wrongdoing. Their excuse was that it was merely entertainment, but, in other circumstances, they admitted that there was more to it than that. And this is precisely what the Hopis found repulsive (Keith 1984; Anonymous 1980).

All of these groups have consistently misinterpreted, misrepresented, and idealized Hopi reality. The problem has continued unabated through the decades, and even though the Tribal Council has tried to control the situation by providing a neutral meeting-place for tourists and Hopis at the Cultural Centre on Second Mesa and by issuing rules of conduct, some villages have had to close their limits to White tourists during the Snake Ceremonial.[3] The former chief of Oraibi, Mina Lansa, even went so far as to close the village for several years to Whites (except for those who supported the Traditionalists).

The Politics of Prophecy

Whether the White brother motif in the emergence myth came before or after the appearance of Europeans is unimportant here. It cannot be proven one way or another. What is important is that the Hopis believe that their clan traditions have prophesied not only the advent of the Whites but also an astounding series of signs and events.

In the course of my work, I designed a catalogue and typology of Hopi prophetic statements that have appeared in print in one form or another during the period of 1858–1961. I have furthermore compared these statements with contemporaneous social and political affairs throughout the last century and a half. The largest body of prophecies, constituting eighty per cent of the corpus, were concerned with the White brother (over fifty per cent concerned him alone), the Mormons, various intramural clan affairs, and the purification by Maasaw. The rest of the corpus involved the emergence myth and the land. What is interesting for this paper is that over seventy per cent of the prophetic statements came from the hostile faction prior to World War Two and the Traditionalist Movement after that time. During the period of 1962 to the present, almost one hundred per cent of the prophetic statements, which have appeared in print, stem from the Traditionalist Movement, and about ninety per cent of them from three men: Dan Qötshongva (Katchongva), David Monongya, and Thomas Banancya. All three are from Third Mesa, the first two were leaders of the Traditionalist Movement and the latter functioned as their spokesman.

During 1948 a group of leaders met on several occasions to discuss the bombings of Hiroshima and Nagasaki. They were convinced that the "ash bomb" motif of their mythology was a prophecy of the atomic bomb and that it was a crucial sign indicating that the advent of Maasaw and the end of the world were near. During the meetings, the traditions of the various clans were collated into a corpus of prophecies that were to be spread throughout the world in preparation for the coming apocalypse. Four young men who were knowledgeable in the White man's ways and could speak fluent English were appointed as spokesmen and interpreters. These leaders and their interpreters became what came to be known as the Traditionalist Movement.

The movement developed a political ideology that was clearly anti-American. They claimed that the US government had no legal authority over their sovereign nation and that the Hopi Tribal Council did not represent legitimate, "traditional" villages. Neither had the right to sell Hopi land and the only rightful leaders were the "Hopi Traditional Chiefs." Thus the inviolability of tradition was reaffirmed and served as the point of departure for their analyses of past, present, and future events.

The main problem with the movement was that it was not what it purported to be. That traditionalists are not necessarily traditional is a well-known sociological insight, but the problem for the Traditionalists was that they had few legitimate claims to authority. Furthermore, the movement became just as much an instrument of change as the Tribal Council was. In fact, the Traditionalists were notorious for changing their "traditions" to fit the audience and were therefore radically involved in cultural change. The Traditionalists were deeply engaged in reformulating their religion, including its prophecies, and they attempted to change the local, agricultural concerns of traditional Hopi religion to universalistic and missionary ones. The attempt failed, at least during the heyday of the movement, but they did succeed in recruiting White Euro-Americans to the cause even though they failed to mobilize their own people.[4] This resulted in a curious situation where from a local, Hopi perspective the movement functioned as a political type of nativism, whereas seen from without, it demonstrated all the characteristics of a millenarian movement

Finally, it should be noted that the Traditionalist Movement could neither maintain a clear divide between traditionalism and progressivism— the very bastion of their political platform—nor maintain a clear distinction between itself and the Tribal Council—perceived as being their major opponent—in neither means nor ends. In order to offset the advantages of the Tribal Council, the Traditionalists were forced to adopt their opponent's methods.

Literacy and Prophecy

In my opinion, literacy played a major role in making the Movement a partner in acculturation. Drawing on the work of anthropologist Shuichi Nagata (1968, 1977, 1978) as well as previously unpublished archival material and obscure pamphlets and newspaper items, I identified the following consequences that literacy had on Traditionalist prophecy.

In the first place, English became adopted as the *lingua politica*. This gave rise to a new form of leadership in the Traditionalist Movement consisting of secular "spokesmen" whose only redeeming qualities were loyalty to the Movement and a command of English. In the second place, the reproduction of Traditionalist prophecies in a foreign medium resulted in two important factors of change: (1) disparate clan traditions were summarized for the first time into a common corpus, and (2) prophetic discourse changed languages and, with it, audiences.

New genres were employed by the Traditionalists which became incremental to their political tactics, namely, the frequent use of letters, petitions, statements, and communiqués sent to the US government as well as to English-speaking support groups, for instance, Americans, Canadians, Europeans, and other Indians. But even though these tactics gave them access to a greater arena, they also became instruments of acculturation. Thus, the implacable stance of resistance is set in apocryphal terms, but it is offset by deliberate and/or implicit invitations to a foreign authority to help remove political rivals or to improve the democratic principles and constitutional rights on the Reservation—the latter otherwise described as foreign impositions!

The mass media have neither changed the style, nor the generative process, of the oral communication reproduced in print. It is still oral knowledge imparted by knowledgeable specialists. But in 1949 the Traditionalist Movement abandoned the indigenous contexts of the secrecy of knowledge as a political ploy. This has had serious consequences. The ploy not only placed Hopi prophecies in another context, it also removed the prophecies from the whole indigenous context with the intricate social relationships and postures necessary for obtaining prophetic knowledge.

Recent literary criticism warns that writing only serves to keep readers and writers apart by a text which "like a two-sided mirror can only reflect back upon them their own images" (Smith 1985). Writing codifies language and carries it to new contexts beyond the control and comprehension of the writer. The written text does not clarify; it primarily invites contention and fixes it in an expanded context of temporal and spatial persistence. This can certainly be claimed about Traditionalist prophecies. Literacy has frozen prophetic tradition into texts which have carried that tradition beyond the reach, understanding, and control of its bearers. Thus, what was once a body of knowledge, restricted to formalized and ritualized indigenous contexts becomes accessible to a broader public which also consists of non-Hopis. Secondly, the publication of Hopi prophecies has indeed invited contention, especially in connection with the indelible proof of constant manipulation and change.

Literacy led to three results: (1) it created a greater impact on the national arena, (2) it led to a greater degree of extramural dialogue, and (3) it led to a greater degree of intramural dialogue.

Concerning the impact on the national arena, it is first of all evident that the written media gave the Traditionalists the trappings of power, which they did not possess, through the consistent use of the rhetoric of power. Secondly, it gave them a useful tool for discrediting the Tribal Council and for promoting their own hegemonic dialogue. Thirdly, it provided legal channels hitherto unavailable to them. Examples show that all three factors were consistently staged in apocryphal terms.

Concerning the greater degree of extra mural dialogue, it has turned out that making Hopi prophecy available to the public domain brought with it an implicit invitation to non-Hopis to participate in a more or less conscious orchestration of apocryphal dialogue. This made Hopi thought more accessible to like-minded movements, but it also allowed the needs, topics and terminology of Euro-American and Indian supporters to influence Hopi prophecies. Secondly, the introduction of a newsletter gave the Traditionalists the possibility of constructing and controlling their own public image. Examples of propaganda show that the Traditionalists knew whom they were addressing and what types of metaphors and images worked best for them.

Concerning the greater degree of intramural dialogue, it can be seen that the new availability of secret knowledge in the news media gave Hopi young adults the chance to express ethnic identity as well as to gain access to ethnic knowledge; it also allowed opponents one of the few opportunities to express their mutual criticisms to each other; and it served as a meeting place for all parties to develop an apocryphal consensus.

Thomas Banancya, Traditionalist Spokesman

One of the most interesting personalities attached to the Traditionalist Movement was their spokesman from Kykotsmovi, Thomas Banancya. Shuichi Nagata described Banancya in his 1978 publication on the founder of the movement, Dan Qötshongva (Katchongva). Banancya was born in 1902 in a highly acculturated family in Moenkopi and was one of the first Hopis to receive a college education, though he did not complete it. Being a member of the Coyote clan, he did not play a significant part in the traditional ritual hierarchy. In his early political career he was somewhat against traditional authority, but during the Second World War he grew disillusioned by the Indian policy of the American government and was imprisoned for his campaign against compulsory military service.

Soon after, he became the right-hand man to Dan Qötshongva and became a highly articulate spokesman for the Traditionalist Movement. Thus, he was a successful example of the above-mentioned innovation in recruiting members whose talents were not based on traditional values and social status but in their ability to deal with the White world. Richard Clemmer noted Banancya's marginality, but glossed it over with an inventive explanation tendered by his informants (1978, 71). But Banancya's marginality is a fact and not an issue. The issue lies in evaluating the depth of his insight and the authenticity of his interpretations. Banancya has spent thirty years on the lecture circuit, and even though his interpretations have changed, he has had a tremendous impact on his non-Hopi public and is probably responsible for the fact that the Traditionalist Movement did not die out sooner than it did. Travelling around the world with his drawing of the so-called prophecy rock east of Oraibi pasted onto a large posterboard with an old map of Hopi territory as its backdrop, Banancya was successful in recruiting Euro-American supporters with his colourful apocryphal exegesis.

Comparative analysis shows that he not only changed his interpretations for changing audiences, but he also changed his drawings to fit the interpretations! From activist meetings to ecology magazines, New Age journals, and Hollywood press conferences, Banancya developed more and more imaginative prophecies. He demonstrated a talent for attuning Hopi prophecy to dominant concerns in the American public. But, by the end of the 1970s, Banancya's audience changed drastically and, with it, his prophecies. Euro-American acclamation was gone. Now, his audience was Hopi, with the result that Banancya's exegesis fell more in line with traditional interpretations.

From Entrepreneur to Syncretist

By the end of the 1970s, the Traditionalists had developed a long catalogue of prophecies and signs of the end of the world, but the acclaim they enjoyed internationally was equalled by the criticism and shame they generated among their fellow Hopis. Most Hopis simply said they were lying; many, in deeper anger, called them traitors and manipulators. Any analyst of the late 1970s could hardly foresee the developments of the 1980s. Who, for instance, could have foreseen that one of the spokesmen for the Traditionalist Movement, Caleb Johnson, would run for the 1989 chairmanship of the Tribal Council with a political platform hardly distinguishable from his opponent? Of interest here, it would also surprise many that the general Hopi public and the representatives of the Tribal Council would finally take Thomas Banancya's prophecies seriously.

Since there is little space to introduce the reader to the substance of Hopi prophecies in comparative perspective—for instance, Traditionalist prophecies compared to earlier Hopi prophecies—I can only refer to my book *The Invention of Prophecy* (1992) for detailed evidence. The following catalogue is a sample of Banancya's prophecies and represent without exception the invention of tradition. During the 1970s Banancya addressed the Temple of Understanding's Spiritual Summit Conference V at the Cathedral of St. John in New York City in October 1975. His address was interspersed with a series of sensational prophecies. Maasaw, who is now equated with the Messiah in the Bible, met the Hopis in the beginning of this world and presented them with the spiritual path, telling them what to expect in the future. The Hopis were then given the duty to take care of the entire North American Continent—a crucial stance held by the Traditionalists. Then followed the story of the stone tablets and the two brothers: If the White Brother leaves the true path he will change the circle to the cross and will try to tempt his Hopi brother from the true path with the promise of ever new inventions. Then he listed the issues which indicate that the end is near: the destructive mining on Black Mesa, the use of chemical fertilisers, housing programmes, water and sewage lines, smog, all of which are signs that the true Hopis should go to the United Nations and find support there. Then follows a listing of all the inventions which Hopi prophecy purportedly knew about—couched in crypto-primitive terminology: carriages pulled by animals (buckboard wagons), carriages running by themselves (automobiles), trails in all directions (highways), cobwebs in the sky (telephone lines), closing the windows and doors but hearing and talking over the mountains (radio and television), the invention of a gourd full of ashes (atomic bombs), roads in the sky (air travel), man messing around with the moon and the stars (space travel), wars, violence, natural catastrophes, interfering with male and female (feminism), inventing human beings (genetic technology), and so on.

He claimed that two powerful nations—one with the swastika, the other with the sun symbol—were given the sacred mission of purifying themselves and thereby warning others. A third nation will arise wearing the red paint on the Powamuy rattle, and will come by flying saucers. If the third nation does not bring on the purification, a fourth nation from the west will destroy everything. If they also fail, then the Hopis must ask the Great Spirit for the complete destruction of the world.

But if all goes well, Maasaw will lead humanity into a paradisic life everlasting, where the earth will be renewed and all people will speak one tongue and believe in one religion—understood here as being the Hopi religion.

By the end of the 1970s, things were changing in the United States, and the religious scene was quickly becoming occupied with other topics such as the cult scare with accusations of brainwashing in Asian cults and the drastic measures employed by concerned parents. The Hopis were left to themselves.

Of signal importance is the fact that Banancya appeared again eight years later, only this time the audience was quite different than he was used to: it consisted of other Hopis! Banancya attended the Second Hopi Mental Health Conference in 1983, arranged by the Hopi Health Department. He showed his illustration of prophecy rock to a Hopi audience, and gave them a somewhat modified interpretation. The modifications clearly demonstrated a change of policy for the Traditionalist Movement: where doom was the theme of so many decades and alienation from mainstream Hopis, the hope of reconciliation during the 1980s brought other prophecies with it. The story is more in line with the "traditional"—not "Traditionalist"—story again. As the dwindling support by Whites faded with the turn of the decade, the only possible choice available was reconciliation with the rest of the Hopi people.

Hopi Mental Health

At the First Hopi Mental Health Conference, held by the Hopi Health Department at Kykotsmovi in 1981, the Hopi Prophecy Workshop Committee under the direction of a Hopi artist by the name of Terrance Talaswaima, formulated a number of astute observations about the nature and function of Hopi prophecy:

> The forementioned issues of Hopi prohecy and the Hopi view of mental health hold important lessons for those who wish to assist members of the Hopi population in need. One cannot ignore the legitimacy of prophecy and underlying beliefs in mental health. Prophecy provides one with a strong direction in life. It illustrates definite patterns of evolution in this world, lets individuals know what to expect for the future, and as such prepares them for the inevitable. By taking note of prophecy and recognizing the signs of its fulfilment, people can adjust their lives in accordance with the ways of the universe and, by doing so, prolong the existence of this world. There is a definite strength in prophecy: it provides a clear recognition of present-day realities, it calls for an acceptance of disharmony and corruption in spirit, and it points towards the importance of self-sufficiency, self-discipline, and attentiveness to Hopi teachings and practices in preparation for the next world.
>
> Unfortunately, few Hopis appear to be taking note of prophecy and adjusting their lives for the better. Mental health and social problems are getting worse. Most people express frustration and depression when talking about prophecy; they throw up their hands in a kind of helplessness and declare that there is nothing one can do to improve the present climate and situation.
>
> Prophecy has been used as an excuse to avoid personal responsibility in improving the qualities of life and behaving in a way that follows Hopi teachings and beliefs. There runs a tremendous pessimism throughout Hopi that things will only get worse. This has immobilized a great deal of the population to either watch life deteriorate from a distance, or join in on the fun and go downhill as well. People who wish to help others and lead productive lives are frustrated at every turn. As such Hopi prophecy becomes a self-fulfilling prophecy—the people help to make it happen sooner. (Hopi Health Department, n.d., 51)

At the next Mental Health Conference in 1983 the Hopi Prophecy Workshop Committee was expanded to include both Progressives, such as the now-deceased Percy Lomakwahu from Hotevilla, and Traditionalists such as Thomas Banancya, who have been concerned with prophecy for many decades. The result was not only admirable but signal, even though the Chairperson Leigh Jenkins, then Assistant Director of the Hopi Health Department, hastened to add that "The following information ... is not meant to be the authoritative 'word' of the Life Plan, but rather a perspective of various interpretations and viewpoints" (Robin 1983, 35).

The report contains nothing less than a chart depicting the *qatsivötavi*, "life path," or the mythical history of the Hopis. This is accompanied by Banancya's interpretation of prophecy rock and is concluded by a systematic examination of the major prophetic statements in Hopi tradition, quoted in Hopi, wherein the statements are compared with statistics and other information *as proof of the legitimacy of each statement*. But the catalogue of dire signs is first introduced by positive and soothing words of hope. Once again, Hopi prophecy has been transformed, this time in the face of other needs:

> All Hopi informants say the same thing: That it is *our generation* which is witnessing the fulfilment of the Life Plan made known to us at the time of Emergence. All informants noted that the signs are quite clear as to the current stage of life we have entered into—a perilous period of life preceding an event known in Hopi theology as the punishment, purification and the judgment of all mankind by the Creator.
>
> We have reached a point in life where we must begin to work together so that we reach the right decisions. We have to look at ourselves so that we can again have respect for our fellow man, for the world, for if we don't, then we will all be judged accordingly for our mistakes. (Hopi elder)
>
> So is there hope for mankind? A simple Hopi proverb might kindle a measure of hope: Kaiitsivu, kapustamokca, konakopanvungya hakapii hihita ung kyataimanii! He who is slow to anger, frustration and self-pity *will live* to see and wonder at the many changes. (Robin 1983, 43)

The report then examined "those predictions that are in the process of occurring or those which are yet to occur." This section of the report provides a unique insight into the combination of prophetic cognition and Western methods of inquiry which characterize the Hopi cognitive environment today. The catalogue of prophecies includes global over-population, the conquering of the United States by a foreign power, the advent of coastal earthquakes, catastrophic changes in the weather, the rise of starvation and pestilence, the political machinations of the Navajos, the presence of mineral development and exploitation, the discovery of life on another planet, the conquest of death by scientific technology, the dominance of women in political affairs, and other matters.

By instruction, I will quote the section on the meaning of the prophecy of the ash bomb:

ASH FALLING FROM THE SKY

Hopi informants hold various interpretations as to the true meaning of this prophecy. Let us examine a few of them.

**Nuclear Fallout: If current world trends continue, the final outcome will most likely be nuclear war and subsequent radioactive fallout. At present, the Soviet Union has 12,000 nuclear warheads aimed at American cities while the United States points 9,000 warheads in their direction. The continuation of current tensions may well lead to a final confrontation between these two global powers.

**A Volcanic Eruption: This refers to our previously discussed prediction of the eruption of the San Francisco Peaks. Ash from the sky?

**Air Pollution: Can one imagine the valley between Ozaivi and Second Mesa being filled with polluted air? It is indeed possible in this day and age! Huge clouds of polluted air now occasionally reach Hopiland. Flagstaff now generates enough industrial smoke and automobile emissions to create a haze known as smog... (Robin 1983, 48 f.)

These prophecies and interpretations indicate that despite acculturation and borrowed forms of argumentation, there is no indication of secularization or decline in the Hopi traditional way of thinking. The prophecies have placed, and still do place, the Hopis squarely in the centre of world events in Hopi thought, and they continue to serve as mechanisms of evaluation and systematization in the computer age. But the quotes are eloquent examples of the syncretistic process where the catalyst for most of his career was despised for his free-wheeling interpretations and his pandering to impressionable Whites and, yet, in a new context in which Hopi ethnic identity and Tribal Council policy converge with Traditionalist rhetoric, we find a meeting of minds, and with them a meeting of prophecies.

At the Third Hopi Mental Health Conference in 1984, which had the theme "Prophecy in Motion," the mainstream of Hopi religious thought followed the universalism of the Traditionalists by comparing the prophecies of the Bible with Hopi prophecies. The *a priori* position of the workshop was that "serious students of theology do not negate the possibility that men of all races actually may have received their religions from the same God or Creator, each religion designed to speak to a specific culture" (Jenkins and Kooyahoema 1984, 64). The results of their comparison were that "both Hopi and Biblical teachings presented surprisingly similar warnings, and that current events seemed to match those warnings almost to the letter" (65). The workshop called for mutual understanding between denominations and "helping one another prepare for the Judgement to come" (66). In a single elegant stroke, Hopi religion is placed on an equal footing with at least one of the major universal salvation religions!

The point here is that Hopis who are in positions of authority, both tradi-tional and contemporary forms of authority, have analysed their situation and have found and articulated the resolution to their problems. Whether the resolutions can be realized by the populace at large is another question entirely. The Hopis have solved their problems before, and they will do it again.

Prophecy has been identified by the Hopis as a relevant and viable vehicle of self-help, and that functional solutions are provided along with ideologi-cal ones. One of the major mechanisms that helped to transform and update prophetic tradition was the ideological body that invented it. Thus the in-vention of tradition in cultural collision became a viable solution in cultural collusion.

Notes

1. This paper is based on my book *The Invention of Prophecy* which was published by the University of California Press in Los Angeles in 1994. The original edition was delivered at the University of Aarhus for the post-doctoral degree of philosophy: *The Invention of Prophecy: Continuity and Meaning in Hopi Indian Religion*, Knebel: Brunbakke Publications, 1992. See as well Geertz 1987, 1989, 1991, 1992b, 1993a and 1993b. The University of California edition is abridged and revised. My study is based on fieldwork conducted on the Hopi Indian Reservation in northern Arizona in 1978–1979, and for shorter periods in 1982, 1988 and 1992 plus ten years of tran-scribing, translating and reflecting on the taped interviews I conducted during my visits.
2. The *kiva* is the cult house of the secret brotherhoods.
3. See, for instance, the following articles in the Hopi newspaper *Qua' Töqti*: "Villages to Develop Own Control Policies" (15 July 1982); "Visitor Control at Dance Successful" (26 Aug. 1982); and "Snake Dance Closed to Non-Indians" (4 Aug. 1983). White participation at dances was prohibited for much of 1992.
4. Local support probably never reached more than ten per cent of a population of eight or nine thousand.

References

Anonymous. 1980. "Hopis Condemn Smoki for Performing Dances." *Qua' Töqti* 6(8) (11 Sept. 1980): 1.
Baird, R. D. 1971. *Category Formation and the History of Religions*. The Hague and Paris: Mouton & Co.
Brand, S. 1988. "Indians and the Counterculture, 1960s–1970s." In *History of Indian-White Relations*, ed. W. E. Washburn, 570–72. Handbook of North American Indians, 4. Washington: Smithsonian Institution.
Bureau of Indian Affairs. 1955. *Hopi Hearings. July 15–30, 1955*. Keams Canyon: Hopi Agency.
Clemmer, R. 1978. *Continuities of Hopi Cultural Change*. Ramona: Acoma Books.

Courlander, H. 1982. *Hopi Voices: Recollections, Traditions, and Narratives of the Hopi Indians*. Albuquerque: University of New Mexico Press.

Geertz, A. W. 1987. "Prophets and Fools: The Rhetoric of Hopi Indian Eschatology." *European Review of Native American Studies* 1: 33–45.

—1989. "A Container of Ashes: Hopi Prophecy in History." *European Review of Native American Studies* 3: 1–6.

—1991. "Hopi Prophecies Revisited: A Critique of Rudolf Kaiser." *Anthropos* 86: 199–204.

—1992a. *The Invention of Prophecy: Continuity and Meaning in Hopi Indian Religion*. Knebel: Brunbakke Publications.

—1992b. "The Archaic Ontology of the Hopi Indians: On John Lofti's Interpretation of Hopi Religion." *Anthropos* 87: 537–43.

—1993a. "Theories on Tradition and Change in Hopi Studies." *Anthropos* 88: 489–500.

—1993b. "Archaic Ontology and White Shamanism: A Review Article." *Religion* 23: 369–72.

Green, R. 1976. "The Pocahontas Perplex: The Image of Indian Women in American Culture." *The Massachusetts Review* 16: 698–714.

Hallowell, A. I. 1963. "American Indians, White and Black: The Phenomenon of Transculturation." *Current Anthropology* 4: 519–31.

Hopi Health Department, n.d. *Report on the First Hopi Mental Health Conference*, Jan. 1981. Kykotsmovi: Hopi Health Department.

Jenkins, L., and M. Kooyahoema. 1984. *Report of the Third Hopi Mental Health Conference: 'Prophecy in Motion'*. Kykotsmovi: Hopi Health Department.

Keith, C. 1984. "Simple Ceremonies." *Arizona* (15 July): 4, 12, 14.

Nagata, S. 1968. "Political Socialization of the Hopi 'Traditional' Faction." Special Collections, University of Arizona, Tucson.

—1977. "Opposition and Freedom in Moenkopi Factionalism." In *A House Divided? Anthropological Studies of Factionalism*, ed. M. Silverman and R. F. Salibury. St Johns: Memorial University of Newfoundland.

—1978. "Dan Kochongva's Message: Myth, Ideology, and Political Action among the Contemporary Hopi." *The Yearbook of Symbolic Anthropology* 1: 73–87.

Robin, R. 1983. *Report of the Second Hopi Mental Health Conference: Crossroads of Cultural Change*. Kykotmovi: Hopi Health Department.

Schweidlenka, R. 1987. "Eberhard Kohler: Ein christlicher Esoteriker legitimiert den Völkermord." *Informationsdienst Indianer Heute* 4: 29–31.

Sider, G. 1987. "When Parrots Learn to Talk, and Why They Can't: Domination, Deception and Self-Deception in Indian-White Relations." *Comparative Studies in Society and History* 29: 3–23.

Smith, F. 1985. "A Metaphor for Literacy: Creating Worlds or Shunting Information?" In *Literacy, Language, and Learning: The Nature and Consequences of Reading and Writing*, ed. D. R. Olson, N. Torrance and A. Hildyard. Cambridge: Cambridge University Press.

Whitely, P. M. 1987. "The Interpretation of Politics: A Hopi Conundrum." *Man* 22: 696–714.

Part V

CATEGORY PROBLEMS AND THEORETICAL SUSPENSE

INTRODUCTION TO PART V

The presentations in Part V each present a solution to the problem of syncretism on very different levels. Representing the stance of social science, the anthropologist Charles Stewart points out different significant discourses on syncretism that have been active in anthropology, with decisive results in political as well as religious life. He suggests that the problems of the category are due to the discursive entanglement of the concept. Ulrich Berner, a historian of religions, swears by the historical and descriptive approach in the attempt to solve the problem of definition. He presents a model for the classification of syncretism for heuristic and comparative purposes in historical studies. Luther Martin, also a historian of religions, recommends that we turn to biology to explain the phenomenon of syncretism. He also suggests that the cognitive sciences may give the category some explanatory value that can discharge former misconceptions of the term.

These three presentations differ in theoretical outset; nonetheless, they are all equally important contributions in the overall attempt to solve the problems of the category syncretism. The three pieces suggest competing theories. However, the intention is not just to set them up against each other in order to discuss their differences; rather, the goal of this part is to emphasize the necessity of confronting the issues concerning distinct levels of discourse and theory, because this best reflects the complexity of the phenomenon.

The Predisposed Discourse

It may not come as a surprise that the subject of syncretism is primarily discursive. Therefore, in his effort to get a picture of the entanglement of discourses related to the notion, Charles Stewart examines the research history of anthropology to find the answer to the misconceptions of the category. According to Stewart, there are different approaches towards syncretism in the historical onset of European and North American anthropology, each of which reflect, in comparison to the seventeenth-century syncretistic controversies, an irenic and a negative version of syncretism. He observes that the discourse of syncretism in British anthropology, from the starting point of European colonization, was related to the negative attitude towards syncretism of the European Church. Consequently, British anthropology has continued to use the negative discourse of syncretism so that it came to influence later African scholarship. It was followed by "insider and outsider"—controversies and reluctance against being called a "syncretist" in some of the

African churches. On the other hand, he points out that politics of acculturation and nation-building drove the American school of anthropology towards the irenic attitude of syncretism. The different motivations inside these schools of anthropology, with dissimilar "localizing strategies," have accordingly formed opposing discourses about syncretism. Thereby, Stewart observes how the questions concerning the category are to be found in the outskirts of other discourses. These very political discourses put into question the usability of syncretism as a scientific category, because as Stewart remarks, the term continues to reflect the aversion to cultural mixture.

Nonetheless, the term seems to be inordinately viable in resisting all attempts to abolish it. Stewart tells us that in contemporary social studies, syncretism has come back because of an increased interest in subjects such as "globalization." Now severed from the problematic discourses of acculturation and replaced in the frame of cultural dynamics without former days' idea of purity, the "essence" of syncretism changes to "hybridization." The reference of this analogy to biology gives the term an appearance of naturalness. But, as Stewart concludes, even processes termed "hybridization" will "be dictated by historico-political events and contingencies." Despite the problems of political-discursive factors imbedded in the term he argues for keeping the category, much in the same line as Ulrich Berner. As long as scholars accept the premises of a redefinition of culture and religion that reject the idea of the existence of pure cultures and pure religions, syncretism can be used within the framework of modern sociological theories about culture and cultural change.

Therefore, Stewart dismisses Baird's disputation against the category of syncretism, because he finds that it is convenient as a descriptive term from the point of view of social science and shows the efficiency of discursive processes. In reference to what he names "circumlocution," Stewart understands the impact that the term syncretism has on forming folk theories of culture and "directing the invention of traditions." It is in this recognition of the enduring problem of the notion that he points to how "syncretism" is socially related to power. This is a fact, which speaks for including a social level of inquiry into the larger frame of theory of syncretism. But, still more can be said on how to describe the phenomenon of syncretism. Stewart expresses doubt as to whether syncretism refers to stable conditions or to ongoing processes. It is, as he points out, the dilemma, or tension, between "structure" and "process." In noting this tension between what seems to be two incompatible poles in the nature of syncretism, Stewart confesses that the dilemma is a problem of social-science enquiry in general; in other words, the continuing debate over the relation between theory and practice. Despite his attempt to grasp the nature of the phenomenon Stewart admits to its fluidity and describes it, more or less in accordance with Michael Pye's definition of the syncretistic process, as a "momentary state of mixture … in a process which can lead in any direction." He seems to be caught between the ambiguities of the stabilization of tradition, in particular concerning scriptural religions, and the ongoing innovative processes, while he acknowledges a difference in "syncretic potentials" between scriptural and non-literate religions. This dilemma between stability contra process, or structure and process, reminds us that we may have to look elsewhere to find an explanation of this type of dynamics, for example, along the lines of Luther Martin's focus on syncretic processes as being the "trial and error" processes in culture and religion.

However, Stewart's contribution to the study of syncretism is that he frames the problem of the category as a mainly discursive one. He suggests, therefore, an "anthropology of syncretism" that is not concerned with whether "this" or "that" religion is or is not syncretistic, but instead he recommends that we study the adversary discourses on the blending of religion. A suggestion that expresses much of the outlook of this volume.

Cognitive Explanations of Syncretism

In a tone similar to Robert Baird's criticism of the category syncretism as nothing but a historical truism, Luther Martin declares that the category explains nothing in itself; rather, he accentuates that the formations which we call syncretistic are the problem that needs to be explained. In his response to Michael Pye (represented in Part II of this book), he refutes the descriptive definition of syncretism as scientifically sound, because it preserves the historic assumption about cultures as stable systems. This paradigm of syncretism can at best describe, as he disputes along with Baird, the self-evident factor that all religions are historical formations. In a recent article, Martin warns against "normative points of reference to non-syncretistic origins characteristic of earlier usages" (Martin 2001, 390) as the generalization of a historical generative pattern that envisages syncretistic formations to be the result of "mixing" or "blending" of different religious progenitors. This is, he states, a reminder of the classical idea of "pangenesis" of the pre-Darwinian biology (392–93). In the present essay (as well as in this his recent article), Martin suggests that we may have to turn to recent biological theory in order to find explanations that revise the earlier problematic suppositions about syncretism.

Martin turns to the cognitive sciences to find scientific criteria that can explain the old problems of syncretism in a new way. He agrees with the anthropologist Pascal Boyer (1994, 114–15), who argues against the idea that religions should be shared systems of ideas. From Boyer's observations, it is not because humans share a system of thought that religious representations have similar features, but because we transmit a paradigmatic "culture" or "symbolic system" through the process of socialization. Thus it is argued that culture is the product of the human mind; contrary to historians' traditional assumption when they refer to culture as the product of historical and haphazard contingency. Accordingly, religious ideas involve or contain innate cognitive structures that may reveal to us their "learnability" and the causes for their acquisition. Consequently, Martin establishes that syncretistic formations in cultural constructions may be explained from their founding in cognitive constraints. Analogous to language, Martin suggests, syncretistic formations are constrained by selectivity and combinatorial systems that do not (con)fuse or mix their semantics. Turning to the studies of how the brain works, Martin succeeds in refuting the classical assumption of syncretism as simply the "mishmash of religions"—not everything goes.

The Systemic Character of Syncretism

In his recent work, Martin proposes that we use the Darwinian theory of natural selection as a model for the underlying mechanisms of syncretism. Dan Sperber's epidemiological model is suggested as a means of characterizing the processes of cultural transmission, with reference to his reformulation of the theory of the biologist Richard Dawkins. In Dawkins's theory of cultural transmission, a cultural unit of replication, named a "meme," is considered analogous to the genetic transmission of genes (Dawkins 1976): "memes propagate themselves in the meme pool by leaping from brain to brain via a process which, in broad sense, can be called imitation" (quoted in Martin 2001). Sperber, however, emphasizes the "mutational element" of cultural transmission in his model whereby he understands the mechanism of Darwinian selection not so much as a transmission of cultural replicates, but as the process of cultural transformations (in Martin 2001, 396). From this point on Martin assumes, accordingly, that syncretistic formations are not replications or some kind of blending of non-syncretistic religious origin; it is more exactly "the collective product of cultural input only as that input is processed by human minds" (ibid, 396).

Martin's explanation of the systemic character of syncretistic formations suggests that religious elements transform according to generative rules of "learnability" similar to those of language (i.e. to learn is also to change), which basically are the outcomes of cognitive selective and constraining mechanisms. In consequence, this means that humans discriminate amongst the information they receive from more or less intuitive and unconscious recognitions of similarities. Hence, the outcome may be that the brain has not developed to copy information, but rather to use information to construct something new of its own; that will explain, consequently, how conceptual "mutations" take place. Concerning syncretic formations, this theoretical paradigm of cognition may help explain the "normality" of syncretistic imagination. Yet, it is still essential to question the social constriction on syncretistic formations with reference to, for example, the power-relations that were discussed in Part IV; or how different modes of religion act upon syncretistic "mutations" of religion. The main point is that Martin overcomes the classical theological bias implanted in the category by invoking the cognitive perspective on cultural processes akin to syncretism, which he compares to processes of "trial and error" (2001, 398–99). In his recent work "To Use 'Syncretism,' or Not to Use 'Syncretism'" Martin concludes that "The theoretical identification of cognitive principles can not only establish the constraints upon such historical formations as religious syncretisms but also an analytical architecture for their historical explanation" (2001, 400).

The Historical-Descriptive Sense of Syncretism

The presentation of the "heuristic model of syncretism" was the outcome of a research project ("Sonderforschungsbereich") on syncretism which Ulrich Berner contributed to in the late 1970s at the University of Göttingen in Germany.[1] This "terminological model" of syncretism was intended for use in an interdisciplinary workshop for philological-historical research. In Berner's own words voiced in a later work: "This multiplicity and variety of terms, however, may be perceived as unnecessarily complex when the context and function of an 'heuristic model' designed for interdisciplinary study is not recognized" (Berner 2001, 503). In a commentary on his contribution to this volume he states:

> Looking back, twenty-five years after drafting the "Heuristic Model of Syncretism," the impression is ambivalent: on the one hand, the model looks very complex, comprising a lot of definitions, on the other hand it appears now as rather limited, covering only a part of the field that Religious Studies are concerned with. If the model remains a useful instrument within a limited context of research, however, this very fact might have interesting implications concerning the relationship between different approaches to the problem of syncretism. (Personal communication with the editors)

Setting aside for a later discussion the many interesting points in the "table of content" or typology of syncretisms, which is represented in the essay, we will instead focus on the main discussion of this part—the theoretical displacement of the category of syncretism. With respect to the descriptive use of the category, Berner's heuristic model of syncretism represents in many ways a "no-problem-theory" as long as historians of religions will agree upon discharging the "old" misconceptions of syncretism. In a recent work, he defends his heuristic model by dismissing (analogously to Gustavo Benavides, Part IV, this volume) theories, which claim that religions have a core and boundaries or are "systems." He emphasizes that there is no problem with the concept in itself as long as we do not "presuppose any assumption about the previous state of that system as somehow 'pure' or 'essential'" (Berner 2001, 500). He thus defends the descriptive strategy of his model, however, strictly for historical researches; Berner realizes the problem of the "moral" dimensions of what he refers to as the "inference between meta-language of research and the object-language of religion" (2001, 500). In a personal communication to the editors, Berner recognizes that the model is limited to Near East studies that belong to the field of historical research and are restricted to philological studies. Berner writes:

> Historical-philological studies often have the tendency to focus on the religion of the educated elites or even on "theology" as produced by religious professionals. The Heuristic Model also leaned towards this side and this may contribute to widening the gap between historical and anthropological research on syncretism.

Inspirations behind the Model

Nevertheless, if we adjust Berner's heuristic model to Stewart's focus on discourse, then Berner's model may, from the methodological point of view, survey the discursive research on syncretism; in another sense, it is ruled out by the restriction of the model to a particular form of historical research—that of the philological school. This in fact questions Berner's defence for the descriptive usage of the category syncretism, which unattended accommodates Luther Martin's criticism of the descriptive usage because the philological use of syncretism contains so much of former prejudiced outlooks on syncretism. However, Berner has recently been reconsidering his model according to its applicability to a different field of study because he has been involved in a new collaborative research centre that focuses on the concept of globalization and emphasizes fieldwork in Africa (see Berner 2001). Accordingly, he states in his commentary: "Additionally, more attention was given to the situation in which syncretistic processes occur: distinguishing between different kinds of syncretistic situations may be another step towards theorizing about syncretism."

I could not agree more with Berner because, if we accept Martin's cognitive explanation, the main issue concerning the category might not be about a "normality" innate to the phenomenon itself; rather the definitions of the category are fixed by external factors with reference to the discursive and power-related problems illustrated by Stewart and the other scholars discussing syncretism predominantly in relation to Christianity and its encounter with other religions. In that respect Berner is right to conclude in his commentary to this volume that:

> It remains an open question, however, whether there will emerge a new model, which is more appropriate for anthropological fieldwork. In any case, it would not make sense looking for the "essence" of syncretism or discussing which concept of syncretism is the "right" one. Every conceptual model that is consistently constructed could be useful, because every concept of syncretism that is clearly defined possibly opens up a new perspective on the complex cultural phenomena. (letter to the editors)

Berner here draws a very important lesson from the philosophy of science: there is nothing in the world that generates a concept, no "essence" that tells us how we should interpret it and on which we may decide its rightness of "fit." Rather, it is by virtue of having concepts constructed in such a manner that they become heuristically useful that we may produce new insight. This goes no less for matters that belong to the worlds of humans and to social affairs. Finally, it is worth mentioning that Berner's systemic organization of his model, inspired by the sociological systems theory of Niklas Luhmann, into a "system level" and "element level" is very convincing, in that it gives an almost semiotic description of the processes of syncretism. As such, Berner's heuristic model proves to be both useful and relevant as a descriptive frame of research. However, it cannot stand alone, without some theoretical insights as to what kind of phenomenon we are dealing with when speaking of syncretism. Therefore, to contest all the many normative pitfalls inclusive of the notion of syncretism we need to include both the discursive and the cognitive aspects alongside the descriptive use to justify the application of the category in the scientific studies of religion.

Note

1. The results of this research centre were published as "Göttinger Orientforschungen. Veröffentlichungen des Sonderforschungsbereiches Orientalistik an der Georg-August-Universität Göttingen," Wiesbaden (Harrassowitz). There were six series: Syriaca; Studien zur spätantiken und frühchristlichen Kunst; Iranica; Ägypten; Biblica et Patristica; Hellenistica. An additional series was called "Reihe Grundlagen und Ergebnisse," including G. Wiessner, ed., *Synkretismusforschung. Theori und Praxis* (Wiesbaden: Harrassowitz, 1978) and U. Berner, *Untersuchungen zur Verwendung des Synkretismus-Begriffes* (Wiesbaden: Harrassowitz, 1982).

References

Berner, Ulrich. 2001. "The Notion of Syncretism in Historical and/or Empirical Research." *Historical Reflections/Réflexions Historiques* 27(3): 499–509.

Dawkins, Richard. 1976. *The Selfish Gene*. New York: Oxford University Press.

Martin, Luther, H. 2001. "To Use 'Syncretism' or Not to Use 'Syncretism': That is the Question." *Historical Reflections/Réflexions Historiques* 27(3): 389–400.

Sperber, Dan. 1996. *Explaining Culture: A Naturalistic Approach*. Oxford: Blackwell.

Relocating Syncretism in Social Science Discourse[*]

Charles Stewart

The Meanings of "Syncretism"

Syncretism is considered a pejorative term in some quarters today; certainly it acquired deprecatory overtones in the past, and these negative associations have caused anthropologists to doubt whether the term can or should be used in current writing. The first issue to consider is which histories and which regional ethnographic traditions, if any, anthropologists should feel themselves governed by.

One could start, for example, with the first-century AD Roman writer Plutarch who first coined the term "syncretism" (*Moralia* 2.490b) with wholly positive connotations. For him it was a form of brotherly love whereby normally inimical Cretan tribes sank their differences and united in the face of attacks by forces from beyond Crete. It was this banding together of Cretans (*Kretes*, "Cretan")—similar in many respects to the temporary segmentary fusions described among the Nuer (Evans-Pritchard 1940)—which Plutarch termed "syncretism" (*syn-kretismos*).

The term acquired overriding negative connotations in the seventeenth century when, in the wake of the Reformation, the Lutheran theologian Georg Calixtus (1586–1656) advocated the unification of the various Protestant denominations and ultimate reunion with the Catholic Church (McNeill 1930). His irenic vision of an ecumenical Christianity found some favour among Calvinists but was rejected by orthodox Lutherans and disdained by the upper echelons of the Catholic hierarchy. On the view of his opponents,

Calixt's proposed reunion threatened an heretical and inconsistent jumble of theologies—a syncretism—and the ensuing debates which carried on for the rest of the century came to be known as the "syncretistic controversies" (Schmid 1846). A negative assessment of religious mixture was perhaps to be expected, especially from the Catholic Church which was concerned to safeguard the integrity of its doctrine and practice throughout the world.

This negative view of syncretism would remain very much in place during the ensuing period of missionary expansion lasting well into the twentieth century. Syncretism became a term of abuse often applied to castigate colonial local churches which had burst out from the sphere of mission control and begun to "illegitimately" indigenize Christianity instead of properly reproducing the European form of Christianity which had originally been offered. Protestant missionaries were no less aware of the "danger" of syncretism than their Catholic counterparts, and a prime example may be found in the writing of the Church of Sweden (Lutheran) missionary Bengt Sundkler who served his Church in South Africa over a five-year period beginning in 1937. Sundkler distinguished two types of Independent Church: the Ethiopian Churches, which had seceded from parent mission churches for racial or ethnic (political) reasons but nonetheless still stuck closely to the missionaries' form of Christian practice; and the Zionist Churches, which had further separated from the Ethiopians through theological innovations such as speaking in tongues, healing and purification rites, observance of taboos and claims to possess the power (or medicine) to fight traditional Zulu diviners' arsenal of sorcery (Sundkler 1961, 55). In Sundkler's eyes, Zionism amounted to a "nativistic-syncretistic" interpretation of Christianity and in following this Church the Zulus were borne, as if over a "bridge," back to "the African animism from where they once started" (1961, 297).

With the case of Sundkler we can see how the negative attitude of European Churches towards syncretism was transferred from the theological debates of the seventeenth century, through missionary policy and ideology, and finally, through the field research of an individual missionary, delivered at the very doorstep of academic anthropology. The second edition of Sundkler's *Bantu Prophets of South Africa* (1961; first edition 1948), was published by the International African Institute, then under the directorship of Darryl Forde, Professor of Anthropology at University College London. This organization also provided Sundkler with a research grant assisting him in preparing the second edition.[1] I do not mean to suggest that British social anthropologists of this period were unaware of the differences between themselves and missionaries. Certainly the writings of Evans-Pritchard would have done much to advance the professional attitude that missionaries were people whom anthropologists could respect—especially for their linguistic skills—but with whom one did not share the same intellectual agenda. In a famous passage at the very end of his *Nuer Religion* (1956, 322), Evans-Pritchard expressed the opinion that when it came to analysis anthropologists occupied a position distinct from theologians. Anthropologists could describe and elucidate the socio-cultural context and form of religious beliefs, but they were not in a position to judge the validity or veracity of these beliefs. While anthropologists were, in principle, conscious of their differences from missionaries, I would contend that these boundaries could blur; and occasionally concepts such as "syncretism" could enter the anthropological vocabulary still laden with church/mission associations instead of passing through critical scrutiny and possible recasting. As we shall see below, during this very same period the term was given more positive connotations in the anthropological discourse of other regional traditions. Among Africanists, however, the term "syncretism" retained a negative spin.

This negative assessment was undoubtedly reinforced when African scholars as well as the leaders of various South African Independent Churches became familiar with the concept of syncretism and, predictably enough, reacted strongly against it (Pato 1990; Stewart and Shaw 1994, 15). At a recent conference in South Africa leaders of the South African Ethiopian Church spoke out and denied that the terms "sect" or "syncretist" could be used in a sociological, morally neutral, sense. Furthermore, "they roundly condemned any attempt to understand the [Zionist] Church of Lekhanyane in these analytical terms" (Kiernan 1992). This statement echoed views that had already been registered years earlier by the South African anthropologist Martin West (1975, 3). Granted this ambience, many latter-day Africanist anthropologists have also grown uncomfortable with the word and some have argued against its applicability by asserting that independent African Churches have faithfully adapted Christianity to local cultural contexts (for instance Kiernan 1992), and should not, therefore, be considered syncretic. Still other anthropologists have largely bypassed the word or developed alternatives such as "selective conservatism" (Wilson 1961, 548) or bricolage (Comaroff 1985, 12).[2] This lexical avoidance has not, however, prevented these latter writers from making important contributions to our understanding of independent African Churches as forms of resistance to colonial hegemony and means of preserving valued cultural resources.

On the other side of the Atlantic a much more positive attitude towards the concept of syncretism has prevailed among social scientists. The simultaneous existence of two such different positions may perhaps be attributed to the relative lack of interchange between American and British anthropology in the 1940s and 1950s. This mutual isolation was reinforced by a regional division of labour whereby British or British-trained social anthropologists largely monopolized research in Africa while American-trained anthropologists carried out the majority of studies in the New World. The two opposed discourses of syncretism—thus amounted to different "localizing strategies" (Fardon 1990)—regionally generated theoretical contributions which in this case addressed the very same concept and term. These differing theoretical discourses on syncretism did not result solely from the differing intellectual orientations of the British and American "schools" of anthropology. African and New World societies presented quite different political situations, and this made for very different fieldwork experiences for mid-century anthropologists.

Whereas most sub-Saharan African societies were still under colonial rule up until the 1950s, most New World societies had already gained independence in the preceding century and were actively engaged in attempts to consolidate national cultural identities. Many North and South American countries publicly espoused versions of a "melting-pot" ideology as a strategy of nation-building. The melting-pot is the analogue of syncretism in the ethno-political domain, and it would have been difficult to criticize the one without simultaneously undermining the other. In this sense, it could be argued that American (in the broad sense of North and South American) anthropologists were culturally or historically predisposed to take a different attitude toward cultural mixture since they themselves were raised, and lived as members of, these societies.

The influential mid-century anthropologist Melville Herskovits, for example, considered syncretism a valuable concept for specifying the degree to which diverse cultures had integrated (1958; Apter 1991); it was not a bridge leading to religious relapse, but rather a stage (for Negroes and other minorities) on the road towards the ideal of cultural assimilation and integration. Similar views were expressed by the Brazilian sociologist, Gilberto Freyre, who, like Herskovits, was trained in anthropology under Franz Boas at Columbia University. Freyre considered Brazilian society to be fundamentally a synthesis of different "races" and cultures (1945).

This optimistic view of syncretism, and "acculturation" generally, was inherited and embraced by the succeeding generation of American anthropologists, an example being Hugo Nutini, who began his research in Mexico in the late 1950s. As Nutini autobiographically writes, "Since I began anthropological research in Mesoamerica, I have conceived of syncretism as a special kind of acculturation ..." and he cites the research of Herskovits in Haiti which aided him in formulating his views (n.d.). Nutini's account of his entry into the study of syncretism evidences no suspicion that the term might have pejorative overtones, and he has gone on to publish numerous studies mapping out the various forms and modes of syncretism (for instance, Nutini 1988), thereby introducing a neutral analytical conception of syncretism to the current generation of anthropologists. Numerous other American Mesoamericanists have also approached syncretism as a valid, unproblematic object of analysis (Edmonson *et al.* 1960). It becomes apparent, then, that syncretism has received positive or negative connotations depending on the regional scholarly tradition within which one encounters it.

Church and State Discourses

If Africanists' conceptions of syncretism have differed from Americanists' conceptions this may be attributed, as the foregoing survey suggests, to the pervasive influence of two different larger institutional discourses on the two anthropological traditions. In Africa, it was the European Churches' negative view of syncretism that swayed anthropological usage, while in the New World sociologically-grounded state visions of ethnic synthesis and integration imbued syncretism with positive overtones. On closer examination the discourses of these two institutions—the Church and the state—were actually quite similar. Both envisioned a teleological process of acculturation, or assimilation, whereby initial differences would be eliminated on the way to adopting a dominant standard.

To be sure, different Church and state social theorists often allowed that some degree of original particularity might remain even at the stage of final acculturation. Nonetheless, I think there was an overriding conviction in both institutional discourses that a stable, final phase of cultural homogeneity could be reached. For the Church, the main phase of acculturation would ideally happen in the short space of the catechistic period prior to baptism, at which time the converts became full, bona fide Christians. State sociology recognized a longer period of a generation or more for full assimilation to occur. One important difference was that this dominant standard was, in the case of Africa, externally imposed under conditions of colonialism, while in the Americas it was internally generated in a context of independent nationism.

We have seen how missionaries/social scientists such as Sundkler mediated the institutional view of the Church to the anthropological community. A parallel case can be made for the mediatory role of social scientists such as Herskovits in the New World. Herskovits had one foot very firmly in the academic anthropological community; indeed he was instrumental in establishing the discipline at Northwestern University in Chicago. He was the only anthropologist on the staff when first hired in 1927, but by 1938 he had managed to motivate the establishment of an Anthropology Department proper (Jackson 1986, 110). In 1947, with support from the Carnegie Corporation, he founded the first African Studies programme in the United States and he continued as an influential figure in this field until his death in 1963 (p. 123).

Herskovits was certainly no stranger to the administrators of large foundations and government granting authorities. From the 1920s onward he was a frequent recipient of such grants, and he was often called upon for advice. As a spokesman for the Boasian position he stressed the adaptability of American minorities to new cultural and environmental surroundings and this led to a strong integrationist viewpoint. In 1925 he argued that American

Negro culture had already assumed the same pattern as white culture. The Negro population, he contended, had largely assimilated with white culture, changing itself and the tone of the dominant culture in the process (p. 102). Later, during the 1930s—especially after his first field research in Africa—Herskovits developed the idea that American Negroes unconsciously preserved a number of Africanisms, mainly in the areas of religion, folklore and music. He thus represented a unique and sometimes unpopular position between total assimilationism—which he had earlier tended towards—and the insistence on Negro particularity advocated by a number of Black American sociologists and commentators. Herskovits's post-1930s viewpoint offered one example of how a conviction in "acculturation" could accommodate a degree of lingering ethnic particularity. Africanisms could survive among American Negroes, but they were often matters of unconscious cultural behaviour such as rhythm, or forms of greeting and etiquette which he termed "cultural imponderables" (Apter 1991, 241). These cultural traits were "focal" for African-Americans, but not for the dominant culture, thus their continued existence did not negate the sharing of a common culture (Herskovits 1958, xxvi; Jackson 1986, 112).

In one of his best known books, *The Myth of the Negro Past* (1941), Herskovits presented an elaborate account of his views on Africanisms among New World Negroes by comparing data from Surinam, Haiti, and the United States. One of the objectives of this exercise was to argue against the idea that the experience of slavery had completely destroyed the Negro's history, leaving blacks a deracinated social group in the present (Apter 1991, 237). In making his case for Africanisms he appealed to the concept of syncretism to depict how African customs were used to "reinterpret" New World realities in a distinctive process of acculturation (p. 240). As Herskovits put it in the introduction to the second edition of *The Myth of the Negro Past*,

> Considered in the light of the theory of culture-change, it seemed to me that the syncretizing process really lay at one pole of the continuum that stretched from situations where items from two or more cultures in contact had been fully merged to those situations where there was the unchanged retention of pre-existing ones. (Herskovits 1958, xxii)

An example of syncretic cultural reinterpretation was African polygamy which he identified as being transformed in the New World environment into a recognizable social phenomenon which he labelled "progressive monogamy" (Herskovits 1958, 168; Apter 1991, 240). Another example was the manner in which Haitian Negroes reinterpreted chromolithographs of Catholic saints according to their understanding of African deities. St. John, for example, was identified with an African thunder deity because Catholic images usually depicted him with a lamb, and the ram was the emblem of the god of thunder in Dahomean and Yoruban cosmology (Herskovits 1937, 639).

Syncretisms not only contained "survivals" of the Negroes' past, but offered a mode of uniting the past and the present. Surveying his contribution in the introduction to the second edition (1958) of *The Myth of the Negro Past*, Herskovits wrote,

> The conclusion that we reach is that in Africa, as in the New World, the cultural processes that will be operative will be those of addition and synthesis to achieve congruence with older forms, rather than of subtraction and substitution, with their resulting fragmentation. (1958, xxvii)

It is perhaps less well known that *The Myth of the Negro Past* was written in the space of one year, commissioned by the Carnegie Corporation as part of a large-scale study of the American Negro. The Swedish economist Gunnar Myrdal was invited to direct this project, an appointment for which Herskovits was indirectly responsible, for when consulted by the director of the Corporation he had recommended the appointment of a foreign social scientist, and preferably one from a country without an imperialist tradition (Jackson 1985, 231). Such a person, he argued, would bring a greater degree of objectivity to the investigation. With substantial funds at his disposal, Myrdal commissioned twenty different specialists on the American Negro to prepare "memoranda" which he would then have the advantage of reading before submitting his final report (Myrdal 1964, liv). Herskovits composed *The Myth of the Negro Past* in accordance with this brief. It was a building block for Myrdal's classic *An American Dilemma* which appeared in 1944 and would have enormous influence in the USA for the next two decades at least.

Myrdal's central argument was that racial segregation and discrimination stood as large, disturbing contradictions in a nation espousing democracy, freedom and equality for all—in short, the treatment and predicament of the Negro population contradicted the "American Creed." Writing during World War II, Myrdal stressed the analogy between American attitudes towards Negroes and Nazism, and he used this parallel to goad American moralism into rethinking and rationalizing popular attitudes. At the same time he pointed out that once Negroes received equality of rights and employment, a great many of the problems in interracial relations would be structurally resolved and the society would inevitably move towards greater integration and social justice. On the issue of culture, Myrdal took a strong assimilationist line: "We assume that it is to the advantage of the American Negroes as in individuals and as a group to become assimilated into American culture, to acquire the traits held in esteem by dominant white Americans. This will be the value premise here" (1964, 929).

The high water mark in the reception of *An American Dilemma* came in the Supreme Court's 1954 *Brown v. Board of Education* decision where Chief Justice Earl Warren cited Myrdal's book in passing the decision outlawing school segregation (Jackson 1985, 264). Echoes of Myrdal's ideas are also discernible in Martin Luther King's famous "I Have a Dream" speech where he exhorted America "to live out the true meaning of its creed" (p. 265). These examples illustrate the degree to which the Carnegie Corporation-sponsored study of the American Negro affected national policy and perceptions.

The involvement of Melville Herskovits in this project may thus be pointed to as a prime example of the close relationship and mutual influence which social science and American public sector social policy exerted on each other. Herskovits did not entirely agree with Myrdal's findings, or vice versa. Myrdal was sceptical of Herskovits's thesis about Africanisms (1964, 930), and Herskovits was much less optimistic than Myrdal about the actual progress of assimilation and the real prospects for interracial harmony.[3] As we have seen, from the early 1930s Herskovits increasingly emphasized the African past of New World Negroes, and the influences which this history continued to exercise over present cultural forms. His ideas on these matters set him apart from the majority of contemporary liberal social scientists, who, like Myrdal, placed greater confidence on the process of assimilation. From today's perspective we might view his conceptions of syncretism and cultural reinterpretation as indicative of resistances to domination, or as pointing to sites of struggle for cultural survival (Apter 1991). Herskovits's notion of syncretism thus anticipated recent studies of syncretism which have elaborated this framework of resistance and the politics of culture (cf. Stewart and Shaw 1994). Although out of fashion in the 1940s and 1950s, Herskovits's work on the history of the American Negro dramatically gained in popularity in the 1960s, especially with the rise of the black power movement in the United States (Jackson 1986, 123).

Institutional Changes

The year 1963 represents a watershed in the historical development of Church and state perspectives on key issues affecting the concept of syncretism. This was the second year of the Second Vatican Council (1962–65) and also the year that Glazer and Moynihan published *Beyond the Melting Pot*. Vatican II revised Catholic practice on many points so as to render it more compatible with contemporary realities. It recognized that science and culture were domains separate from religion and legislated greater pursuit and expression in these areas (Abbott 1966, 165). Furthermore it promulgated the translation of Latin liturgical texts into the vernacular languages of each particular congregation (ibid., 150). In the drive to increase public comprehension of the Christian message, the Church did not stop at translation, but also offered that its message could be accommodated to the cultural conventions of foreign societies:

> Living in various circumstances during the course of time, the Church, too, has used in her preaching the discoveries of different cultures to spread and explain the message of Christ to all nations, to probe it and more deeply understand it, and to give it better expression in liturgical celebrations and in the life of the diversified community of the faithful.
>
> But at the same time, the Church, sent to all peoples of every time and place, is not bound exclusively and indissolubly to any race or nation, nor to any particular way of life or any customary pattern of living, ancient or recent. Faithful to her own tradition and at the same time conscious of her universal mission, she can enter into communion with various cultural modes, to her own enrichment and theirs too. (Abbott 1966, 264)

It is certainly true that since ancient times the Church has necessarily worked through cultural translation to communicate the gospel message to peoples living around the Mediterranean Sea. The reiteration of this idea in the Vatican II decrees was a significant response to the actual predicament of Catholic churches in areas of the recently missionized and now de-colonized world. Vatican II expressly allowed, for example, that where initiation rites are found in mission lands that, "elements of these, when capable of being adapted to Christian ritual, may be admitted along with those already found in Christian tradition" (Abbott 1966, 159). Likewise, a 1563 decree from the Council of Trent was cited approvingly: "If certain locales traditionally use other praiseworthy customs and ceremonies when celebrating the sacrament of matrimony, this sacred Synod earnestly desires that these by all means be retained" (161). The institution of the Catholic Church was, in effect, redrawing the boundaries around syncretism by recognizing that a degree of cultural adaptation would not affect the content of the Christian message.

Widening the range of allowable cultural expressions made syncretisms more difficult to identify, but it certainly did not lead to an abolition of the concept. There was still the possibility that some adaptations of Christianity could distort or misapprehend divine revelation. A deepened understanding of cultures on the part of the Church would not only help in finding suitable local forms through which to express the true Christian message, but would also be necessary in ruling certain syntheses out of bounds:

> A better view will be gained of how their customs, outlook on life, and social order can be reconciled with the manner of living taught by

divine revelation. As a result, avenues will be opened for a more pro-found adaptation in the whole area of Christian life. Thanks to such a procedure, every appearance of syncretism and of false particularism can be excluded, and Christian life can be accommodated to the genius and the dispositions of each culture. (Abbott 1966, 612 f.)

Clearly "syncretism" still receives a negative meaning in Vatican II usage, but many practices that might have been disparaged as syncretism in decades previous would henceforth be allowed as valid, culturally specific expressions of the one faith. This shift of "frame" is a matter to which we shall return.

Glazer and Moynihan's *Beyond the Melting Pot* is nowhere near as important a document as the decrees of Vatican II. I call attention to it because its well-known title captures the new *Zeitgeist* which began to take hold in mid-1960s America and soon flourished in a host of movements articulating ethnic pride. *Beyond the Melting Pot* was one of the first nails in the coffin of the optimistic assimilationism of the Myrdal era. As Glazer and Moynihan wrote in their preface:

The notion that the intense and unprecedented mixture of ethnic and religious groups in American life was soon to blend into a homogeneous end product has outlived its usefulness, and also its credibility ... The point about the melting pot ... is that it did not happen. (1970, xcvii)

They go on to elaborate that all immigrants have acculturated in the United States; it is not the case that they remain fully Irish or Italian in a fashion consistent with the current inhabitants of those countries. But neither do they become fully homogenized Americans. Instead they create a new identity and recognize themselves and are recognized by others as members of distinctive groups (ibid., 13).

An account of the post-1960s politics of ethnicity in the United States is beyond the scope of this study. It is sufficient for my purposes simply to note that subsequent debates over ethnic politics, and more recently, multiculturalism, have generally fought over the boundaries between the demands of a national culture and the rights of ethnic groups to express their particularity and have these expressions acknowledged and respected. To put it simplistically, the debate can be viewed as a contest over cultural mixture: how much should be allowed, and at what socio-political level? Under the guidance of social science, ethnic politics began to take a new course after 1963, one which elaborated ethnic differences and then—in some versions at least—urged public recognition and tolerance rather than accepting the blanket assimilationism of the previous period. In this respect the discourse of social science apparently came to diverge from the Church discourse which it earlier paralleled.

Since 1963 the Catholic Church[4] has expanded its acceptance of culturally-mixed religious expressions where once it would have scorned many of these as syncretic. The American state, on the other hand, under the pressure of popular movements, has been forced to concede that what it once thought it had forged in the way of a common culture must now be unravelled. But such a contrast may be superficial and the two discourses might actually still be on a parallel course towards increased promotion of syncretism. It is possible that multiculturalism may lead to a greater and more profoundly integrated common culture. Under the melting-pot ideology citizens were mainly formed according to a Eurocentric, indeed a heavily Anglo-centric, master narrative. It is not certain that a new master narrative of American identity will now replace this, but if one does, then, granted the stimulus of learning about other cultures in school and in other public spheres, there is a chance that it will be more profoundly syncretic. It may be that instead of just rolling back previous syncretic progress, the current phase of multiculturalism is actually a means of redirecting further syncretization (cf. Baumann 1995).

Syncretism Today

In contemporary social theory, processes such as globalization, international migration and the formation of diasporas are subjects of great interest. In this body of literature the word "syncretism" has begun to reappear alongside allied concepts such as cultural hybridization and creolization as a means of capturing the dynamics of actual global processes. In the process of exploring cultural hybridity writers such as Edward Said (1993), Paul Gilroy (1993) and James Clifford (1988) have lifted syncretism out of the framework of acculturation—syncretism is no longer a transient "stage" which will disappear when, with time, assimilation occurs. Cultural borrowing and interpenetration are instead seen as part of the very nature of cultures. To phrase it more accurately, syncretism describes the process by which cultures constitute themselves at any given point in time. Today's hybridization will simply give way to tomorrow's hybridization, the form of which will be dictated by historico-political events and contingencies.

The idea of cultural purity has become entirely suspect in anthropology, and largely replaced by the view that cultures are porous to external influences which may be adopted or resisted, but either way come to affect the form of social life in any given place. Culture is not a coherent structure which is successfully transmitted across generations, but rather the outcome, at any particular moment, of historical and social processes (Bourdieu 1977; Ortner 1984). "Syncretism" can be used within this theoretical framework to focus attention precisely on issues of accommodation, contest, appropriation, indigenization and a host of other dynamic intercultural processes.

If we accept the premise that there are no pure cultures, then we are led to suppose that there are no pure religious traditions either. Historians of religions have, indeed, long expressed this view (van der Leeuw 1938, 609; cf. Droogers 1989, 9 f.). Acceptance of this observation puts to rest the frequently-heard criticism that syncretism necessarily assumes the existence of ideal pure traditions in contrast to which other traditions are mixed, or syncretic. All that need be accepted is that syncretism involves the amalgamation of elements from two or more different traditions. But if we accept that all religions are syncretic, how useful can this term be? As Baird has objected, "to say that 'Christianity' or the 'mystery religions' or 'Hinduism' are syncretistic is not to say anything that distinguishes them from anything else and is merely equivalent to admitting that each has a history and can be studied historically" (1991, 146).

While I agree with Baird's point, I think that he only rules out placing undue optimism in the theological, analytical potential of the concept. His observation does not change the fact that all religions are composites at present and will continue to innovate and forge new hybrid forms in the future. Syncretism remains valid as a descriptive term to refer to this aspect of religious traditions and cultural forms generally. This is where social science takes over. Social scientists have begun to recognize that syncretism, perhaps referenced by a synonym or circumlocution, can also form part of folk theories of culture. As such, it plays a role in directing the invention of traditions or the aggressive dismissal of neighbouring traditions. A case in point might be those Hindu nationalists who insist that their religion syncretically encompasses the Islam of their Indian co-nationals (van der Veer 1994).

The syncretic-ness of all religions may be an unexceptional fact, but pointing this out socially often amounts to an expression of power differentiation and social control. It is a term that has historically been applied to someone else's body of religious practice. The bearers of a given tradition rarely acknowledge that it might be syncretic—although I think they can, and should. When at the beginning of this century theologians pointed out that Christianity itself was syncretic, they were met with disapproval on the part of western Christians (Baird 1991, 143). The study of how a people contest, negotiate and act on attributions of syncretism, if, that is, they do act at all, requires a switch from theology, to the sociology of theology in both scholarly and popular forms. Furthermore, denials of syncretism, whether by academic analysts or the people under study, are every bit as interesting as cases where the compositeness of religious traditions is recognized and accepted.

In putting an anthropology of popular theology into practice there are a number of pitfalls which European and North American anthropologists must negotiate. Chief among these is the degree to which our own notions of religion, and religious integrity, or non-syncretic-ness, are informed by Judaeo-Christian ideas. I can use myself by way of example here.

Recently I published a study (1991) of local religion in Greece concentrating on the discrepancies between Greek Orthodox doctrine and apparently anomalous local beliefs in demons, called *exotiká* in Greek. The names and features of certain of these demons can easily be shown to come from ancient Greek religion. Their appearance within contemporary Christianity thus poses a clear example of syncretism. In the introduction to my book I argued that these theologically non-standard elements were incorporated into Greek Orthodoxy in the early centuries of Christianity when ancient (pagan) religions were still viable traditions followed by large numbers of adherents. By the sixth or seventh centuries, in Greece at least, most of the adherents of ancient religions had converted to Christianity, which became the primary religion left in Greece. I considered the first five centuries of Christianity to be a time of active syncretism between Christianity and paganism, a period in which Christianity triumphed by absorbing paganism within its theological and cosmological structure. When paganism ceased to be a vital, alternative form of religion I judged Christian-Pagan syncretism to have ceased. Since this occurred more than a millennium ago, I wrote that Orthodox Christianity should be considered a synthetic as opposed to a syncretic religion, attempting to differentiate between an active, ongoing process of syncretism and the completed results of such a process. I pointed out, in addition, that contemporary practitioners of Greek Orthodoxy consider themselves as exclusively that, and they practise a religion that is theologically unified. For them their religion is an integrated Christian whole (1991, 7).

Having reconsidered the question, I would now insist that Greek Orthodoxy is syncretic in so far as it has historically absorbed and incorporated influences from Judaism, Egyptian religion and other religious traditions located around the Mediterranean in the first centuries of our era. That people now experience it as a unified Christian faith is a significant observation, but it does not change the fact of the fundamental syncretic-ness of Christian theology and cosmology. What is, I now think, most objectionable in my earlier view is the assertion that Orthodox Christianity reached a point of stability in the early Middle Ages. Once the idea of stable traditions is introduced, how far away can the notion of pure traditions be? This, then, is pitfall number one for the European anthropologist writing about syncretic situations, especially where Christianity is one of the religions involved. Just because Christianity "triumphed," and assimilated alternative, pagan elements within its structure does not make it non-syncretic. Furthermore, I think my position was influenced by the popular theological opinion, itself conditioned by professional theology, that Christianity is an integral, non-syncretic religion. Other religions are syncretic, but not ours. Historians of religions may have disputed this, but their opinions have not significantly revised widespread and well-entrenched popular attitudes to the contrary.

The issue of historical time deserves special consideration in this example; it is a feature of the Greek case which does not differentiate it from other situations of syncretism. Anthropologists of Buddhism similarly argue about whether this religion may be considered syncretic. Buddhism has, manifestly, absorbed and retained numerous elements from Hinduism. The Buddha began life as a Hindu, much as Christ began life as a Jew, and went on to found a new religion which incorporated many ideas from this pre-existing tradition. Yet several scholars of Theravada Buddhism have argued that it is not syncretic. Most notably, Richard Combrich (1971, 48) has contended that Hindu gods have featured in Buddhist practice since the religion began, and are therefore traditional features of it. On my view this is precisely why Sri Lankan Buddhism is basically syncretic. Its form may be "orthodox"— that is, consistent with its earliest forms and most important precepts—but considering it "syncretic" does not necessarily throw this orthodoxy into doubt. Syncretic religions can be orthodox, just as they can be experienced as an integral whole.

The fact that Christianity, like Buddhism, possesses a long literate history may be another feature which originally caused me to view Greek Orthodoxy as stable, or synthetic. I was focused on a long written tradition of doctrine and scripture which on the one hand was armature for Christianity against the pressures of change, but furthermore a source of deception for the latter-day scholar who may think that because the doctrine was stable the actual local practice of the religion was also uniform and stable. Local historical evidence which might reveal an alternative picture of heretical excrescence and exogenous influence is sometimes difficult to find, but it was almost surely the case. In any event, this was what my own research showed, using contemporary fieldwork to paint a picture of heterodoxy beneath the orthodox surface of the contemporary Greek Church.

Because Christianity is our own tradition with a long historical record of theological refinement and precision behind it in the West, we are easily led to assume that Africans' or Melanesians' scant century-long versions of Christianity must necessarily be syncretic, or at least more syncretic than ours. If we do look at European Christianity as it is actually practised, we will see much to convince us of its syncretism, and of the vitality of its syncretism either in competitive relationship with New Age religions, or in its response to secular social forces such as feminism or science.

Process and Stability

The concept of syncretism alerts us to an important tension between stable condition and ongoing process. The very word, and its adjectival derivatives "syncretic" or "syncretistic," teeter like gerunds on the border between the verbal and the nominal. We can speak of syncretism as a condition/state— for instance "Mayan-Christian syncretism"—or we may speak of a process of syncretism thereby designating something dynamic and ongoing—for instance "Hindu-Muslim syncretism intensified during the Middle Ages." In respect of this tension between structure and process, syncretism does not radically differ from most other social phenomena. In part this dilemma may be an artefact of social-science enquiry, which requires the researcher to act like a photographer converting fluid social action into still frames, for analysis. This dilemma is probably not finally resolvable; it is an essential anthropological tension. When viewed at a certain moment in time, continuing processes do take on the appearance of discrete states and not only do social scientists frequently perceive social and cultural forms to be established and enduring, but the social actors they describe often work with this premise as well.

So syncretism is a momentary state of mixture between two or more different religions, but this is a temporary balance in a process which can lead in any direction—whether toward further accretive mixture, or toward the unravelling of past syntheses. This transitoriness of syncretic combinations may be obscured by the existence of written texts which, in the form of holy scriptures, ritual handbooks and theological commentaries can have the effect of stabilizing a tradition or, at the very least, of creating an orthodox standard by which divergent local traditions are evaluated, if not regulated (Goody 1986). In the cases of Christianity and Islam, these features are all present and give rise to a strong sense of religious boundaries; existing laws and theological pronouncements prevent one from freely innovating. Unauthorized innovators run the risk of being labelled heretics or practitioners of another faith. These features of religions of the book work to suppress, or punish, spontaneous syncretism from within particular regional and historical traditions. I think some difference in syncretic potential must be acknowledged between religions of the Book and non-literate religions such as local Nigerian religious practice which is basically more receptive to the incorporation of diverse, exogenous deities into its repertoire of worship (Peel 1968).

There are, then, differences worth observing between, on the one hand, Pagan-Christian syncretism, which finished more than a thousand years ago and involved the disappearance of paganism as a separate tradition, and on the other hand, the syncretisms between indigenous African religious traditions and Christianity which began much more recently and are still ongoing.

In Africa, African religion and Christianity remain vital traditions, and in between the two, depending on the place, there even exists a choice of syntheses, such as Zionist or Ethiopian Churches in South Africa. A distinction between active, ongoing and past, finished processes should be retained, even though the results of each should nonetheless be termed syncretic.

What needs to be stressed in the Greek case, however, is that Christian Orthodoxy did not cease to be actively syncretic when paganism disappeared. On the contrary, it immediately began to absorb influences from Islam. The eighth-century controversy over iconoclasm, for example, can be understood as the effect of an Islamic aesthetics of non-representation on a Greek tradition rich in iconography. Interestingly, in the late Middle Ages and up to the modern period, Greek Orthodoxy seems to have absorbed less from surrounding religions and I think this is in part due to the effect of the collapse of the Byzantine Empire and the degree of inimicality between Orthodoxy and Catholicism on the one side, and Orthodoxy and the Islam of the Ottoman Turks on the other. In this period, consciousness of religious boundaries was greatly raised; religious autonomy was inextricably bound up with political autonomy and this is what the Byzantines were fighting for.

At the fifteenth-century Council of Florence, convened to discuss the reunion of the Orthodox and Catholic Churches, the Greek representatives vigorously disputed seemingly minor issues such as the use of unleavened bread in the Eucharist, or the inclusion of the *filioque* clause, holding that the Holy Spirit emanates from both the Father and the Son, in the Creed. After much wrangling over these matters (Gill 1959), the Byzantine contingent did, finally, accede to Catholic demands and they signed a decree of union. However, no sooner had they disembarked back in Constantinople than they began to repudiate and openly campaign against the implementation of the agreement. The Council of Florence was an attempt to gain European military support by entering into full communion with the Catholic Church. Had the decree been widely supported and accepted in Byzantium there is a chance that the Emperor would have received enough aid to enable him to repel the encroaching Ottomans. As it was, the preservation of religious boundaries proved more important than this, and the Byzantine Empire fell a scant fourteen years after the Council of Florence.

Similarly, during the long period of Ottoman rule from 1453 until the nineteenth century, Orthodoxy mixed relatively little with Islam because of the politicized and highly sensitized nature of the boundaries between the two religions. The Ottomans never demanded that Christians convert; on the contrary, they respected all religions of the Book within their domain, and administered them through their religious leaders. The Greeks were lumped together with other Orthodox Christians, like Serbs and Bulgarians, under the leadership of the Patriarch of Constantinople. Orthodoxy was granted considerable autonomy by the colonizers thus enabling it to preserve its integrity and discreteness.

Of course, syncretism was always possible in these periods—between Judaism, Catholicism, Orthodoxy and Islam primarily—and good regional historical research (for instance, Hasluck 1929) reveals its nature—mutual patronage of shrines and cults. My impression, however, is that there was not that much amalgamation because of the freedom of religious expression and the importance of religion as practically the sole indicator of group identity. It is in the period since Greek independence (1832) that Greek Christianity has been more permeable to influences such as Protestantism, Jehovah's Witnesses, and New Age sects and cults. Notably none of these is tainted by association with the primordial "other" religious traditions of the region during the Ottoman period: Islam, Catholicism and Judaism. Now, with around 96 per cent of the populace at least nominally Orthodox, religious boundaries and identity have become more assumed than defended, although the recent neo-Orthodox movement, now growing in magnitude, is concerned to reverse any inroads made by "European" Christianity into Greek Orthodoxy.

Frame

If historical time is one parameter affecting the pace of syncretism, and sometimes even the recognition of it altogether, then what I here refer to as "frame" poses similar problems. Granted that we can recognize two different religious traditions in a given social field, how can we ascertain that they have indeed mixed rather than simply stand juxtaposed to one another? In brief, how can we differentiate syncretism from religious pluralism?

If we go to a hospital, for example, and see that Chinese acupuncture—or acumoxa—is being administered in one room whereas laser surgery is being performed in the next room, we would not seriously consider this a syncretism of Chinese and Western medicine.[5] To offer another example, in Trinidad one may encounter Hindu followers of three different religions: Hindu Kali Mai cultists, Shouter Baptists and adherents of Shango, all subscribing to very similar beliefs and practices regarding possession (Vertovec 1992). At first one might be tempted to consider this the result of mutual borrowing, or syncretism, but closer inspection reveals that the possession phenomena in question can be accounted for as internal features of each of the separate religious traditions. Furthermore, none of the actors involved attributed these similarities to borrowing, but rather just to coincidental convergence (ibid.). In this case, we must once again rule out syncretism on the grounds that no "mixture" may be discerned either from our own or from the actors' points of view.

The issue of frame emerges most importantly, for our purposes, in the very definition of religion itself, especially in the boundaries which are set between religion and culture. As we have seen, the Catholic Church's opening towards "inculturation," beginning with Vatican II, posed one example of how religious specialists may themselves reconsider and re-draw the boundaries between religion and culture. Is the symbol of the lamb, for example, essential to the Christian message, or might it be replaceable by an equivalent symbol in regions where sheep and goats are not herded? Likewise, as Schreiter asks, can we allow the bread and wine of the Eucharist to be replaced by other foods in regions where they are not known (1985, 8)?

In his study of Sinhalese Catholics, Stirrat (1992) has shown how the Catholic Church initially forbade the use of drums in Christian rituals and the wearing of white as a colour of mourning. The Church identified these practices as "Buddhist" and therefore as incompatible elements from a different religion which should not be mixed with Catholicism. After independence, however, when Buddhism began to set the tone of Sinhalese culture, it became important for Sri Lankan Catholics to participate more fully in this national culture rather than to be seen preserving sub-cultural practices which linked them with western colonialism. Encouraged by the Vatican II pronouncements, the use of drums and the wearing of white for mourning were reclassified as acceptable elements of Sinhalese culture which did not threaten the integrity of Catholicism. Numerous other examples, such as Mende (Sierra Leone) debates over whether participation in women's initiation rites is consistent with Islam (Ferme 1994), can be cited to show how widespread is this problematic division between participation in local, or national, culture and religious integrity.

Ultimately these frames are not stable, as clearly emerges in the case of Catholicism, and even the separate frames maintained on Trinidad may one day be altered, or collapsed altogether. What is important to see and study sociologically, I think, is that the implementation of these frames is socially, politically and historically contingent. This is true whether it comes as a theological pronouncement or as an academic observation. As an example, we may once again refer to Gombrich's study of Sri Lankan Buddhism (1971). We have already seen that he discounted the possibility of syncretism on the grounds that elements of Hinduism were time-honoured components of Buddhism. But he offers another ground as well, namely that Buddhism is fundamentally soteriological and only practices directed at salvation properly qualify as elements of Buddhist religion. The Hindu deities drafted into the Buddhist pantheon are primarily appealed to for mundane, "this-worldly" ends such as gaining prosperity or curing illness. Given the narrow frame which he sets up for Buddhism, then, Hindu gods are excluded; they are not aspects of Buddhist religion, hence one more reason why Sri Lankan Buddhism is not syncretic (p. 49).

This position contrasts with my own study of Greek Orthodoxy (1991, 11) where I considered that there was a certain core of cosmological structure and a "salvation idiom" which were essential to Christianity and which, if significantly contradicted, would be grounds for ruling an innovative cult non-Christian. The panoply of demons that I studied, such as the Hindu deities within Buddhism, did not perhaps conform to the letter of Christian doctrine, but neither did they contradict the basic kernel of Christian Orthodoxy. I considered them tolerable variations, the stuff of local religion, but not elements which fall outside the frame of Christianity. Thus I deem the coexistence of non-Christian demons within the basic structure—or frame—of Orthodoxy to be a clear example of syncretism. Gombrich concedes something similar when he describes Buddhism as "accretive" (1971, 49), but he then seems to draw a tighter frame around Buddhism such that accreted Hindu deities and the this-worldly concerns expressed around them fall outside of Buddhism proper. That other anthropologists of Buddhism have disputed the description of Buddhist "religion" as limited strictly to eschatology (cf. Gellner 1990, 103) only further indicates the subjectivity and variability besetting the demarcation of frames.

Conclusion

Ultimately the anthropology of syncretism is not concerned with pronouncing whether Buddhism, or any other religion, is or is not syncretic, but rather with studying the various arguments made for or against the notion of religious mixing. I think it should be concerned with competing discourses over mixture, whether syncretic or anti-syncretic. Wherever syncretism occurs, or has occurred, it is usually accompanied by a parallel discourse which might be termed meta-syncretic: the commentary, and registered perceptions of actors as to whether amalgamation has occurred and whether this is good or bad. A strictly objectivist view could never be sufficient.

In order to implement this anthropology of syncretism, I think we need to proceed with the broadest and most general definition of syncretism: the combination of elements from two or more different religious traditions within a specified frame. This much founds a consistent starting point. We can establish that two or more different traditions are involved, and what the relevant frame is, either on the basis of what the actors involved say, or on the basis of our own analytical reasoning as long as we clearly indicate when we are taking which perspective.

Of course these differences of perspective introduce another difference in frame—that between insiders and outsiders, or between subjective and objectivist views—and it might be the case that we will often end up studying how a given social group negotiates the claims of outsiders such as the

Catholic Church, or influential individuals such as the Oxford Professor of Sanskrit. Sociological assessments do enter into and affect the social contexts they pronounce upon, sometimes as the undergirding to government policy, sometimes as legitimating support for various positions in the social field. In agreement with Droogers (1989, 20) I consider the social-science study of syncretism to be crucially about the various discourses which seek to control the definition of syncretism in a given social field, whether promulgated by insiders or outsiders.

Most previous definitions of syncretism stipulate that a syncretism must fuse disparate, disharmonious elements, or that it necessarily contravenes the tenets of one or more of the initial religious systems, that it involves ambiguity, or any number of other criteria. From the perspective that I advocate here, these sorts of assertions need to be examined as part of the strategic social negotiation of religious synthesis, rather than as definitive of syncretism altogether. Decisions about whether certain religious forms are theologically inconsistent, or give rise to ambiguous "dual systems" of belief (Schreiter 1985, 144 f.), are part of power struggles over syncretism. Social anthropologists and sociologists should try to identify where these contests are taking place and render accounts of them, rather than allow themselves to be trapped into contributing to them.

Notes

* I would like to acknowledge my debt to Rosalind Shaw who engaged in many rich discussions of syncretism with me during our collaboration in editing *Syncretism/Antisyncretism: The Politics of Religious Synthesis* (1994). Our introduction to that volume, titled "Problematizing Syncretism," is the point of departure for the present chapter. I also thank Göran Aijmer and all the participants in the IASSA (The Institute for Advanced Studies in Social Anthropology, University of Gothenburg, Sweden) conference on syncretism for their stimulating exchange of ideas on various issues surrounding syncretism.

1. Although some passages in *Bantu Prophets in South Africa* appear objectionable today—such as the ones I have cited—Sundkler's overall contribution can be viewed in a positive light as establishing a new missionary awareness of African forms of Christianity (Kuper 1987, 155).

2. In earlier works Comaroff makes greater use of the concept of syncretism (for instance, 1981) and the term does appear in *Body of Power, Spirit of Resistance* (1985).

3. It should also be noted that Herskovits was not entirely pleased to be engaged in a project which, in retrospect, possessed characteristics of "social engineering." It has been amply demonstrated that Herskovits dogmatically eschewed applied social science and even refused to join the NAACP (National Association for the Advancement of Colored People) at first—although he agreed with its main goals and did later join—because he thought this would compromise his scientific objectivity (Jackson 1986, 115 ff.;

Fernandez 1990, 151). Herskovits believed that it was sufficient for social scientists to produce knowledge and that this would itself lead to the amelioration of unfortunate social situations. If Blacks were to read his *The Myth of the Negro Past*, for example, or simply learn of its findings, it would enable them to discover that they have a past, and provide assurance that they have a future as well (1958, xxvix).

4. Protestant Churches adopt similar stances, especially regarding missionization (Pickering 1992).

5. This example arose in discussions with Elisabeth Hsü at the IASSA conference.

References

Abbott, W., ed. 1966. *Documents of Vatican II*. London: Geoffrey Chapman.

Apter, A. 1991. "Herskovits's Heritage: Rethinking Syncretism in the African Diaspora." *Diaspora* 1: 235–60.

Baird, R. D. 1991 [1971]. *Category Formation and the History of Religions*. 2nd ed. The Hague and Paris: Mouton & Co.

Bourdieu, P. 1977. *Outline of a Theory of Practice*. Cambridge: Cambridge University Press.

Clifford, J. 1988. *The Predicament of Culture*. Cambridge, MA: Harvard University Press.

Comaroff, J. 1981. "Healing and Cultural Transformation: The Tswana of Southern Africa." *Social Science and Medicine* 15b: 367–78.

—1985. *Body of Power, Spirit of Resistance: The Culture and History of a South African People*. Chicago: University of Chicago Press.

Combrich, R. 1971. *Precept and Practice: Traditional Buddhism in the Rural Highlands of Ceylon*. Oxford: Clarendon Press.

Droogers, A. 1989. "Syncretism: The Problem of Definition, the Definition of the Problem." In *Dialogue and Symcretism: An Interdisciplinary Approach*, ed. J. Gort, H. Vroom, R. Fernhout and A. Wessels, 7–25. Amsterdam: Editions Rodopi.

Edmonson, M. *et al.* 1960. *Nativism and Syncretism*. Middle American Research Institute, Publication 19. New Orleans: Tulane University.

Evans-Pritchard, E. E. 1940. *The Nuer: A Description of the Modes of Livelihood and the Political Institutions of a Nilotic People*. Oxford: Clarendon Press.

—1956. *Nuer Religion*. Oxford: Clarendon Press.

Fardon, R. 1990. *Localizing Strategies: Regional Traditions of Ethnographic Writing*. Edinburgh: Scottish Academic Press.

Ferme, M. 1994. "What 'Alhaji Airplane' Saw in Mecca, and What Happened When He Came Home: Ritual Transformation in a Mende Community (Sierra Leone)." In Stewart and Shaw, eds. 1994, 27–44.

Fernandez, J. W. 1990. "Tolerance in a Repugnant World and Other Dilemmas in the Cultural Relativism of Melville Herskovits." *Ethos* 18: 140–64.

Freyre, G. 1945. *The Masters and the Slaves*. New York: Knopf.

Gellner, D. 1990. "What is the Anthropology of Buddhism About?" *Journal of the Anthropological Society of Oxford* (Special Issue: The Anthropology of Buddhism) 21: 95–112.

Gill, J. 1959. *The Council of Florence*. Cambridge: Cambridge University Press.

Gilroy, P. 1993. *The Black Atlantic: Modernity and Double Consciousness*. London: Verso.

Glazer, N., and D. P. Moynihan. 1970 [1963]. *Beyond the Melting Pot: The Negroes, Puerto Ricans, Jews, Italians and Irish of New York City*. 2nd ed. Cambridge, MA: MIT Press.

Goody, J. 1986. *The Logic of Writing and the Organization of Society*. Cambridge: Cambridge University Press.

Hasluck, F. W. 1929. *Christianity and Islam Under the Sultans*. Oxford: Oxford University Press.

Herskovits, M. 1937. "African Gods and Catholic Saints in New World Negro Belief." *American Anthropologist* 39: 635–43.

—1958 [1941]. *The Myth of the Negro Past*. 2nd ed. Boston: Beacon Press.

Jackson, W. 1985. "The Making of a Social Science Classic: Gunnar Myrdal's *An American Dilemma*," *Perspectives in American History*, NS 2: 221–67.

—1986. "Melville Herskovits and the Search for Afro-American Culture." In *Malinowski, Rivers, Benedict, and Others*, ed. G. Stocking. Madison: University of Wisconsin Press.

Kiernan, J. 1992. "Slaves No More: The Creation of Independence by Religious Synthesis." Paper, 2nd EASA Conference, Prague.

Kuper, A. 1987. "The Magician and the Missionary." In *South Africa and the Anthropologist*. London: Routledge.

Leeuw, G. van der. 1938 [1933]. *Religion in Essence and Manifestation*. New York: Macmillan.

McNeill, J. T. 1930. *Unitive Protestantism*. New York: Abingdon Press.

Myrdal, G. 1964 [1944]. *An American Dilemma*. 2nd ed. New York: McGraw–Hill.

Nutini, H. 1988. *Todos Santos in Rural Tlaxcala: A Syncretic, Expressive, and Symbolic Analysis of the Cult of the Dead*. Princeton: Princeton University Press.

—n.d. "Talk on Syncretism at the University of Gothenburg." Notes for the IASSA Conference on Syncretism, June 1993.

Ortner, S. 1984. "Theory in Anthropology Since the Sixties." *Comparative Studies in Society and History* 26: 126–66.

Pato, L. 1990. "The African Independent Churches: A Socio-Cultural Approach." *Journal of Theology for Southern Africa* 72: 24–35.

Peel, J. D. Y. 1968. "Syncretism and Religious Change." *Comparative Studies in Society and History* 10: 121–41.

Pickering, W. S. 1992. "Introduction: Old Positions and New Concerns." *Journal of the Anthropological Society of Oxford* (Special Issue: Anthropology and the Missionaries: Some Case Studies) 22: 99–110.

Said, E. 1993. *Culture and Imperialism*. London: Vintage Books.

Schmid, H. 1846. *Geschichte der synchretischen Streitigkeiten in der Zeit des Georg Calixt*. Erlangen: Carl Heydner.

Schreiter, R. 1985. *Constructing Local Theologies*. London: SCM Press.

Stewart, C. 1991. *Demons and the Devil: Moral Imagination in Modern Greek Culture*. Princeton: Princeton University Press.

Stewart, C., and R. Shaw, eds. 1994. *Syncretism/Anti-Syncretism: The Politics of Religious Synthesis*. London: Routledge.

Stirrat, R. L. 1992. *Power and Religiosity in a Post-Colonial Setting: Sinhala Catholics in Contemporary Sri Lanka*. Cambridge: Cambridge University Press.

Sundkler, Bengt. 1961 [1948]. *Bantu Prophets in South Africa*. 2nd ed. London: Oxford University Press.

Veer, P. van der, ed. 1994. "Syncretism, Multiculturalism and the Discourse of Tolerance." In Stewart and Shaw, eds. 1994, 196–211.

Vertovec, S. 1992. "Ethnicity and the Perception of Religious Convergence: Shango, Spiritual Baptist, and the Kali Mai Traditions in Trinidad." Paper, 2nd EASA Conference, Prague.

West, Martin. 1975. *Bishops and Prophets in a Black City*. Cape Town: David Philip.

Wilson, M. 1961. *Reaction to Conquest*. London: Oxford University Press.

285

SYNCRETISM, HISTORICISM, AND COGNITION: A RESPONSE TO MICHAEL PYE[*]

Luther H. Martin

"Syncretism" is a central category for the modern study of religion, the sense of which remains, nevertheless, anchored in the historical orientation of its nineteenth-century definition. The overriding historiographical goal during this century was an understanding of human history "wie es eigentlich gewesen," to cite Leopold von Ranke's historistic dictum (1824, *Vorrede*). This positivistic assumption concerning the accessibility and nature of the past informed a view of religions as more or less coherent systems of belief in which a primordial or original "hierophany" became progressively diluted or contaminated through historical transmission. In the succinct formulation of Ioan Couliano, this view can be summarized as the search for "origins and transgressions" (1990, 57). The cardinal historical process whereby the integrity of a particular religious system might be violated was termed "syncretism."

1. Some Early Uses of "Syncretism"

The notion of "syncretism" was first given academic currency by von Ranke's younger contemporary, the German historian, J. G. Droysen, who described, in his *Geschichte des Hellenismus* (1980; originally published in 1836), the "east-west mixture of people" that occurred in the aftermath of Alexander's far-flung conquests in the fourth century BCE (Martin 1983, 134–37). This descriptive model of mutual cultural influence during the Hellenistic period remains the classical model for any discussion of syncretism. Although not much used in social-scientific research,[1] "syncretism" has become a central category in studies of religion, largely through the influence of the German *Religionsgeschichtliche Schule* (Rudolph 1979, 196). Syncretism, in other words, refers almost exclusively to religious syncretism. To cite one definition based on the Hellenistic model, syncretism is "a blending of religious ideas and practices, by means of which either one set adopts more or less thoroughly the principles of another or both are amalgamated in a more cosmopolitan and less polytheistic shape" (Moffatt 1922, 157).

This understanding of syncretism, however, is based on the Greek verb, *synkerannumi* ("to mix together"), the quite literal Latin translation of which is *confusio*—hardly a helpful designation?[2]

From about the same time that "syncretism" began to be used to describe religious disorder, it also began to be employed by Biblical theologians to characterize Greco-Roman paganism in contrast to the normative and exclusivistic claims of Christian origins;[3] and, subsequently, by Protestant theologians to characterize the historical corruptions they attributed to Roman Catholicism[4] (Smith 1990, 1–26). This idiosyncratic usage, the sense of which is derived from the same Greek root, *synkerannumi*, is exemplified by Hermann Usener, who wrote of syncretism as a "*Religionsmischerei*" ("mishmash of religions") in contrast to the "faith of the fathers" (1948, 337, 340). If, however, we are to retain notions such as "syncretism" as categories of religious knowledge, then the processes of their formation and the performing of their organization must be explained on the basis of more or less scientific criteria.

2. What Does Syncretism Explain?

In recent theoretical discussions, syncretism has been understood as the consequence of historical, social, and/or cultural processes to be described. One of the foremost proponents of employing "syncretism" as a description of ongoing religious histories has been Michael Pye. Already in 1971, Pye argued that syncretistic situations must "be understood *entirely* in terms of the dynamics of religion" (1971, 93, emphasis added).

Whereas the rehabilitation of a descriptive over a normative use of the category represents a clear theoretical advance, problems remain. One problem with descriptions of syncretistic formations is a tendency to retain historist assumptions about stable cultural systems against which they are measured.[5] In his oft-cited definition, Clifford Geertz, for example, writes that culture is "an historically transmitted pattern of meanings embodied in symbols, a system of inherited conceptions expressed in symbolic forms by means of which men communicate, perpetuate and develop their knowledge about and attitudes toward life" (1973, 89)—itself an understanding influenced by Weber's historicism[6] (Comaroff and Comaroff 1991, 249). Upon such assumptions, Carsten Colpe concludes: "It can be stated as a principle that syncretism, when verifiable, is a late stage in a particular epoch of the history of religions" (1987, 226). This notion of religious syncretism as a symbolic or ritual complex derived from two or more antecedent systems would seem to retain much of its earlier shape as a category of religious change as defined in terms of western/Christian assumptions about an original religious integrity against which syncretistic formations may be measured.[7]

Such "canonical" views of cultural integrity have been identified by the anthropologist, Pascal Boyer, as representing a "theologistic bias," which "consists in the assumption that the religious representations of a given group, 'culture,' or 'society' constitute an integrated and consistent set of abstract principles." Such a bias leads to descriptions of syncretistic formations "in which [antecedent] religious beliefs are presented as consisting of shared, context-free statements"[8] (1994, 40). Boyer emphasizes, however, that

> ... people [just] do not live in simple cultural environments where an integrated "cultural scheme" is shared by most members of the group and unambiguously displayed in various episodes of social interaction. More realistically, we must conceive that, at any time, cultural assumptions are available in many different variants. ... People live in cultural environments where constant undirected variation is the rule rather than the exception. (1994, 256)

If stable or normative religious contexts from which religious variations may be differentiated do not, in fact, exist, then syncretism simply describes the historical and cultural complexity that is characteristic of all religious formations. In the words of Jonathan Z. Smith, "there is no primordium—it is all history" (1982, xiii), a view already suggested at the end of the last century.[9] Syncretism, in other words, is a category that describes all religions as historical formations, but is, in itself, discriminatory of none. Although Pye, too, affirms this conclusion (1971, 92), he argues, nevertheless, that syncretism is "the *temporary* ambiguous coexistence of elements from diverse religious and other contexts within *a coherent religious pattern*" (1971, 93, emphasis added) which may, at some point, be dissolved (1971, 92; reaffirmed 1994, 220)—a curious suggestion of historical reversal suggestive of earlier essentialistic views of religion.

An inverse sense of syncretism describes the simplification of culture, not its complexification. Rather than describing a devolution from original simplicity into historical intricacy, syncretism, in this second, Hegelian sense[10] (Préaux 1987, vol. 1, 7), is held to describe a synthetic consolidation of the dialectical complexity that characterizes all cultures and their religious formations—except, of course, those held to be revealed *de novo*. Again, it is

Boyer who argues that although "religious representations within a group often have similar features" resulting in the postulation of "some overarching, super-organic 'culture', [or] 'symbolic system' ... transmitted through 'socialization'," "what is observed is certainly *not* that people 'share' a system of ideas" (1994, 114–15). Descriptions of religious syncretisms as theological syntheses are, in other words, artificial constructs. The *locus classicus* of Hellenistic syncretism, Lucius' prayer to Isis in Book XI, 5 of Apuleius' *Metamorphoses* (Martin 1983, 137), already represents such a construct, based upon the author's neo-Platonic agenda. Actually, religious practices during the Hellenistic period conformed less to the syncretistic construct proffered by Apuleius than to the dynamic model of henotheism recently argued by H. S. Versnel (1990; 1993), and suggested for syncretistic processes generally by James Moffatt already in the 1920s.[11] Syncretism, in this second sense, is a category that describes a categorical construct which may be imposed upon any religion, but is faithful to the specific histories of none. This problem is well-recognized by Pye who insists, to the contrary, on a case-history approach that emphasizes the historical idiosyncrasy of every syncretistic formation.

Finally, however, it has been recognized by cognitive scientists and illustrated most dramatically by language acquisition and competence theories that cultural formations such as syncretisms—no matter *how* they might be described—explain nothing; rather they are the problem to be explained.[12] While critiques by cognitive science of the historical and cultural explanations for religion, such as those exemplified by Pye, are only now beginning to be explored, enough has been suggested so that the field would do well to take seriously findings in this new area of interdisciplinary research (Boyer 1992, 1993, 1994; Lawson and McCauley 1990, 1993a, 1993b). Because of the inherently complex nature of all cultural forms, however, not to mention the inexhaustible source of new complexity introduced by their transmission, such explanations have generally been neglected.

3. The Contribution of Cognitivist Theorizing

Unlike the cosmos, which some scientists now propose may simply be more complex than our brains (Johnson 1994, 1), culture is the product of human minds. Its influence, cognitive scientists now argue, "is never ... random" (Boyer 1994, 20); the consequence of trial and error (Boyer 1994, 27); on the one hand, or determinative, on the other. Rather, as Boyer concludes: "cultural material ... given to subjects through social interaction may be said to under-determine adult religious ideas. The only way fully to account for adult representations is to posit some preexisting cognitive structures, which constrain the learnability of religious ideas" (Boyer 1994, 28). And, as he subsequently elaborates:

> Religious concepts could not be acquired, and more radically could simply not be represented, if their ontological assumptions did not confirm an important background of intuitive principles ... The stable elements, which are recurrent in the religious systems of many different human groups, are not ... historically contingent assumptions. They consist in principles derived from intuitive ontologies. The major mistake of anthropological theories [and those of the history of religions] ... was to assume that, because religious judgments differ from one human group to another, the only elements that can constrain them must be cultural. In fact, they are mostly constrained by the activation of intuitive ontologies, that is, by something that is not transmitted culturally and in fact is not "cultural" at all. (Boyer 1994, 154)

The issue suggested by cognitive science, in other words, is not a contrast between assumptions about cultures as historically constructed systems and about cultures as artificial constructs, but that the systemic scaffolding of complex cultural constructions like syncretisms seem to be erected upon the constraints of cognition itself, constraints that would account for the *systemic* character of syncretistic formations (see Martin 1983). This conclusion in no way denies the cultural *content* of such formations; it is to suggest, however, that syncretisms, like all cultural representations, are the products of cultural input only as processed by human minds (Pinker 1994a, 125).

One of the reasons why minds create such complex cultural formations as syncretisms is to provide redundant sources of information for domain-specific contents, decreasing, thereby, the margins for error. It has been estimated that English texts, for example, "are two to four times as long" as they need to be for their information content (Pinker 1994a, 181; on "redundancy" see also Barsalou 1992, 248–50), and all students of Hebrew are familiar with the superfluity of written vowels for a native reader. In the presence of multiple domains of information, however, such as that occasioned by cultural contact and pluralism, minds compensate for the increased possibilities of ambiguity by discriminating among the surfeit of available information. Rather than "a jumble where socialized subjects eventually find what they need in order to become competent members of the group" (Boyer 1994, 40), cultural formations such as syncretisms may be understood as a selective reinforcement of a cultural content.

Selection as a significant feature of syncretistic formations has been noted in passing,[13] though it is generally neglected in favour of behaviouristic assumptions of cultural determinism. The question remains: why, in a particular syncretistic formation, is just A selected from one culture rather than B or just C from another rather than D? How, in other words, in any specific instance of religions in contact, do minds construct just the religious formation they do rather than some other configuration that the conditions of cultural complexity and plurality render possible (Martin 1983, 139)? What demands description is not simply individual examples of historical-cultural choice but, rather, the underlying mechanisms of selection.

To describe the selective process in relationship to specific cultural stimuli is to describe a set of cognitive processes which "constitute a plausible causal explanation" for the observed recurrence of religious representations and the patterns of their transmission (Boyer 1994, 14). Selectivity, in other words, is a function of the human cognitive system. Although people can make errors when presented with similar stimuli, they nevertheless select between different types of information to an impressive degree (Barsalou 1992, 83). Without this ability, "the cognitive system would function [as] chaotically" as, in the definition of many, do syncretistic formations[14] (Barsalou 1992, 85).

We might suggest that syncretistic formations are produced, like those of language, as the selective consequence of a discrete combinatorial system (Pinker 1994a, 237). According to the generative rules of language, "phonemes snap cleanly into morphemes, morphemes into words, words into phrases. They do not blend or melt or coalesce: *Dog bites man* differs from *Man bites dog*, and believing in God is different from believing in Dog" (Pinker 1994a, 163).

Might not the possibilities of religious representation be both created and constrained by analogous cognitive processes?

Boyer has argued that all humans "are equipped with similar inferential mechanisms, which restrict the range of generalizations they can produce" (1994, 116). Although generalizations about similarities among religions may be constructed upon conscious and even intentional representations of similarities, they are most often the products of intuitive and unconscious recognitions. To the extent that the mind can be characterized as a conglomerate of "information-processing mechanisms *designed to pursue certain goals*" (Pinker 1994b, 34, emphasis added), the systemic nature of syncretistic formations, in which the value or significance of each element results from the simultaneous presence of the other constitutive units of the system (to paraphrase Saussure 1966, 114; see Martin 1983), is a consequence of cognitive shaping and not historical or cultural accident. These intuitive recognitions of similarities might suggest a basis also for "comparative" study (Barsalou 1992, 277; Boyer 1994, 189; on the recognition of similarities for category formation generally, see Barsalou 1992, 171–73; Boyer 1994, 62–68, 170–73).

Comparative studies of religious representations have generally focused on the culturally-specific "counterintuitive claims" that constitute the explicit as opposed to the tacit nature of religions; cognitive processes, on the other hand, constitute species-specific, "cross-cultural universals" (Boyer 1994, 111). While syncretistic formations document the proliferation of culturally-specific religious representations, they also offer historical examples for the possibility of conceiving an architecture for comparative study based not on artificial analyses of idiosyncratic similarities and differences but upon the given or natural blueprint of human cognition.[15]

Notes

* This article is a slightly revised version of a presentation to a conference on "Religions in Contact," sponsored by the Czech Association for the Study of Religion in Brno, Czech Republic, 23–26 August 1994. The original paper appeared in the conference proceedings (Dolezalova *et al.* 1996).

1. Although there is a brief entry for "syncretism" in the one-volume *Encyclopedia of Anthropology* (Hunter and Whitten 1976, 378) which equates syncretism with cultural change, there is no entry for the term in either the multi-volume *Encyclopaedia of the Social Sciences* (Seligman and Johnson 1930–1935), nor *the International Encyclopedia of the Social Sciences* (Sills 1968–1976).

2. Alternatively, "syncretism" is derived from *synkretizō*, used by Plutarch (*De fraterno amore*, 19) to describe the coming together of the normally factious Cretans in the face of attack (see Martin 1983, 134–37).

3. Anonymous, "The Octavius of Minucius Felix," *Fraser's Magazine for Town and Country* 47, 1853, 293–95. The second edition of Droysen's work (1877) was more influential than the first (Austin 1981, "Preface").

4. Ironically, the notion of "syncretism" had been employed irenically by some seventeenth-century Protestants over against Catholicism; see the discussion by Moffatt (1922, 155–57).

5. This essentialistic assumption is the basis, for example, of the typology of syncretistic usage developed by Ulrich Berner (1979, 70–71).

6. In *The Protestant Ethic and the Spirit of Capitalism*, for example, Weber writes that "historical reality" is not grasped "in abstract general formulae, but in concrete genetic sets of relations which are inevitably of a specifically unique and individual character" (1958, 48).

7. This observation has been made by the Comaroffs concerning the use of this category in discussions of African religious traditions (1991, 249).

8. The remainder of this paper is largely dependent upon my reading of the thesis argued by Boyer in this book.

9. "Indeed it would be hard to find in any of the great religions of the world an utter absence of syncretism, or the union of apparently hostile religious ideas" (Griffis 1895, 192). Griffis anticipates Robert Baird's more well-known objection that "no real purpose is served by applying" the term "syncretism" to describe an historical process which is "both inevitable and universal" (Baird 1971, 146).

10. This Hegelian model was, of course, also the basis of the so-called Tübingen school of biblical studies, associated with the mid-nineteenth-century work of F. C. Baur (Kümmel 1972, 132).

11. "The tendency of syncretism, when broadly viewed, was to henotheism" (Moffatt 1922, 157).

12. For an application of competence theory to the study of religion, see Lawson and McCauley (1990; especially chapter 4).
13. Judith Berling defines syncretism as "the borrowing, affirmation, or integration of concepts, symbols, or practices of one religious tradition into another by a process of *selection* and reconciliation" (1980, 9, emphasis added).
14. Even the body's immune system operates by recognition, that is, as a selective system (Levy 1994, 65).
15. See Jonathan Z. Smith's critique of the conventional comparative enterprise in these terms (1990, 51).

References

Austin, M. M. 1981. *The Hellenistic World from Alexander to the Roman Conquest*. Cambridge: Cambridge University Press.

Baird, Robert. 1971. *Category Formation and the History of Religions*. The Hague: Mouton.

Barsalou, Lawrence W. 1992. *Cognitive Psychology: An Overview for Cognitive Scientists*. Hillsdale, NJ: Erlbaum.

Berling, Judith A. 1980. *The Syncretic Religion of Lin Chao-en*. New York: Columbia University Press.

Berner, Ulrich. 1979. "Der Begriff 'Synkretismus'—ein Instrument historischer Erkenntnis?" *Saeculum* 30: 68–85.

Boyer, Pascal. 1992. "Explaining Religious Ideas: Elements of a Cognitive Approach." *NUMEN* 39: 27–57.

—1993. *Cognitive Aspects of Religious Symbolism*. Cambridge: Cambridge University Press.

—1994. *The Naturalness of Religious Ideas: A Cognitive Theory of Religion*. Berkeley: University of California Press.

Colpe, Carsten. 1987. "Syncretism." In *The Encyclopedia of Religion*, vol. 14, ed. Mircea Eliade, 218–27. New York: Macmillan.

Comaroff, Jean, and John Comaroff. 1991. *Of Revelation and Revolution: Christianity, Colonialism, and Consciousness in South Africa*, vol. 1. Chicago: University of Chicago Press.

Couliano, Ioan P. 1990. *The Tree of Gnosis*. San Francisco: Harper.

Dolezalova, Iva *et al.*, eds. 1996. *Religions in Contact*. Brno: Czech Society for the Study of Religions.

Droysen, J. G. 1980. *Geschichte des Hellenismus*. 3 vols. München: Deutscher Taschenbuch. [Orig. 1836–1843; 2nd ed. 1877; new ed., Erich Bayer, 1952–1953.]

Geertz, Clifford. 1973. *The Interpretation of Cultures*. New York: Basic Books.

Griffis, W. E. 1895. *The Religion of Japan*. New York: Charles Scribner's Sons.

Hunter, E. R., and P. Whitten, eds. 1976. *Encyclopedia of Anthropology*. New York: Harper.

Johnson, George. 1994. "Cosmic Noise: Scaling Lofty Towers of Belief, Science Checks its Foundations." *The New York Times* (The Week in Review) Sunday, July 10: Sec. 4.1.

Kümmel, Werner Georg. 1972. *The New Testament: The History of the Investigation of Its Problems*. Trans. S. McL. Gilmour and Howard C. Kee. Nashville: Abingdon Press.

Lawson, E. Thomas, and Robert N. McCauley. 1990. *Rethinking Religion: Connecting Cognition and Culture*. Cambridge: Cambridge University Press.

—1993a. "Crisis of Conscience, Riddle of Identity: Making Space for a Cognitive Approach to Religious Phenomena." *Journal of the American Academy of Religion* 61: 201–33.

—1993b. "Connecting the Cognitive and the Cultural." In *Natural and Artificial Minds*, ed. Robert G. Burton, 121–45. Albany: State University of New York Press.

Levy, Steven. 1994. "Dr. Edelman's Brain." *The New Yorker*. May 2: 62–73.

Martin, Luther H. 1983. "Why Cecropian Minerva? Hellenistic Religious Syncretism as System." *NUMEN* 30: 131–45.

Moffatt, James. 1922. "Syncretism." In *Encyclopedia of Religion and Ethics*, vol. 12, ed. James Hastings, 155–57. New York: Charles Scribner's Sons.

Pinker, Steven. 1994a. *The Language Instinct*. New York: William Morrow and Co.

—1994b. "Is There a Gene for Compassion?" Review of Robert Wright, *The Moral Animal*. *The New York Times Book Review*. September 25: 3, 34–35.

Préaux, Claire. 1987. *Le monde héllenistique*. 2 vols. Paris: PUF.

Pye, Michael. 1971. "Syncretism and Ambiguity." *NUMEN* 18: 83–93.

—1994. "Syncretism versus Synthesis." *Method & Theory in the Study of Religion* 6: 217–29.

Ranke, Leopold von. 1824. *Geschichten der romanischen und germanischen Völker*. Leipzig: G. Reimer.

Rudolph, Kurt. 1979. "Synkretismus—vom theologischen Scheltwort zum religionswissenschaftlichen Begriff." In *Humanitas Religiosa: Festschrift für Haralds Biezais zu seinem 70. Geburtstag*, 194–212. Stockholm: Almquist & Wiksell.

Saussure, Ferdinand de. 1966. *Course in General Linguistics*, ed. C. Bally and A. Sechehaye in collaboration with A. Riedlinger; trans. W. Baskin. New York: McGraw-Hill.

Seligman, E. R. A., and A. S. Johnson, eds. 1930–1935. *Encyclopaedia of the Social Sciences*. New York: Macmillan.

Sills, D. L., ed. 1968–76. *International Encyclopedia of the Social Sciences*. New York: Macmillan.

Smith, Jonathan Z. 1982. *Imagining Religion: From Babylon to Jonestown*. Chicago: University of Chicago Press.

—1990. *Drudgery Divine: On the Comparison of Early Christianities and the Religions of Late Antiquity*. Chicago: University of Chicago Press.

Usener, Hermann. 1948 [1896]. *Götternamen*. Frankfurt: G. Schulte-Bulmke.

Versnel, H. S. 1990. *Inconsistencies in Greek and Roman Religion*. I: *Ter Unus. Isis, Dionysos, Hermes*. Three Studies in Henotheism. Leiden: E. J. Brill.

—1993. *Inconsistencies in Greek and Roman Religion*. II: *Transition and Reversal in Myth and Ritual*. Leiden: E. J. Brill.

Weber, Max. 1958. *The Protestant Ethic and the Spirit of Capitalism*. Trans. Talcott Parsons. New York: Charles Scribner's Sons.

THE CONCEPT OF "SYNCRETISM": AN INSTRUMENT OF HISTORICAL INSIGHT/DISCOVERY?

Ulrich Berner

Recent years have seen a growing interest in the phenomenon of (religious) syncretism. This can be followed in two areas: On the one hand, the concept of syncretism is encountered with increasing frequency in discussions of contemporary religions—the final chapter in the *Handbuch der Religionsgeschichte* by C. Colpe is entitled "Syncretism, Renaissance, Secularization and the Formation of New Religions in the Present Day" (Colpe 1975). This heading apparently places the concept of syncretism on the same level as the concept of secularization. When taking account of the post-Christian religions in his book on the religions of Africa, E. Dammann remarks that "Syncretism is characteristic of all these formations" (1963, 278); it could be concluded that the concept of "syncretism" plays a particular role as a designation of a phenomenon of modern religiosity (Dammann 1963).

In recent years, we have seen the publication of the results of a number of symposia dedicated to the phenomenon of "syncretism" in different and separate fields of the discipline of the study of religion (*Religionsgeschichte*).[1] The collaborative research centre (*Sonderforschungsbereich* 13) at Göttingen is especially concerned with syncretism in the Near East in Late Antiquity. Linking the theme to the contemporary religion scene renders this historical research into syncretism particularly interesting. A theory of syncretism as an analytical tool, allowing insights into the conditions leading to certain "syncretistic" processes, should also throw some light on contemporary developments.

However, achieving such a theory faces the unsurprising obstacle formulated at the first of the symposia mentioned by H. Ringgren: "The term syncretism is often used without a clear and unambiguous definition" (1969, 7).

If the meaning of the concept of "syncretism" is not clearly defined, then—obviously—it is impossible to establish a theory of syncretism. A definition alone would not, however, suffice: if one takes a broad approach, various types of "syncretism" will have to be distinguished (Dunand 1975, 153 ff.). If the definition of "syncretism" is narrow, then alternative concepts must be defined next to the concept of "syncretism." A whole catalogue of concepts would thus be required. Additionally, such a catalogue would still have to be linked to conventional usage if the continuity of the research linking historical and contemporary material is not to be interrupted. Yet, ordinary usage is itself not exactly uniform. Given the contrasting use of both narrow and broad definitions, one encounters a confusing diversity of possibilities when viewing the use of the term "syncretism" in the study of religion (*Religionsgeschichte*).

In an older study of religion in Japan, in W. E. Griffis's *The Religions of Japan*, "syncretism" is used as a basic concept. "Indeed, it would be hard to find in any of the great religions of the world an utter absence of syncretism, or the union of apparently hostile religious ideas" (1904, 192). In a more recent work on Egyptian religion, *Conceptions of God in Ancient Egypt: The One and the Many*, E. Hornung defines the concept very narrowly: "Syncretism" is understood exclusively as a very specific form of association of two divinities (1982, 91 ff.). Hornung uses it for a transitory "inhabitation (of one god in another)," and distinguishes this from other associations such as "fusion" or "identification"—which are conventionally also understood as syncretism (Biezais 1975a; 1975b, 374). The situation is also complicated because other concepts, such as "synthesis," are used as alternatives or synonyms (Spiegel 1953, §341, n. 7). Aside from this, many authors also employ metaphorical descriptions linking phenomena which may be quite distant from one another.[2] There are also differences in the evaluation of syncretistic phenomena. Whereas, for example, G. von Rad perceives syncretism as a menace to the pure Yahweh belief in his *Theologie des Alten Testaments*, W. Pannenberg has recently employed the term in a positive sense, characterizing the syncretism of Christianity as a "singular power" (von Rad 1958, 70; Pannenberg 1971, 270, n. 33).

This short introduction of an arbitrary selection from the wealth of sources using various meanings of the concept of "syncretism" illustrates the problem. Moving on, it should no longer appear surprising that in one of the best-known discussions of the Egyptian religion, Morenz suggested that "we ought to abandon the infelicitous term 'syncretism'..." (1973, 140). However reasonable this consistent demand appears to be, in our opinion, it is impossible to obey unless one is prepared—from the very start—to block every theoretical approach based on the comparability of the historical materials dealt with in the various disciplines. The lack of uniformity in ordinary usage hints at the difficulties facing any effort to suggest a binding terminology for research into syncretism. On the other hand, however, the very lack of such an instrument makes it almost impossible to give a general interpretation of the results of the various historical research projects.[3] A binding terminology must be transparent—using clear definitions—while the concepts must also be easily recognizable as terms of a meta-language. On the other hand, the terms cannot deviate significantly from conventional scientific usage, to assure continuity. Any adjustments to conventional usage must not only be justified by the necessity of uniformity and transparency, but the terminology must also be useful. It must be justified with application and practical experience in historical research, in other words, through heuristic value. The work on a theme defined by the continuity of a collaborative research centre (*Sonderforschungsbereich*) is potentially the best condition for accomplishing such a programme. The method must be that of developing a terminology as a model which can incorporate the experience of "blind" historical research before testing and improving it by continual application in confrontation with historical material. It was in exactly this fashion that the following terminology for syncretism was developed, tested and improved.[4]

The model presented below is based on the idea that the introduction of the concepts "system" and "element" is the most suitable means of resolving the difficulties mentioned given the terminological challenges.[5] Every religion and every individual interpretation of a religion in the sense of a "theology" will be understood as a (religious) system, with "religions" understood as "religious systems" (*Religionssystem*). In the following, a "religious system" will be understood as an association of elementary thoughts (and the related representations and acts), providing humans with an irreducible explanation of the world, and giving them behavioural norms which are likewise absolute and untraceable.[6]

This concept of system not only covers a carefully reflected theoretical construction, as, for example, the theology of Origen.[7] The theology of the Syrian martyr legends, for example the legend of the holy Behnam, contains only a few elements, "God as the creator of all things," "Jesus as the physician of the weak," "forgiving the sins for the faithful," and so on (Wiessner 1978, 119–33). Such texts also offer a system that fulfils the given condition for their authors and later readers. The distinction between the system of Origen, for example, lies—aside from the number of available elements—in the degree of reflection. Two levels related to the concept of "syncretism" are therefore already clear:

Syncretism can be viewed as a process in the historical development of religion, which takes places on the system level where two systems enter into an association, which remains to be defined. It can also be a process on the elemental level, where the association concerns only elements, but not the entire associated systems.

To be distinguished on the system level is the question whether the faithful in any religious system dispute the "correct" or binding interpretation of their system or whether the process affects two different religious systems. The latter would be designated a "systematization," the former a "rationalization." This has consequences for the specific meaning of the system concept. In the case of a systematization, "syncretism on the system level" would signify that it involves two religious systems. In the case of rationalization, "system" could signify either an individual interpretation of a religious system—as in the case of Origen mentioned above—or instead a partial system, as, for example, the royal dogma in the context of the Egyptian religious system, whether on the level of the official priestly theology or that of "popular religion." Such a partial system is an internally closed and sensible association of elements, but only a relatively independent one which ultimately owes its meaning to the larger religious system.

With these distinctions between systematization and rationalization, the system and element levels, there are already—in outline—three different levels recognizable, so that the conditions for more precise descriptions of the processes of religious history can be created.

Beginning with the system concept has an inherent double advantage. It permits the elimination of metaphorical descriptions from syncretism research. This is not intended to claim that the heuristic use of metaphors has no value (Harré 1959–60). Expressions such as "fusion of gods" or "syncretistic ferment" need, however, no longer be accepted as precise descriptions, and should thus be avoided where the goal is a theory of syncretism. This approach also illuminates the subject of the discourse: whether "syncretism" designates the relationship between two religions or characterizes a religion as such, or indeed individual conceptions. Moreover, none of the meanings possible in conventional usage will be excluded from consideration by the decision on the definitions.

However, this only creates a framework for a differentiated approach to the concept of syncretism. One means of getting to the subject matter follows from this observation: Every system of the above-mentioned type is exposed to continual testing in the course of history. As it does not invariably fulfil its function without difficulties, it remains subject to constant change, and in extreme cases it can be rendered completely inoperative. These difficulties can come from within, if the adherents experience changes which threaten the plausibility of the explanatory and normative roles of a system. They can also be external, if one system is destabilized by doubts arising through the encounter with another.[8] These problems can also arise in combination given the possibility of enduring competition between different systems for a long period. The processes of rationalization and systematization in religious history can be understood as a response to these two basic forms of testing.

"Syncretism on the system level" can now be interpreted as one of the possible reactions to such destabilizing tendencies, throwing doubt upon the capacity of the system to explain and exhort. It would thus be the reaction which endeavours to overcome the doubts, removing the boundary between the systems, and thus the competitive character. This interpretation can also be transferred to the element level. This can also serve a more precise definition of the loose colloquial concept of syncretism, fulfilling the double challenge of clearly defining the concept while respecting conventional usage.

A preliminary, formal and substantial distinction and interpretation of the concept of syncretism is thus achieved. This can be taken further with the conceptual model in the context of establishing alternative concepts to designate related processes which would all otherwise fall under the same unfocused heading.

Terminology as a Heuristic Model: "Syncretism"

"Systematization" designates the processes, serving to solve the problems arising from the encounter of different systems or from enduring competition.

A.1. Progressive Systematization

When the tendency of the process of systematization aims at raising doubts among the adherents of a competing system and gaining for one's system, then the concept of "progressive systematization" is used.

A.2. Stabilizing Systematization

When the tendency of the process of systematization aims at raising confidence in one's own system, confirming the adherents in their confidence, then the concept of "stabilizing systematization" is used.[9]

A.3. Vertical Systematization

Where the conflict is between systems with different functions (e.g., where one system is a "religion" and the other is "science") but with differing degrees of overlapping roles, "vertical systematization" is the concept used in order to identify the difference in the levels; where the overlap in the functions is virtually zero, the transition approaches "reacting rationalization" (*infra* B.3)

B. Rationalization

"Rationalization" is used to designate those processes solving problems that do not arise from confrontation with other systems, but which are rather the result of disturbances within a system.

B.1. Perfectionizing Rationalization

When the tendency of the process of rationalization aims at transcending the given state of the system and reaching a perfect state, "perfectionizing rationalization" is the concept used. The conceptual goal of the "perfect state" can be drawn from a vision of the future or the past; it can be presented as either an explanation or as a reduction of the system.

B.2. Stabilizing Rationalization

When the tendency of the rationalization process aims at a hardening of a given state in the face of competing interpretations of the system (e.g., as "heresy") in order to confront the danger of decay or fission, "stabilizing rationalization" is the concept.

B.3. Reacting Rationalization

Where a conflict of systems involves systems which do not overlap (e.g., where a religion is confronted with a new economic system), "reacting rationalization" is the concept.

I: Syncretism on the System Level

"Syncretism (on the system level)" designates those processes where the boundary—and thus the competitive relationship—between the systems is eliminated. This can happen in very different ways, some with relations on the element level or linked with syncretisms on the element level. A hypothetical example:

> Sargon of Agade had the goal "of unifying the Sumerian and Semitic religions in a syncretism" (Dijk 1971, 437). If van Dijk's presentation is to be understood as meaning that Sargon's enterprise was intended to eliminate the boundary between what were originally two different religions, so that (in contrast to the religion of the Old Testament) the confrontation of the religions of the migrants and the natives should be eliminated and thus the competition of the two should disappear, this would be a syncretism on the system level.

II: Meta-Syncretism or Pseudo-Synthesis

These concepts designate the process whereby a new system emerges, one which is clearly and consciously distinct from the earlier systems, and does not contain new elements, but one which consists exclusively of elements from the preceding systems. Syncretism is thus taking place on a level beyond the preceding systems and can thus be designated a "Meta-Syncretism." In contrast to the synthesis (*infra* section III) as a creative process, this is a "pseudo-synthesis." The result of this process can be termed a "syncretistic religion" or a "syncretistic system." This characterization as "syncretistic" would thus be clearly defined and distinguished from the processes of syncretism. A hypothetical example:

> In his lecture on "The Syncretism of Mani," A. Böhlig emphasized the "new" in Mani's system (1975, 169). Should the predicate "new" characterize Mani's system such that it would incorporate new combinations and (re-)interpretations of elements which were all known from the preceding systems, this would be a Meta-Syncretism or a pseudo-synthesis.

III: Synthesis

"Synthesis" designates an irreversible and creative process where the conflict between different systems leads to the emergence of new elements of one of the systems; this new system is thus not simply the sum of selected elements from the preceding systems. The new elements cannot be traced to ancestors in the earlier system, but are only roughly related to elements in the preceding system. A hypothetical example:

> V. Maag describes the emergence of the religion of the Old Testament with a number of concepts and metaphors of which only a single example will serve: "The New emerged in the power field of the polar relationship between nomads and settled peoples and thus transcended both" (Maag 1958, 1964, 1966–67). The expression "transcend" gives weight to the interpretation of this process as a "synthesis."

IV: Evolution

"Evolution" designates an irreversible and creative process within a system, where new elements emerge which then function as the centre of a new system. The result of this process can be identified as a "new religion," in contrast to a new syncretistic religion (*supra* II). A hypothetical example:

> Buddhism emerged in India from the prevailing religious system and not through a conflict of Brahmanism with another foreign system. Should it be demonstrated that the central ideas of Buddhism, for example, that of "Nirvana" cannot be identified in Brahmanism, then the original Buddhism can be understood as the result of an evolution.

V: Determination of Relations on the Systemic Level

"Determination of Relations" designates the process determining the proportions representing the relative contribution of a system with respect to competing systems. Determination of Relations can be total or differentiated. The relationship to competing systems can be determined by one of possibilities enumerated hereafter, or it can occur in a differentiated fashion whereby several of the possibilities may be simultaneously involved.

A.1. A harmonizing determination of relations appears where the boundary between the systems is preserved but the competitive relationship is eliminated. A hypothetical example:

> Following F. Heiler's presentation, Ramakrishna came "to the conviction … that all religions are true and lead to the divine community. He avers 'that I have tried all religions: Hinduism, Islam and Christianity, and I have found that it is the same god to which all strive in different ways.'" (Heiler 1962, 409 ff.)

In this version, the boundaries between the religions are not eliminated, as it is not claimed that they all teach the same. However, the religions are placed on the same level through the claim that they all strive for the same goal. A reservation that the different ways offer differing degrees of security or speed in reaching the goal is not made—at least not in the quote. The emphasis on the unity of the goal—the truth of the religions and the possibility of "testing" different routes eliminates the competitive relationship, so that the concept of a "Harmonizing Determination of Relations" appears reasonable.

A.2. A hierarchic determination of relations is involved where the border between the systems is preserved and the competitive relationship limited as all of the systems concerned are recognized.

A.2.1. Hierarchic relationing in evaluation: The systems are judged differently. A hypothetical example:

In his discussion of the relationship between Hindism and Buddhism in Indonesia, P. Zoetmulder introduces a story of the brothers Gagang Aking and Bubaksah which is preserved in several versions. The story relates that the younger brother, who remained an adherent of Buddhism, reaches the highest heaven, whereas the older brother, a Shaivite, must be content with a less elevated position. "Shaivism and Buddhism are brothers where the first is indeed the elder, but the younger reaches a higher degree of perfection—these are interpretations with parallels recorded in recent times on Bali and Lombok" (Zoetmulder 1965, 271). This description appears to fit the scheme of a hierarchic relationing in evaluation: the systems of Buddhism and Hinduism, or Shaivism, are clearly distinguished and identified as ways to the same goal, with the reservation that the one way leads to the goal more quickly and nearer. The evaluation restricts the competitive relationship.

A.2.2. Hierarchic determination of relations in the epistemological sense: The systems are assigned to different levels of insight and truth. A hypothetical example:

H. von Glasenapp's work (1948) on "Shankara's philosophy of the All-Unity" is subtitled "The steps leading to the divine." This indicates that there are several steps in the system of this Hindu thinker and reformer. Shankara knows an absolute and a relative truth. Whoever reaches the point of absolute truth recognizes the unity of all being, the non-duality (*advaita*); from the other position, however, all possible views of the relationship of god to the world can be developed (Glasenapp 1948; Strauss 1973, 243 ff.; Hacker 1950). Such a theoretical approach also implies the possibility of bringing different systems into a hierarchic relationship.

A.2.3. Hierarchic determination of relations in the chronological sense: The validity of different systems is limited to different periods of time. A hypothetical example:

The Tendai school of Japanese Buddhism attempted to link all of the tendencies of Buddhism and their scriptures to a specific interpretation of Buddhism and the underlying literary work. As W. Gundert put it, "This purpose served the critically differentiating steps of teaching (*kyohan*) which form the dogmatic accomplishments of the Tendai school. According to this, Buddha's teaching is initially divided into five periods ..." (1943, 60). This assumption of the different periods of the "Revelation" allows the possibility of relativizing the various Buddhist systems in their validity, by relating them to the periods of the teachings of Buddha. Their new system necessarily corresponds to the final and highest teaching of Buddha.

A.2.4. Hierarchic determination of relations in the genetic sense: The validity and the claims of competing systems are limited by assigning other systems a dependency relationship to another system. A hypothetical example:

> Among the arguments of early Christian apologetics was the claim that the Greek philosophers borrowed from the Old Testament and thus those philosophical systems were only true insofar as they were dependent upon the Biblical Revelation and thus from the Christian system.[10]

A.2.5. Hierarchic determination of relations in the inclusive sense: One's own system is allegedly comprehensive insofar as it always included the central elements of the competing systems. A hypothetical example:

> Origen claims in his apologetic work, *Contra Celsum*, that the scientific method is not specific to pagan philosophy, but rather was always present in the Christian system and was pursued just as assiduously. (Berner 1978)

A.3. A distancing relationship is characterized where the boundary and the competitive relationship between systems is preserved and the very existential value of the competing systems is thrown into doubt. A hypothetical example:

> Early Christian apologists, such as, for example, Justin, condemned the Mithraic religion in its entirety as expressed in particular with claims that central elements of the Mysteries of Mithras can be traced back to the influence of the devil or evil demons.[11] All of these relations can be either explicitly or implicitly formulated. This depends upon the literary genre of the relevant sources. In those Early Christian works expressly termed "apologies," for example, the relationships to the competing systems were explicitly formulated. In the Syrian legends of the saints, for example, the relationships of the competing systems (e.g., Judaism) were only implicitly formulated so that the historical-philological interpretation of the sources (which precedes the use of a Determination of Relations concept) is thus more complicated. (Wiessner 1978)

VI: Syncretism on the Element Level

Syncretism on the element level designates:

(a) those associations of different elements where the boundary between the elements is terminated so that the adherents of the system concerned perceive them as a unity;

(b) the superposition of an element by means of other interpretations;

(c) the emergence of a element in analogy or as an equivalent to a competing element.

B.1. An absorbing syncretism appears where an element acquires the additional function of another element, thereby expelling the other so that the composite structure can only be recognized in secondary analysis. A hypothetical example:

> In his presentation of Greek religion, O. Kern discusses the phenomenon—for which he has several examples—where "the god of the heavens is the heir of many mountain gods" (1926, I, 198). Kern assumes, for example, the existence of a pre-Greek mountain god at Olympus, whose character can no longer be established. If the facts in these cases mean that the Indo-Germanic god of the Heavens, Zeus, expelled a mountain god who was part of the native religion, and assumed one of his roles—even if only as representative of this or that mountain—and thus a function which he previously did not have (of which the adherents of the Greek religious system were no longer conscious), this is a process of "absorbing syncretism."

B.2. An additive syncretism will be found where the boundary and thus the competitive relationship between different elements is eliminated without one of the elements being absorbed so that the ensuing combination of the existing elements can be recognized as composite by the adherents of the system concerned. When this involves elements which have diametrically opposed meanings, then it is a "*complexio oppositorum*," which is an exceptional case of additive syncretism. A hypothetical example:

> W. Westendorf reconstructs the ancient Egyptian religion as a "System where the vital forces preserve themselves in an 'eternal' cycle consisting of two polar elements which are occasionally unified corporally" (Westendorf 1974, 137). He establishes the following thesis: "As a rule, the gods of the Egyptian pantheon (insofar as they are not hybrids) can be ordered in terms of nHH- or D.t-eternity ..." (ibid., 139). These two eternities constitute that "system where the vital forces preserve themselves in an 'eternal' cycle." Westendorf assigns the god Re to the nHH-eternity, and the god Atum to the D.t-eternity.
>
> Under this supposition, the emergence of the divine name "Re-Atum" can be identified as an "additive syncretism in the sense of a complexio oppositorum": Two gods, who are polar opposites in the system of the Egyptian religion—as Westendorf interprets in the above-mentioned fashion—are thus "associated to form a new unity" in the formula of this double name ("Hybrid-name"). This formula permits the two

preceding elements to be clearly recognized and is clearly distinguished from the solution of the "absorbing syncretism."

B.3. An agglomerating syncretism appears where an element is suppressed by other meanings.

B.3.1. An identification appears where different elements are explicitly explained as being identical or appear to be interchangeable under all circumstances. A hypothetical example:

"And thus El, the god who was the equal of his sibling gods, was understood as a past revelation of that God who later announced himself as Yahweh. The way was thus paved for Yahweh to appropriate much from El" (Fohrer 1969, 95). If one follows G. Fohrer's description in his "History of the Israelite Religion," this process of equating the Canaanite El with the so-called sibling gods of the Israelite religion—as well as the equation of Yahweh which Fohrer had earlier explicitly stated (ibid., 94)—can be assigned to the concept of "Identification" and thus understood in terms of an "agglomerative syncretism on the element level." This syncretism on the element level—if one hypothetically assumes that this description is correct—does not by any means demand a syncretism on the system level (cf. *supra*: the hypothetical example of the synthesis concept).

B.3.2. A transformation appears if an element undergoes a change in meaning in the course of a conscious re-interpretation. A hypothetical example:

At the meeting of the German orientalists in 1968, G. Wiessner gave a lecture entitled "On the Confrontation between Christianity and Zoroastrianism in Iran," taking an example of a Syrian legend of a saint and martyr, the Qardag novel. By comparing this with the Ardashir novel, he noted "how genuine Persian-feudal heroic traditions and their vision of humanity were preserved and changed in the world of the Christian Iranians" (Wiessner 1969, 415). Wiessner then raised additional questions by—leaning on Widengren—noting that in this Persian "vision of heroism … the historical report is combined with elements of myth" (416). Of decisive importance in this connection is the conclusion, "that the Qardag-novel seems to have a parallel in this mythical-historical struggle of the Iranian heroic model in the Ardashir-novel" (416). Wiessner confirms that the specific correlations are "too striking for them to be assigned to the creative imagination of the author of the Christian novel alone" (417). He therefore poses the question of "whether the Christian tale is another historizing version of the Iranian myth … Such a historicizing transfer of the Iranian myth to a Christian hero would mean that the Christian hero was identified with that power against which the Zoroastrian heroic model fought. The Zoroastrian dualistic cosmic conception would thus have undergone a complete transformation in the Christian version, whereby the Persian king no longer appears as the leading warrior of the Ahuric, but rather as an evil Ahuric world, whereas his opponent would have become the representative of the good pole" (417). This reversal of the motif can only be understood as a conscious revision whereby certain elements of the Iranian system were "preserved and changed." This example would thus fit precisely into the category of "transformation."

B.3.3. A functional change occurs when an element of a system is taken as an element in another system without this being consciously revised. A hypothetical example:

Origen develops a highly specific version and explanation of the resurrection concept. In *Contra Celsum* IV, 57, Origen introduces his understanding such that the Resurrection is presented as a case of the more general thought that the "basic underlying material" can assume all properties which God or the Demiurge can give it. Here, Origen has combined a number of concepts of Greek philosophy which have either nothing or very little in common with the Biblical tradition, to form a conceptual model—and thus he is working within the framework of contemporary philosophical discourse—in order to use this as an interpretation for the concept of a resurrection and thus as an element introduced into his Christian system (Berner 1978). If one assumes that Origen was not deliberately re-interpreting, but was rather of the opinion that he was drawing on a philosophical conceptual model which was compatible with the Christian system and thus suitable for use as an interpretative instrument for an element of the Christian system, then one can refer to this as "Functional Change."

B.3.4. A substitution appears where an element of one system is marginalized such that it is dismissed together with the system to which it belongs in the course of creating a distancing relation (cf. *supra* V.A.3), while its function is assumed by a newly created or transformed element of the competing system. A hypothetical example:

In Mongolia, Buddhism of a lamaistic type displaced Shamanism. W. Heissig recorded that "The lamaistic missionaries replaced the function of the Shaman with similar features from the lamaistic world ..." (Heissig 1970, 341). It was, in particular, two kinds of lamaistic clerics who offered themselves "as substitutes for the ecstatic function of the shaman and his exorcism" (343). It is particularly interesting that the clothing of the Gurtum-Lama, which transformed him into a Bodhisattva, included "a typically shamanistic emblem, a silver mirror" (344).

This phenomenon can be understood as a hint that an element here—the role of Gurtum-Lama—may not have been newly created, but did have to be changed in order to perform the function of the displaced element—the role of the shaman. If this interpretation is correct, then this is a Substitution.[12]

B.4. An equivalence syncretism appears where an element emerges in a system which is intended to be equivalent to an element in a competing system. A hypothetical example:

P. Kawerau describes and interprets the phenomena which characterize the parallel existence of Christianity and Islam in Jerusalem in the following fashion: "While the Christians in Jerusalem enthusiastically celebrate Holy Week each year, the Moslems celebrate a festival in honor of Moses at the same time, in order to have an Islamic celebration of equal significance during the Christian Easter" (1972, 199). This description of the actual facts—two competing systems: Easter as one element and Islamic festival as the other—and the interpretation that the Moslems wanted to place an equal Islamic festival beside the Christian Easter would appear to fulfil the criteria of the concept of "equivalence syncretism."

VII: Determination of Relations on the Element Level

"Determination of Relations on the element level" designates the proportional relationship of different elements which does not eliminate the boundary separating them, so that they are preserved as members of a relation and remain recognizable to the adherents of the system concerned.

C.1. The determination of relations can take the form of a bimorphic model. A hypothetical example:

The ba-concept of the Ancient Egyptian Religion can in general be understood as belonging to general conceptions of the soul (e.g. van der Leeuw 1970, 314, n. 1). The ba is generally depicted as a bird, and it is ascribed the capacity to release itself from the (dead) body, but it is also closely connected to the body. This image—however it is to be understood—is apparently a basic component of the ancient Egyptians' conception of the complex composition of the human being. This anthropological conception served as a point of departure to place different elements of the religious system into their relative positions, explaining both their dependent and independent roles. W. Schenkel understands the process thus: "The theological-speculative" fusion of the gods is "primarily based on the concept of the 'ba' insofar as the thought processes are clearly articulated. What is probably the earliest example is at the same time one which (over the course of time) became one of the most thoroughly examined: the fusion of the polar-opposites Re (god of the heavens) and Osiris (the god of the Nether-world). During the Middle Kingdom (ca. 2000–1600 BC), the solution of the problem was sought in terms of the unification of the two gods as a being with two ba's. Later, as in other cases, one god—Re—will be understood as the ba of the other god—Osiris understood as the 'body'."[13] Accordingly, two elements—Re and Osiris—are set into a relationship which is a figurative representation of anthropological conceptions. The relationship between the two gods is presented as an analogy to the relationship between the ba and the (dead) body. The concept of the human being after death and the relationship to the ba provides an operative context uniting different entities and can be designated as a "biomorphic" model, and the transfer of this conception to the relations between different elements can be understood as "Relationing through a biomorphic model."

C.2. The determination of relations can take the form of a sociomorphic model. A hypothetical example:

In his *History of Greek Religion*, O. Kern writes, "Following the model of the human community, this Olympic religion created a divine state headed by Zeus as the celestial Anax" (1926, vol. 1, 201). According to this version, the relations between and among the gods were formulated in analogy to the hierarchical order of a social system. One can say that such a divine state represents the result of defining relations with a sociomorphic model.

C.3. The determination of relations can be accomplished with a technomorphic model. A hypothetical example:

In a hymn to Khnum, the ancient Egyptian god of the potter's wheel, J. Assmann translates, "He formed mankind and modeled the gods ..." (1975, No. 145B, v. 15). This statement establishes a relationship between various divinities. This relationship arises through a figurative representation from the sphere of the techniques of human craftsmen. This process can be defined as "Defining Relations through a technomorphic model."

C.4. The determination of relations can be established through an ontological model. A hypothetical example:

In the context of his discussion of the syncretism of Buddhism and Hinduism or Shaivism in Java, P. Zoetmulder cites a hitherto unpublished text, Tantular's "Sutasoma": in this text, "the gods endeavor to calm raging Kalaruda, Shiva's terrifying manifestation who strives to kill the hero Sutasoma, an incarnation of Buddha, by reminding him that Buddha and Shiva cannot be distinguished. Even if they are named by different names, two of them cannot be made; for the essence of Buddha (*jinatva*) and *Shivatattva*) is identical. Although different, there is no duality in Dharma" (1965, 269). The link justifying the use of the concept of "ontological defining of relations" is the abstraction *jinatva* and *shivatattva* which stand in relation to the claim that the elements concerned—Buddha and Shiva—are ultimately identical—but only on this level—for the difference on the level of manifestation is not contested. Zoetmulder suggests that ontological considerations are involved by using the concept of essence, which is derived from the Western tradition of ontology. Distinctions between different levels of being produce the apparently paradoxical statement about Buddha and Shiva being simultaneously identical and unequal. This case is thus to be distinguished from identification where only the difference between the names remains, and can be hypothetically interpreted as an Ontological Definition of Relations. (Berner 1976)

C.5. A local determination of relations appears where elements of one system are set into the geographical environment of another system. A hypothetical example:

> Discussing the religions of India, J. Gonda emphasizes the complexity of the process of Sanskritizing or Hinduizing in the Dravidic parts of India. One of the examples introduced in this context appears to fit the scheme of a "Local Determination of Relations": "Another process consists of transferring the acts and deeds, the life and death of the great figures of Brahminism, e.g., the major roles of the Ramayana, into their own region" (1963, vol. 2, 12). In this way, the Dravidic peoples relate central elements of the Brahminic system by placing them into their own geographical environment, which was the local context for their own religious system. Thus, this local defining of relations can also be placed in the context of the Determination of Relations on the element level.

A Note Concerning the Validity and Application of the Model

The model presented here does not raise a claim to have covered every one of the possible and actual processes of syncretism and the related processes.

The model is thus meant to be enlarged, either through new sets of alternative concepts on one of the three levels, or through further differentiation of one of the suggested concepts. The model has the heuristic function of permitting the historical material to be examined from new standpoints, inquiring whether all of the definitional criteria of any given concept can be discovered in a concrete historical process. Where an historical process fails to fall under one of the previously defined cases, it should be possible to formulate a new concept and place it into the model. The model contains four distinct possibilities of employing the concept of syncretism:

1. Syncretism only on the system level (where the Determination of Relations would be on the element level).
2. Syncretism only on the element level (where the Determination of the Relations on the system level would be possible).
3. Syncretism on both the system and element levels simultaneously.
4. Meta-syncretism.

Application of the model thus avoids a restricted definition of the concept while the clear distinction of the possibilities guarantees that equivocations and pseudo-controversies should be excluded. The most important feature allowing the interpretation of the concept of syncretism in terms of content is the juxtaposition of "syncretism" and "synthesis."

The application of the model depends upon the conventional methods of historical-philological work, as a *conditio sine qua non*. In the course of the interpretation of the documents involved, those key points must be identified which permit the application of one of the meta-level concepts of the model. Where a religious document is itself strongly analytical, direct links may permit a close correspondence between the language processes of the object and the meta-level description. For instance, in the preface of his *Contra Celsum*, Origen carefully reflected on the uncertain situation, adumbrating his intention of rhetorically stabilizing the system and thus allowing his thoughts to be construed in precisely this fashion. However, there can be a significant discrepancy between the original understanding forming the basis of a system and the historical description of the same. It is, therefore, conceivable that an author will him/herself have viewed his/her work only in terms of an existing tradition and expected to be read as such, while an historical analysis could conclude that the author's work actually represents a synthesis of two traditions.

The concepts of this model were conceived in descriptive terms and they should be able not only to describe and interpret the conception of the authors, and the intentions of their system, but also—and significantly—the processes which are not reflected in the introspective role, but rather implicit in that of exposition, which suggest latent intentions. Discrepancies, such as those suggested above, can emerge from the historical-descriptive character of the model, and the stepped character of the model thus appears to be essential in order to describe such complicated processes exactly. The model should establish the conditions necessary for a theory of syncretism.

The apparently boundless variety of one aspect of the historical processes of religions should thus be organized by applying the model. The first result is thus that exactly comparable processes should be placed in the same categories despite completely different contexts in space and time.[14] Hypotheses about the conditions leading to certain processes can also be experimentally examined using historical materials since clearly organized material is already available. It is thus possible that in this way eminently scientific theoretical insights in the form of historical explanations could be gained without abandoning proven historical methods. These could then allow for further prognoses for the development of contemporary religions.

Notes

1. We can mention Hartman, ed. 1969; Dietrich, ed. 1975; Dunand and Lévêque 1975.
2. Cf., e.g., Nilsson 1961, vol. 2, 728: "The ensuing building is the so-called syncretism"; Thomsen 1969, 132: "The Japanese religious soil is in a constant ferment of syncretism."
3. We cannot expect any help from the phenomenology of religion, insofar as it belongs to the hermeneutic science of religion (*Verstehende Religionswissenschaft*). Its basic theoretical religious and scientific premises blur the boundaries separating the language of religion from that of the science of religion. Separating these two linguistic levels—as object- and metalanguage—is an essential prerequisite for the present goal of a theory of syncretism, seeking to incorporate historical explanations in a very narrow sense, as has been discussed since the formulation of the Hempel-Oppenheim scheme of scientific explanation (Berner 1975, 57–72).
4. For discussions from which improvements were gained, I am obliged to G. Wiessner and the other collaborators of the *Sonderforschungsbereich 13*. The use of the model was most recently demonstrated and discussed, using a number of examples, at the colloquium "Synkretismusforschung—Theorie und Praxis" (Göttingen, October 1977). The papers of this colloquium have since been published (Wiessner, ed. 1978).
5. The choice of these basic concepts was not a mere borrowing of N. Luhmann's familiar sociological system theory: the capacity of the abstract system concept inspired the use of the model. It will, however, only be later—when theoretically organizing the historical material—that further stimulation from the actual system theory can be considered.
6. This concept of religion was initially conceived without any restrictions on content, which would, e.g., allow a distinction between historical religions from the allegedly pseudo-religions or ideologies of the modern age. In my opinion, the most important justification for such a limit in the features of religious studies would be that which G. Wiessner considers. He posed the question of "whether it is not the peculiar character of religious claims-to-truth that they are presented as a systemic formation realistically describing reality in the mode of the personality?," at the end of his article, "Prolegomena zu einer Religionsphänomenologie als einer systematischen Religionswissenschaft" (1974, 208).

7. Characterizing the theology of Origen as a system should not be confused with taking a position in the discussion on the issue of whether Origen was a "systematizer" (cf., e.g., Kettler 1966, 1 ff.).

8. Cf. Berger and Luckmann 1971, 116 f., where the authors approach the problem, but do not take up the theme of "syncretism."

9. A.1. and A.2. can appear separately and must therefore be clearly distinguished; they are not, however, mutually exclusive insofar as they can appear together in one and the same document.

10. Cf., e.g., Origen, *Contra Celsum* IV, 39; V, 15; VI, 19; VII, 30.

11. Justin, *Apologia* I, 66, 4; Dialogue with the Jew Tryphon, 78, 6.

12. Heissig himself comes close to this form of expression: "The form in which Tantrism succeeded in Mongolia as a substitute for the forbidden Shamanism, was as applied, systematic magic" (Heissig 1970, 342, n. 45).

13. Schenkel 1975, vol. 2, 723. The concepts "biomorph," "sociomorph" and "techno-morph" were introduced by E. Topitsch (e.g., 1972, 15).

14. This has already been achieved in detail in a few points of the work in *Sonderfor-schungsberich* 13: G. Wiessner found a transformation in Syrian Christianity (cf. *idem* 1978 and the example in B.3.2. "Transformation"); W. Schenkel found an example of a transformation in Coptic Christianity (cf. *idem* 1977, 121 ff., esp. 130).

References

Assmann, J. 1975. *Ägyptische Hymnen und Gebete*. Zürich and Munich: Artemis-Verlag.

Berger, P. L., and Th. Luckmann. 1971. *Die gesellschaftliche Konstruktion der Wirklichkeit: Eine Theorie der Wissenssoziologie*. Frankfurt am Main.

Berner, U. 1975. "Bemerkungen zum Verhältnis von Religionsgeschichte und Religions-phänomenologie." *Göttinger Miszellen* 18.

—1976. "Überlegungen zur Übertragbarkeit des Komplimentaritäts-Begriffes auf ägyptische Gottesvorstellungen." *Göttinger Miszellen* 20: 59–71.

—1978. "Der Synkretismus in der origeneischen Darstellung des Auferstehungsglaubens in 'Contra Celsum' IV, 57." In Wiessner, ed. 1978, 39–57.

Biezais, H. 1975a. "Transformation und Identifikation der Götter im Synkretismus." *Temenos* 11: 5–26.

—1975b. "Baltische Religion." In *Germanische und Baltische Religion*, ed. Å. V. Ström and H. Biezais. Stuttgart/Berlin/Mainz: W. Kohlhammer.

Böhlig, A. 1975. "Der Synkretismus des Mani." In Dietrich, ed. 1975.

Colpe, C. 1975. "Syncretism, Renaissance, Secularization and the Formation of New Religions in the Present Day." In *Handbuch der Religionsgeschichte*, vol. 3, ed. J. P. Asmussen and J. Laessoe in association with C. Colpe, 441–523. Göttingen: Vanden-hoeck & Ruprecht.

Dammann, E. 1963. *Die Religionen Afrikas*. Stuttgart: W. Kohlhammer.

Dietrich, A., ed. 1975. *Synkretismus im syrisch-persischen Kulturgebiet. Bericht über ein Symposion in Reinhausen bei Göttingen in der Zeit vom 4. Bis. 8. Oktober 1972*. Göttingen: Vandenhoeck & Ruprecht.

Dijk, J. van. 1971. "Sumerische Religion." In *Handbuch der Religionsgeschichte*, I, ed. J. P. Asmussen and J. Laessoe in association with C. Colpe. Göttingen: Vandenhoeck & Ruprecht.

Dunand, B. F. 1975. "Les Syncrétismes dans la Religion de l'Égypte Romain." In *Les Syn-crétismes das les Religions de l'Antiquité*, ed. F. Dunand and P. Lévêque. Leiden: Brill.

Fohrer, G. 1969. *Geschichte der israelitischen Religion*. Berlin: W. de Gruyter.

Glasenapp, H. von. 1948. *Der Stufenweg zum Göttlichen: Shankaras Philosophie der All-Einheit*. Baden-Baden: H. Bühler.

Gonda, J. 1963. *Die Religionen Indiens II*. Stuttgart: W. Kohlhammer.

Griffis, W. E. 1904. *The Religions of Japan*. New York: Charles Scribner's Sons.

Gundert, W. 1943. *Japanische Religionsgeschichte*. Stuttgart: D. Gundert.

Hacker, P. 1950. *Untersuchungen über Texte des frühen Advaitavada. 1. Die Schüler Sankaras*. Mainz: Akademie der Wissenschaften und der Literatur. Abhandlungen der Geistes- und Sozialwissenschaftlichen Klasse, No. 26.

Harré, R. 1959–60. "Model and Mechanism." *Proceedings of the Aristotelian Society*, N.S. 60: 101–22.

Hartman, S., ed. 1969. *Syncretism. Based on Papers Read at the Symposium on Cultural Contact, Meeting of Religions, Syncretism held at Åbo on the 8th-10th of September 1966*. Stockholm: Almqvist & Wiksell.

Heiler, F. 1962. *Die Religionen der Menschheit in Vergangenheit und Gegenwart*. Stuttgart: Reclam.

Heissig, W. 1970. "Die Religionen der Mongolei." In *Die Religionen Tibets und der Mongolei*, ed. G. Tucci and W. Heissig. Stuttgart: W. Kohlhammer.

Hornung, E. 1982. *Conceptions of God in Ancient Egypt: The One and the Many*. Ithaca, NY: Cornell University Press.

Kawerau, P. 1972. *Das Christentum des Ostens*. Stuttgart: W. Kohlhammer.

Kern, O. 1926. *Die Religion der Griechen*, vol. 1. Berlin: Weidmann.

Kettler, F. H. 1966. *Der ursprüngliche Sinn der Dogmatik des Origenes*. Berlin: A. Töpelmann.

Leeuw, G. van der. 1970. *Phänomenologie der Religion*. Tübingen: Mohr.

Maag, V. 1958. "Der Hirte Israels." *Schweizerische theologische Umschau* 28.

—1964. "Tod und Jenseits nach dem Alten Testament." *Schweizerische theologische Umschau* 34.

—1966–67. "Das Gottesverständnis des alten Testaments." *Nederlands Theologisch Tijdschrift* 21.

Morenz, S. 1973. *Egyptian Religion*. Ithaca, NY: Cornell University Press.

Nilsson, M. P. 1961. *Geschichte der griechischen Religion*. 2 vols. Munich: Beck.

Pannenberg, W. 1971, "Erwägungen zu einer Theologie der Religionsgeschcihte." In *Grundfragen systematischer Theologie. Gesammelte Aufsätze*. Göttingen: Vandenhoeck & Ruprecht.

Rad, G. von. 1958. *Theologie des Alten Testaments*. Münich.

Ringgren, H. 1969. "The Problems of Syncretism." In Hartman, ed. 1969.

Schenkel, W. 1975. "Götterverschmelzung." In *Lexikon der Ägyptologie*, vol. 2, ed. W. Helck and E. Otto, 723. Wiesbaden: Harrassowitz.

—1978. *Schenkel, Kultmythos und Märtyrerlegende: Zur Kontinuität des ägyptischen Denkens*. Wiesbaden: Harrassowitz.

Spiegel, J. 1953. *Das Werden der altägyptischen Hochkultur*. Heidelberg: F. H. Kerle.

Strauss, O. 1973 (rpd). *Indische Philosophie*. Liechtenstein [orig. Münich 1925].

Thomsen, H. 1969. "Non-Buddhist Buddhism and Non-Christian Christianity in Japan." In Hartman, ed. 1969.

Topitsch, E. 1972. *Vom Ursprung und Ende der Metaphysik*. Münich.

Westendorf, W. 1974. "Zweiheit, Dreiheit und Einheit in der altägyptischen Theologie." *Zeitschrift für ägyptische Sprache und Altertumskunde* 100.

Wiessner, G. 1969. "Zur Auseinandersetzung zwischen Christentum und Zoroastrianismus in Iran." In *Zeitschrift der Deutschen Morgenland-Gesellschaft, Supplementa I, XVII Deutscher Orientalistentag vom 21. bis 27. Juli 1968 in Würzburg, Vorträge*, ed. W. Voigt, Part 2. Wiesbaden: Harrassowitz.

—1974. "Prolegomena zu einer Religionsphänomenologie als einer systematischen Religions-wissenschaft." In *Theologie und Wirklichkeit: Festschrift für W. Trillhaas zum 70. Geburtstag*, ed. H. W. Schütte and F. Wintzer. Göttingen: Vandenhoeck & Ruprecht.

—1978. "Die Behnam-Legende." In *Synkretismusforschung: Theorie und Praxis*, ed. G. Wiessner, 119–30. Göttinger Orientforschungen. Reihe Grundlagen und Ergebnisse, 1. Wiesbaden: Harrassowitz.

Zoetmulder, P. 1965. "Die Hochreligionen Indonesiens." In *Die Religionen Indonesiens*, ed. W. Stöhr and P. Zoetmulder. Stuttgart: W. Kohlhammer.

Part VI

CURRENT APPROACHES TO SYNCRETISM
IN THE STUDY OF RELIGION

INTRODUCTION TO PART VI

The current approaches to syncretism are not so much concerned with defining the notion in relation to its problematic past in theology—instead, the three presentations in this part attempt to understand mechanisms behind the phenomenon/a that we refer to as syncretism. However, the task of defining the notion of syncretism was, all along, a search to free a controversial category from a troublesome essentialism and to replace it with a better explanation of the nature of religious transformations and innovations such as syncretistic formations. As such, there is good reason for wanting to define the nature or rather natures of syncretism without confusing it, or them, with a prejudiced essentialism, as was the case with the theologian use of the category. Reading the amount of work represented in this volume has not been an easy assignment, especially because the scholarly discourses have tended to form new issues from the various definitions, which are, then, in need of yet more definitions. This has been the difficult task for the contributors to this book: to find a way to describe the category syncretism as useful for the study of religion and anthropology through this cobweb of definitions. However, this has led the study of syncretism to some conclusions about the formation of religion in general. Moreover, in later years, the study has gained, from linguistics and cognitive studies, a theoretical background against which to explain various mechanisms that relate to the formation of religion. This is also the case with the work of the last three contributors to this volume. Timothy Light contributes his insight into linguistic and cognitive studies to the study of syncretism. He demonstrates how syncretistic formations are linked to the acquisition of religious categories from childhood. That may help us explain different attitudes toward syncretism without falling back on biased definitions. Panayotis Pachis, a historian of religions, relates a theory of cognition to an analysis, which includes power-issues, of the use of syncretism in contemporary Greece. He describes how the "golden age" of Antiquity is a construction of contemporary life and, as such, he invalidates the definition of syncretistic formations as being some kind of "survivals." Kirstine Munk, also a historian of religions, relates syncretism with the psychological redirection of the mind in contemporary Zulu rites of crisis. In her view, syncretistic formations are means to negotiation between the clashes of cultural as well as of social patterns on a personal basis in the Zulu tradition of today. Most interestingly, Munk relates the dynamics of syncretism to the individual maker of religion.

The Acquisition of Religion

The notion "ortho-syncretism" invented by Timothy Light speaks for itself. By now we should be well aware that today's orthodoxy relates to yesterday's mixing. However, Light explains this as a matter of fact, just like Martin did, in the terms of cognitive theories. In this way, he describes the phenomenon "syncretism" as a normal human development. The problem about the notion of syncretism is not that it refers to an abnormal phenomenon, because, according to Light, "melding" is the way religion and other cultural products change in peoples' minds. He states, more precisely, the problem to be that humans are only able to think in *unitary wholes*. The "melding" of religion is therefore, when we follow Light's argument, partly a psychological problem of group-identity, and partly a phenomenon that emerges quite naturally from the ways we acquire religion.

This manner of considering the acquisition of religion according to cognitive theories comes close to the linguistic theories about language acquisition and *creolization* (see Part IV of this volume). Light confirms, in his approach to syncretism, that the acquisition of new religious elements is a process similar to the acquisition of a foreign language. He is in agreement with Bickerton (see Part IV of this volume) and other linguists who believe that learning is a reiterative or reformulating process; even though he does not suggest a particular period of "childhood's creolization" as different to adult acquisition. As an alternative, he presents a more elementary chronological process from simple acquisitions into more complex ones, which further entails that our learning-ability is flexible and dynamic throughout life. The chart of his own religious development demonstrates how he sees the different stages of acquisition happening through a life. The three steps from childhood, through adolescence to maturity, give us a good implication of how the integration of emotionally powerful symbols to more complicated processes of learning occur. It is worth noticing, with his reference to Rudolph Otto, the significance he lends to the numinous enhancement of religious symbols and the effects of symbols on memory-systems. Chart III, more specifically, illustrates the three stages as expressed with reference to syncretism: a process that goes from the "discrete-point acquisition" to the "multidimensional webbing," which also continues throughout life. Learning is not, then, just a question of innate mechanisms of the brain. Light states that the more elaborated our knowledge about a culture becomes the more our new learning is constrained. That is, new learning is dependent both on innate patterns of cognition and cultural categories of interpretation.

Light's cognitive model of syncretistic acquisition is in effect very hermeneutical, in particular with reference to the interaction between "symbols" and "categories." There is no suggestion of a model similar to Chomsky's theory of "universal grammar," but rather the idea that our cognitive apparatus

319

functions like a system of inferences. His focus on the interplay between symbols and categories shows that the transformative mode of syncretism is mainly interpretive; because with our cognitive abilities we do not just copy religious meaning through generations of religious praxis. We make innovations through reinterpretation as a part of the acquisition of new religious elements.

Light's cognitive model on syncretistic acquisition not only proves that all religions are syncretistic, it also explains that the causes of conflict over the "melding" of religion are because some categories are more reluctant to change than others, since they are basically important and, we might say, innate to their respective cultural or religious systems. This explains, as well, why there is resistance to syncretistic innovation in some areas of one religion, and in another, the same may go unnoticed. This helps us to get an idea of where to look for the roots of conflict in power-related discourses of syncretism. Furthermore, his model may also help us to structure a typology of syncretism, similar to the one Berner engineered, only based on categorial differences in religions.

Light's use of theories from linguistics and cognitive studies contributes to a new understanding of syncretism, wherein the *phenomenon* of syncretism becomes explained by learning abilities of the brain; along with this, he gives us an explanation, psychological as well as hermeneutical, of why the *notion* of syncretism may cause a problem in religion and in social life. Yet, with regard to the importance he places on religious categories and the "numinousity" of symbols, we might take a further step and question whether the reason for "anti-syncretism" is to be found in particular modes of religion. This may finally help us get over the discrepancy between the Christian use and the scholarly use of the notion.

Principle of the Past as a Dynamic Element of Syncretism

In Herskovits's introduction to his concept of "Africanism," we already touched upon the concept of "survivals" as a prevalent element of the dynamics of syncretism. This is taken up anew in Panayotis Pachis's discussion of the revival of "Hellenism" in contemporary Greece. Here, Pachis points out that the idea of an idealized "Hellenism" is a powerful tool in contemporary political and religious propaganda. When present religions in Greece are moulded upon the "principle of the past," it serves to guarantee authority to their current worldviews. Ancient Greek culture has thus, according to Pachis, become a "creative hybrid creation" that is syncretistic in nature. He mentions the neo-Pagan invention of the "golden age" of ancient Greek culture as mixed with more or less folk-scientific ideas of today's ecological problems and postmodern naturalism; or the nationalistic and fascist political tendencies in Greece which, with the help from the Orthodox Church, emphasize the bonds between religion and nationalism. According to Pachis, we can detect a blend of different religious and political interests in the contemporary religious discourses that are responsible for the invention of a new mythology about the past, and that, because of the inclusive intention to return to a more traditional mono-culture, can be dangerous in the context of a modern society.

Thus, the Greek example is another case of power-related "syncretism." However, Pachis sees these syncretistic formations of the past mainly connected to the way people think in contemporary society. This observation invalidates Herskovits and the early anthropological view of syncretistic elements as "survivals." As an alternative, Pachis describes how it is the symbolic character of the past that enhances the current religious reality and which likewise provides the frame of revision of religious elements. As he states, people are simply not aware of the source of their ideas, and how they use them as standardized models to adjust their conduct in the present. Inspired by both Luther Martin and Timothy Light, Pachis understands syncretism as a cognitive phenomenon that refers to the formative process of cultural categories. The point is to go behind the surface of the operation, and look for the structure of how ideas of the past are formed and reformed in the minds of people. Therefore, his Greek illustration serves as an interesting example of how the cognitive and the semantic levels are intertwined with the social level. This resembles Gustavo Benavides's definition of religious syncretism as a means for power and legitimation (see Part IV of this volume) and how religion of the past finds a renaissance in the present by serving as an authority for religio-political struggles. However, in Pachis's definition, syncretistic formations are part of a set of "criteria of selection" connected to our cognitive apparatus. If we accept this more-or-less evolutionary approach and accept the idea that "eclecticism is a function of the human cognitive system," then we have a very good argument for the general nature of cultural processes as being basically syncretistic.

Syncretism as a Means of Negotiation

Kirstine Munk describes syncretism as playing a vital part in the cultural reformation going on in present-day South Africa where a crisis between traditional Zulu practices and modernity is taking place. Her description of the healing practices or "rites of crisis," that occur as a consequence of the cultural clashes between Zulu values and Western lifestyle, focuses on syncretism as an element of negotiation between incompatibilities present in the social life of South Africans of Zulu descent. First, on a small scale, syncretism concerns the process of reconstructing and reinterpreting the traditional healing practices as a mutual collaboration between the healer and patient. Secondly, on a larger scale, it concerns the reason of crisis; that is, the patient's problematic relationship with his or her social reality. These are the reasons for seeking comprising and "syncretistic" solutions between conflicting interests of moral, social and economical issues.

In Munk's view, the phenomenon of syncretism is involved more with the sensuous rather than intellectual experience of religion and it appears to be more active in rituals with individual and magical references. She opposes the idea that the magical rites are involved in reproducing particular world-views as closed-meaning systems—along the lines of criticism from cognitive theories, represented, for example, by Luther Martin (Part V of this volume). Instead, she states that these rites concentrate on the intentionality of the patient. Therefore, patients are given a greater opportunity to influence the ritual process. Consequently, it is the flexibility of this type of rites that render them suitable for solving questions of new matters that cannot be answered by any other institution. This may explain why the "rites of crisis" form a matrix of syncretism, in addition to the way they are already cut out to handle social contradictions (e.g., witchcraft) in the traditional Zulu context. There is no doubt that Munk is right in emphasizing the involvement of syncretistic elements as particularly salient in rites dealing with personal well-being. For instance, it is worth noting that there are only few participants in such rituals to negotiate about old and new matters. This undoubtedly makes syncretistic inputs a less problematic issue than it would be in the official Christian Churches of South Africa, as, for instance, Charles Stewart points out in his essay in this volume (see Part IV).

Magic versus Religion?

Are we then forced to admit a dual perspective when it comes to syncretism—one that confirms the traditional differentiation between "magic" and "religion" by referring to magical traditions as being more inclined towards syncretism? It is not Munk's intention to neither confirm nor refute this issue. On the contrary, she stresses, by way of her examples, the very dynamics of the constitution of the "rites of crisis" in Zulu tradition. In that respect she is right of course to point out that rituals are not just coherent or tight "meaning systems."

However, we cannot yet discharge the questions about the theoretical dichotomy between, on one hand, the view of religion as "meaning systems," and on the other hand, magic as a more client-oriented approach, simply because we have discovered that individuals play a larger role than expected in the constitution of rituals. However, they do so within the confines of semantic spaces and ritual frames that can be brought to make sense;

322

novelties that were beyond all cognitive, semantic or social rules would probably not be of much ritual use. We must also accept the fact that not all rituals may be the same. Clearly, there are a whole group of rituals, various initiation rites, shamanistic rites, divination, and so on, which are, similar to the magical practices of the Zulu tradition, founded on a person-to-person basis. However, other rituals are simply constructed to confirm and reproduce a particular tradition or institution; let us for lack of a better concept call them "meaning systems." For instance, in a Christian church service, there are rules of participation, such as when to pray, when to stand up, when to sit down, and so on, that do not involve individual innovation—just the opposite, it confirms a particular theological system that is performed, whether the participants believe in it or not.

Indisputably, syncretistic formations are constrained differently by different modes of rituals and/or religions. It is actually quite simple. We do not have to accept Kraemer's and others' prejudiced views of particular religions as having an innate capacity for syncretism in order to consider with Munk that different religious institutions have different constraints in relation to syncretistic input. Therefore, Munk's example of the healing practices in South Africa confirms that some religious institutions are more open to syncretistic inputs than others. The "rites of crisis" form an interesting matrix for syncretistic blending, in contrast to an otherwise anti-syncretistic culture. Munk observes that this is because the blending is based on a structure of negotiation of personal and social matters between healer and patient, and not on the grounds of theology or worldview. Furthermore, this may confirm Timothy Light's argument about the interplay between symbols and categories. In the case of Munk's Zulu friend's visit to the "*isangoma*," the syncretistic input, such as western medicine blended with traditional herbs or the fake leopard fur, does not seem to transgress the frame of the traditional category of a rite of crisis. "The bombardment of senses" enforced by the syncretistic input seemed to be the expected in Theleki's case, whereas in the case of Munk's meeting with the white *isangoma*, David Myburgh, the "syncretism" becomes a paradox of contradictory categories. The magic performed and the things said challenged Munk's own sense of reality.

According to Munk's criticism of the static definition of the concept of worldview, she has proved, with both of her empirical examples, that people do not have coherent worldviews (that they quite often think that they do is another issue). She has also pointed to particular rituals that use syncretistic inputs to prompt our senses so that we may redirect our "worldviews." Or, is it maybe better to use Light's classification to demonstrate Munk's position? That the human mind is structured by sets of categories that may seem similar to a worldview, or classification system, especially when it is redirected by challenging and strange new categories. We may further learn from Munk's examples that the way people react to "syn-cretistic redirection" all depends on the social-psychological frames the religious practice is set in.

Hence, Munk is able to turn the interest in syncretism away from the problematic focal point of the concept to the more intriguing question about the phenomenon, and its impact on the individual maker of religion. Her account of the white *isangoma* David Myburgh presents a fascinating example of religion in making; how one person can form a cross-field of syncretism, racially, religiously as well as politically and make up a new religious category based on the encounter of cultures.

ORTHOSYNCRETISM:
AN ACCOUNT OF MELDING IN RELIGION[*]

Timothy Light

1. Introduction

Like all other human phenomena, religions constantly change over time. They change in response to new circumstances. They change as a result of new perceptions and interpretations by succeeding generations. Just as do other human phenomena, religions change particularly when they come into intimate contact with other religions. Even when the contact is contemporaneously interpreted only in terms of conflict (e.g., the Christian religious wars, and the Confucian disdain of Buddhism in China), religions—and other cultural phenomena—borrow and learn from each other.

Religions have multiple sources in their histories. That leads to a major religious conundrum: Today's form of any religion has many antecedents from yesterday. Yet the truth claims of most religions require that the past be seen as unitary and inevitably leading to today, and even to an implied permanence in interpretation of how things are structured in the world. Understanding human religious behavior must include understanding that contradiction and accounting for the human capacity to absorb and assimilate multiple, often contradictory, sources while interpreting their sum as unitary and frequently as derived from the same origin.

Syncretism is the term which is generally given to religious mixing. This paper is an initial attempt to describe the cognitive mechanisms which lead to syncretism as an inherent part of human religious behavior. Although other scholars have attempted to define syncretism in ways that include some kinds of religious mixing and exclude other kinds (e.g., Baumann 1994;

Pye 1993, and elsewhere; Schreiter 1993), I shall use the term to mean simply "religious melding," leaving for another time further refinement. I do this because the central issue is not the taxonomy of mixing, but the prevelance of the phenomenon itself. That issue is central not only because the claim of religious truth tends to deny it in the face of obvious predominance, but, more importantly, because the human capacity to simultaneously mix cultural material and to claim that cultures are unitary is one of the principal (if not *the* principal) building blocks of our ability to have cultures.

2. The Cognitive Structure of Religious Knowledge

I suggest that at the highest level of observable abstraction in human behavior, our religious knowledge, contains three cognitive entities:

1. Symbols
2. Categories into which those symbols are arranged
3. Organizational rules which relate the categories of symbols

The symbols of religion—gods, saints, demons—are *on the surface* the most important entities to us because it is they to which we turn in reverence, worship, fear, and so on. It is symbols which are learned first in the transmission of religion. It is symbols to which loyalty is sworn and which are used to define religious groups. It is symbols around which we unify and symbols over which we fight. As Sperber (1975), Boyer (1990, 1994), and Lawson and Macauley (1990) have shown, the transmission of symbols from generation to generation or from group to group may not necessarily imply transmission of meaning or interpretation of those symbols. Adherents of a given religious tradition may frequently have quite different interpretations of the symbols which draw the attention of the body as a whole.

The categories into which those symbols are arranged, and the definition of those categories, give meaning to the symbols. We are less aware of these categories than we are of the symbols themselves because the latter are ostensible objects of the most intense attention. But it is the categorization of our symbols which really defines our religious understanding and behavior. When religions change, it is the changes in categories and organization which mark true change.

The greatest change occurs when categories themselves are redefined or altered. The rules regarding the arrangement of categories, therefore, imply the most serious characterization of our religious understanding and behavior.

Light *Orthosyncretism*

Chart I.A *Christian Perceptions at Four Years Old*

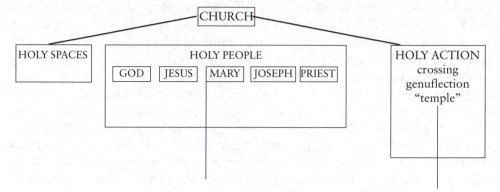

Chart I.B *Christian Perceptions as an Adolescent*

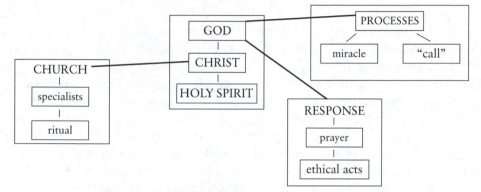

Chart I.C *Christian Perceptions as a Late Middle-Aged Man*

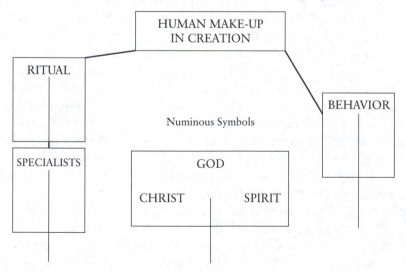

An example is in order. At the risk of embarrassment, Charts I.A, B, and C above give an analysis of my own religious understanding at three stages of life. I use myself because that is the easiest source to abuse in this way. I list three stages of life and the different understandings that occur at those three stages as an illustration of the truth of the constant *individual*, as well as *group*, changes that occur in religion. I begin with individual development because I think that the dynamics of religious development are precisely the same as those of religious borrowing and adaptation throughout life for the individual or the group. And I begin at home because the forces that lead to syncretism are generally identified in other people's religious traditions rather than in those of us who have grown up in the West with our exclusivist monotheistic heritage. My belief—even as a practicing Christian—is that we are no different in our religious behavior than anyone else.

Because of the limits of space, I will not further analyze these charts except to note that the genesis of religious development is no different from the development of other learning. (The cognitive mechanisms accounting for this process are discussed at the end of the paper.) And the acquisition of vocabulary items (*church, cross, God*) is the same process throughout the lexicon. One acquires the term, and then meanings are made progressively precise as one acquires other terms, especially those which are frequently used together with the targeted one.

For example, my earliest religious memory is that at some point around the age of three or four, I learned the word *temple* in the ordinary way that one acquires vocabulary, through one's own (ersatz) analysis of the functions that the word seems to have in others' use. For me, *temple* was associated with the darkness of the church, the music, the hushed tones of people entering the church, and, of course, the formal ritual activity. *Temple* became for me the symbol of the feelings that Rudolf Otto assigns to encounters with the numinous. Because I could not yet read, when hymns were sung (and like all children, I wanted to participate) I joined in calling out "temple, temple, temple" to (my version) of the tune. Later on, of course, I gradually learned more precise definitions of the term *temple* along with acquiring a host of other terms dealing with religion. Human memories are layered rather than entirely replacive, so that even today the word *temple* carries an extra load of meaning for me, despite my conscious understanding of that term—and use of that term—in multiple contexts where it is simply a denotator with a specific referent of no more significance to me than *table, chair,* or *ball*.

Learning the (generalized and hence undefined) symbol—and adhering to the symbol with strong emotional devotion—occurs nonverbally as well. Children brought up in a Christian tradition which practices genuflexion, crossing oneself, and kneeling for prayer initially acquire the act of genuflecting as a generalized acknowledgment of, and participation with, the sacred and not as a specific act that is triggered by the precise and limited circumstances which the Church assigns to them. The generalized power of such acts throughout one's life is striking. The movie and comic-book parodying of religious behavior under trying circumstances certainly evidences the underlying reality. In comedies where a risk is being taken or fear is evident, participants will ostentatiously and furiously cross themselves. The *rapprochement* between France and Germany in the late 1950s and early 1960s was epitomized in de Gaulle and Adenauer going to Mass together. This was a public act which carried immense authority in legitimizing the new friendly relationship. It did so not because all of the German and French populations were Catholic, for they most assuredly were not. Quite to the contrary, in fact. Still heir to the categorical rationalism of the late-eighteenth-century Revolution, France was still legally governed by late-nineteenth-century attempts to excise all religion from public life, and Germany was still so much the heir to the religious wars among Christians that the state gave financial support to all the contending parties, officially legitimating them. The photographs, newsreels, and televised images of the two men going to church together took their power not from the precise meaning that the act might have had—that both men were Catholic—but from a generalized, unstated and thoroughly undefined acceptance that in those two cultures, approaching the shared symbols of the sacred is a sign of acknowledgment of adherence to authority higher than that which produced the conflict between them. Had the act been further specified, it would have had the opposite effect because it would have required individual (and hence conflicting) meanings to be asserted by the viewers. As long as it was the most general of religious acknowledgments, it served to draw on primordial, nonverbal adherence to the power of the symbols being used.

3. Examples and Analyses

Consider five examples of quite different forms of religious mixing. Although recounted briefly, I believe that it is evident that they can be understood as operating with essentially the same dynamics as the personal Protestant Christian example given earlier. The first of these examples will be analyzed at greater length both because it reflects my own direct observation and because it illustrates with ostensible opposition quite similar phenomena to the Christian case I have just mentioned above.

3.1. Example 1: Acquiring a God in Chinese Religion

It is common for Chinese merchants to maintain a small shrine-altar in their place of business. On the altar are the image(s) of a god or gods. Offerings such as fruit, wine, or other foods are placed in front of the divine image. Most of the businesses that I have visited over the past thirty-five years have made sure that the offerings are fresh so that the shrine-altar is an attractive part of the business establishment. This custom is followed by Chinese merchants throughout the worldwide Sino-diaspora as well as in Chinese territory itself (i.e., Mainland China, Taiwan, Hong Kong, Macau). In whatever part of the world in which they may be found, the images that are kept on these altars derive from the Chinese past. Most of the images are of deities whose genesis is either a historical or legendary part of the past which defines what being Chinese means. That is entirely fitting, as the outer-bound of Chinese religion is formed by the sense of *China* itself. Historically, except for Buddhism, all the sources of Chinese religion (the received ancestral tradition, Confucianism, Taoism) are all indigenous. Until 1911, the chief religious specialist was the emperor, and even now the symbol of China itself remains the most numinous of all the religious ideas in Chinese religion. Among the most common images is *Guan Ti* (or *Guan Gong*), a deity based on Guan Yu, a general of the third century CE, whose intense loyalty so epitomized this cardinal Confucian virtue that his popular canonization was long ago embraced by the nation as a whole. Other frequently-seen gods are *Cai Shen*, the God of Prosperity, and *Shou Sheng Gong*, the God of Longevity, both of which are, of course, functionally mythological, as would be the gods of the kitchen, stove, wind, and so on. Another frequently-seen image is that of *Guan Yin*, the Goddess of Mercy. *Guan Yin* derives from the male figure Avalokitesvara imported to China with Buddhism and transposed into a female in China centuries later. Less common outside of Hong Kong, but with growing popularity as long-term residents or natives of Hong Kong migrate to other places is the image of *Wong Tai Sin*, the divinized form of Wong Cho Ping (ca. 284–364 CE) (Lang and Ragvald 1993: 3–9; Ma 1993: 251–54).

Irrespective of earliest source and of relative antiquity, even irrespective of whether the deity was initially Chinese, all of these figures are fully Sinicized. Their physical images conform entirely to the aesthetic and devotional expectations of Chinese custom. Their names are not only Chinese, but widely familar, and even the most rarely seen of them fit at least loosely into a general pantheocratic arrangement. They sound like Chinese gods and they look like Chinese gods, even though *Guan Ti* was apparently canonized almost two thousand years ago and continuously revered, and *Wong Tai Sin* (possibly cononized not long after and then forgotten) revived only at the end of the nineteenth century (Lang and Ragvald 1993: 11–18).

In contrast, many Chinese businesses in Singapore (population approximately 75 percent Chinese) support a deity whose image is decidedly not Chinese, but, most likely, Thai in origin. When asked about what seems an anomaly to the outside visitor, merchants initially say that the figure is simply another Chinese god. When the observer insists that he doesn't look like a Chinese god, the merchant is willing to acknowledge that he probably came from Thailand, but, "Now for us, he is Chinese."

The categories which organize the symbols in Chinese religion can be defined as follows:

A. The entity of China and the Chinese people. This is the overarching religious idea in China—as seems to have been the case in ancient Rome. It is evidenced by the Sinicization of foreign borrowings; by the principal religious specialist having been the emperor for the two thousand years prior to 1911; by the discourse on religious thought, which interprets the principal foreign borrowing, Buddhism, not to its Indian origins but to native Taoism and Confucianism; and by the conflictedness of intellectuals formally disdaining Buddhism, and yet practicing and explicating their Confucianism with distinctly Buddhist elements.

B. The largely abstracted superhuman agent *Tian* (heaven, sky) and the works of that agent—*Tianming* (mandate of heaven; often in practice seen as little more than *ming* [fate]); the very ancient and largely absent *Shangdi* (high god). Although prominent in Confucian works and given lip service in speech, in fact *Tian* figures little on overt religious behavior, and *Shangdi* today is most frequently heard as the term which the Protestant missionaries chose to use as a translation for the term God. Hence, this category is put in parentheses in Chart II indicating optionality.

C. Gods and spirits—including popular local gods, gods that were at one time legitimated through governmental sanction, imported or adapted deities, buddhas, etc.

D. Special persons not (yet or widely) deified, including sages (e.g., Confucius, Laozi, Zhuangzi, etc.), patriarchs, arhats, etc.

E. Religious specialists, monks, priests, spirit-mediums, heads of family.

F. Rituals of maintenance and exchange.

G. "Classics" (i.e., sacred books) and oral explanation.

H. Processes: iterative deification; recognition of the specially marked: spirit-mediums.

Charted schematically, these categories and some of their members would look like Chart II.

Chart II. *Chinese Religion: The Major Categories*

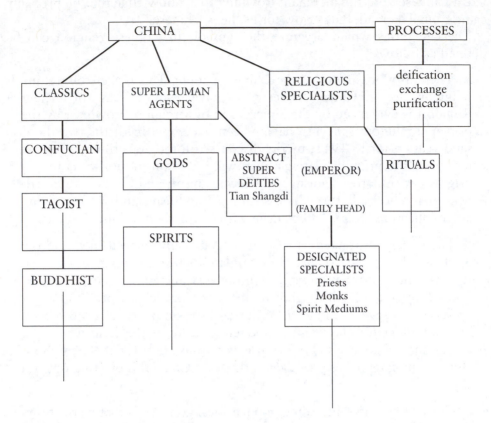

Note: Parenthesis indicate optional or highly infrequently appearing categories; thin lines within a category indicate the openness between that category and the numinous.

This chart, of course, displays the hierarchical relationship. It also displays the fact that only the category of the nation is entirely exclusive to one member. *Tian* (and even more *Shangdi*) is frequently so inoperative in people's concepts, reporting, and religious behavior that it must be considered an optional category. All the categories of deities/spirits, special persons, religious specialists, and religious exegeses are open, which means that they may be both added to and subtracted from and that individuals and groups may legitimately select from among the members of the categories and quite happily ignore the remaining members with no adverse consequences. The process of deification is technically closed, as it is a single process, but, of course, that process itself is by definition unlimitedly repeatable and therefore it, too, is in effect a fully open class. The chart format obscures one critical characteristic of Chinese religion as a nationally non-native phenomenon.

The more educated and closer to traditional social elites, the more strictly are the lines between the categories maintained. The more "popular," the more some lines are blurred. Thus, at the most "popular" level, the abstract agent *Tian* hardly bears a presence, and the emphasis of attention is entirely placed on gods, spirits, and the deification (or the ability to be deified) of special persons of the past, of which the lines between the two are weak at best.

Understanding Chinese religion in this way makes the following quite predictable:

(i) A Chinese Buddhist temple in Kuala Lumpur, Malaysia, watched over by nuns. Prominent in the temple are glass cases containing scores of god figures. When asked, the nun in charge acknowledges that, while they are certainly gods, she has no idea of who each one is or its function because her devotion is to *Guan Yin*.

(ii) A Chinese proprietary temple in Singapore dedicated to the somewhat evanescent deity *Tai Bo Gong*. The temple keeper characterized the deity as the king of the underworld. A purported cognescento argued that he is the god of gamblers.

(iii) The Chinese temple in Panama City, Panama is dedicated to *Guan Ti*. Many of the frequent worshipers are also Catholic Christians and regularly attend Sabbath Mass.

(iv) In her excellent book, *Changing Gods in Medieval China, 1127–1226* (1990), Valerie Hansen relates that her initial interest in Chinese deities and deification processes stemmed from being told one day that an associate had just gone to pray to a new god because of hearing that the new god was very efficacious.

3.2. *The Virgin of Guadalupe*

In 1531, Juan Diego, a Christianized native Mexican, encountered the Virgin on top of Tepeyac Hill near Guadalupe. The Virgin addressed him in Nahuatl, his own language, and when his vision was not believed by the Church hierarchy, she caused roses to flourish in a sterile location on the hill. Following her instructions, Juan Diego gathered the roses in his cloak and took them to the bishop. When he opened the cloak, the image of the Virgin was miraculously imprinted on the cloak. This demonstration of miraculous visitation resulted in a shrine being built upon Tepeyac Hill. The cult of the Virgin of Guadalupe thereupon spread rapidly and today she is understood to be the Mexican national symbol—even to the degree that churches dedicated to her frequently have the colors of the Mexican flag painted on their roofs.

Eric Wolf's famous description of the development of the cult of Guadalupe stresses that in pre-Hispanic times Tepeyac Hill had been the site of a temple dedicated to "the earth and fertility goddess *Tonantzin*, Our Lady Mother, who—like Guadalupe—was associated with the moon" (Wolf 1958). This temple, like its modern successor, the Basilica of the Virgin of Guadalupe, was the site of large pilgrimages. Following records left by Catholic priests, Wolf asserts that the converted faithful often continued to call the Virgin by the name of *Tonantzin*, a practice discouraged as Satanic by Catholic priests. As the Mexican national symbol, then, the apparition at Tepeyac is a merger of Catholic Mary and Nahuatl *Tonantzin* and called by both names. Interestingly, Louise Burkhart's recent study shows that it is unlikely that *Tonantzin* was ever the name of a Nahua deity, since in Nahuatl that term is not a name, but merely a title that could be applied to any appropriate deity. It is a normally formed word made up of three morphemes: *to-* "our," *-nan-* 'mother', *-tzin* (reverential suffix).

> The Indians were not perpetuating memories of pre-Columbian goddesses but were projecting elements of their Christian worship into their pre-Christian past, conceptualizing their ancient worship in terms of Mary ... In colonial records, indigenous myths are often adapted in response to Christian teachings ... Priests, incapable of viewing Indian religion except in terms of idolatry vs. Christianity, were oblivious to many of the subtle adjustments and compromises the Indians were making both in their memories of "idolatry" and their practice of Christianity. (Burkhart 1993: 208)

Presuming that Burkhart's greater linguistic sophistication renders her analysis more accurate, we can conclude that the adoption of the Virgin of Guadalupe as the Mexican national symbol resulted from a bi-cultural readiness for a paramount sacralized earth-mother figure so that Guadalupe is indeed as epitomizing an example of syncretism as can be found. Part of the genius of this figure, however, is that the conscious interpretations of the figure conflicted seriously, while the behavior of both cultures was ironically the same. For both native Nahua and the Spanish Catholics, the appearance of the Virgin in Mexico gave a new symbol for expressing prior meanings which were then reified in that new symbol. Not only did the Nahua reformulate the Virgin back to a deity which did not previously exist by using standard religious honorifics to refer to her and then describe her, but the colonial Spanish preserved legends surrounding her appearance that are strikingly parallel to the accounts of similar appearances in Spain long, long before New World exploration was ever thought of (Burkhart 1993: 214–18). For the Indians, this reformulation was merely appropriate behavior for adapting to the Conquest. For the Spanish it was called idolatry. Yet they shared allegiance to Guadalupe and for rather similar reasons.

3.3. African (Christian) Healing

[E]very Church in Africa is concerned with Christian healing. We distort our subject if we just think of Christian healing in terms of a special kind of faith healing ... "We are here to heal," a leader of the Church of the Twelve Apostles told Dr. Baeta, when asked what his Church stood for. "This is not a church, it is a hospital," unashamedly proclaimed one prophet to his Zionist congregation, according to Dr. Sundkler ... The *direct* healing of man's physical and mental illnesses by Almighty God, often without the use of any medicine, either European or traditional, is procliamed as of the essence of the Gospel. (Mitchell 1963: 47; italics original)

These remarks begin a talk at a conference convened by the World Council of Churches' Department of Missionary Studies to discuss "independent" or "separatist" African Christian churches. Mitchell's words are both explicatory and also perhaps a bit plaintive. Healing seems to be a central province of so many indigenous religious specialists in Southern and West Africa that in Africa healing must be seen as an integral part of the definition of religion itself. (The point is generally confirmed by Baeta 1962; Berglund 1976; Daneel 1970; Oosthuizen 1968; Pauw 1975; and Sundkler 1961, 1976.) If the Christian Church is to deal effectively with its environment in Africa, healing must then be a part of its mission. However, healing under what regimen? Separatist churches openly sponsor "faith healing" by clergy and prophets. 'Mainline churches', in contrast, manage hospitals and send *medical* practitioners as missionaries alongside clergy and other specifically religious workers. Standing firmly within the cultural tradition that has recently been molded by the applied effects of the Scientific Revolution, Mitchell notes that "some women who might be helped to have children are led on and on by promises [from separatist faith healers] that they will become fertile. Men who have tuberculosis and who could be cured by drugs are kept from that cure" (1963: 51). Of course this raises an ethical dilemma: the independent churches receive greater welcome by ostensibly fitting in with indigenous expectations, but through the dissemination of their Christian-based faith (i.e., through spreading Christian symbols) they keep needy people away from definite and proven cures. For the "mainline" churches the dilemma is pregnantly summed up in Mitchell's final sentence: "What responsibility does the Church have positively to teach Western scientific culture in Africa today?" (1963: 51).

Less than a century before, few Christians would have raised this question. The basic science that lies behind the medical discoveries which have produced so many cures was seen by many to be a direct challenge to the claims of Christianity. For many others, the emergence of science was at least a matter troubling the prospects of faith and worthy of extensive debate and discussion. The discomfort that Christians continue to have trying simultane-ously to maintain religious participation and absorb scientific discovery has by no means disappeared, as evidenced by the fact that Barbour's 1989–1991 Gifford Lectures concerned just that matter (Barbour 1990). Extensive prayer and certain rituals have been (and often still are) a prominent part of the Christian response to illness throughout Christian history. The Christian churches of the broad Catholic tradition still maintains healing and exorcism rituals in their formal books of worship. Whether that is called "faith heal-ing" or not probably depends on individual definitions of the function of prayer and the potential of faith healing. But, whatever it is named, it is cer-tainly a clear linkage between calling on the transcendent and the hope for relief. Such specific religious responses to illness (and other catastrophes) have diminished in popularity among Western Christians as the certainty of cure by medicine has grown. Correspondingly, the effective definition of God—or at least *how* and *why* God works—has changed as well. Science does not admit the direct action of any transcendent power contrary to natu-ral laws. Science sees no connection between the moral state of any indi-vidual (i.e., biological host) and any disease (i.e., invading parasite). The Scientific Revolution has caused God to recede to a much more remote position for post-scientific Christians.

Although it is in a Christian missionary context, Mitchell's question con-cerning the Church's obligation to spread Western science along with the Christian Gospel ironically asks as well that we consider where the actual *religious mixing* is. Are the independent churches with their emphasis on faith healing (and the possible negative consequences thereof unwelcome syncre-tists? Or, because prior to the scientific revolution, Christian and African views of disease were rather similar, should the "independent" or "separa-tist" faith healers be understood as approaching Christian orthodoxy and the scientifically-oriented churches be understood as the deviants?

3.4. The Tao in the American Nursery

In the 1920s A. A. Milne published his immensely popular children's fan-tasies about a little boy's personified stuffed animals, led by his teddy bear "Winnie The Pooh." The Pooh stories reflect the nursery ethos that pre-vailed among the British wealthier classes at the end of the nineteenth century. The background also to such equally popular stories as Travers's *Mary Poppins* and J. M. Barrie's *Peter Pan*, this safe world that contains no real dangers and no genuine choices was commanded by distant parents, but directly overseen by understanding nannies—one of them even being a fully cognizant dog. Milne's Pooh stands out because he is passive in contrast to the frenetic and often confused behavior of those around him who behave like adults (particularly a cranky donkey and a silly rabbit). Being "a bear of little brain," Pooh is not expected to understand or accomplish much. In reality, through accident or through the excesses of others, Pooh seems to hit the target and in superficially bland or even inane observations provides the author's moral comment. The general burden of Pooh's wisdom is that children with few pretensions are generally more deeply seeing than adults with all their plans and actions.

Of course, by the time the Pooh stories appeared, the effectiveness of the world they portrayed had already been shattered, and the possibility of the safe nursery as the locus of upbringing for the ruling classes was in decline. The tragedy of World War I destroyed illusions of there being a chance of maintaining a world that was as protected, controlled and isolated as the British nursery. A scant few years later, World War II saw the end of the empire itself. The Pooh stories seem to have correspondingly grown in popularity, particularly among late adolescents and young adults. Presumably, despite being written for children, these stories provide a happy refuge of escape at later times of life when the complexities of reality are overwhelming.

In the 1980s Benjamin Hoff merged the world of Pooh with that of the *Tao* of the Chinese classics, the *Tao Teh Ching* (or *Laotzu*) and the *Chuangtzu* in two books that are regularly seen in college student backpacks today, *The Tao of Pooh* and *The Teh of Piglet*. While there is indeed an escapist strain in religious Taoism and while a small portion of the *Chuangtzu* reflects that theme, the main burden of the *Chuangtzu* and the full focus of the *Tao Teh Ching* are intensely realistic, concentrating on a world defined by uncertainty, violence, conflict, and a primal force (the Tao) which was mediated and interpreted by shamans and other mediums and which treats human beings "like straw dogs." Hoff's transportation of the Tao into the lost nursery world of a few percent of late-nineteenth-century British families redefines both the Tao and the nursery in ways that would probably have been unrecognizable to actual participants in either. Hoff's effort is one of scores of similar appropriations of the *Tao* (*The Tao of Physics, Sex, Islam, Leadership*, etc.) as a blank numinous symbol on which a late-twentieth-century American author can write his own meanings and through the use of which those meanings are graced with transcendence.

3.5. Christian "Pluralism"

Among the liveliest movements in Christian theology of the past decade or so has been the attempts of several thinkers to relate their Christianity to interpretations of experience that originate with Asian religions. Christian scholars working in this mode include both European Caucasian Christians who were raised with fairly conventional Protestant understandings of their faith, but who have come into contact with various Asian religious practices and concepts, as well as Asian Christians who have reflected on the indigenous traditions which surround them. To be found in this group would be thinkers such as Cobb, Eck, Lee, Hick, Koyama, and Suh, to name just some representative figures. The products of these thinkers differ notably, but they share two common features.

First, their definition of the transcendent is considerably more abstract than the notion of a personal God which many Protestants are raised. The transcendent, moreover, is understood to be a much richer term than can be encompassed in any concept of *God* as labeled in a single human term. Eck's principal encounter has been with Hinduism, and the continuous interplay in Hinduism between the unitariness of God as a concept and the multiplicity of God's manifestations in many gods has given Eck's marvelous phrase "the manyness of God." Hick has been particularly touched by generally strict (and somewhat academic) Buddhism; so that, like Guruge (1982), he understands that the ineffability which is the hallmark of monotheism can be even more profound in a possibly atheistic religion where the object of religious attention is a state to be achieved by the mind through "skillful means." Growing up and practicing in Korea, the Asian society which has most embraced Christianity and which therefore has most assimilated it to indigenous norms, Suh and others have developed *Min Jung* theology, a Christian interpretation which draws extensively on native religious practices and understanding and which, for example, finds an honorable place for Christian shamanism.

Second, while not denying common Christian practices such as the Eucharist and other public worship, practitioners of pluralist Christianity have especially identified meditation as a practice which draws individuals into closer understanding of the transcendent. This adaptation of a means for clearing the mind and thus approaching the transcendent which derives from Buddhism and Taoism (and which was, in fact, advocated by neo-Confucianism as well) does not by itself replace traditional prayer, but inevitably meditation becomes defined as a function for which prayer had been used, and in turn prayer becomes defined far more as approaching the transcendent than as petition, supplication and so on.

4. Analyzing the Examples: The Force to Integrate

The various instances of religious mixture cited above are major and open to easy observation. They range from the addition of a deity—a process that is certainly not unknown in many polytheistic religions—to a radical change in interpreting received symbols, an adaptive procedure that has been engaged in many times throughout the histories of Judaism, Christianity, Islam, Buddhism, Confucianism, and Taoism. While any fieldworker may easily find other, and dramatically different, examples of mixing, these five give a reasonable picture of the extent of the mixing that can be found among human religions. Consider now the salient features represented by these examples.

From a monotheistic viewpoint, the acquisition of a new god seems the most dramatic form of syncretism possible. Whether that new god is a borrowing from another tradition, as in the case of Singapore Chinese merchants, or a revivification of a figure which may (or may not) have been recognized as a deity in the past (as in the case of Wong Tai Sin), or a switch in allegiance (Hansen 1990), such alteration appears traumatic to the religious system. However, *within* the Chinese religious system, changing gods is an ordinary act, fully expected and supported by the system itself. In contrast to the monotheistic viewpoint, what would be shocking in Chinese religion would be a constraint prohibiting such a variation. It is for this reason that the category of "deity" remains an open class and that the category of "religious processes" includes deification. Because alteration in deities is a normal, expected practice in Chinese religion, this syncretic act is understood as merely a characteristic of the religion itself. That is the reason why Ching's textbook on Chinese religion (1993) identifies syncretism as the commanding feature of this religious tradition. At the same time, it is the reason why *syncretism* as a practice or as a label has long been merely a descriptor and not a pejorative term for this tradition.

In contrast, the irony of the Christian missionaries in Africa when dealing with faith healing represents a minor shift within the Christian tradition, but one that would be traumatic in the Chinese or African traditions. Although heirs to a long history of faith healing themselves, Christians define God as omniscient and omnipotent. For human beings to change their understanding of how God expresses those powers is interpreted as a *human* alteration, not as a change in the deity. For faithful participants in the Chinese tradition to acknowledge that healing comes only via scientific means would require both a redefinition of the notion of deity and the elimination of a major religious process. Or, in short, the variation within each of the two traditions is a normal change within that tradition, *but would be a drastic and traumatic alteration in foundational understanding from the viewpoint of the other tradition.*

Hoff's appropriation of the term *Tao* as an essentially empty numinous symbol to which he gives content is a particularly familiar American act. Although less sophisticated in approach, as a response to reality, it differs but little from similar appropriations by the nineteenth-century "transcendentalists" Thoreau and Emerson. Indeed, the habit of identifying a single entity—whether transcendent like the Hoff's Tao, Aristotle's unmoved mover, or conceptual such as Royce's loyalty, Marx's history, or Smith's "invisible hand"—is a basic interpretive process in the Western European tradition. Invoking this process engages others in a debate over whether the proposed entity is correctly identified and defined, but not whether the practice of seeking such an entity has merit. That is presumed to be a given truth.

In contrast, the use by Cobb, Eck, Hick, Sub, and others of Asian religious understandings to reinterpret Christian symbols seems a radically different act. That appears particularly so since, for many Hindus, the only way to incorporate the Christian notions of God and Christ as *one* among innumerable deity figures rather than as *the* symbol for the whole of Deity, and for many Buddhists (as Hick also acknowledges), the whole notion of deity is repugnant (Guruge 1982). Fundamentally, however, the pluralists are engaged in largely the same enterprise as Hoff and his predecessors. For one of the major adaptive responses throughout Christian history has been the willingness to reinterpret the commonly held symbols in the light of new perceptions. Within Church history, such adaptations are understood principally in terms of the debates at the time of the adapting revision. Thus the distinction between Aquinas and Anselm on the proofs of God continues today to be an important subject of seminary teaching. However, from the viewpoint of religion as a whole, Christianity undertaking attempts to prove the existence of God by whatever system of logic is the major adaptation. In an earlier era, although Church history identifies the precise definition of the Trinity as the issue, from the outside, the main adaptation was the amalgamation of the Hebrew monotheistic tradition with pan-Mediterranean soteriological concerns and Platonic understandings of the twofold structure of reality. However defined in retrospect, it was that merger which was dramatic. The function of Church history's identification of the definition as the issue has been to obscure the initial amalgamation of multiple sources.

Juan Diego's experience apparently leading to a reinterpretation of both Christian and Nahua traditions (assuming Burkhart to be correct) at first seems to be a singular instance and calls into question Wolf's famous interpretation of syncretism because, instead of being a kind of symmetrical contribution of each tradition into a new symbol which becomes the Mexican National Symbol under the dual name of *The Virgin Mary/Tonantzin*, the process apparently caused the retroactive establishment of *Tonantzin* as a deity after the vision of the Virgin. If we examine each of these examples carefully, what we see is that each new adaptation results in a major reinterpretation of the past on a scale that is no less dramatic than the retroactive creation of a deity in a conquered polytheistic tradition. However, we also find that each of these examples occurs within a framework of basic symbols and categories and processes which makes it expected, just as does the vision of Juan Diego in both the Iberian Catholic and Mexican Nahuatl traditions.

What happens in these cases of mixing and change can be interpreted within the framework which is used in this paper as instances of alteration of symbols within the categorial and hierarchical traditions given by tradition. Where categories are altered, only one is changed at a time so that participants sense the renewal of continuity in the midst of change. Two principles of religious syncretism summarize this process:

1. *The Principle of Religious Change.* In the normal process of religious change (including change induced by contact with other religious traditions), every attempt will be made to retain the same religious symbols and the categorical arrangements thereof. When successful adaptation requires substantial alteration, that change will take the path of the least disruptive and system-defined most expected behavior. Open categories will admit new symbols or, where the relevant category is closed, reinterpretation through re-arranging hierarchy and definition will occur. Internally the tradition's understanding of what happened in the alteration will be interpreted as continuity, despite the appearance to the outside of radical change.

2. *The Principle of Cognitive Integrity.* We perceive ourselves as, and act as though, we are integrated wholes. Individuals and groups see themselves as integrated wholes, not as bundles of contradictory and chaotic mixtures. The Timothy Light whose religious notions are schematically described in the three charts at the opening of this paper appears to himself as a single person whose reactions and perceptions are somehow consistent and coherently related. The Principle of Religious Change is a manifestation in religion of this more fundamental human characteristic. All of us know from observation that every society and every individual to a greater or lesser degree simultaneously holds on to mutually contradictory propositions, beliefs, and habits of action. And yet we operate as, and consider ourselves as, unitary wholes, and we talk about ourselves as single entities and about our societies as cohesions definable by shared characteristics. An individual who does not have this sense of integration and cannot behave as though it were there is termed abnormal. A society lacking such definition disintegrates.

5. A Cognitive Framework for Learning Religion as Religious Change

I shall briefly outline a scheme attempting to account for the human cognitive apparatus which makes religious change, including syncretism, a normal human development. The proposal is based on the work of cognitive scientists, most specifically on the work of Karmiloff-Smith (1992), but also on work that I had previously done on how we learn foreign languages. The heart of cognitive acquisition is a reiterative process which begins with the isolated mastery of individual items of information. *Information* here refers both to mental concepts and to behavioral acts. The child reared in a religiously participatory environment in much of Asia learns early on to remove his or her shoes in designated sacred spaces, or in a Catholic environment to genuflect and/or cross him/herself when particularly sacred symbols are present. Like my first acquisition of *temple* as an all-purpose sacred term discussed above, these acts are acquired with so imprecise a meaning as to be denotationally meaningless, but nevertheless powerfully *meaningful* in the sense that they are isomorphically associated with the signs and feel of the numinous.

After a time, the natural course of learning development results in enough information related to a given sphere—in this case to what a society defines as religion—for links to develop among the individually acquired items. Those items form a structure of relationship. It is through that relationship that the meaning of each is determined and the meaning of the whole is arrived at. Still further learning results in the links of meaning to be deeply integrated so that everything that is somehow termed "religious" is related to all other things so termed, and the resulting "webs" of connection not only provide ever finely graded meanings for specific acts and terms, but also provide the possibility of extensive exegeses of the acts and terms which make up participation in the religion. This process leading from single acts of worship learned apparently by rote to the practice of complex theology and philosophy explaining those acts and their relationships is reiterative in the sense that it continues throughout the life of the individual and the group. That is, we are always learning new items which relate to the spheres of our cultural belonging. Initially, those items are acquired in isolation and without context. Gradually the stages of learning—from discrete-point to linking and finally to multi-dimensional webbing—weave the new items into our prior learning. The new items are thereby defined by that prior learning, but the new items, joining their place in our linkages and webs, in turn contribute to the definitions of what has already been learned.

We learn only what we are ready for, and the more our system of understanding in any cultural sphere is elaborated, the more our new learning is constrained to acquiring that which either fits directly into "slots" prepared by prior learning or that which is easily interpreted by prior learning, irrespective of what it may have meant before should it be an item which comes from another culture. The Chinese absorption of a Thai deity fits the Chinese framework of deities so that no new categories or processes need be designed to accommodate it. The notion of *Tao* in the earliest Taoist classic, the *Tao Teh Ching*, is rather far in content from that of Benjamin Hoff. But Hoff, like the dozens of authors who have appropriated the term *Tao* in the titles of their books, selects *Tao* as an empty symbol which brings merely the sense of numinousness and exotic origins so that he can give the term his interpretation.

The scheme just outlined is graphically summarized in the following chart:

Stage One: Discrete-point Acquisition	Stage Two: Integration	Stage Three: Webbing
Single ritual acts Single behavioral precepts	Ritual acts linked Precepts linked to consequences and hierarchy	Ritual acts linked to precepts and together linked to rest of perceptions
Single exegeses	Explanations linked to some acts and precepts	Exegeses incorporate ritual practice
Role of sacred space	Sacred space delineated for acts and precepts	Sacred space incorporate within exegeses
Retrievable only as single items	Retrievable only as sets of acts and consequences	Integrated worldview—verbally articulated—becomes explanation of how things are and values that are taught

Chart III. *The Ongoing Process of Developing a Religion (Or Any Other Cultural Norm)*
[a synthesis of Light 1987 and Karmiloff-Smith 1992]

This chart is intended to illustrate a process that continues throughout life. While we go through irretrievable stages in our maturation from infancy through adolescence to adulthood, we also preserve as a continuous dynamic process the ability to acquire new learning and thereby to modify old learning. The most significant features of this process are:

(i) It moves from single-point or discrete learning to integrative learning.
(ii) It is completely recursive so that the output of any stage in the process can be input of any other stage.
(iii) Consequently, while in infancy and childhood, the contents of our mental workings are primitive "representations" (i.e., decompositions of perceptions into length, shape, color, etc.); later, our minds work principally on fully integrated "representations," which are close to our accounting thereof.
(iv) As the final stage is verbally recoverable and expressible, verbal reflections on, or exegeses of, our perceptions (i.e., theology or philosophy) are direct materials for learning and processing.
(v) In the version given below, the points are derived from the experience of already extant religion and refer to passing it on. The same process occurs when perceptions are turned into a religion. Note that nothing is implied about what is specifically integrated with what so that change is implicit in the framework.

6. Orthosyncretism

If I have been at all successful in the previous pages, readers will have understood that normal human religious knowledge derives from multiple sources, and normal human religious behavior is adaptive. Those two statements are true of all human knowledge and all human behavior. What distinguishes the various kinds of knowledge and behavior that we exhibit are the symbols which we cluster under the headings of our major culture endeavors (e.g., religion, politics, society, etc.), the ways in which we arrange those symbols, and the processes which we attribute to those symbols. What we share with each other within our human groupings—and what thereby gives us communal unity and belongingness—is a common set of symbols. How we each organize those symbols and the power of process that we each attribute to them may or may not be fully shared. When we pass on our traditions to succeeding generations, we transmit symbols, but how those symbols are understood (what they mean) may differ greatly from generation to generation and individual to individual. Lying behind our differences in understanding our common symbols are, of course, different circumstances to which we adapt and how we treat those circumstances. Most critical is that latter clause. Our treatment of circumstances, that is our interpretation of all data that come to us, is what defines those data for us. We interpret experience by our own lights. We interpret what our societies teach us by our own lights.

If these points are understood and accepted, then it is no great leap to declare that all religion is syncretic and that orthodoxy is a matter of time, not permanence. The systems of human behavior and human interpretation are constantly changing. Language changes, politics change, society changes, religion changes. The description of the system at any given moment can be quite accurate, but the choice of moment is ultimately arbitrary. What gives the appearance of permanence is the persistence of symbols as they are passed from generation to generation. How those symbols are arranged and what they can do—that is, what the whole structure means—is determinable only for given times, given places, and given people.

With this understanding, it is only mildly amusing in an ironic sort of way—*but entirely natural and to be expected*—that the Christian missionades in mid-twentieth-century Africa were wondering how much new science they should teach as a part of their mission to people whose healing beliefs are quite close to those of Christendom throughout most of its history. With this understanding, it is thoroughly expected that someone like Hoff might go around the world to find a symbol which he could interpret entirely within his own framework to make a hortatory point to his own society. After all, that is what Thomas Aquinas did in an immeasurably more sophisticated and learned way in linking the Aristotelianism borrowed from the Arabs to the Mediterranean salvation religion which he had received via his northern European society. And, with equal sophistication and learning, that is what Zhu Xi (Chu Hsi) and his contemporaries did in reinterpreting received Confucian humanism in the light of the Taoist and Buddhist practice and metaphysics which they ostensibly disdained. And, of course, that is (again, with considerable sophistication) precisely what religious pluralists are doing right now in reinterpreting both Christianity and certain Asian traditions harmoniously.

Orthosyncretism as a title was admittedly chosen because peculiar (not to say barbaric) neologisms tend to capture attention. But, cute though the term may be, it expresses a fundamental truth: today's orthodoxy is the result of yesterday's mixing, and it has never been otherwise.

Note

* My debts in preparing this paper are immense to the point of far exceeding my ability to enumerate them here. I am most especially grateful to two wonderful colleagues, Tom Lawson and Byron Earhart, for encouragement, hours of discussion, many reading suggestions and constant ideas. I am also grateful to students in the seminar "Religions in Contact" which I taught in the winter term of 1995 at our university. Naturally, the many errors and infelicities herein are my own doing and not theirs.

References

Armstrong, Karen. 1993. *A History of God: The 4000–Year Quest of Judaism, Christianity and Islam*. New York: Alfred A. Knopf.

Baeta, C. G. 1962. *Prophetism in Ghana: A Study of Some "Spiritual" Churches*. London: Student Christian Movement Press.

Barbour, Ian. 1990. *Religion in an Age of Science*. San Francisco: HarperSanFrancisco.

Baumann, Martin. 1994. "The Transplantation of Buddhism in Germany: Processive Models and Strategies of Adaptation." *Method and Theory in the Study of Religion* 6(1): 35–61.

Berglund, Axel-Ivar. 1976. *Zulu Thought-Patterns and Symbolism*. New York: Holmes and Meier.

Bond, George, Walton Johnson, and Sheila S. Walker. 1979. *African Christianity: Patterns of Religious Continuity*. New York: Academic Press.

Boyer, Pascal. 1990. *Tradition as Truth and Communication*. Cambridge: Cambridge University Press.

—1994. *The Naturalness of Religious Ideas*. Berkeley: University of California Press.

Burkhart, Louise M. 1993. "The Cult of the Virgin of Guadalupe in Mexico." In *South and Meso-American Native Spirituality from the Cult of the Feathered Serpent to the Theology of Liberation*, ed. Gary H. Gossen with Miguel Leon-Portilla. New York: Crossroad.

Ching, Julia. 1993. *Chinese Religions*. Maryknoll, NY: Orbis.

Daneel, M. L. 1970. *Zionism and Faith-Healing in Rhodesia: Aspects of African Independent Churches*. The Hague: Mouton.

Dumezil, Georges. 1952. *Les Dieux des Indo-Europeens*. Paris: Presses Universitaires de France.

Eck, Diana L. 1993. *Encountering God: A Spiritual Journey from Bozeman to Benares*. Boston: Bacon Press.

Gort, Jerald D., Hendrik M. Vroom, Rein Fernhout, and Anton Wessels, eds. 1989. *Dialogue and Syncretism: An Interdisciplinary Approach*. Grand Rapids, MI: Eerdmans.

Guruge, Amanda W. P. 1982. *The Miracle of Instruction: Further Facets of Buddhism*. Colombo: Lake House Investments.

Hansen, Valerie. 1990. *Changing Gods in Medieval China, 1127–1276*. Princeton, NJ: Princeton University Press.

Hayward, Victor E. W., ed. 1963. *African Independent Church Movements*. Edinburgh: Edinburgh House Press (for the World Council of Churches Commission on World Mission and Evangelism).

Hick, John. 1980. *God Has Many Names*. Philadelphia: Westminster Press.

—1993a. *Disputed Question in Theology and the Philosophy of Religion*. New Haven: Yale University Press.

—1993b. *The Metaphor of God Incarnate: Christology in a Pluralistic Age*. Louisville, KY: John Knox Press.

Hick, John, and Paul F. Knitter, eds. 1992. *The Myth of Christian Uniqueness: Toward a Pluralistic Theology of Religions*. Maryknoll, NY: Orbis Press.

Hoff, Benjamin. 1983. *The Tao of Pooh*. New York: Penguin Books.

—1992. *The Te of Piglet*. New York: Dutton.

Jonas, Hans. 1991. *The Gnostic Religion: The Message of the Alien God and the Beginnings of Christianity*. 2nd ed. Boston: Beacon Press.

Karmiloff-Smith, Annette. 1992. *Beyond Modularity*. Cambridge, MA: MIT Press.

Kleeman, Terry F. 1994. *A God's Own Tale: The Book of Transformations of Wenchang, the Divine Lord of Zitong*. Albany, NY: SUNY Press.

Lang, Graeme, and Lars Ragvald. 1993. *The Rise of a Refugee God: Hong Kong's Wong Tai Sin*. Hong Kong: Oxford University Press.

Lawson, E. Thomas, and Robert N. McCauley. 1990. *Rethinking Religion*. Cambridge: Cambridge University Press.

Lee, Virginia Fabella, Peter K. H. Lee and David Kwang-sun Suh, eds. 1992. *Asian Christian Spirituality*. Maryknoll, NY: Orbis Press.

Ma, Shutian. 1993. *Hua Xia Zhu Shen: Dao Jiau Zhuan*. Taipei: Yun Long Press.

Martin, Luther H. 1987. *Hellenistic Religions: An Introduction*. New York: Oxford University Press.

Matsunaga, Alicia. 1969. *The Buddhist Philosophy of Assimilation: The Historical Development of the Honji-Suijaku Theory*. Tokyo: Tuttle (for Sophia University).

Milne, A. A. 1926. *Winnie-the-Pooh*. New York: E. P. Dutton.

—1928. *The House at Pooh Corner*. New York: E. P. Dutton.

Mitchell, Robert C. 1963. "Christian Healing." In Hayward, ed. 1963, 47–51.

Oosthuizen, G. C. 1968. *Post-Christianity in Africa: A Theological and Anthropological Study*. Grand Rapids, MI: Eerdmans.

Pauw, B. A. 1975. *Christianity and Xhosa Tradition: Belief and Ritual Among Xhosa-speaking Christians*. Capetown: Oxford University Press.

Pye, Michael. 1993. "Syncretism vs. Synthesis." *Method & Theory in the Study of Religion* 6(3): 217–29.

Schreiter, Robert J. 1993. "Defining Syncretism: An Interim Report." *International Bulletin of Missionary Research* 17: 50–53.

Seidel, Anna K. 1969. *La divinisation de Lao Tseu dans le taoïsme des Han*. Paris: Ecole Francaise d'Extrème-Orient.

346

Sperber, Dan. 1975. *Rethinking Symbolism*. Cambridge: Cambridge University Press.

Suh, David Kwang-sun. 1991. *The Korean Minjung in Christ*. Hong Kong: Commission on Theological Concern, The Christian Conference of Asia.

Sundkler, Bengt G. M. 1961. *Bantu Prophets in South Africa*. London: Oxford University Press (for The International African Institute).

—1976. *Zulu Zion: And Some Swazi Zionists*. New York: Oxford University Press.

Wolf, Eric. 1958. "The Virgin of Guadalupe: A Mexican National Symbol." *Journal of American Folklore* 71: 34–39.

Religious Tendencies in Greece at the Dawn of the Twenty-first Century—An Approach to Contemporary Greek Reality

Panayotis Pachis

In the setting of postmodern relativism and after the withdrawal of political ideologies a new phenomenon emerges in Greek reality: the vision of "real Hellenism" which is set within the universal tendency to return to particular ethnic and religious traditions. This phenomenon is best expressed in two trends, which tend to become characteristic examples of contemporary Greek reality. We must mention, of course, at this point that these cover *only a part and not the whole* of the religious tendencies of current Greek reality. The first one is related to the attempt to revive ancient Greek religion, which is set within the wider universal neo-Pagan movement. The second one is associated with the tendency to interrelate and identify Hellenism and Orthodoxy, which is characterized by the fundamentalist features.

Neo-Paganism, under its diverse forms and, especially that of polytheism, forms one of the new religions that flourished in the middle of the seventies (Papalexandropoulos 1999, 23–24). Besides, the openness of modern society allows the introduction of new creeds or new interpretations. In this way, new forms of religiosity are created, as happened in this case with neo-Paganism. These form part of the universal religious system. Many of these new religions are based on past forms. Naturally, this way of thinking does not come as a surprise if we take into account that in many religions it is assumed that the only way to shape the modern way of thinking is for it to be moulded on principles of the past. For this reason believers insist on preserving forms of the past, which they consider criteria of stability and an expression of their whole worldview.[1] On the other hand, it is typical for groups that use oral traditions, as happens also in the case of the Greek neo-Pagan movement, to assert that they act in accordance with the practices of their ancestors. Naturally, the only affirmation for the practices of their ancestors is formed by the practice of their descendants (Boyer 1994, 231, 258–59; Beyer 1998, 25; Light 2000, 162, 184). With these tactics the circular character of these groups creates, in accordance with the declarations of their followers, the clearest guarantees for the correctness of the views that characterize their worldview.[2]

Greek neo-Paganism forms an especially interesting movement for the study of religion. The study of the sources of its birth and development, of the currents from which it is formed, reveals its particularity within contemporary Greek society (Papalexandropoulos 1999, 23–28). Greek neo-Paganism as a member of the wider religious system should be considered a phenomenon of alternative religiosity, which is differentiated from the rest of the socio-religious whole.[3] Besides, the re-use of a term that is distinguished by a polemical character makes it very clear where this movement stands within a society that is considered mono-cultural.[4] We should not forget, however, that the appearance of new divinities or new religious forms affects, according to the views of these societies, syncretism (Shaw and Stewart 1994, 1–26). Besides, the members of the above societies usually believe that that kind of practice could destroy the purity of their tradition (Martin 1996, 216; Martin 2000a, 280; Veer 1994). They consider syncretism to be a way towards discovery of a spiritual truth, which is expressed universally, be it imperfectly, in its local variations. This fact constitutes a traumatic reality for their whole system, as confirmed by the view of L. H. Martin: "…syncretism still tends to be used with reference to some norm to designate corrupted or impure religious phenomena and to be used, as such, as an explanatory category rather than a set of transformed data to be explained" (Martin 2001a, 400). This tendency is opposed to the liberal scientific traditions of comparison (Martin 2000a, 280).[5] This situation supports the views of this group on respect for the free expression of one's feelings. In any case, it is appropriate for a modern state that it should not consider all these groups minorities, but equal members of the broader social whole.[6]

The appearance of this movement is related to the social context and the transformation that occurs in the context of the globalization of society. According to P. Beyer, the transformations of religion are also related, "to the gradual formation or differentiation that occurred during the last two centuries within the simple global religious system. The ideas of differentiation and system are essential in this case" (1998, 3). The religious system forms an established expression of the category of religion (Beyer 1998, 9). A social system forms an entity formed by the continuous and periodical production of inter-connected series of communication. According to the same scholar, "these communications (and not the people) form the basic elements of a social system" (ibid.). Only because of meaning can new communication appear; this periodical repetition leads to the closure or limitation of the system. In this way, the system is distinguished from the factors that do not belong to the environment of the particular system. Human religious behaviours are characterized, further, by their ability to accept and assimilate many and contrary meanings (Beyer 1998, 10). They believe, indeed, that these views are reinforced if they incorporate them in a unified whole that is often regarded as their common source of origin. In general, the change of view related to the way of expression of such forces from the divine environment does not form a real change but simply an alteration of form. In this practice the normal process of every religious change is related to the effort to preserve the same religious creeds as well as its absolute arrangements.[7]

When we take into consideration that international communication becomes all the easier as more and more people gain access to the Internet, the influence of West-European and North-American Paganism will most probably grow perceptibly in Greece in the immediate future (Xydias 1999, 14). Nevertheless, at present—and from the middle of the eighties onwards—this movement has been gaining ground within the Greek state. In this setting, the new admiration of ancient Greek culture in Greece is neither unusual nor original. To begin with, it claims to be the continuation of the modern Greek hellenocentric tradition that can be noticed during the nineteenth century and in the inter-war period. These views are placed within the positivistic assumptions of the nineteenth century, as well as the ideas of linguistic, racial and cultural purity that dominated Europe during this period (Stewart 1994; Martin 2000a, 280). We should not forget, moreover, that the views of the German classicists may be considered a cornerstone for the creation and development of corresponding nationalistic ideologies. Contemporary admiration of the ancient Greek tradition is not limited to the activity of a few intellectuals, as in the past. There are certain people who seek to revive the ancient Greek religion and dedicate themselves to this issue. Publishers are even more active in this direction because the interest of the reading public for matters concerning ancient Greek culture keeps increasing. There are also many associations that focus their attention on the study of ancient Greek tradition and culture and, lastly, certain cases are recorded of admirers of antiquity that consider the Ancient Hellenistic current to be fashionable and are involved in it in exactly this way (Mênê 2000, 360–62). But at the same time there are also many representatives of modern Greek art (painters, architects, etc.) that use this trend in their work.[8] Their results present, in this latter case, an exquisite representation of a creative hybrid creation that yields a real renaissance in this sector of contemporary Greek intellectual reality. This situation is also supported by the view of L. H. Martin, who characteristically says: "the selection and transformation of available cultural information as occasioned by cultural contact and pluralism is syncretistic. [Such] transformed ... representations, syncretisms [are] not named ... corruption but ... innovation" (Martin 2001a, 400).

Among the adherents of the ancient Hellenistic spirit, various groups can be included, which differ from each other.[9] The common feature of the Greek admirers of Antiquity is the turn to the past and the expression of a spontaneous love towards it (Xydias 1999). The description that follows is indicative and clearly demonstrates the ancient Hellenistic current in Greece. In brief, we notice that ideological framework of this group is based on three concepts: love for country (*philopatria*), love for beauty (*philokalia*) and love for gnosis (*philosophia*). The first concept refers to a continuous involvement in community affairs based on equality and the principles of democracy. The goal of every culture should be that people are considered to be in charge of their own decisions, just like the Greeks of the Classical period. The second concept relates to the admiration of anything beautiful and to the natural environment. The third one, finally, refers to the love of knowledge and wisdom.[10] It is worth mentioning that the two latter concepts are mainly related to a deeper knowledge of the natural environment. Followers of such movements believe that we must "adopt the most important teaching of our ancestors and deify Mother Nature."[11] Thus, in this case the tendencies of a feminist ecology prevail, with the consideration of the domination of the great mother goddess Earth. This tendency formed the motivating force of current Greek neo-Paganism towards the view of "chthonic religion" as the only authentic one. This is exactly why they are particularly interested in contemporary ecological phenomena. At this point, we must admit that this post-ecological conviction of admirers of ancient Greek culture may pose diverse problems, but is not anachronistic in any way. In their view, ecological problems stem from the dominance of the layperson's approach to life, and they can be solved by a return to the dominance of the divine, the highest form of which can be found in Nature. This is why they do not consider that the "issue of ecology is a purely scientific issue. It is above all a moral and religious one" (Verettas 2002, 67–68). Furthermore, they define the concept of religion on the premises of the following questions: "what is the world," "what is a human being?" and "what should be the values ruling our lives?" (Marinis 2002, 94).

The cartography of the domain attests that there are extravagant and sober-minded groups, as well as quaint and serious ones, as with every new ideological movement. Among them, there are also those that adopt the extreme fascist Western European models of the purity of the Greeks. For certain followers of this movement the acquisition of purity is obtained with the establishment of an Apollonian class, while for others it is the result of an ecstatic Dionysian function (Xydias 1999, 18). In the context of this postmodern naturalism (an amalgam of rationalism and irrationalism that mixes old and new scientific theories of contemporary physics, etc.), the neo-Pagan admirers of ancient Greek culture succeed in blending "traumatic" religious feelings with essential humanist values (ibid.). In this way a situation of a "golden age" is presented: a utopian situation where neither people nor their religion contained anything derogatory. Everything is perfect. Followers of this tendency, as opposed to the ones of syncretistic views, always imagine the existence of an "ideal" religious situation or model from which can arise better, but—often—also worse, forms of religious study (Papalexandropoulos 1999, 27).

The most fundamental pivot of the admiration of ancient Greek culture is the idea that Greece is the "cradle of civilization." This idea relates to a tendency to exaggerate that one could attribute to a guileless enthusiasm. It is simply understood as a one-way progress route of humanity from "barbarism" to "civilization." Here we have another alteration of the original humanistic idea, beyond the tactics of propagandistic ideology, of the Greek origin of civilization. They believe in the superiority of the Greeks. They are opposed to contemporary ecumenism and the globalization of culture, believing in ethnic purity and a Hellenism based on that (Xydias 1999, 8–9). In this way, through their generalizations, the primary and strong antagonism between "us" and "them" is increasingly reinforced.[12] This concept is not expressed by all members of this group, but mainly by those who harbour nationalistic feelings. For them, these ideas of "Greek supremacy" form, of course, a preferential ground for their fascist and extreme rightwing tendencies (Schoinas 1999, 34–35; Georgalas 1997; Pleuris 1998).

Another pivot of the Hellenocentric movement is the view on the communication of ancient Greek civilization with extraterrestrial gods and with lost civilizations (Atlantis). In this case we have to do with "theories" that may be judged on the grounds of "common sense," but we have to do with a new type of mythology, which could well form the basis for the "common sense" of the future. Many followers base the core of a new metaphysical ideology, of a new postmodern public reason, of a new common sense along this line of thought.[13]

It is worth mentioning at this point, that the problem that this tendency presents is that its contributors move within the spirit of an absolutization of the ancient Greek religion, which leads to a subjective improvement and, thus, to an unhistorical remodelling (Schoinas 1999, 29–30). We should consider however, that "Greek religion as a monolithic entity never existed … the various city-states' religions overlapped sufficiently to warrant the continued use of the term 'Greek religion' … Religious historians often give a relatively static picture of the archaic and classical age. As if during this period religion remained more or less unchanged until the Hellenistic age. Admittedly, it is not easy to keep a proper balance between a synchronic system and diachronic development. Yet a modern history should at least try to stick to a minimal diachronic perspective" (Bremmer 1994, 1–2; Price 2000; Vernant 1987, 99, 101).

The truth is that in the last few years an effort has been made to overcome more petty differences. Various organizing bodies and committees appear as representatives of an official and regular religion demanding respect for its monuments and symbols, both from the state and from individuals. Likewise, an important part of their activity is devoted to the preservation of ancient monuments, especially of the temples, which they consider "holy shrines" where the ancient cult should be revived. Indeed, here and there, the sporadic organization of archaic rites has begun—marriages, "baptisms," nature-worshipping rituals, celebrations of historical anniversaries, animal offerings, libations, etc. (Xydias 1999, 11).[14] In this they follow, as we mentioned above, the examples of equivalent neo-Pagan movements of other countries, with which, as it appears, they maintain ties and develop close cooperation. Representatives from Greek neo-Pagan groups took part in the first World Council of Ethnic Religions, which was organized in Lithuania in 1999, having as a central theme: "Unity in Difference" (Xydias 1999, 11).

At the opposite end of the spectrum from the tendency presented above, there is another faction that believes in the continuation of ancient Greek culture and Christianity and, in this sense, in the unity of Hellenism and Orthodoxy, according to which the Orthodoxy forms the main source of our ethnic identity.[15] It is worth mentioning at this point that this phenomenon reached its heyday in the 1990s but is today receding. This tendency has rekindled the discussion that started two decades ago in Greece on the relations among Hellenism, Orthodoxy and the West, a discussion that defined especially the features of a renewed Christian and Greek identity within the polarity East–West. Naturally, this phenomenon is not unknown, but it is a feature of the same groups since the nineteenth century and flourished especially during the post-war period (from 1949 on).[16] This movement lost momentum during the inter-war period (Vergopoulos 1978; Petrou and Tsironis, forthcoming).

This whole development is related further to the ideas of the contemporary hellenocentric currents. It forms a clear ideological position that expresses the views of the adherents of these groups and is manifested, especially during the last decade, in ecclesiastical circles and in some circles of the intellectual elite (Metallinos 1992, 13–38; Petrou 2001, 262, 268; Manitakis 2000, 67–97, 112–44; Vakalopoulos 1968). They believe that only through the right tradition is it possible to attain the purity of contemporary social and religious life. Many of them create a composite mode of thought and expression that demonstrates, even more, the ideological coexistence of the two tendencies mentioned above. They consider this the only way to acquire salvation and purity. Of course, this "salvation" is selective and is limited exclusively to the members of their group. Another characteristic feature is the well-known statement of these groups, that Orthodoxy is not a religion but a way of life (Meskos 2000). Thus, they believe that Orthodoxy expresses the primary mode of authenticity. This view is not only typical of Greek-Orthodox religious reality, as it is a common feature of all contemporary religions, which try, in this manner, to emphasize this "untouched mark of reference" as a higher goal, one that states its connection with its power and legitimacy.

The question that one should ask in this case is whether all these views are relevant for persons living in both traditional and contemporary societies. To answer this question one should consider the differences that clearly define the form of these two societies. In the former, religion dominates, and usually imposes its authoritarian objectives by means of a hierarchy; while in the latter, individuals seek to shape their own way of thinking and, therefore, a collective identity is not imposed by anyone. In this latter case religion is not a dominating factor of daily life, as it is in traditional societies.

It should not escape our attention, however, that this tendency is especially dangerous for the framework of a modern society because it emphasizes the *sui generis* character of religion. In this way, religion forms the regulating factor par excellence not only of the religious but also of the political problems of the contemporary world.[17] Its adherents seek the return of traditional and one-dimensional society and not the maintenance of society in the setting of a modern state. Therefore, on the one hand, there are efforts to interfere with society on a religious foundation, and on the other, of upgrading the role of religion in a pluralistic world. In this manner, the adherents demand that their views be accepted on their own "absolute authority" and, at the same time, that they form a common rule of life. Thus, ways, views and problems of the past are introduced in the present and form the factor par excellence of people's way of thinking. This means, however, that they are ignorant of or overlook the fact that these views are the products of adaptations to the cultural standard of that period. This dimension applies absolutely to the subject of their views. They see human activity within standardized models and structures of the past (Manitakis 2000, 163–201). The closed mentality that the Orthodox Church cultivated has contributed to the essential detachment of many from the Church, even if they uphold nominal relations. The turn of the Church to the past made it distant and contributed to the development of indifference. It is truly inconceivable that certain people believe that our forefathers had the right to create their world in whatever way they thought most appropriate and that we are obliged to follow what they created. The same society, especially during the last decades, is free to form the setting within which its members move. Restrictions disappear and Greek citizens are allowed to shape their world, a world that is characterized by openness, cosmopolitanism and freedom. Especially important, however, is the fact that the cultural juxtapositions and changes have created a pluralistic situation in Greek society (Petrou 2001,

269–70; Petrou and Tsironis, forthcoming, 1–2, 8–9; Giddens 1990; Lash and Friedmann 1992).

Moreover, a citizen does not need to be an Orthodox Christian to be Greek. We should, of course, not forget that there is a close relation between these two, as between state and church (Manitakis 2000, 23–66, 171–74; Petrou 2001, 267). The specification of a person's religion on the identity card forms an important statistical factor and, for this reason, the terms above are considered identical. Church authorities as well as the members of various extreme nationalistic groups, which uphold and emphasize these views, base them on this fact.

The concept of Helleno-Christianity (*Ellenochristianismos*) and the concepts of "Homeland–Religion–Family" (*Patris–Threskeia–Oikogeneia*) loomed large in the vocabulary of the nationalistic postbellum politic (1949 and afterwards) and especially of the military juntas (1967–1974); echoes of it may still be heard in the rhetoric of conservative politics and nowadays of clerics—this in obvious contradiction to socialist and communist platforms, which favour a greater degree of separation between social/political and religious life (Stewart 1991, 195–96).

At this point, it is worth referring to one more fact that is diametrically opposite to the phenomenon mentioned above. Many of the important intellectual representatives of the modern Greek state (nineteenth and twentieth centuries) already moved along the same line of turning to Antiquity. They tried to show that many features of Orthodox reality are morphologically related to pre-Christian religiosity. They identified the cultural structures of Orthodoxy with those of Ancient Greece and found their own bridge to "authentic" Hellenism, without any need to be cut off from the main body of contemporary Greek Christianity.[18] Of course, this view is opposed by numerous representatives of the Church as well as many intellectuals who are of the opinion that there is no relation whatsoever between ancient Greek religion and Christianity. In fact, in order to justify the existence of all these practices, they consider them as part of the framework of "customs" and popular "folklore."

On this point I must also mention that the practice of choosing elements from two or more important cosmologies and combining them in a religious practice—and perhaps in this way a new cosmology—is defined by anthropologists and scholars of religion as syncretism. For this reason, they suggest that some of the survivals mentioned above confirm the syncretistic character of religion in contemporary Greece.[19] Charles Stewart affirms that this practice is not accurate in the case of contemporary Greek religion (1991, 7). Of course we cannot deny the fact that many elements of the ancient Greek reality exist in contemporary religious practice, but Orthodox Christians in the whole of Greece partake consciously in this reality without regarding themselves as belonging to something that relates to their cultural past. Ancient Greek religion as a vital cosmology belongs to the past.

Naturally, many elements of contemporary reality, as we mentioned above, are morphologically related to ancient Greek reality. Besides, religion in Greece is considered the result of a long internal development process. Transfer of elements from one to the other cultural reality (as in the case of transfer from Antiquity to Christianity) is characterized by Eric Wolf as "first-order formations that concern those which are intimately connected with the bases of life and which would be relatively unaffected by the objections of theologians and bishops" (in Gregory 1986, 241; Martin 2000a). However, these need to be considered and examined as symbolic and ideological additions in relation to the entire religious reality and not only as surviving features and remnants of folk tradition. Those who observe customs follow the traditional view. Many of those, especially in the environment of urban centres, have a clearly symbolic character.

The above allows us to relate conclusively that syncretisms that are created in corresponding cases are the result of a cultural category as a creation of the human mind.[20] Jonathan Z. Smith notes that the "evolutionary approach" is always created with the "dynamic of change and persistence" (1982, 24). On the other hand, in order to understand religious syncretism, we must realize that a basic factor lies in the problem of copying and in the transformation of religious aspects that characterize every syncretistic formation (Martin 2001a, 2001b). These religious similarities should be perceived and understood as consequence of similar religious practices that exist in a historical-cultural environment from which it receives constructive influences (Martin 2000b, 51). Of course, the historical examples of syncretism are presented according to the criteria of selection.[21] The same issue is also encountered by researchers when they come across "new world orders" (Martin 1997, 149). In other words, eclecticism is a function of the human cognitive system. It is an eclectic operation that allows certain factors to prevail over others (Martin 1996, 220–21). Many contemporary religions form an eclectic revision of the past with new views that are added due to the instability of the current global social context.

Notes

1. In general about neo-Paganism, see Mênê 2000, 21–28, 31–47, esp. 23, where reference is made to the definition of this phenomenon by its North-American (Pagan Educational Network) and British representatives (The Pagan Federation).
2. Concerning the causes of paganistic revival and forms as well as various neo-Pagan groups, see Mênê 2000, 29–30, 63–65.

3. About the religious alteration as a tramatic phenomenon to the religious system of a mono-cultural society, see Light 2000, 178. On the phenomenon of alternative religiosity in Greece, see also Christodoulou 1999.
4. For the meaning of "paganism" as a polemical term, see Cancik 1986, 1990 and 1998; Brown 1999; Roussele 1999.
5. On comparativism, see also Smith 1990; Martin 2000b.
6. For the issue of religious freedom in Greece, see Beis 1997; Threskeftike Eleftheria 2000; Papastathis 2000.
7. Light 2000, 180, 184. Another typical reference is that made by the author (185) claiming that: "today's orthodoxy is the result of yesterday's mixing, and it has never been other-wise."
8. Indicatively, let us note, at this point, works by Greek artists, such as K. Parthenis, N. Engo-nopoulos, G. Stathopoulos and Al. Fassianos. Another typical example is the movement of Greek architects whose works are considered part of the so-called postmodern architecture.
9. In regards to the different ways of thinking of these groups in Greece, see Panagos 1987; Rassias 1992; Marinis 1997; Xydias 1999, 12, nn. 7, 8.
10. See Verettas 2002, 52–56. Margaritidou 2000, 44–46, mentions the names of the several Greek neo-Pagan groups.
11. See Verettas 2002, 61, also 47, 55, 65, 67–68. With regards to the ecological interests and views of this group, see also, Mênê 2000, 21, 24–25, 47–53, 59, 60–61, 93–95, 294, 307, 326–30, 333–36, 362; Anastasakis 2002, 17, 18, 20–27, 28, 34–35; Marinis 2002, 101; Demopoulos 2002, 86–88; Mênê 2002, 161, 162, 166, 167; Mytilinaios 2002, 179, 181; Spyropoulos 2002, 218–21, 227–30; Toutountzi 2002, 235, 237, 241–44; Tsagrinos 2002, 281–84; Xydias 1999, 17; see also Mênê 2000, 333.
12. About the distinction between "we" and "the Others" see Konstantopoulou 1999.
13. See Xydias 1999, 18–21. These views are supported by members of the following groups: The *Group E* and the *Group of National Restoration*. The members of these groups are influenced, mainly, by the theories of E. von Däniken. Cf. also Leukofridis 1975; Phanos 1997; Mênê 2000, 324–35.
14. Xydias 1999, 11. See also about "*Prometheia*," the celebration organized by Tryphon Olympios at the feet of Olympus. See also Margaritidou 2000, 45. Prof. Dr Tr. Olympius (University of Stockholm) is the founder of the so-called "School of Philosophy of Mt. Olympus" and among the first who performed his wedding according to ancient Greek rites.
15. See Petrou 2001, 261–62; Petrou and Tsironis (forthcoming), 2–4; Paparigopoulos 1955; Veremis 1997.
16. Petrou 1992, 141–90; 2001, 262–69; Petrou and Tsironis (forthcoming), 2; Paparigopoulos 1955; Vergopoulos 1978; Dimaras 1985; Tsoukalas 1983; Veremis 1983; Rozakis 1983; Alivizatos 1979; 1983; Stewart 1994, 128–37; Skopetea 1998; Zacharopoulu 1998.
17. About the role of religion as a *sui generis* phenomenon, see McCutcheon 1997. The author's subtitle, "*The Politics of Nostalgia*," reflects contemporary Greek reality in the most characteristic manner.
18. Wachsmuth 1864; Politis 1871; 1909; Lawson 1999 [1910]; Kyriakidis 1922; 1956; Kakridis 1967; Herzfeld 1982; Kyriakidou-Nestoros 1978; 1983; Alexiou 1978; 1985; Danforth 1984; Gregory 1986; Kokoslakis 1987; Stewart 1991; 1994, 138–42; 1999.
19. Stewart 1991, 6–7. Also Martin 2000b, 51, who aptly remarks: "the views of religious 'survivals' gained theoretical support from evolutionary theories borrowed from biology and was illegitimately adapted to social development." Cf. also Smith 1982, 24.

20. About the connections between "syncretism" and "cognition," see Martin 1996; 2000a, 284; 2001a, 396; Light 2000; Martin and Leopold (forthcoming). See also Pinker 1994; Boyer 1994.
21. Concerning selection as one of the characteristic features of syncretism, see Martin 1996, 220–21; 1997, 149; Beyer 1998, 10–11. We also find the phenomenon of selection in the ideas of the Greek neo-Pagans; see Demopoulos 2002, 78–79.

References

Alexiou, A. 1978. "Modern Greek Folklore and Its Relation to the Past: The Evolution of Charos in Greek Tradition." In *The 'Past' in Medieval and Modern Greek Culture*, ed. S. Vryonis, 221–36. Malibu, CA: Undena Publications.

—1985. "Folklore: An Obituary?" *Byzantine and Modern Greek Studies* 9: 1–28.

Alivizatos, N. C. 1979. *Les institutions politiques de la Grèce à travers les crises 1922–1974*. Paris: R. Pichon and R. Durand-Auzias.

—1983. "'Έθνος' κατά 'λαού' μετά το 1940." In *Ελληνισμός- Ελληνικότητα. Ιδεολογικοί και βιωματικοί άξονες της νεοελληνικής κοινωνίας*, ed. D. Tsaousis, 79–90. Athens.

Anastasakis, R.A. 2002. "Έρως προς το Θείο. Ο Ελληνικός Δρόμος." In *Η αναβίωση τηςαρχαίας ελληνικής θρησκείας*, ed. E. Aulidou, 15–42. Thessaloniki.

Beis, K., ed. 1997. *Η Θρησκευτική Ελευθερία. Θεωρία και Πράξη στην ελληνική έννομη πράξη*. Athens.

Beyer, P. 1998. "The Religious System of Global Society: A Sociological Look at Contemporary Religion and Religions." *NUMEN* 45(1): 1–29.

Boyer, P. 1994. *The Naturalness of Religious Ideas: A Cognitive Theory of Religion*. Berkeley: University of California Press.

Bremmer, J. 1994. *Greek Religion*. Oxford: Oxford University Press.

Brown, P. 1999. "Pagan." In *Late Antiquity: A Guide to the Postclassical World*, ed. G. W. Bowersock, P. Brown and O. Grabar, 625. Cambridge, MA and London: Belknap Press.

Cancik, H. 1986. "Nutzen, Schmuck und Aberglaube. Ende und Wandlungen der römischen Religion im 4. und 5. Jahrhundert." In *Der Untergang von Religionen*, ed. H. Zinser, 65–90. Berlin: Reimer.

—1990. "Apolegetik/Polemik." In *Handbuch religionswissenschaftlicher Grundbegriffe*, II, ed. H. Cancik, B. Gladigow and M. Laubscher. 29–37. Stuttgart: W. Kohlhammer.

—1998. "Paganismus." In *Handbuch religionswissenschaftlicher Grundbegriffe*, vol. 4, ed. H. Cancik, B. Gladigow and K.-H. Kohl. 302. Stuttgart: W. Kohlhammer.

Christodoulou, D. 1999. *Νομικά Ζητήματα. Θρησκευντική Ετερότητα στην Ελλάδα* (Σειρά Μελετών. Κέντρο Ερευνών Μειονοτικών Ομάδων, vol. 2. Athens.

Chuvin, P. 1991. *Chronique des derniers Païens*. Paris: Belles Lettres/Fayard.

Danforth, L. M. 1984. "The Ideological Context of the Search of Continuities in Greek Culture." *Journal of Modern Greek Studies* (May): 54–85.

Demopoulos, M. n.d. "Η Οικολογία στην αρχαία Ελλάδα και η Βίβλος." *ICHÔR* 15.

—2002. "Οι Έλληνες πρέπει να επαναμφανισθούν! Η αρχαία Ελληνική Παράδοση ως πηγή έμπνευσης και όχι αντιγραφής." In *Η Αναβίωση της αρχαίας ελληνικής θρησκείας*, ed. E. Aulidou, 70–92. Thessaloniki.

Dimaras, K.Th. 1985. *Ελληνικός ρομαντισμός*. Athens.

Georgalas, G. 1997. *Κοσμοεξουσιαστές*. Athens.

Giddens, A. 1990. *The Consequences of Modernity*. Cambridge: Polity.

Gregory, T. E. 1986. "The Survival of Paganism in Christian Greece: A Critical Essay." *American Journal of Philology* 107: 229–42.

Herzfeld, M. 1982. *Ours Once More: Folklore, Ideology and Making of Modern Greece*. Austin: University of Texas Press.

Kakridis, J. 1967. *Die alten Hellenen und neugriechischen Volksglauben*. Munich: Heimeran.

Kokosalakis, N. 1987. "The Political Significance of Popular Religion in Greece." *Archives des Sciences Sociales des Religions* 64: 37–52.

Konstantopoulou, C. *et al.* 1999. *"Εμείς" και οι "Άλλοι." Αναφορά σε τάσεις και Σύμβολα*. Athens.

Kyriakidis, St. 1922. *Ελληνική Λαογραφία*, Μέρος Α΄: *Μνημεία Λόγου*. Athens.

—1956. "Αρχαία Ελληνική Θρησκεία και Χριστιανισμός," *Πρωτόκολα του Α΄ Συνεδρίου για τον Ελληνο-Χριστιανικό Πολι-τισμό*, 91–102. Athens.

Kyriakidou-Nestoros, A. 1978. *Η θεωρία της ελληνικής λαογραφίας*. Athens.

—1983. "Η λαϊκή παράδοση. Σύμβολο και πραγματικότητα." In *Ελληνισμός. Ελληνικότητα. Ιδεολογικαί και βιωματικοί άξονες της νεοελληνικής κοινωνίας*, ed. D. Tsaousis, 249–56. Athens.

Lash, S., and J. Friedmann. 1992. *Modernity and Identity*. Oxford: Blackwell.

Lawson, J. C. 1999 [1910]. *Modern Greek Folklore and Ancient Greek Religion*. Cambridge Cambridge University Press.

Leukofridis, G. 1975. *Κοσμοσκάφος ΣΤΑ—ΓΥΡΟ ΕΨΙΛΟΝ—το ''Οργάνων' Όργανο του Αριστο-τέλη*. Athens.

Light, T. 2000. "Orthosyncretism: An Account of Melding in Religion." In A. W. Geertz, R. T. McCutcheon, eds., *Perspectives on Method and Theory in the Study of Religion. Adjunct Proceedings of the XVIIth Congress of the International Association for the History of Religions, Mexico City, 1995* (special issue of *MTSR*) 12(1–2): 162–86.

Manitakis, A. 2000. *Οι σχέσεις της Εκκλησίας με το Κράτος—Έθνος. Στη σκιά των Ταυτότήτων* (ΝΕΦΕΛΗ—ΙΣΤΟΡΙΑ). Athens.

Margaritidou, St. 2000. "Νεοσαμάνοι και Έθνικ." *AVATON* (April–May): 43–46.

Marinis, P. 1997. *Η Ελληνική κοσμοθέασις*. Athens.

—2002. "Καιρός να γνωρίσουν όλοι την πατρογονική μας Θρησκεία!" In *Η Αναβίωση της αρχαίας ελληνικής θρησκείας*, ed. E. Aulidou, 93–107. Thessaloniki.

Martin, L. H. 1996. "Syncretism, Historism, and Cognition." *Method and Theory in the Study of Religion* 8(2): 215–24.

—1997. "Akin to the Gods or Simply One to Another? Comparison with Respect to Religions in Antiquity." In *Vergleichen und Verstehen in der Religionswissenschaft. Vorträge der Jahres-tagung der DVRG vom 4 bis 6. Oktober 1995 in Bonn*, ed. H.-J. Klimkeit, 147–59. Studies in Oriental Religions, 41. Wiesbaden: Harrassowitz.

—2000a. "Of Religious Syncretism, Comparative Religion and Spiritual Quests." In A. W. Geertz and R. T. McCutcheon, eds., *Perspectives on Method and Theory in the Study of Religion. Adjunct Proceedings of the XVIIth Congress of the International Association for the History of Religions, Mexico City, 1995* (special issue of *MTSR*) 12(1–2): 277–86.

—2000b. "Comparison." In *Guide to the Study of Religion*, ed. W. Braun and R. T. McCutcheon, 45–56. London and New York: Cassell.

—2001a."To Use 'Syncretism' or Not to Use 'Syncretism': That Is the Question." *Historical Reflections/Réflections Historiques* 27(3): 389–400.

—2001b. "Comparativism and Sociobiological Theory." *NUMEN* 48: 290–308.

Martin, L.H., and A. Leopold (forthcoming). "Comparative Approaches to the Study of Syncretism." In *New Approaches to the Study of Religion*, ed. P. Antes, A.W. Geertz and R. Warne. Leiden: Brill.

McCutcheon, R. T. 1997. *Manufacturing Religion: The Discourse on Sui Generis Religion and the Politics of Nostalgia*. New York and Oxford: Oxford University Press.

Mênê, Ch. 2000. *Νεοπαγανισμός. Η αναγέννηση της αρχαίας θρησκείας*. Thessaloniki.

—2002. "Ελληνική Θρησκεία: Μια δυναμική Αντίσταση!" In *Η Αναβίωση της αρχαίας ελληνικής θρησκείας*, ed. E. Aulidou, 155–77. Thessaloniki.

Meskos Ars. (Father). 2000. "ποιο είναι το μέλλον του νεοπαγανισμού." *AVATON* 8 (April–May): 50.

Metallinos, G. 1992. *Ορθοδοξία και ελληνικότητα*. Athens.

Mytilinaios, St. 2002. "Ελληνισμός: Φιλοσοφία—Πολιτισμός και όχι Θρησκεία!" In *Η αναβίωση της αρχαίας ελληνικής θρησκείας*, ed. E. Aulidou, 178–207. Thessaloniki.

Panagos, S. 1987. "Η Πολιτεία του Ολύμπου." *Daulos* 70 (October): 3908–10.

Papalexandropoulos, St. 1999. "Ο Νεοπαγανισμός ως νέα θρησκεία." *SYNAXI* (Special issue: *Ελληνικός Νεοπαγανισμός*) 69 (January–March): 23–28.

Paparigopoulos, K. 1955. *Ιστορία του Ελληνικού Έθνους*. Athens.

Papastathis, Ch., ed. 2000. *Θρησκευτική Ελευθερία και επικρατούσα Θρησκεία*. Εταιρεία Νομικών Βορείου Ελλάδος, 36. Thessaloniki.

Petrou, I. 1992. *Εκκλησία και πολιτική στην Ελλάδα (1750–1909)*. Εκκλησία–Κοινωνία–Οικουμένη, 3. Thessaloniki.

—2001. "Nationale Identität und Orthodoxie im heutigen Griechenland." In *"Gottes auserwählte Völker." Erwählungsvorstellungen und kollektive Selbstfindung in der Geschichte*. PRO ORIENTE. Schriften reihe der kommision für südeuropäischen Geschichte, Bd. I, ed. A. Moser, 261–71. Frankfurt am Main.

Petrou, I., and Ch. Tsironis (forthcoming). "Orthodoxy and Cultural Identity in Modern Greece," 1–12.

Phanos, St. 1997. *Οδηγός των βιβλίων για την αρχαία Ελλάδα*. Athens.

Pinker, S. 1994. *The Language Instinct*. New York: William Morrow.

Pleuris, K. 1998. *Από το ψεύδος στην αλήθειαν*. Athens.

Politis, N. 1871. *Μελέτη στη ζωή των Νέο-Ελλήνων*. Athens.

—1909. "Λαογραφία." *Λαογραφία* 1: 3–18.

Price, S. 2000. *Religions of the Ancient Greeks*. Key Themes in Ancient History. Cambridge: Cambridge University Press.

Rassias, G. 1992. *Υπέρ της των Ελλήνων Νόσου*, vol. 1. Athens.

Roussele, A. 1999. "Paganism." In *Late Antiquity: A Guide to the Postclassical World*, ed. G. W. Bowersock, P. Brown and O. Grabar, 625–26. Cambridge, MA: Belknap Press.

Rozakis, C. 1983. "Η Ελλάδα στον διεθνή χώρο." In *Ελληνισμός. Ελληνικότητα. Ιδεολογικοί και βιωματικοί άξονες της νεοελληνικής κοινωνίας*, ed. D. Tsaousis, 91–120. Athens.

Schoinas, F. 1999. "Ελληνισμός και Χριστιανισμός: Ρήξη ή ζεύξη," *SYNAXI* (Special issue: *Ελληνικός Νεοπαγανισμός*), 69 (January–March): 29–41.

Shaw, R., and Ch. Stewart. 1994. "Introduction: Problematizing Synthesis." In *Syncretism/ Anti-Syncretism: The Politics of Religious Synthesis* (European Association of Social Anthropologists), 1–24. London and New York: Routledge.

Skopetea, E. 1998. *Το πρότυπο βασίλειο καιη Μεγάλη Ιδέα. Οψεις του εθνικού προβλήματος στην Ελλάδα (1830–1880)*. Athens.

Smith, J. Z. 1982. *Imagining Religion: From Babylon to Jonestown*. Chicago: University of Chicago Press.

—1990. *Drudgery Divine: On the Comparison of Early Christianities and the Religions of Late Antiquity*. London: School of Oriental and African Studies, University of London.

Spyropoulos, I. 2002. "Αρχαιοελληνική Θρησκεία: Η απαντηση στις κατάστροφικές συνέπειες του πολιτισμού." In *Η Αναβίωση της αρχαίας ελληνικής θρησκείας*, ed. E. Aulidou, 208–30. Thessaloniki.

Stewart, Ch. 1991. *Moral Imagination in Modern Greek Culture*. Princeton, NJ: Princeton University Press.

—1994. "Syncretism as a Dimension of Nationalist Discourse in Modern Greece." In Stewart and Shaw, eds. 1994, 127–44.

—1999. "Μαγεία και Ορθοδοξία." *Archaiologia* (special issue: *Η Μαγεία στη Νεότερη Ελλάδα*) 72 (September): 8–13.

—2000. *Θρησκευτική Ελευθερία και Δημοκρατία* (Κίνηση Πολιτών κατά του Ρατσισμού). Αθήνα.

Toutountzi, O. N. 2002. "Η μεγάλη επανάσταση του νέου Διαφωτισμού! Η αναγέννηση της εθνικής μας θρησκείας και του εθνικού μας πολιτισμού." In *Η Αναβίωσης αρχαίας ελληνικής θρησκείας*, ed. E. Aulidou, 231–49. Thessaloniki.

Tsagrinos, G. 2002. "Οι ζωντανοί θεοί των Ελλήνων! Ο κόσμος των θείων δυνάμεων στην ελληνική φιλοσοφοθρησκευτική παράδοση." In *Η Αναβίωση της αρχαίας ελληνικής θρησκείας*, ed. E. Aulidou, 250–96. Thessaloniki.

Tsoukalas, K. 1983. "Παράδοση και εκσυγχρονισμός. Μερικά γενικότερα ερωτήματα." In *Ελληνισμός. Ελληνικότητα. Ιδεολογικοί και βιωματικοί άξονες της νεοελληνικής κοινωνίας*, ed. D. Tsaousis, 37–48. Athens.

Vakalopoulos, A. 1968. "Byzantinism and Hellenism: Remarks on the Racial and the Intellectual Continuity of the Greek Nation." *Balkan Studies* 9: 101–26.

Varelidis, E. 1998. "Για το Αρχαιοελληνικό Δωδεκάθεο." *Anichneuseis* 23 (March–April): 25–26.

Veer, P. van der. 1994. "Syncretism, Multiculturalism and the Discourse of Tolerance." In Stewart and Shaw, eds. 1994, 196–211.

Veremis, K. 1983. "Κράτος και Έθνος στην Ελλάδα: 1821–1940." In *Ελληνισμός. Ελληνικότητα. Ιδεολογικοί και βιωματικοί άξονες της νεοελληνικής κοινωνίας*, ed. D. Tsaousis, 59–67. Athens.

—ed. 1997. Εθνική Ταυτότητα και εθνικισμός στη νεώτερη Ελλάδα. Athens.

Verettas, M. 2002. "Φιλοπατρία, Φιλοκαλία, Φιλοσοφία. Σκέψεις για την αναβίωση της Αρχαίας Ελληνικής Θρησκείας." In *Η αναβίωση της αρχαίας ελληνικής θρησκείας*, ed. E. Aulidou, 43–69. Thessaloniki.

Vergopoulos, K. 1978. *Εθνικισμός και οικονομική ανάπτυξη. Η Ελλάδα στον Μεσοπόλεμο*. Athens.

Vernant, J.-P. 1987. "Greek Religion." In *The Encyclopedia of Religion*, vol. 6, ed. M. Eliade, 99–116.

Wachsmuth, C. 1864. *Das alte Griechenland im neuen*. Bonn: M. Cohen.

Williams, M. A., C. Cox and M. S. Jaffee, eds. 1966. *Innovation in Religious Traditions*. Berlin: Mouton de Gruyter.

Wolf, E. 1966. *Peasants*. Englewood Cliffs, NJ: Prentice-Hall.

Xydias, V. 1999. "Οι 'Έλληνες' ξανάρχονται," *SYNAXI* (special issue: Ο ελληνικός Νεοπαγανισμός) 69 (January–March): 5–22.

Zacharopoulou, E. 1998. *Η ελληνική παρουσία στο Μόναχο με ειδική αναφορά στην κοινότητα της Salvatorkirche. Η ίδρυση και η εδραίωση της κοινότητας με βάση τα Βαυαρικά κρατικά αρχεία*. Diss. Thessaloniki.

MEDICINE-MEN, MODERNITY AND MAGIC: SYNCRETISM AS AN EXPLANATORY CATEGORY TO RECENT RELIGIOUS RESPONSES AND MAGICAL PRACTICES AMONG URBAN BLACKS IN CONTEMPORARY SOUTH AFRICA

Kirstine Munk

In recent years there has been a tremendous upsurge in the quest for traditional magical practices among modern South Africans, and the traditional Zulu healers, the *inyangas* and the *isangomas*, are more popular and numerous today than ever before. This rise in popularity is seen especially in urban areas where traditional religious experts specialize in modern problems such as unemployment, traffic accidents, HIV/AIDS and crime (Munk 1997). The healers have medicines to protect a person from being shot, and medicines to evade the police. They can offer a client medicine to win a court case as well as to make him or her popular. If the medicine does not work, you can simply return to the healer and get your money back. However, clients seldom do (Munk 1998).

More than 85 per cent of the black population use traditional healers, and the healers draw their clientele from an extensive geographical and social range. Patients willingly travel across the vast country to a healer who has reportedly treated their kind of ailment with particular success, and among the patients are Zulu bourgeoisie, namely politicians, teachers and business people, as well as rural and urban poor. According to the traditional health system, disease is considered a social as well as a biological or psychological dysfunction, and it therefore allows room for treatment of marital problems, depression and crime as well as strokes or broken limbs. The health system is intimately bound to the cultural and religious construction of reality (Kleinman 1980), and cosmological classifications are central to the classifications of disease.

Zulu cosmology is based on the bold supposition that this world is fundamentally a beautiful place without blemish (Asmus 1939). The ancestral spirits, who live in the world below, guard their offspring and provide them with fertility, happiness, health and good luck. In exchange, the descendants must pay respect to the ancestral spirits with offerings of beer and cattle and they have to live according to traditional Zulu values and ethics. Otherwise, the ancestors will punish them with afflictions such as marital problems, infertility and bad luck. Although most Zulus have converted to Christianity, they still maintain the traditional ancestor cult along with their Christian faith. These two religious systems coexist in urban areas today, but the traditional thought-patterns prevail.[1]

Zulu values and ethics are included in the concept *ubuntu*, which denotes humanity, good character, generosity, and respect. The ideal is embedded in an African way of life that securely attaches the individual to the social group, and the social aspect of personality is highly pronounced: "A person becomes who he or she is through others," as a common proverb says.[2] We are what we are through our social interaction and through the social position given at birth. Zulu society is highly hierarchical, and attempts to transcend a certain position must often be sanctioned. Successful and entrepreneurial people are therefore always at risk of being accused of witchcraft, or they may provoke jealousy and become a victim of witchcraft themselves. Young women are especially vulnerable in this respect.

Witchcraft is quite common in modern South Africa. It is believed to be the main cause of severe illnesses such as cancer, AIDS, strokes, and calamities such as poverty, marital problems and unemployment. Together with ancestral wrath it is one of the most common etiological explanations to illness and affliction (Ngubane 1977). Therapeutic intervention is always based on etiology and the most important task of the traditional healers is therefore to determine the cause of the problem.

Primarily this is done by the *isangomas* who do so by means of throwing divination bones or by entering a state of ecstatic trance. The *isangomas* have been directly chosen by one of their ancestral spirits to divine the will of the ancestors, to find witches and to cure diseases. These healers derive their authority, their knowledge and their powers from their enduring and intimate relations with their ancestral spirits. Much of their potency also relates to their personal history of suffering and to their control of dangerous and destructive forces in their own lives. When an ancestral spirit chooses a future *isangoma*, the person usually becomes very ill and is forced to undergo a ritual of initiation that exhibits all kinds of liminal traits, during which a close contact between the novice and the ancestral spirit is established (Berglund 1989). The spirit will continue to guide the *isangoma*'s work, either through dreams or empathy, and show what medicines to use. In exchange, the *isangoma* must promise to behave "nicely," that is, to live according to Zulu tradition. The ancestral spirits are very conservative and severe in their punishment if tradition is not properly honoured.

An *inyanga* is a traditional medicine man who has special knowledge of particular ailments. He has obtained this special knowledge from his father who learned it from his father, and so on, so that any *inyanga* will depend on the knowledge and experience of a line of *inyangas* before him. An *inyanga* might experiment a little personally, but generally people have faith in him precisely because the tradition he draws upon is unbroken and has been well tested over the years. Many of the traditional healers are reputedly able to do the most fabulous things that are not explicable within a normal explanation frame. A healer might suddenly manifest fire out of nothing in the middle of a ritual, or make stolen things return to the client through a closed wall. These acts, *umlingo*, are manifestations of the spiritual power of the healer and confirm his authority. Hence, the more "magic"[3] the healer performs, the more clients he will generally have. The most popular healers are conscious of innovation and they will indeed introduce new ways to deal with modern ailments, but the efficacy and the potency of the magical concoctions and the rites they perform are always dependent on the rites and practices being representations of "original" ritual forms. Researchers have often stressed the great amount of conservatism that is found in this belief-system, and the conscious use of tradition has been explained as a symbol of resistance to the increasing penetration of white hegemonic culture (Hammond-Tooke 1989; Wilson 1971). Considering the political history of South Africa, this seems to be a very likely explanation.

The healers are associated with ancestors, prosperity, tradition, in-group, daytime, life, light, good health, and harmony, while witchcraft is associated with the opposite categories in the Zulu belief-system: Witchcraft is the inversion of social order. It limits and denies life, and the more foreign and strange the practice, the greater its potency for death and destruction (Berglund 1989). Because of this categorization concerning the familiar and the strange, the traditional and the new, the social and the anti-social, the healer and the witch, one would anticipate that the healers in modern South Africa would exhibit a basically *anti-syncretistic* response in dealing with new matters (Stewart and Shaw 1994). But the opposite is actually the case and the most popular healers are those that seem to exhibit the most syncretistic traits.

David Myburgh, a South African *isangoma* of white descent, is an example of this.[4] He is one of the most famous *isangomas* in the country, has an immense amount of clients and many black trainees. The South African media covers his actions eagerly, and rumours tell that he is a great magician, a charlatan, a political trickster with a sinister past, and many other things. He seems difficult to place. Raised on a farm in the countryside he had an early and close contact with Zulu culture through his Zulu age-mates. David's parents were conservative Christians, and as a young man he joined AWB, a radical, racist, rightwing movement.[5] Later in life, when he served as a soldier in the Angolan war, he had a nervous breakdown and when the doctors seemed unable to help him, he finally consulted a Zulu *isangoma*. This *isangoma* told David that his only rescue was to become an *isangoma* as this was what the spirits wanted. Then followed a long training period of six years that turned David's life upside down. He now travels the country as a magician and healer, and gives courses for black *isangomas* and *inyangas* on new magical practices such as "manifestations of fire."

My meeting with David wasn't anything I had expected. Instead of a cultural renegade in a traditional *isangoma* attire, he looked so ordinary that, when he came to visit, I mistook him for the plumber. His worldview and cosmology is in many respects strongly affected by white culture and cosmopolitan New Age thought, but significantly, David never prays or sacrifices to his own ancestral spirits. Instead he works with the spirits of the Zulu healers that trained him. When I asked him why he, being a white *isangoma*, is so extremely popular among the black population, he stated: "This is an insecure time. People are afraid and they seek the *isangomas* for protection. But they also know that I know more than most. My time of training was very long, much longer than it is for most people, and I have been living under the river.[6] It is a dangerous time. Either you die, or you return to life with renewed power. I learned how to manifest fire. The spirits spoke to me in a language that doesn't exist anymore. It resembles Hebrew. And I acknowledged that truth is not confined to one culture. It is my strength, that I have the wisdom from several cultures to draw upon."[7]

David claimed that he is consulted by members of all political parties from Afrikaner Weerstandsbeweging to ANC, blacks as well as whites, who all want to know what the future will be. As I had just acquired some old divination bones,[8] I asked David if he could show me his art. He accepted, but since the bones were not his own, he had to "cleanse" them first and after breathing on the bones for a while, he asked for a saucepan, a bit of water and some methylated spirits. "People don't believe this," he said, and took my saucepan with the water and spirits in it, placed it on my table with the old bones right under and began to pronounce a strange abracadabra in something that sounded like Hebrew. As he spoke, concentrated and quickly, he suddenly grabbed my hand and held it over the saucepan the second it burst into fire! I gasped and stared at the long blue flames that rose towards the ceiling. David quickly removed the pot, cast the bones aside, and began to tell me about my life and my future. It all sounded surprisingly correct, but he ended with a statement that seemed somewhat disturbing: "You are very psychic, your third eye is wide open, and basically you are an *isangoma* yourself. God will reveal himself to you soon."

The thought of becoming a traditional Zulu healer did not appeal to me. David sensed my reservation and decided to demonstrate my "psychic channel" in order to see for himself if I really was an *isangoma*. To this end he requested a small piece of tinfoil. We went into the kitchen where we found what he wanted. He made a small pellet out of the tinfoil and moistened it with some water from the tap. Then he placed the wet pellet in my hand, said one of his magical formulae, and waved his hand in the air. "Here, place your hand here," he suddenly said, and when my hand was exactly where David pointed, the pellet in it became scorching hot, and within a split second I felt the heat as an immense pain. David quickly removed the tinfoil and threw it in the sink. "It only heats because you have access to the divine power," he said. "Did it hurt you badly?" I nodded and stared at the burn in my hand. Then I looked for the tinfoil pellet. It had turned into ashes.

Syncretism is always highly pronounced in the magical rites that are performed by the famous South African healers, and it is noteworthy that the magical rites generally only occur as part of a divination ritual. It therefore seems that *umlingo* has a ritual meaning that goes beyond the sheer manifestation of the religious power. I will return to this later. But syncretism is also an important part of the ritual design when one visits the less famous healers.

Some time before my meeting with David, I accompanied a good friend of mine to one of the local *isangomas*. My friend Theleki, a bright and entrepreneurial young Zulu woman, was suffering from a persistent headache and we came to the *isangoma* for an explanation and a cure. A consultation with a healer usually takes place in a secluded hut where all the healer's ritual regalia and medicines are kept. A ritual hut is quite small, stuffed and seems a bit "messy," exposing an overload of contrasting symbolism. Some of the traditional medicines are kept in used plastic containers such as empty Coca Cola bottles. Others, such as dead snakes, bath salts, soap and monkey skulls just lie scattered on the floor where the client is also asked to sit down. And some of the medicines are a blend of traditional and modern: Western pharmaceutical pills of all kinds are mixed into dried medical plants.

At the beginning of a divination ritual the patient will always be very quiet and will never disclose to the healer why he or she has come. It is solely up to the healer to account for the patient's symptoms. Otherwise one will never know if the healer is trustworthy and has a good contact with the spirits. The ancestral world is a reversed world in which darkness is light, up is down, left is right, and so on, and the ritual hut is therefore kept in darkness inside for the spirits to see. The patients also sit in a reversed order in the ritual setting due to the reversed order of the spirit world; men to the left and women to the right—a position that would be unthinkable in any other situation. At the most sacred place in the back of the hut, meat from sacrificial animals hangs suspended from the roof, so that the spirits may eat. In this case the *isangoma* was a member of an African independent church, and under the meat was a Christian altar containing traditional medicine as well as candles, crosses, and other types of Christian symbolism.

The crisis ritual began soon after we had entered the room.[9] The *isangoma* was wearing her ritual attire that is a modern variation of a traditional ritual gown. It is usually made of fake leopard fur in polyester. She was covered in a huge rug with images of traditional Zulu spears and shields, and she wore noisy chains of beer bottle caps around her ankles. On her head was a braided wig with enormous coloured plastic beads, and in her hand she held an oxtail. When the healers flick an oxtail through the air the zipping sound invokes the spirits. An *isangoma* might also use a drum for the same effect or stamp her feet on the ground so the bottle caps ring.

The *isangoma* lit a bundle of dry evergreens on the altar in order to invoke her ancestral spirits. Soon smoke filled the room and she inhaled it as she prayed to the spirits and asked them to come. She spoke faster and faster and gasped for breath. Suddenly the spirits manifested themselves in the room by loud whistling sounds that came from the top of the roof somewhere around the area where the sacrificial meat was hanging. The *isangoma* had entered into a trance, and when she turned towards us, her movements were suddenly those of an old man. She bellowed loudly and spoke so fast and strangely that it was very difficult for us to grasp everything she said. She listed a number of symptoms—among those were headache—and she told my friend that her calamities were all due to witchcraft. People were jealous of all the things she had accomplished and the money she earned. It was witchcraft of the worst kind, and nothing could be done to prevent it. All hope would soon be over.

When the *isangoma* reached this dramatic point, she told us that she had to stop. The trance was over and she became again the friendly young woman she had been before the ritual began. She had a long conversation with my friend about the things that had just transpired in the liminal phase, and they elaborated on the passages that Theleki thought were of particular importance: Theleki had lost her father at an early age so she has had immense responsibilities at home as a co-provider for her younger siblings. She is an ambitious and successful woman, and she therefore knew that she would be prone to witchcraft. She also knew that, according to traditional Zulu ethics, this was partly her own fault, because her success disturbed the delicate balance between her and her poorer, distant kin. But she argued that due to the responsibilities she now had to her close family because of her father's death, she had to do her best to earn money and provide her mother with a good home, and pay the children's school fees. In fact she had just applied for a better job with chances of promotion. "One cannot just sit around and do nothing!" she exclaimed. The *isangoma* agreed—"no, you have to do something," and then she gave Theleki some medicine for her headache and a medicine to give her luck at her job interview.[10]

It was a very sombre prediction that Theleki received from the *isangoma* during the trance and the *isangoma* was unable to help her much besides giving her the medicines. She could not remove the cause of Theleki's problems, because the witchcraft was too strong, and Theleki would therefore always have to fight the ill will of others and their grudges against her. But even though the prediction was bleak, Theleki had—to my surprise—had a very good experience in the *isangoma*'s hut, and she left it with a big smile and a sparkle in her eyes.

This kind of discrepancy, one that we often find in rituals, is quite puzzling. Anthropologist Bruce Kapferer suggests in his recent book that the answer may be found in the capacity of human beings to redirect their consciousness actively into the world and thereby to make and unmake the realities of themselves. Rituals of crisis are especially suited for that. The phenomenological philosophers that inspire this line of thought remind us that reality is never something fixed. It is closely connected with the intentionality of our own being. From this perspective, ritual practice is not just a representation of meanings; rather it is the very dynamic of their constitution (Kapferer 1997).

There are basically two different ways of dealing with rituals. The most common approach perceives the rites as representations. Researchers of this observation investigate how belief-systems, thought-patterns and ideals create human acts. This interest inevitably leads to a perception of rituals as models that approximate the world. Rituals mirror a classification system, i.e. they reflect a cosmology. This heuristic approach is mainly found in various structuralistic methodologies where researchers focus on the ritual structure and on the mental classification system that the rituals articulate. Because religious thinking is expected to create religious acts, the model-mirror trope has resulted in a tendency to focus on religious experts, their meaning system, and the ways in which tradition is passed on, foremost during initiation.

The other, more client-oriented approach, basically sees rituals as *creative acts*. The ritual process is here perceived as a virtual reality in which humans construct their own reality, reconstruct themselves and get a chance to examine the social roles that they play. This latter approach makes good sense in a Zulu context as neither the patients nor the healers are very interested in cosmological issues. They have instead a strong pragmatic focus. But the two ritual perspectives probably always coexist in a multistable relation, such as the drawing we know from gestalt therapy, which may be viewed either as a goblet or as two faces opposite one another. They are both there at the same time in the same illustration, and they are mutually dependent, although one's focus will inevitably be on either the one or the other. People do not engage in a ritual of crisis simply in order to have their cosmology articulated, and even though there is a homology between cosmological design and ritual practice as it clearly has been demonstrated by Lévi-Strauss (1968) and others (e.g. Eliade 1958), it still remains a mystery how a homology in itself establishes any effect. On the other hand, if we focus on the creative aspect of rituals, we must still be aware of the fact that meanings, values and realities are historically and culturally constructed.

Phenomenological philosophers argue that we always create experiences as *meaningful* occurrences. We are faced with a myriad of impressions and perceptions every second of the day, but we never experience all of it. Our consciousness is intentional, it is always directed at something, and it will continuously and actively make a selection of possible impressions from which only some configure into something that is personal and meaningful— an experience. The reason why rituals have a creative impact is, from a phenomenological point of view, because of the overload of *signifiers*, which we find especially in the liminal phase. This is due to the fact that participating in a ritual is foremost a *sensuous* rather than an intellectual experience (Friedson 1996). Our senses become exposed to a multitude of strange and unfamiliar perceptions and we are inevitably forced to make new configurations of meaning.

Magic, *umlingo*, can be used to prod the senses and create realities that are conducive to transformations of consciousness: The surprise when my saucepan suddenly burst into fire prevented me from having the same analytical and distanced approach to the things David told me during the divination ritual as I had had during our conversation. And as David finally told me something that was very hard for me to accept, a magical ritual of highly syncretistic character was again used to loosen up my perceptual boundaries between the possible and the impossible, the likely and the unlikely, in order to pave way for some kind of useful interpretation of his statement.

Zulu crisis rites are generally dramatic events that force the patients to play a very active part, as it was the case for Theleki. From the very beginning the patient is made bewildered and perplexed by a number of strange sensory inputs: peculiar smells, strange sounds from unexpected places, a solid symbolism, the mess, the smoke, the trance, the reversed order of the setting, the bellowing, the darkness, and on top of this, too much verbal information. The healer speaks so fast that the patient must *actively select* bits and pieces of information and throughout the ritual try to configure it all into various meanings. However, this process is at the same time jeopardized by the other ritual aspects that compel attention. The bombardment of the senses is used to redirect the consciousness of the patient, and the ritual process can be likened to the old alchemist method; *solve et coagula*. The ritual helps to dissolve attitudes and explanation models that

369

are not useful to the patient any more and it forces him or her to actively configure a new pattern of meaning.[11]

Patients always contribute something in this way. They bring meaning into the rituals and there is therefore more at stake here than what simply reduces to tradition or worldview. The regalia of the traditional healer contribute significantly to this effect. They induce a new state of mind by means of cultural opposites that are constantly played out against each other in a typical syncretistic and competing way. Consider the traditional oxtail together with the Christian cross; the traditional wig with the enormous plastic beads of modern design; the fake leopard fur of polyester; chains of beer-bottle caps around the ankles; traditional medicine in the Coca Cola bottles, and so on. As we know from research on syncretism, a new element is never simply being incorporated. It has to be improved, it has to become more powerful than it was before (Colpe 1977). Often we see that an incorporated element conveys three or more meanings. In the case of the leopard fur of polyester, the leopard denotes tradition, power, aristocracy and *ubuntu*, whereas polyester is a western fabric; it is practical and cheap, and people wear it for everyday purposes. But the combination of leopard and polyester signifies the authority of the modern *isangoma* and of the rituals in which the moral negotiations take place today. Yet, all the different meanings are there at the same time. Therefore, we find in syncretism an enormous ability to contain paradoxes and contradictions. The syncretistic process creates a multivocality and contributes in this way significantly to the conceptual confusion that is at stake.

The ritual messiness and the bombardment of the senses is crucial. The German philosopher Martin Heidegger said in *Der Satz vom Grund*, that the thought is a listening, that sees (1958). There is a creative relationship between our senses and the thoughts they produce. In Zulu crisis rites, it is very much the manipulation of the senses that forces the intentional consciousness to make a redirection. Without the sensuous confusion that forces the individual to actively make new configurations of meaning, these rituals would not work. Since humankind's intentional consciousness is incorporated and situated, as we have to be somewhere in space, human beings create themselves and the world through their senses (Kirkeby 1998). In addition, when a patient's perceptions are being manipulated in the way it happens here, then his or her consciousness can be redirected and the world will look different.

Most of the problems that face the Zulus today are very much the result of the acculturation process. It is difficult for many, as it was for my friend Theleki, to unite traditional moral standards with modern economic demands. Many Zulus are, due to their various social roles and their risk of becoming a victim of witchcraft, not likely to show initiative and conceit when looking for a job—but they have to in order to succeed! During a

crisis ritual the patient is then given the opportunity to make a moral negotiation, and see the world in a new way. The patient is no longer subjected
to a horrible double bind situation formed by a lock of modern demands and
traditional structures, but through the ritual, she becomes free to choose
from diverse repertoires and to test different options in a virtual space. The
ritual puts her in the centre of negotiations, and she can thereafter leave the
medicine man's hut with a slightly different look at the world and with the
self-assurance that is necessary to face whatever difficulties she may have.
Despite the anti-syncretism that one would anticipate due to the belief-
system, the empirical case studies show that syncretistic elements in rituals
of crisis become both necessary and crucial parts of the process of human
reformation in modern South Africa and other places, where people have to
recreate themselves and the order of their worlds in new and foreign
contexts.

Notes

1. The Zulus converted to Christianity in great numbers after the British conquest in the
   late nineteenth century, and it is estimated that 74 per cent of all South Africans are
   Christians today (Kritzinger 1985). Most Zulus belong to the so-called main-line
   churches and maintain their traditional beliefs along with their Christian faith. This
   kind of Christianity is not mixed with the traditional cult, but the two religious systems
   live together side by side in a relation that could best be termed *symbiosis*—"life
   together with." It should be noted, however, that the African Independent Churches
   (AICs) have gained momentum in recent years, and that these congregations now have
   almost as many followers as the main-line churches. The AICs mix traditional Zulu
   religion with Christianity in various ways, but church members often combine the healing rituals in the church with visits to traditional healers. Others do not (Oosthuizen *et
   al*. 1994).
2. "*Umuntu ngumuntu ngabantu*" means literally: "A person is a person through others."
3. I use the word magic as a translation of the culture-specific term *umlingo*, which
   denotes any unusual, strange, awe-inspiring performance or trick that seems to break
   with the laws of nature. *Umlingo* occurs in many contexts and should *not* be understood in any Durkhemian sense of the word as opposed to "religion proper."
4. More white people have become traditional healers in recent years (Hall 1994;
   McCallum 1992). This particular interest in black South African spirituality is probably
   connected with New Age and the search for the "original" unspoiled religion. Black
   South Africans accept white *isangomas* quite easily. Their approach to healers is a
   pragmatic one: Are they any good? Besides, people of white complexion fit very well
   into the Zulu belief-system, since white is the colour of spiritual strength (Berglund
   1989).
5. AWB (Afrikaner Weerstandsbewegeng) was founded in 1973 and is by its own definition a cultural organization dedicated to defending a Christian Afrikaner nationalism.
   The organization is highly militant and recruits its members among the religious right
   in the Afrikaans-speaking part of the white population (Chidester 1992).

6. The spirits will sometimes give an *isangoma* esoteric wisdom by holding him/her captive in a cavity under a river together with snakes. After a year or so, the person returns with great spiritual powers.
7. This interview with David took place during my fieldwork in South Africa in 1993.
8. Divination bones are very small bones that are taken from the neck of sacrificial animals. South African healers throw the bones on the ground and interpret the meaning of their position.
9. The ritual recorded here took place during my fieldwork in 1993.
10. The medicine Theleki was offered for her headache was a dried powder from the fever tree (*Acacia xanthophloea*) to be inhaled. Powdered barks and roots have traditionally been used against malaria and the symptoms that are connected with this disease, including headache (Hutchings 1996; Watt and Breyer-Brandwijk 1962). The medicine Theleki bought for the job interview is a very common medicine called *isimonyo*. It is said to make a person more popular. The medicine consists of fat from various luck-bringing animals such as the python and the hippopotamus. It is mentioned in the old literature, where it was used by young women who wanted to make a good impression on the king in order to be accepted into the royal harem (Dlamini 1986). Today the medicine is used whenever people want to make changes in their lives that involve the acceptance of others. Hence a new ingredient has been added to this old medicine, namely a strong red dye because red is the symbol of transformation and change. The medicine is applied on the cheeks like rouge and it has a very nice smell. The *isangoma* "prays over" the medicine, and the efficacy of the medicine is dependent on the powers of her ancestral spirits. Hence the better the *isangoma* is—and this is tested during the divination ritual—the stronger is the power of her spirits, and the more effective will her medicines be. This *isimonyo* was sold in a small cosmetic plastic container of western style.
11. The active involvement of the patient has also been pointed out by other researchers (Peek 1991).

References

Asmus, Gustav. 1939. *Die Zulu.* Essen: Essener Verlagsanstalt.

Berglund, Axel-Ivar. 1989 [1976]. *Zulu Thought-Patterns and Symbolism.* London: Hurst & Co.

Bourguignon, Erika, ed. 1973. *Religion, Altered States of Consciousness, and Social Change.* Columbus: Ohio State University Press.

Campbell, Susan Schuster. 1998. *Called to Heal: Traditional Healing Meets Modern Medicine in South Africa Today.* South Africa: Zebra Press.

Chidester, David. 1992. *Religions of South Africa.* London: Routledge.

Colpe, Carsten. 1977. "Syncretism and Secularization: Complementary and Antithetical Trends in New Religious Movements?" *History of Religions* 17(2).

Dlamini, Paulina. 1986. *Servant of Two Kings.* Compiled by H. Filter. Ed. and trans. S. Bourquin. Pietermaritzburg: University of Natal Press.

Eliade, Mircea. 1958. *Patterns of Comparative Religion.* London: Sheed & Ward.

Friedson, Steven M. 1996. *Dancing Prophets: Musical Experience in Tumbuka Healing.* Chicago: University of Chicago Press.

Geertz, Armin W., and Jeppe Sinding Jensen, eds. 1991. *Religion, Tradition, and Renewal.* Aarhus: Aarhus University Press.

Hall, James. 1994. *Sangoma: My Odyssey into the Spirit World of Africa*. New York: Touchstone.

Hammond-Tooke, David. 1989. *Rituals and Medicines: Indigenous Healing in South Africa*. Cape Town: A.D. Donker Books.

Handelman, Don. 1990. *Models and Mirrors: Towards an Anthropology of Public Events*. Cambridge: Cambridge University Press.

Heidegger, Martin. 1958. *Der Satz vom Grund*. Pfullingen: Günther Neske.

Hutchings, Anne. 1996. *Zulu Medical Plants: An Inventory*. Pietermaritzburg: University of Natal Press.

Kapferer, Bruce. 1997. *The Feast of the Sorcerer: Practices of Consciousness and Power*. Chicago: University of Chicago Press.

Kirkeby, Ole Fogh. 1998. *Begivenhed og kropstanke. En fænomenologisk-hermeneutisk analyse (Event and Body-Thought: A Phenomenological-Hermeneutic Analysis)*. Copenhagen: Handelshøjskolens Forlag.

Kleinman, Arthur. 1980. *Patients and Healers in the Context of Culture: An Exploration of the Borderland between Anthropology, Medicine, and Psychiatry*. Berkeley: University of California Press.

Kriege, Eileen Jensen. 1950. *The Social System of the Zulus*. Pietermaritzburg: Shuter & Shooter.

Kritzinger, J. J. 1985. *´N Statistiese beskrywing van die godsdienstige verspreiding van die bevolking van Suid-Afrika*. Pretoria.

Lévi-Strauss, Claude. 1968. "The Effectiveness of Symbols." In *Structural Anthropology*, 186–205. London: Penguin Press.

McCallum, Taffy Gould. 1992. *White Woman Witchdoctor: Tales from the African Life of Rae Graham*. Miami: Fielden Books.

Munk, Kirstine. 1997. "Traditional Healers, Traditional Hospitals, and HIV/AIDS among Urban Zulu." *AIDS Analysis Africa* 7(6): 10–12.

—1998. *De døde lever! Religion, tradition og kulturmøde i Sydafrika (The Dead are Alive! Religion, Tradition and Acculturation in South Africa.)* København: Munksgaard.

Ngubane, Harriet. 1977. *Body and Mind in Zulu Medicine: An Ethnography of Health and Disease in Nyuswa-Zulu Thought and Practice*. Oxford: Academic Press.

Oosthuizen, G. *et al*. 1994. *Afro-Christianity at the Grassroots: Its Dynamics and Strategies*. Leiden: Brill.

Peek, Philip M., ed. 1991. *African Divination Systems: Ways of Knowing*. Bloomington: Indiana University Press.

Sartre, Jean-Paul. 1977. *Sketch for a Theory of the Emotions*. London: Methuen & Co.

Stewart, Charles, and Rosalind Shaw, eds. 1994. *Syncretism/Anti-Syncretism: The Politics of Religious Synthesis*. London: Routledge.

Turner, Victor. 1968. *The Drums of Affliction: A Study of Religious Processes among the Ndembu of Zambia*. Oxford: Clarendon Press.

—1975. *Revelation and Divination in Ndembu Ritual*. Ithaca: Cornell University Press.

Watt, J. M., and M. G. Breyer-Brandwijk. 1962. *The Medicinal and Poisonous Plants of Southern and Eastern Africa*. London: Livingstone.

Wilson, Monica. 1971. *Religion and the Transformation of Society: A Study in Social Change in Africa*. Cambridge: Cambridge University Press.

Part VII

CONCLUSION

CONCLUSION

That the task of defining syncretism is an ambiguous affair should be obvious to the reader now after having read the essays of this book. In short, we have seen that there is a disagreement between the normality of the phenomenon, the fact that all religions are syncretistic formations, and the complexity of the notion which largely derives from the reluctance to accept the normality of the phenomenon. If we are to conclude anything from the readings of this volume, we shall find that there are two tasks involved in "defining syncretism"; one task concerns the phenomenon of syncretism, the other task relates to the notion of syncretism. The two are intimately related, of course, but they are also different.

Two Tasks of Defining Syncretism

We now know that the category of syncretism is replete with definitional controversies. Apart from Robert Baird, however, all the presentations in this volume are in favour of keeping the category as long as the grounds for using it can be agreed upon. This does not mean that we have to reach one agreement on *one* all-embracing definition. There is much consideration in Ulrich Berner's proposal to judge every concept of syncretism, that is clearly defined, a valuable new perspective (see the introduction to Berner's essay, Part V). Definitions may thus be considered points of departure for arranging different subjects within an extensive analysis of syncretism. If we were to make a survey of the many definitions presented in this volume, it would ease the undertaking if we divided, roughly, the task into two sections. That is to distinguish between issues to do with the notion of syncretism, and issues to do with the phenomenon of syncretism.

Overall, the majority of the readings debate the consequences of the pre-dispositions in past scholarship concerning the notion of syncretism. One group of contributions may be categorized as explicitly concerned with the discourse on the notion of syncretism (see Pye, Rudolph, Apter, Benavides, Droogers, Stewart, and Martin). Research into the discourse or discourses of syncretism is important because we thereby sort out the "mal effects" of the discourses that have rendered the notion a tricky category for scientific use, for instance because it has caused the misrepresentation of (in particular) non-Christian religions and cultures (see Geertz in this volume). However, we do not make the mistreatment of cultures disappear by expelling the notion of syncretism. There is a chance, though, if we discuss the matter reflectively in our scholarly discourses, that we thereby may improve our

376

understanding of the subject and prevent some unintended consequences of its use in the future (see Apter and Stewart in this volume). As such, the analysis of discourses about the notion of syncretism is also a way to constrain the use of it. Even if we find that the scholarly discussion tends to reiterate the same questions over and over again, it is through these discussions that we make up our minds about the notion, and of how the notion can influence the view of the phenomenon that we want to know more about.

After reading the mass of theoretical and empirical data presented in the essays, we can deduce that the phenomenon of syncretism relates to several other phenomena that outline its "nature." It relates to power—not just because of the notion and its supplementary discourses, but also because, as André Droogers suggests, the phenomenon of syncretism refers to more stocks of meanings that can become a means of achieving power in different ways (see also Bastide, Apter, Stewart, Benavides, and Geertz in this volume). The manner in which the phenomenon of syncretism relates to power makes it a *social* phenomenon that evolves not just from the encounter of different religions but also from the encounter of cultures, peoples, classes, and not the least, discourses. Syncretistic formations or innovations are very often transmitted through discourses. "Discursive syncretism" does not necessarily evolve from real-life encounters of peoples and their religions; they are, however, assembled through the reinterpretation, and transformation, of religious meaning whether it stems from external or internal sources. "Discursive syncretism" may be used to negotiate between old and new standards of life such as to redirect or manipulate people's minds and worldviews in political as well as ritual life (Munk and Pachis in this volume). Along with Armin Geertz we may emphasize that the rule of syncretistic reinterpretation is fundamentally based on misrepresentation and misunderstanding. Alternatively, as Michael Pye states, the syncretistic meaning expresses an ambiguity that can go in any direction. In every sense, therefore, syncretism is also a *semiotic* phenomenon. On a semiotic level the dynamic power of syncretism equals a metaphor in the ways in which it is capable of "bridging" and "blending" or even redirecting the meaning of things that are otherwise classified dissimilar in religious or cultural affairs (Droogers, Vroom, Pye, Munk). Questions about the phenomenon's presumable nature of ambiguity, compatibility or incompatibility etc., therefore, should be examined according to the semiotics of the particular religious mode or cultural context. Consequently, the phenomenon of syncretism has to do with how we acquire religious and cultural knowledge (Light, Martin, and Benavides). Therefore, syncretism is also, as Luther Martin suggests, an altogether *cognitive* phenomenon (see also Light and Pachis).[1] That further explains both the cause and mechanism of syncretism on the grounds of human cognitive architecture. If we accept the fact that knowledge is never passed on from mind to mind infallibly, but that it mutates during the process of acquisition and transmission then we have an explanation of the underlying predictability of syncretism (Martin and Light). The mind's associative way of blending different conceptual or mental domains is, one might say, the "cognitive optimum" for the mechanism of syncretistic formations. Timothy Light provides a good illustration of how the cultural categories, which we learn through our upbringing, form basic cognitive categories wherein we arrange and interpret various conceptual inputs—old as well as new, and known as well as foreign. We can therefore "blame" syncretism on the plasticity of our human brain and the riches of our semantic systems.

Three Levels of Analysis of Syncretism

So far, we may conclude that we can divide the topics relating to syncretism into two analytical positions. One position concerning the notion of syncretism includes the historical background of the term and the accompanying analyses of the discourses regarding the notion. On this level of enquiry, we will find the actual controversies of defining the category together with the persisting debate of "whether to use or not to use syncretism" (see Martin). The other position concerns the classification of the actual phenomenon of syncretism in regard to its "nature." The two levels, the notion and the phenomenon, are of course interconnected in the same way as a "signifier" and the subject it "signifies" form a hermeneutic circle of referentiality: The notion, as a concept, refers to something in the world of human affairs, which is going on whether we care or not, but we should never be able to talk about the goings-on if we did not have a concept that could hold together (*con-cipio*) our thoughts and impressions.

In addition, to avoid complicating the definition of syncretism further, I suggest we divide our study of the nature of syncretism into three analytic levels that take into consideration the divergence of the subject matter attached to the category (see in the same line Berner's heuristic model, Part V, and Rudolph, Part II). The first level is the *social* to which we may assign issues of power to syncretism. This also concerns the different politics and modes of religion with regard to the encounter of religions and religious innovation notwithstanding the antonym "anti-syncretism." The second level is the *semiotic* where we must bear in mind the hermeneutical and transformative impact that syncretistic formations have on religion. This has to do with the mechanisms of change and innovation in religious meaning that many scholars refer to as the dynamics of syncretism (see van der Leeuw). The third level is the *cognitive*, here seen as the basic level underlying the two other levels because it explains the nature of conceptual blending and religious categorizing from the structure of human cognition that may also help explain the transformative manner of "syncretistic semiotics" as well as the various constraints against syncretism in religious systems.

The Social Level of Syncretism

Kraemer claimed that syncretism is innate to particular non-Christian religions (see Part II), whereas history demonstrates that anti-syncretism is mainly an invention of Christianity. The case studies in this volume concerning power and cultural interpenetration are connected with the history of Western colonialism together with Christianity on the domineering end of the leash (see Bastide and Part IV). Ironically, Christian Mission has been a major generator of syncretism in modern times despite a general anti-syncretistic attitude among the Christian churches. This ambiguity rests upon the Christian mode of religiosity as being dogmatic and universal at the same time. However, there is now a theory available, in the work of the British anthropologist Harvey Whitehouse, which can substantiate the causes of both syncretism and anti-syncretism. Based on Melanesian ethnography, he has constructed a theory which combines theories of memory from the field of cognitive science with the study of social and political mechanisms in religion. He does so in order to specify two very different modalities of religious activity: The one is a doctrinal mode of religiosity in which the emphasis is on standardized beliefs, repetitive sermonizing, wide dissemination of the tradition, and the institutionalization of religious authorities as guardians of orthodoxy. The other is an imagistic mode of religiosity in which emotionally laden imagery is evoked in rare and climactic rituals, triggering intensely personal experiences, and establishing enduring cohesion within small communities of participants. It is common for both modes to be present in any given religion.[2] Nevertheless, some religions emphasize one mode of religiosity over the other. Subsequently, Christianity is one religion that is particularly entrenched in the doctrinal mode of religiosity.

Even though we know that syncretism is a general phenomenon, we have also observed how some religions are relatively xenophobic in their struggle to protect themselves from foreign religious input. Hence, if we understand such phenomena as "syncretism" and "anti-syncretism" as the consequences of divergent modes of religiosity, some of the conceptual confusion regarding the reasons for anti-syncretistic or pro-syncretistic attitudes may fall into place. To start with, we can observe that syncretism is a salient problem to religions of the doctrinal mode. The reason for this is, as Whitehouse points out, that the system of sanctioning in doctrinal transmission relates religious revelation to moral issues (Whitehouse 2000, 63). This is how homogeneity together with political stability is secured in large-scale Christian society (63, 125). Right from the beginning, universal transmission of faith has been an imperative of Christianity. However, this adds to syncretism in the form of re-codification or reformulation of dogma in different cultures. It is understandable that the frequency of syncretistic innovation will be much higher in "large-scale" societies than in "small-scale" imagistic societies, because "multicultural" societies offer more concerning "syncretistic innovations" than "monocultural" societies do. Then again, in societies where both modes of religiosity are represented and with the doctrinal mode as the domineering part—which has been the situation of many of the case-stories in this volume—the frictions between the modes will at the same time generate new religious forms and distinct social groups together with the increasing pressure to be in command of the innovations (see Bastide, Benavides, Geertz, Wilson, Droogers).

As much as one may disagree with Kraemer's value-laden differentiation there is no getting around the fact that Christianity has fought against the incorporation of alien elements more forcefully than most other religious traditions. Consequently, the anti-syncretistic trend in Christianity has been taken for granted either as a sign of true revelation or of false discrimination. Because of the political complexity of the term syncretism, not many have dared imply, since Kraemer, that there might be a fundamental difference in the "modes" of syncretism in Christian religiosity and other religiosities. Timothy Light's wise suggestion of how we acquire, in all cultures and religions, categories that are particularly prominent to us during a lifetime, explains in a profound way why some categories are more protected against change and innovation than others (see Part VI). Consequently, we may find "anti-syncretism" in every type of human society. However, only in Christianity do we find officially worked-out manifestos against syncretism.

One general question in this volume is whether there may be an advantage in characterizing religions as either "pro-syncretist" or "anti-syncretist." As an addition to Kraemer's statement, we could ask whether we really *can* mark out any innate difference in respect to divergent modes of religiosity and syncretism. We can confirm, so far, that there is in fact an inherent tendency against syncretism in the doctrinal mode of religiosity as it is a consequence of favouring religious centralization and orthodoxy over individual and unauthorized innovation.

The Semiotic Level of Syncretism

In his presentation, André Droogers stated that the capacity to produce symbolic meaning is a universal human capacity that is fundamental for the formation of cultural and social structures. "Meaning-making" has been an all-encompassing resource in the human history in the production and reproduction of culture and religion (Droogers, Part IV). We may propose in line with Luther Martin (Part V) that meaning-making, and in particular "syncretistic meaning-making," can be compared to the processes of "trial-and-error" in the human evolution of culture. All religious activities produce meanings of some kind whether based on ritual iconography or on written texts. However, religious meaning is not static even though religious symbols may stay the same through generations. The meanings of symbols change and become reinterpreted (see Light, Part VI), some would even say misrepresented (see Geertz, Part IV), from generation to generation and from mind to mind. When it comes to the notion of survival it was established by Herskovits to illustrate that some religious symbols are able to survive when being transferred from their original context to a new context. However, the idea of "survivals" has been challenged (see Apter, Part IV), because scholars such as Melville Herskovits and Franz Boas forgot to take into consideration the constant "hermeneutical" relationship that exists between religious symbols and their meanings—especially in the case when it is removed to a different context with a new interpretive paradigm, or, say, another "worldview." For such reasons, syncretism is also a semiotic phenomenon, because part of its dynamics lies in the formulation of the structure of meaning as a new relation between the "signifier" and the "signified."

Vital to the syncretistic production of religion is the underlying mechanism of the selectivity of the human mind (see Martin, Pachis and Berner). However, in order to understand the semiotic properties of syncretism we must expect the cognitive mechanism of selectivity also to depend upon any individual person's cultural impregnation. According to Timothy Light (Part VI), the religious and cultural categories that we acquire during childhood are built into our general cognitive structure of category formation, because the first religious (and cultural/ethnic) impressions we get are often quite "numinous" and thus reside thereafter in the long-term memory system. We may conclude that our acquired cultural knowledge about religion together with our social and psychological profile becomes basic to our taste in the selection of religious styles and artefacts. Therefore, we can defend the idea that the acquisition of new religious elements is based on a fundamental semiotic structure learned from socialization in a particular culture, religion and social class etc., all of which will influence our selection and interpretation of any new input.

Hence, we may deduce that the semiotic function of selectivity constrains the innovative meaning of a syncretistic formation by placing selected material from various sources in a context of available meaning that makes up the paradigm for interpretation. In other words, the combinatorial system of thought underlying a syncretistic formation organizes cultural or semantic difference into a coherent system of meaning (see Vroom, Part III and Leopold 2001, 406). Ferdinand de Saussure's categories *langue* (i.e. the system of language as referring to the combination of rules of grammar, syntax and sound) and *parole* (i.e. the act of speaking) may describe as an analytic illustration this semiotic aspect of syncretism more clearly. When Saussure referred to *langue* as the system of a language and *parole* as the realization of speech, it was his primary concern to determine the units and rules of combination which make up the linguistic system. In short, in separating *langue* from *parole* Saussure also separated what is social from what is individual (Leopold 2001, 407). When we speak of religion, the *langue* of a religion refers to a particular system of beliefs and ritual practices which is shared by members of that religion, whereas *parole* refers to the individual, more private and maybe idiosyncratic ideas and practices. Religious *parole* can typically emerge ad hoc through chains of associations coming from different stocks of information and go in any direction depending, of course, on its *langue* for paradigmatic structure (see Munk, Part VI). For example: to love one's neighbour is a recognized paradigmatic structure in Western secular society even though it stems from, as we know, a Christian *langue*. Nevertheless, *parole* may change and even redirect the structures of a *langue* in general and become so dense with paradigmatic structures that it becomes a new *langue* altogether (see Munk, Part VI). Some groups within the New Age "movement" speak of the combination of the Christ-energy and the Buddha-energy as referring to, simultaneously, a cosmic and an individual process of spiritual evolution which establishes a paradigmatic motif very different from Christian theology and Buddhist teaching (Bertelsen 1989). This is possible because of the semiotic function of selectivity. A specific unit, or aspect, of a religious symbol is selected and joined with a new religious system and in that way is transformed with reference to a new, and emerging, structure of meaning. Generally speaking, the paradigmatic motif, referring to the structure of meaning as the frame of interpretation in any syncretistic formation, is what governs the process of transformation of any religious unit, and not the original context of the unit (Leopold 2001, 417). The semiotic function of selectivity, furthermore, is governed by analogical codification as a vital part of the dynamics of syncretism. Humans often perceive analogies between very different religious phenomena in a mode of naïve comparativity. Lately, shamanism has become very popular in New Age circles where the tendency is to glorify and to bond with "native peoples" who have a shamanistic tradition in order to rescue something of our own "lost" shamanistic past. This is a way of creating an analogy from the base of a paradigmatic motif rather than from documented historical research (see Pachis, Part VI). Religious elements which may appear incompatible, if we compare them in their original historical settings of entire religious systems and cultures, may become compatible when released from them and re-established in new contexts that plead apparent analogies of the select units (see Vroom, Part III). Almost anything can be brought to mean almost anything—with certain constraints to which we now turn.

The Cognitive Level of Syncretism

In conclusion, the syncretistic function of selectivity operates as a function of the cognitive optimum effect so that straightforward associations may take the place of more unintelligible or unidentifiable religious forms. For most people, the motivation to see Buddha as a divinity similar to Christ does not come from years of studying Buddhism and Christianity, respectively. It rather derives from an immediate causality in how we ordinarily construct likeness. The brain organizes knowledge by making "inferences" about given information that is neither random nor a free play of association, but is governed by special principles or mechanisms of handling information. The anthropologist Pascal Boyer claims that these principles are "the mental dispositions for arranging conceptual material in certain ways rather than others." This can be compared to having a "mental encyclopaedia" for distinguishing between concepts and templates in order to create a "walrus" *concept* by using the "animal" *template* (Boyer 2001, 42). Boyer says, that although human minds can produce all kind of variations from the information they receive, then these variations will be shaped by templates in cultural and religious concepts that constrain the variations of culture and religion in general.[3] Likewise, the phenomenon of syncretism is also constrained in respect to selectivity and variation of innovation by the very mechanism which is basic to the way we think.

Again, it lies near at hand to see an analogy between the structure of "conceptual blending" and syncretistic formation. I have already mentioned Gilles Fauconnier and Mark Turner's cognitive theory of blending in the general introduction and elsewhere in the volume. Still, to present the theory in detail would take us too far at this point in the discussion. We can state, however, that conceptual blending is an encompassing and ubiquitous mental capacity used to create diverse conceptual worlds with such features as grammar, complex numbers, and fantasies and hypotheses of all kinds, personal identities as well as rituals and religious worlds. I shall briefly present one of the many examples of conceptual blending from the work of Fauconnier and Turner, as well as a case from the world of religion as an illustration of a syncretistic blend. To exemplify how a blend works on a basically unconscious level, Fauconnier and Turner refer to a boat race that was set up virtually in the minds of the public—as if they were spectators. One of the boats in the race was the clipper, *Northern Light*, which sailed, in 1853, from San Francisco to Boston in 76 days, 8 hours. Up until 1993, Fauconnier and Turner tell us, it was still the fastest on record. However, when the modern catamaran, *Great American II*, set out on the same course, observers were able to declare, a few days before the catamaran would reach Boston, that "at this point, *Great American II* is 4.5 days ahead of *Northern*

Light." The phrasing gives the impression of two boats sailing on the same course during the same period of time in 1993 (Fauconnier and Turner 2002, 63). This fusion of the different time-frames wherein the actual races took place into a single event does not startle us. Nevertheless, we are unconscious of how we do it. The blend has nothing to do "with reality" but it certainly makes sense.

The other example, of religious blending, is taken from the work of Irenaeus of Lyon, a Church Father and Apologetic from the second century AD. It shows that the author is very aware, for apologetic reasons, of why he introduces Jesus Christ as the Word of God in the Garden of Eden in his interpretation of Genesis (Irenaeus 1952). But he is not aware that he is running a mental blend when Jesus seemingly unproblematically becomes a *word* that is walking around in the Garden of Eden talking to Adam and Eve about things to come as well as about the mission of the Christian Church. This point is made by setting up a situation that has some *characteristics* of Jesus Christ, some *characteristic* of the word, and some *new characteristic* of emerging structures of the actual blend. We all know that Jesus was a man of flesh and blood. Again, a word, as far as we know, is not. At least it is not a physical life form and its appearance depends, as we all know, on very complex cognitive and linguistic processes of making meaning in oral or literal form. However, a word has one very special quality that a human does not have: it can be spread as sound or writing in all directions at once, and may rest in many peoples' minds at the same time. It can even cause things to happen subsequent to the enunciation of the original speaker. The presence of the original speaker is not a necessary precondition for the efficacy of the word. In the blend, Jesus acquires the quality of the word—he becomes the word of God that spreads in all directions without the original speaker, God, being present or visible in the world. On the other hand, the word becomes alive in flesh and blood and represents the visible part of the divinity in the world. This is rather interesting because while incorporating new inputs into the old mythology, Irenaeus hopes to redirect his readers' minds to accept his and the Church's version of Genesis as the original true version. Through the running of the blend, we can easily understand the extra dimension that emerges through the analogical coding which transforms Jesus into a word and legitimates the Christian Church as a divinely sanctioned institution.

These two examples demonstrate that syncretistic blending is a kind of conceptual blending that is operating on a fundamentally unconscious level where it creates, without problems, metonymic links between things of dissimilar nature. Still, Irenaeus' deliberate Christological input is a conscious intellectual act to redirect peoples' minds to believe in the new teaching. Whether we can state that "a syncretism" is "conscious" or "unconscious," then, relies on the level of analysis of which we speak, in addition to the kind of data we work with (see Rudolph, Part II). Some people may object to

my characterization of Irenaeus' interpretation of Genesis as being syncretistic! Some would claim that Irenaeus' Christian interpretation of Genesis
is, by and large, a consequence of a Jewish reformation and not an outcome
of "a syncretistic blending" of different mythical paradigms. Clearly, the
question of who is right depends on the analytical level at which we speak;
whether we intend to analyse the *social*, the *semiotic* or the *cognitive* level.
There is no reason to expect the conceptual organization of a religious
enunciation to be directly mirrored in all the levels of the analysis. As we
know, social processes shape and change meanings. A conceptual organization may be syncretic at one level of discourse or, say, stage of history, and
yet change into orthodoxy at a later social or discursive point (see Stewart,
Part V; Light and Pachis, Part VI).

Finally, to conclude about the analytical model of three levels of syncretism, I wish to remind you of the Saussurian semiotic division of language
system (*langue*) and speech act (*parole*). However, for a further understanding of the problem, we find help in the linguist Ronald Langacker's treatment of similar structures in his study of cognitive perspectives in grammar.
He writes:

> There is no reason at all to expect this *conceptual* organization to be
> directly mirrored in grammatical constituency, which is a matter of how
> *symbolic* elements successively combine with one another to form pro-
> gressively more elaborate symbolic structures. Grammar is a tool for
> building up to—and symbolizing—complex conceptualizations, but it is
> not to be identified with those conceptualizations. Constituency too is
> a kind of scaffolding, which enables us to reach the composite semantic
> structure. It is essential not to confuse the scaffolding with the struc-
> ture being build. (Langacker 2001, 184)

In reference to Langacker's statement, we must be aware of a comparable
structure of difference when we talk about the dynamics of syncretism. We
must recognize the three levels, the *social*, the *semiotic* and the *cognitive*, as
representing different modes of dynamics. If we accept, however, that there
is a considerable difference in modes of dynamics concerning for instance,
when we talk about "syncretism and power relations," or "syncretism as
transformator and innovator of meaning," then we will be able to grasp the
causes of the categorical ambiguity. The analytical models proposed here
should make us capable of observing more clearly the different structures of
constraints of the phenomenon at the same time as it may allow us to use
the notion in various ways—as long as we make clear distinctions concerning the levels of syncretism that we study.

The Perspective of Description and Explanation of the Category Syncretism

In Part V we discussed three different theoretical outsets for defining syncretism which roughly support the distinction between the *discursive level of explanation* (see Stewart), *the explanatory approach* (see Martin) and *the historical descriptive level of explanation* (see Berner). I advocate that all three levels must be valid for a clarification of the category syncretism because the category cannot be employed as part of a viable taxonomy if we disregard any of the levels.

In various ways the discursive level overlaps the historic descriptive level of explanation, because the discourses of syncretism, whether in theology or in the study of religion, have repercussions in history that we must take notice of in our study of religiosity in general. For instance, in the study of the "two modes of religiosity" it is valuable information to register either anti-syncretistic or pro-syncretistic discourses as well as to describe various traits by which we can tell the difference between modes of religiosity. A survey of the discourses of syncretism in a general historical perspective is in itself valuable information; one that it is good to have in mind when we discuss religious change in general, in addition to bringing up to date the adjustments of the scientific discourse on the subject. In line with Ulrich Berner's heuristic typology and Charles Stewart's critical survey of discourses, I suggest that we rank different discourses and classifications of syncretism in order to give us a picture of two important aspects—on the one hand, the effects which those discourses and classifications have on changes in religious life; on the other hand, a typology, which groups the outcome of syncretistic change in meanings and in the social and political structure of religion with regard to different modes of religion, will also be supportive of an explanatory theory of syncretism.

In conclusion, we require the descriptive level of explanation to enhance our inquiry on the issues of syncretism. The criticism which some scholars have drawn attention to, and appropriately so, in regard to the descriptive use is when the description of (the notion of) syncretism collapses with the causal explanation of (the phenomenon of) syncretism (see Martin, Part V). However, we must have a descriptive or typological outline of a phenomenon in order to be able to create a scientific category. From the readings of this volume, we can also close the matter of concern about the collapse of phenomenon and definition. There exists, in most of the cases, a hermeneutical circle between the case study and the explanation of the case study, which makes up the analytical level of the definition. However, if we want to make the perception of that relationship more stringent it would be an improvement to adjust our descriptions of the phenomenon/phenomena of syncretism to an explanatory level of theory as is suggested by Luther Martin and above in the analytical model. Things change, as do scholarly categories. The category of syncretism is a very good example of how the "scale creates the phenomenon." This does not imply that the matters that make up the phenomenon are created out of nothing, but simply that, with shifting taxonomies, we make different decisions about what "counts as" part of the phenomenon under investigation. Scholarly categories are also socio-cultural categories—they are, just like syncretism, "social facts" and made by humans. But, they do "hook up to the real world," as we know it, so there is no cause for despair if neither the phenomena nor the categories are simple empirical or material objects (Jensen 2003). The study of things social and cultural, thus also religious, may be as rigorous as the study of anything else. We may not have access to eternal verities, "God's-eye views," nor to things "in themselves," but we certainly can and should uphold the ideals of the validity of scholarly discourse. Only theoretical clarity and reflexivity will take us further on that path.

Notes

1. The author attended the conference "Two Modes of Religiosity" arranged by Harvey Whitehouse and Luther H. Martin at the University of Vermont, August 2002, where historians of religions were invited to contribute to the study of "two-modes" with examples from the history of religions. I contributed with the paper "Syncretism and the Interaction of Modes of Religiosity: A Formative Perspective in 'Gnostic-Christian' Movements in Late Antiquity." The papers by the conference contributors are presently in press. Readers may learn more about this project in Whitehouse (2000, 1–17 and 2002, 293–315).
2. Harvey Whitehouse mentions in his introduction to the papers for the conference on "Two Modes of Religiosity" (University of Vermont, August 2002) that: "routinized religion will tend to generate a profusion of concepts that are easier to represent than theologically correct discourse, because they conform more closely to intuitive knowledge—and in that sense constitute forms of knowledge that are closer to the cognitive optimum." This made me think a little more about how syncretism in certain cases exemplifies such a cognitive optimum effect.
3. Boyer compares "strong" cultural representations such as religion to a type of epidemic: "Human minds are inhabited by a large population of mental representations. Most representations are found only in one individual but some are present in roughly similar forms in various members of a group. To account for this is to explain the statistical fact that a similar condition affects a number of organisms, as in epidemics" (Boyer 2001, 45–47).

References

Bertelsen, Jes. 1989. *Kristusprocessen*. København: Borgen.

Boyer, Pascal. 2001. *Religion Explained: The Evolutionary Origins of Religious Thought*. New York: Basic Books.

Fauconnier, Gilles, and Mark Turner. 2002. *The Way We Think: Conceptual Blending and the Mind's Hidden Complexity*. New York: Basic Books.

Irenaeus. 1952. "Proof of the Apostolic Preaching." In *Ancient Christian Writers*, vol. 16, ed. J. Quasten and J. C. Plumpe, trans. Joseph P. Smith. New York: Paulist Press.

Jensen, Jeppe S. 2003. "Social Facts, Metaphysics and Rationality in the Study of Religion as a Human Science." In *Rationality and the Study of Religion*, ed. J. S. Jensen and L. H. Martin, 117–35. London: Routledge.

Langacker, Ronald W. 2001. "Discourse in Cognitive Grammar." *Cognitive Linguistics* 12(2): 143–88.

Leopold, Anita. 2001. "The Architecture of Syncretism: A Methodological Illustration of the Dynamics of Syncretism." *Historical Reflections/Réflexions Historiques*, 27(3).

Whitehouse, Harvey. 2000. *Arguments and Icons: Divergent Modes of Religiosity*. Oxford: Oxford University Press.

—2002. "Modes of Religiosity: Towards a Cognitive Explanation of the Sociopolitical Dynamics of Religion." *Method & Theory in the Study of Religion* 14(3-4).

APPENDIX

Further Reading on Syncretism

Aijmer, Göran, ed. 1995. *Syncretism and the Commerce of Symbols*. Göteborg: The Institute for Advanced Studies in Social Anthropology (IASSA).

Alles, Gregory D. 2001. "The Greeks in the Caribbean: Reflections on Derek Walcott, Homer and Syncretism." *Historical Reflections/Réflexions Historiques* 27(3): 425–52.

Apter, Andrew. 2002. "On African Origins: Creolization and Connaissance in Haitian Vodou." *American Ethnologist* 29(2): 233–61.

Balutansky, K. M., and M. Sourieau. 1998. "Introduction." In *Caribbean Creolization. Reflections on the Cultural Dynamics of Language, Literature, and Identity*, ed. K. M. Balutansky and M. A. Sourieau, 1–12. Gainesville: University Press of Florida.

Bausani, Alessandro. 1984. "L'Islam: integrazione o sincretismo religioso?" In *Incontro di religioni in Asia tra il III e il X secolo d. C.*, ed. L. Lanciotti, 99–114. Firenze: Leo S. Olschki.

Benavides, Gustavo. 1991. "Sincretismo religioso o resistencia política en los Andes?" *Humanitas* 20: 5–19.

—2002. "Power, Intelligibility and the Boundaries of Religions." *Historical Reflections/Réflexions Historiques* 27(3): 481–98.

Bergman, Jan. 1969. "Beitrag zur Interpretatio Graeca: Ägyptische Götter in griechischer Übertragung." In Hartman, ed. 1969, 207–27.

Berner, Ulrich. 1982. *Untersuchungen zur Verwendung des Synkretismus-Begriffes*. Göttinger Orientforschungen, 2. Wiesbaden: Otto Harrassowitz.

—2001. "The Notion of Syncretism in Historical and/or Empirical Research." *Historical Reflections/Réflexions Historiques* 27(3): 499–509.

Biezais, Haralds. 1975. "Transformation und Identifikation der Götter im Synkretismus." *Temenos* 11: 5–26.

Black, Lydia, T. 1994. "Religious Syncretism as Cultural Dynamic." In *Circumpolar Religion and Anthropology: An Anthropology of the North*, ed. T. Irimoto and T. Yamada, 221–36. Tokyo: University of Tokyo Press.

Böhlig, Alexander. 1975. "Der Synkretismus des Mani." In *Synkretismus im persisch-syrischen Kulturgebiet*, ed. A. Dietrich, 144–69. Göttingen: Vanderhoeck & Ruprecht.

Boholm, Åsa. 1995. "Demonic Blessings: Papal Syncretism and Cultural Pragmatics." In Aijmer, ed. 1995, 121–55.

Brook, Timothy. 1993. "Rethinking Syncretism: The Unity of the Three Teachings and their Joint Worship in Late-Imperial China." *Journal of Chinese Religions* 21: 13–44.

Brosses, Charles de. 1760. *Du Culte de dieux fétiches, ou, Parallèle de l'ancienne religion l'Egypte avec la religion actuelle de Nigritie*. Paris.

Calixt, Georg. 1978. *Einleitung in die Theologie*, vol. 1. Edited by Inge Mager. Göttingen: Vandenhoeck & Ruprecht.

Carlson, Jeffrey. 1992. " 'Syncretistic Religiosity': The Significance of this Tautology." *Journal of Ecumenical Studies* 29(1): 24–34.

Carrithers, Michael. 1992. *Why Humans Have Cultures: Explaining Anthropology and Social Diversity*. Oxford: Oxford University Press.

Cassidy, William J., ed. 2001. "Retrofitting Syncretism?" Special issue of *Historical Reflections/ Réflexions Historiques* 27(3).

Colpe, Carsten. 1977. "Syncretism and Secularisation: Complementary and Antithetical Trends in New Religious Movements." *History of Religions* 17: 158–76.

—1987. "Syncretism." In *The Encyclopedia of Religion*, ed. M. Eliade, vol. 14, 218–27. New York and London: Macmillan.

Diehl, Carl Gustav. 1969. "Replacement or Substitution in the Meeting of Religions." In Hartman, ed. 1969, 137–61.

Dolezálová, Iva, Bretislav Horyna and Dalibor Papousek, eds. 1996. *Religions in Contact*. Brno: CSSR.

Droge, A. J. 2001. "Retrofitting/Retiring 'Syncretism'." *Historical Reflections/Réflexions Historiques* 27(3): 375–88.

Droogers, André. 1989. "Syncretism: The Problem of the Definition, the Definition of the Problem." In Gort *et al.*, eds. 1989, 7–25.

Droogers, André, and Sydney M. Greenfield, eds. 2001. *Reinventing Religions: Syncretism and Transformation in Africa and the Americas*. Lanham, MD: Rowman & Littlefield.

Ensink, Jacob. 1978. "Siva-Buddhism in Java and Bali." In *Buddhism in Ceylon and Studies on Religious Syncretism in Buddhist Countries*, ed. Heinz Beckert, 178–98. Göttingen: Vanderhoeck & Ruprecht.

Fabella, Virginia, and Sergio Torres, eds. 1985. *Doing Theology in a Divided World*. Papers from the Sixth International Conference of the Ecumenical Association of Third World Theologians. Maryknoll: Orbis Books.

Ferme, Marianne. 1994. "What 'Alhaji Airplane' Saw in Mecca, and What Happened When He Came Home: Ritual Transformation in a Mende Community (Sierra Leone)." In Stewart and Shaw, eds. 1994, 27–44.

Ferretti, Mundicarmo M. R. 2001. "The Presence of Non-African Spirits in an Afro-Brazilian Religion: A Case of Afro-Amerindian Syncretism?" In Droogers and Greenfield, eds. 2001: 99–112.

Finnestad, Ragnhild Bjerre. 1988. "Kulturmøter som studiefelt for religionshistorikeren." *Chaos* 10: 5–11.

Friedman, Maurice. 1989. "The Dialogue of Touchstones as an Approach to Interreligious Dialogue." In Gort *et al.*, eds. 1989, 76–84.

Geertz, Armin W. 1993. "Theories of Tradition and Change in Sociology, Anthropology, History, and the History of Religions." In *Religious Transformations and Socio-Political Change in Eastern Europe and Latin America*, ed. Luther H. Martin, 323–47. Berlin: Mouton de Gruyter.

—1997. "From Stone Tablets to Flying Saucers: Tradition and Invention in Hopi Prophecy." In *Present Is Past: Some Uses of Tradition in Native Societies*, ed. Marie Mauzé, 175–94. Lanham, NY: University Press of America.

Gort, Jerald D. 1989. "Syncretism and Dialogue: Christian Historical and Earlier Ecumenical Perceptions." In Gort *et al.*, eds. 1989, 36–51.

Gort, Jerald D., Hendrik M. Vroom, Rein Fernhout and Anton Wessels, eds. 1989. *Dialogue and Syncretism: An Interdisciplinary Approach*. Grand Rapids, MI: Eerdmans; Amsterdam: Rodopi.

Grant, Frederick C. 1953. *Hellenistic Religions: The Age of Syncretism*. Indianapolis: Bobbs Merrill.

Greenfield, Sidney M. 2001. "Population Growth, Industrialization and the Proliferation of Syncretized Religions in Brazil." In Droogers and Greenfield, eds. 2001, 55–70.

Gunkel, Herman. 1903. "The Religio-Historical Interpretation of the New Testament." Trans. W. H. Carruth. *The Monist*, 398–455.

Guss, David M. 1994. "Syncretistic Inventions: 'Indianness' and the Day of the Monkey." In Stewart and Shaw, eds. 1994, 145–60.

Hanegraaff, Wouter J. 1998. "The New Age Movement and the Esoteric Tradition." In *Gnosis and Hermeticism: From Antiquity to Modern Times*, ed. Roelof van der Broek and Wouter Hanegraaff, 359–82. New York: State University of New York Press.

Hannerz, Ulf. 1987. "The World in Creolisation." *Africa* 57: 546–59.

Hartman, Sven S., ed. 1969. *Syncretism*. Scripta Instituti Donneriani Aboensis III. Stockholm: Almquist & Wiksell.

Hsü, Elisabeth. 1995. "The Manikin in Man: Culture Crossing and Creativity." In Aijmer, ed. 1995, 156–204.

Jensen, Jeppe S. 1996. "On Intentionally Putting Religions in Contact." In Dolezãlová *et al.*, eds. 1996, 19–30.

Kamstra, J. H. 1970. *Synkretisme*. Leiden: E.J. Brill.

—1989. "The Religion of Japan: Syncretism or Religious Phenomenalism?" In Gort *et al.*, eds. 1989, 134–45.

King, Karen L. 2001. "The Politics of Syncretism and the Problem of Defining Gnosticism." *Historical Reflections/Réflexions Historiques* 27(3): 461–80.

Kippenberg, Hans G. 1998. "Survivals: Conceiving of Religious History in an Age of Development." In *Religion in the Making: The Emergence of the Sciences of Religion*, ed. A. L. Molendijk and P. Pels, 297–312. Leiden: Brill.

Leopold, Anita M. 2001. "The Architecture of Syncretism: A Methodological Illustration of the Dynamics of Syncretism." *Historical Reflections/Réflexions Historiques* 27(3): 401–24.

—2002a. "Synkretisme: En analyse af illegitime blandinger og tredje-identiteter." *Religionsvidenskabeligt Tidsskrift* 40: 47–57.

—2002b. "Syncretism and Transformation in the Gospel of Truth." In *The Nag Hammadi Texts in the History of Religions*, ed. Søren Giversen, Tage Petersen and Jørgen Podemann Sørensen, 46–53. Copenhagen: The Royal Danish Academy of Sciences and Letters.

Levinskaya, Irina A. 1993. "Syncretism: The Term and Phenomenon." *Tyndale Bulletin* 44(1): 117–28.

Lincoln, Bruce. 2001. "Retiring Syncretism." *Historical Reflections/Réflexions Historiques* 27(3): 453–60.

Lundius, Jan. 1995. *The Great Power of God in San Juan Valley: Syncretism and Messianism in the Dominican Republic*. Lund Studies in History of Religions, 4. Lund: Religionshistoriska avdelningen, Lunds Universitet.

Martin, Luther H. 1983. "Why Cecropian Minerva? Hellenistic Religious Syncretism as a System." *NUMEN* 30: 131–45.

—1996a. "Historism, Syncretism, Comparativism." In Dolezãlová *et al.*, eds. 1996, 31–38.

—1996b. "Syncretism, Historism, and Cognition." *Method & Theory in the Study of Religion* 8: 215–24.

—2000. "Of Religious Syncretism, Comparative Religion and Spiritual Quests." *Method & Theory in the Study of Religion* 12: 277–86.

Martin, Luther H., and Anita M. Leopold. (In press). "New Approaches to the Study of Syncretism." In *New Approaches to the Study of Religion*, ed. Peter Antes, Armin W. Geertz and Randi Warne. Berlin and New York: de Gruyter.

McNeill, John Thomas. 1930. *Unitive Protestantism*. New York: Abingdon Press.

Meyer, Birgit. 1994. "Beyond Syncretism: Translation and Diabolization in the Appropriation of Protestantism in Africa." In Stewart and Shaw, eds. 1994, 45–68.

Moffat, J. 1922. "Syncretism." In *Encyclopaedia of Religion and Ethics*, vol. 12, ed. J. Hasting, 155–57. New York: Charles Scribner's Sons.

Mondloch, James. 1982, "Sincretismo religiosa maya-cristiano en la tradición oral de una comunidad quiche." *Mesoamérica* 3: 107–23.

Morrison, Kenneth M. 1990. "Baptism and Alliance: The Symbolic Mediations of Religious Syncretism." *Ethnohistory* 37: 416–37.

Motta, Roberto. 2001. "Ethnicity, Purity, the Market and Syncretism in Afro-Brazilian Cults." In Droogers and Greenfield, eds. 2001, 71–86.

Mulder, Dirk C. 1989. "Dialogue and Syncretism: Some Concluding Observations." In Gort *et al.*, eds. 1989: 203–12.

Munk, Kirstine. 1998. *De døde lever—Religion, tradition og kulturmøde i Sydafrika*. København: Munksgaard.

Nock, Arthur Darby. 1972. "Ruler-Worship and Syncretism." In *Essays on Religion and the Ancient World*, ed. Zeph Stewart, 551–58. Cambridge, MA: Harvard University Press.

Nouailhat, R. 1975. "Remarques méthodologiques à propos de la question de 'l'hellénisation du christianisme'. Syncrétisme, herméneutique et politique." In *Les syncrétismes dans les religions de l'antiquité. Colleque de Besancon*, ed. F. Dunand and P. Lévêque, 212–34. EPRO, 46. Leiden: E. J. Brill.

Parkin, David. 1970. "Politics of Ritual Syncretism: Islam among the Non-Muslim Giriama of Kenya." *Africa* 45: 217–33.

Pearson, Birger A. 1975. "Religious Syncretism in Antiquity." In *Essays in Conversation with Geo Widengren*. Missoula, MT: Scholars Press.

Peel, J. D. Y. 1968. "Syncretism and Religions." *Comparative Studies in Society and History* 10: 121–41.

Pye, Michael. 1969. "The Transplantation of Religions." *NUMEN* 16: 234–39.

—1996. "Buddhism and Shinto on One Island." In Dolezãlová *et al.*, eds. 1996, 159–62.

Ringgren, Helmer. 1969. "The Problems of Syncretism." In Hartman, ed. 1969, 7–14.

Rose, Herbert J., and Herbert W. Parke. 1970. "Syncretism." In *The Oxford Classical Dictionary*, ed. N. G. L. Hammond and H. H. Scullard, 1029. 2nd ed. Oxford: Clarendon Press.

Rudolph, Kurt. 1992. *Geschichte und Probleme der Religionswissenschaft*. Leiden: Brill.

Schenk, Wolfgang. 1989. "Interpretatio Graeca—Interpretatio Romana. Der hellenistische Synkretismus als semiotisches Problem." In *Innovationen in Zeichentheorien: Kultur—und wissenschaftsgeschictliche Studien zur Kreativität*, ed. P. Schmitter and H. W. Schmitz. Münster: Nodus Publikationen.

Schmid, Heinrich Friedrich Ferdinand. 1846. *Geschichte der syncretischen Streitigkeiten in der Zeit des Georg Calixt*. Erlangen: Carl Heyder.

Schütte, Heinz. 1997. "Magie, Volkskultur, Synkretismen." *Zeitschrift für Missionswissenschaft und Religionswissenschaft* 81: 3–29.

Seiwert, Hubert. 1996. "What is New with Religious Contact Today?" In Dolezãlová *et al.*, eds. 1996, 57–66.

Siller, Herman P., ed. 1991. *Suchbewegungen. Synkretismus—Kulturelle Identität und kirchliches Bekenntnis*. Darmstadt: Wissenschaftliche Buchgesellschaft.

Sjørslev, Inger. 2001. "Possession and Syncretism: Spirits as Mediators in Modernity." In Droogers and Greenfield, eds. 2001, 131–44.

Stewart, Charles. 1994. "Syncretism as a Dimension of Nationalist Discourse in Modern Greece." In Stewart and Shaw, eds. 1994, 127–44.

Stewart, Charles, and Rosalind Shaw. 1994. "Introduction: Problematizing Syncretism." In Stewart and Shaw, eds. 1994, 1–26.

Stewart, Charles, and Rosalind Shaw, eds. 1994. *Syncretism/Anti-Syncretism: The Politics of Religious Synthesis*. European Association of Social Anthropologists. London: Routledge.

Van der Veer, Peter. 1994. "Syncretism, Multiculturalism and the Discourse of Tolerance." In Stewart and Shaw, eds. 1994, 196–211.

Wach, Joachim. 1924. *Religionswissenschaft: Prolegomena zu ihrer wissenschaftstheoretischen Grundlegung*. Leipzig: J. C. Hinrichs.

Werblowsky, R. J. Z. 1990. "Das Ausweichen vom Loyalitätskonflikt (Synkretismus) und der aufgezwungene Loyalitätskonflikt." In *Loyalitätskonflikte in der Religionsgeschichte: Festschrift für Carsten Colpe*, ed. Christoph Elsas *et al.*, 36–41. Würzburg: Königshausen & Neumann.

SUBJECT INDEX

Subject Index

criticism 22
determinism 165–66, 169, 205, 274, 290
imponderables 165–66, 181, 269
interpenetration 94, 104, 379
knowledge 166, 180, 377, 381

Deconstruction (of origins)
Definition(s) 7, 16, 25–26, 152, 208–209
Definition, generalized interpretation as 24
Dialogue 103–111
Diffusion, cultural 5
Discourse 200, 205
scholarly 386
Discrimination, racial 135, 151, 166, 188–91, 270
Dispositions, mental 383
Dissolution(s) 25, 66, 224
Doctrine(s) 42

Eclecticism 242, 321, 345
Egyptian religion 41, 98, 296, 305, 308
Emic-etic distinction 170, 220
Enlightenment, the 198
Eschatology 33
Esotericism 35, 246
Esoteric knowledge 239
Essentialism 2–3, 25, 27, 45, 75, 79, 90–91, 98, 144–45, 151, 160, 169, 197, 262, 286, 287, 318, 350–52, 354
Ethnocentrism 145, 162, 238
Etymology 14, 68
Evolution(ism) 33, 90–91, 144, 301
Evolution, 'spiritual' 382
Evolutionary psychology 3, 321
Exodus, the 208
Explanation(s) 5–7
causal 291
historical 27, 76, 143, 312
of syncretism 11, 74–77, 90, 123, 205, 258, 386
structural 125

Frames, of time 384

Garifuna culture 186
Genesis (Biblical) 384–85
Globalization 257, 274, 349
Gnosticism 33, 196
Grammar 147, 319, 385
Greek religion, ancient 34, 98, 305, 309, 320, 348–56

Hegemony, socio-cultural 150, 155, 166, 177–79, 200, 354
Hellenism/Hellenistic 20, 33, 35, 51, 70, 99, 286, 289, 320, 348–56
Henotheism 289
Heterogeneity 21
Heuristic typology 77, 221, 260, 297–99, 310–

12, 386
Hinduism 42–47, 48, 51, 54–57, 302, 309–310
Historical
context 30
process(es) 11
History 20, 76, 286
History of religions school, the German 20–22, 29, 32–36, 88, 287
Homogeneity 21
Honduras, history of 187
Hopi Indians 149, 157, 237–54
Hybridity 76, 257, 274, 350

Identity 167, 175, 209, 242, 247, 319, 353
Ideology 202
Incompatibility 92, 104–106, 124, 157, 228, 370, 377, 382
Indo-european religion(s) 35
Inferences, cognitive 157, 383
Innovation and orthodoxy 380
Innovation(s) 4, 10, 143, 378
Insider/outsider 11, 23, 56, 73, 81, 93, 220, 256
Integration 10, 17, 95, 135, 162, 224, 247
Interpretatio Graeca 21
Interpretation 90, 105, 109, 115, 162, 174, 297, 326, 337–38, 344, 377
Interpretive paradigm 181, 240–41, 381
Islam 48, 50, 71, 89, 92, 99, 278, 308
Israelite religion 60, 306

Japan 40, 59, 73, 296, 303
Java 39, 309
Jerusalem 35
Jesuits 16, 69
Jesus 46
Judaism 22, 30, 88

Language acquisition 146, 259, 319
Langue/parole 381–82, 385
Legitimation 149, 152, 194, 198
Liberation theology 18, 208–209
Literacy 246, 278
Literature, Jewish 29
Logic 92, 103, 123, 129, 175, 208

Magic (and syncretism) 95, 99, 131–33, 233, 322, 362, 369
Meaning
semantic 380
structure of 90, 147, 322, 382
symbolic 92–93, 380
Meaning-making 63, 153–54, 220–21, 366, 368–70, 380, 384
Melanesia, ethnography of 379
Melting-pot 267, 273
Meme-theory 259
Memory 319, 381
Metaphor 155, 219, 221, 226, 232, 296, 298

395

AUTHOR INDEX

398

5318

402

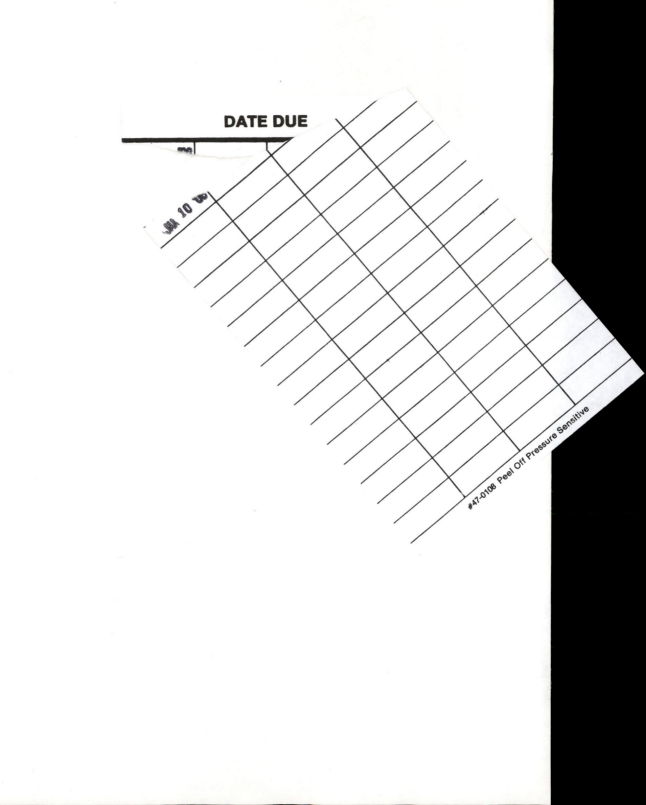

DATE DUE

JAN 10

#47-0106 Peel Off Pressure Sensitive